HER MAJESTY'S TOP GUN

HER MAJESTY'S TOP GUN

and the Decline of the Royal Navy

'Sharkey' Ward

MILL CITY PRESS

Mill City Press, Inc.
2301 Lucien Way #415
Maitland, FL 32751
407.339.4217
www.millcitypress.net

Printed in the United States of America.

Paperback ISBN-13: 978-1-6312-9867-7
eBook ISBN-13: 978-1-6312-9868-4
Library of Congress Control Number: 2020912599

DEDICATION

To the memory of my beloved and gallant eldest son,
Lieutenant-Commander Kristian 'Mental' Ward,
who passed away on 15 November 2018,
and to all his Top Gun peers and predecessors
who stood in harm's way in the Service of Her Majesty.

To the memory of my beloved elder brother, Michael,
who passed away unexpectedly on 16 November 2019.

And to my son, Ashton, who has always been a tower of
strength to me.

Figure 1. Ashton, Michael, self and Kris; 2016.

ACKNOWLEDGEMENTS

To Admiral Sir 'Sandy' Woodward GBE KCB, Commander Carrier Battle Group, for his close friendship and common purpose during the last two decades.

> "If Sharkey Ward had not disobeyed orders, we could not have won the Falklands War".

Figure 2. Admiral Sir 'Sandy' Woodward GBE KCB.

To Dr. Anthony Wells for his active moral support and wisdom.

> "Sharkey's book is terrific, an "All Nighter" for the discerning reader, and a book that should have a major impact on the future of British naval power, in my humble opinion. When I read the draft manuscript, I never put it down. It's that good."

To all those friends and colleagues who, over the past three decades, have kept me up to the mark with respect to the factual details behind the demise of our Naval Service and of the Fixed Wing Fleet Air Arm, including Major-General Julian Thompson CB OBE, Rear Admiral Jeremy Larken DSO, Commodore Michael Clapp CB, Commander Graham Edmonds, Commander Laon Hulme OBE, Lieutenant-Commander Lester May and Commander David Hobbs MBE.

To Leanne Gilroy for the outstanding portrait on the cover of this book.

To Timothy Winrow for his dedicated assistance and advice as my private editor.

TABLE OF CONTENTS

FOREWORD

The public image of a dashing daredevil hero, kicking the tyres and lighting the fires before getting airborne doesn't really do justice to the numerous skills needed to become a good fighter pilot.

Much of the flying conducted by all pilots is relatively mundane, provided that the pilot adheres rigidly to established safety procedures–the laws of physics are never flexible and forgiving! So basic skills include calmness, focus and strict adherence to rules. This is a not unusual skill set, but it is not enough.

Pilots also require a very high level of self-confidence and an ability to work under very high stress, because they must believe that they will be able to cope on those occasions when things do suddenly go wrong. Unlike driving a car, you can't pull up at the side of the road while you sort out problems in the air and re-plan. You have to be able to diagnose and fix all problems while keeping the aircraft safely in the air and on track, which almost invariably creates a sudden and massive increase in workload, and huge corresponding stress.

Being a fighter pilot requires many additional skills, including the superb spatial awareness and hand / eye coordination necessary for "dogfighting" and for very high-speed low-level flight, mastery of an entire additional workload of weapons management on top of the tasks of flying and navigating a supersonic jet, and the ability to remain calm and level-headed while facing an enemy intent on shooting you out of the sky.

Add to that the ultimate challenge for a naval pilot of landing on a short, heaving ship's deck at sea, in bad weather, at night, where you must be accurate to within a few inches in sometimes appalling conditions, and where failure will almost inevitably lead to disaster. These are skills which far exceed the demands on almost any other pilot. It rapidly becomes apparent that the necessary skill set to be a "Top Gun" is both a very broad range of highly unusual skills, and in a very rare combination.

It is no wonder then that very few people indeed have the aptitude to become a Top Gun. While many a teenager may fantasise about becoming one, few actually seek to try. Of those who do apply, most are turned down as it is readily apparent that they don't have the aptitude, and of those who are selected, many do not get through to the end of the long and gruelling journey to become a top front line fighter pilot.

This is the story of one man who made it to the pinnacle of this career in the British Royal Navy, of his fifteen year training program to achieve that goal, of the team who helped to take him there and of his subsequent successful service as one of the very few—the Top Guns of Her Majesty's Royal Navy.

But it is also his reflections on how that same team that helped him to rise to that success has been disintegrating in the years since, due to the complex but naive political system by which military funding has been allocated during this time of peace, and the risks that, once the team has been lost, there will be no one able to train a new generation of the naval aviators needed to protect Britain's strategic and commercial interests around the world. There are those who have claimed that there are other ways to achieve this protection, but this book's analysis lays bare the uncomfortable realities that show this to be false, and that there is little time left before the cost and effort needed to reinstate this capability will rise dramatically or even become impossible.

This is a sobering, but fascinating and truly gripping read, filled with a mixture of drama, humour and uncomfortable analysis and is highly recommended. It is doubtful that the daunting Top Gun "necessary skills list" included great story telling, but Sharkey Ward is undoubtedly a master of that too.

Timothy Winrow

PREFACE

This book provides the reader with a tale of two realities; the making of one of Her Majesty's Top Guns with the instincts and leadership qualities of a war fighter and, in sharp contrast, the demise of Britain's military ability to look after its own maritime security and overseas interests. These two realities are linked by personal exposure and involvement; whether in the front-line at sea or as a fly on the wall in Whitehall and NATO.

The exciting world of Navy fighter pilots flying from aircraft carriers and entering into air combat has been vividly portrayed in the Hollywood blockbuster film, "Top Gun". It has grabbed the attention of the public, many of whom thoroughly enjoy military air displays and the sight and sound of fast jet fighters showing off their paces overhead.

That 'enjoyment' is reflected in the first part of this book and is magnified many times over for the pilot in the cockpit who has an unmatched sense of freedom and of being master of all he surveys, especially his own destiny. The day is never dull when one can take off in dismal weather and hurtle skywards through dense cloud cover into brilliant sunshine. This is particularly so for the Navy fighter pilot launching from the deck of an aircraft carrier at sea. The carrier is his home; a floating airfield that he refers to affectionately as "mother". He depends on her when there is nowhere else to go, just vast expanses of open oceans. And, in combat, she depends on him for her air defence and the control of the skies.

This mutual dependence demands the highest level of professionalism and expertise by all parties, whether below decks in the carrier and its escorts or in the air. The safe and effective conduct of operations in the real world depends entirely on this excellent teamwork and is demonstrated well in the film.

My book does justice to the fact that the Naval Service has been the single most influential and effective UK tool for the projection of military and political power since World War II: confronting and deterring those that would harm us or would attempt to interrupt our vital global trade and energy supplies.

Leading the way in this global maritime defence role have been Aircraft Carrier Battle Groups[1] with their embarked fighter squadrons led by Royal Navy Top Guns, or Air Warfare Instructors as we know them in Britain.

As one of these élite aviators, I shall first endeavour to provide the reader with a detailed insight into my persona and my journey from being an impressionable schoolboy to becoming a fully-fledged Top Gun who had the privilege of leading the Sea Harrier community to air victory in the Falklands War of 1982. This was a journey dominated by job satisfaction, attitude, belligerence and an overriding desire to be the best. Although greatly outnumbered in the South Atlantic, my team willingly stepped into harm's way in defence of our ships and land forces. Without this diligence and aggressive posture, the Falklands War could not have been won. And since then I have not been afraid to challenge those who have fought against maintaining a robust Naval Service, especially the Royal Navy Fleet Air Arm.

---

[1] Carrier Battle Groups consist of one or more aircraft carriers protected by anti-submarine frigates, air defence destroyers, hunter-killer submarines and supported by Royal Fleet Auxiliary logistics vessels.

Figure 3. Author kills a Mirage V.

For the film buffs, I shall then briefly describe the history of the US Navy Top Gun School and the influential part played by Royal Navy Air Warfare Instructors in its formation.

Finally, I shall explore my intimate observations of how and why our Carrier Battle Groups, the fast jet Fleet Air Arm and the Royal Navy as a whole have been forsaken by decades of Government neglect and poor staff-work in Whitehall. It is a disturbing story of misinformation, disingenuous and unjustifiable claims, and propaganda. A cumulative lack of candour has put our National Security at risk and has resulted directly in misguided Defence Budget Expenditure by taxpayers and unjustified Weapon System Procurement that has created the infamous "Black Hole".

Hopefully, the reader will come to recognise and understand the global commitments of the Royal Navy that continue unabated in peacetime and in conflict. Such commitment is revealed when studying the percentage of personnel that are regularly deployed globally in the front line by the Senior Service. The graph below exemplifies this with data showing personnel deployed on active duty at the time of the Libyan crisis in 2011.

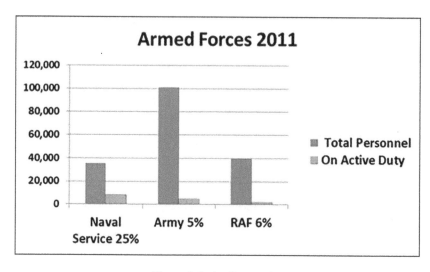

Figure 4. Active Duty ratios.

In the summer of 2019, the Chairman of the House of Commons Defence Select Committee, Dr Julian Lewis was persuaded by circumstance to comment adversely on the "pathetic size" of the Royal Navy. This was in response to the inability of the Naval Service[2] to provide a Carrier Battle Group with enough properly armed aircraft and escorting warships to combat Iranian aggression in the Strait of Hormuz.

The dilemma facing our Whitehall masters now is that investment in the Naval Service has been allowed to dwindle to a level which prevents the effective conduct of that Service's traditional role:

---

[2] The Naval Service comprises surface warships and submarines (The Fleet), fast jet and helicopter combat aircraft (The Fleet Air Arm), the Royal Marines with their associated amphibious warships and the Royal Fleet Auxiliary (logistic vessels that provide the Service with all supplies necessary to maintain an effective global presence).

"ensuring the safe global passage of trade and energy supplies upon which the Nation's very prosperity depends".

It is also important to realise that the effective defence of our Island base cannot be achieved or assured without the flexible military power inherent in the deployment of the Royal Navy's Carrier Battle Groups, surface warships and submarines. My text bears full testament to this statement.

Earlier robust attention to and investment in the Naval Service had the benefit of allowing Britain to conduct its many roles effectively. Those days of threat-related investment appear to be past.

During the journey of life, if one is afraid to tell the truth and to stand up for one's beliefs then that journey will have been wasted. I have followed this code from square one and that is what eventually allowed me to attain my dream of becoming a Naval Fighter Squadron Commander in combat, an Air Warfare Instructor and, for a time, Her Majesty's leading "Top Gun".

Standing up for my beliefs and ignoring 'political correctness' and 'rules for fools' has invited the term 'maverick'. I am persuaded by events that personal integrity and saying it as it is does not fit well with those who seek to maintain a rigid structure to preserve their own often tenuous position in it. A maverick will always choose the former over the latter; often at some personal cost. However, unlike some, I always sleep easy in my bed through having kept my self-respect.

As Plato so wisely said:

"No one is more hated than he who speaks the truth."

Plato appeared to be correct. In the early 1980's I was christened the "Number One Enemy of the Royal Air Force" because I was a lone voice in Whitehall challenging misguided and unjustified investment in various land-based weapon systems.

It is now time that the nation and the public heard the truth about the Nation's military decline despite the extraordinary achievements of Naval Battle Groups – the "Tip of the Spear" of UK global power projection capability. The latter part of this book spells out that truth.

Mini Military Biography:

A Royal Navy Top Gun and Air Warfare Instructor, Sharkey was Senior Pilot of 892 Phantom F4-K Squadron in the aircraft carrier HMS Ark Royal during the Cold War. He personally introduced the Sea Harrier Fighter Aircraft to Naval Service, commanding the Intensive Flying Trials Unit 700A Squadron, 899 Headquarters Squadron and then 801 Front Line Squadron in the Falklands where he was Senior Sea Harrier advisor to the Command on all aspects of the fast jet air war. He flew over sixty war missions by day and night, achieved three air-to-air kills (& one damaged) and was involved in or witnessed eight further kills.

During the war he was awarded the Air Force Cross for services to Harrier Aviation and then decorated with the Distinguished Service Cross for gallantry in the Falklands. He subsequently became Freeman of the City of London and a Member of the Royal Aeronautical Society.

He then served in the Ministry of Defence as Air Warfare and Air Weapons Adviser to the Naval Staff and the First Sea Lord before voluntarily retiring.

PROLOGUE

When disembarking from HMS Invincible to Yeovilton Naval Air Station with my small squadron of jump-jet Sea Harriers late in 1981, I kept my promise to my eldest son, Kris, who was in his first year of boarding at Hazlegrove Prep School in Somerset. I led our six aircraft in close formation at slow speed low over the school at precisely 0900 – during Morning Assembly. Apparently, the noise from our jets was deafening. In the pervasive silence that followed, a good-looking youngster in his first year blushed and blurted out with enormous pride, "That was my Dad!"

That was Kristian – whose long journey towards becoming a much-respected Royal Navy Top Gun in his own right had begun in earnest. As the School Motto so wisely stated, "You can, if you think you can!"

Figure 5. Kris with John Farley & the new Sea Harrier.

Kris and his Navy fighter pilot peers have carried the Air Warfare Instructor/Top Gun ethos into the 21st century with panache. My comments immediately below pay well-deserved tribute to them and to him and are provided to let the reader know that such ethos lives on despite all odds.

It was with a sense of great pride and immense sorrow that I attended my son's Memorial Event at Royal Naval Air Station, Yeovilton on 12 April 2019: the early home of the Royal Navy Fixed Wing Fleet Air Arm.

Figure 6. My Top Gun son, Kristian–by Leanne Gilroy.

Lieutenant-Commander Kristian 'Mental' Ward served his country with honour and distinction as a fighter pilot in the front-line flying Sea Harriers and Ground Attack Harriers from land and sea. His multiple tours in Afghanistan were especially significant, sacrificing his peace of mind and that of his family in order to ensure timely air support to our ground forces and those of our allies.

Imagine if you can, that you are thousands of miles away from home in a bleak, unwelcoming environment with very few creature comforts. You have a critically important role to play in combat operations. You are directly responsible for the close air defence and life-saving support of the Royal Marines, British Army and Allied soldiers fighting on the ground against the fanatical and brutal militant forces of the Taliban and Al Qaeda.

The Harrier fighter pilots of the Naval Fighter Wing and of 1 Squadron, Royal Air Force had this responsibility for several years and took it very seriously. Nothing would stop them from rapidly responding to urgent calls for help from our ground forces engaged in close combat with the enemy.

Our Harrier ground crew and aircrew maintained fully armed aircraft on alert and were ready to go at any time of the day or night. They took pride in being able to get their "wheels off the ground" within 15 minutes of receiving a call for help. This was no mean feat and needed excellent cooperation between the operations team, aircraft ground crew and the pilots.

That cannot be said of the Tornado team who took over from the Harrier in Afghanistan following the 2010 Strategic Defence and Security Review – more of that later. When the Tornadoes arrived in theatre, everything changed.

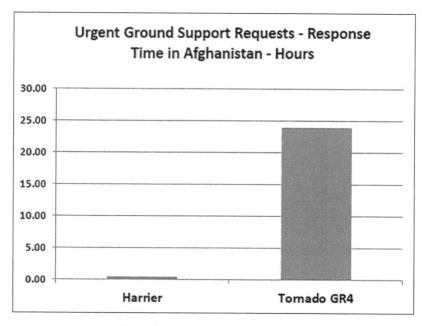

Figure 7. Ground support reaction times.

Armchair Air Marshals dictated that they would require 24 hours' notice to respond to calls for help from our Marines and soldiers on the ground.

> "Too late, too late, the soldier cried; thanks to you, we all died."

Also imagine if you can, the thoughts at the back of the Harrier pilot's mind as he accelerated furiously down the dusty runway at Bagram airbase, tightly strapped into the tiny cockpit of his very small but potent jump jet. There was a job to be done – adrenaline pumping furiously through the veins.

Jet nozzles cracked down momentarily, punching the jet off the runway, then placed aft. Wheels up. Flaps up. Hug the ground at about 10 feet. Reach 500 miles an hour in seconds and then pull maximum 'G' and soar steeply to the heavens to avoid the ground fire that always threatened to come from outside the airfield perimeter. Feverish activity in the cockpit copying details about the target and the disposition of friendly forces: professionalism had taken over and blanked out, at least for a time, the ever-present threat of being shot down and falling into the hands of fanatical terrorists: a fate far worse than death.

This possibility of capture by the inhuman and brutal Taliban fighters did indeed weigh heavily on the minds of all Harrier pilots in theatre. As a result they had a solemn pact between themselves – entirely logical yet mind-blowing:

"If I am shot down and alive, use up your bombs to kill me before I am captured!"

Kris confided this to his brother, Ashton, and to me just two months before he died. He was clearly deeply troubled by the pressures he had faced but being a true Top Gun he never shirked away from his duty and always put the lives of our ground forces first, ahead of his own safety–as did all of his Harrier colleagues.

The Top Gun Harrier boys did not hold back from doing their duty and putting themselves in harm's way – even at very low level over the heads of the Taliban fighters where they were very vulnerable to ground fire. This selfless dedication mirrored the many operational achievements and service of earlier Royal Navy Top Guns, most of whom are no longer with us.

During his four deployments to Afghanistan, my son Kris flew 160-Armed Reconnaissance and Close Air Support missions by day and night in support of coalition ground troops. Towards the end of one mission on the evening of December 2, 2007, when he was running short of fuel and out of ammunition, he was called to the aid of a small team of US Ranger Special Forces pinned down by more than 70 Taliban fighters. They had already suffered one very serious casualty and their radio operator's thumb had been shot off. There appeared to be no way out for the Rangers. But, typical of all Special Force heroes and fighter pilots, there was always room for banter. When Kris contacted the radio operator who was under heavy fire, the latter stated, "Hey, Dude, it's like a war zone down here!" Kris laughed and replied, "It is a war zone, Dude!"

Though low on fuel and at great risk to himself, Kris descended to very low level and, with no weapons left, made several high-speed passes directly over the heads of the Taliban while he called up another Harrier. This brave if dangerous show-of-force kept the Taliban at bay and interrupted the assault; giving the second Harrier time to deliver a 1,000lb airburst bomb on target. The surviving Taliban fighters dispersed.

A few days later two huge, bearded Rangers entered the Harrier operations room. They had travelled a considerable distance to get there to say a very personal thank you. At 6ft 4in, Kris was tall, but one of these soldiers was 6ft 8in "with hands the size of dinner plates". The American picked up the British pilot in a massive bear hug and said: "You saved our lives, Dude!" It was a very special moment.

Such combat events were not the only stress factor.

Sitting alone in a tiny aircraft at medium to high level en route to a target above the bleak and unwelcoming mountainous terrain, the thought that they might never see their loved ones again, their wives, children and families, would often come to the fore. The trauma from this additional stress was difficult to bear but it did not prevent total dedication to the task in hand–the defence and protection of our soldiers.

Figure 8. Ready for Action.

Such gallantry in the face of perpetual danger was clearly "above and beyond the call of duty" and the associated stress was a serious contributor to the PTSD that many of our Harrier boys suffered; including Kris.

You might well ask, how on earth did these Harrier Top Guns overcome and hide their stress when deployed? An email from Kris' Boss, Commander Kev Seymour, to Kris' two children, Jamie and Lucy, gives us a clue:

> "I could not think of anyone better than your Dad to showcase the ability of the Navy fighter pilot. Afghanistan was where Kris shone, his beaming smile keeping everyone going day and night due to him swimming in an ocean of Tommy Hortons coffee!
>
> Nor can I tell you enough about his professionalism as a pilot and as the best Senior Pilot and buddy that anyone could have had on operations. One trip that

we did just before Christmas 2008 epitomized our friendship. We flew together, laughed together, bantered together, dropped all our ordnance together on the Taliban and walked back in together grinning from ear to ear. I cherish those times and you guys can be very, very proud of an amazing Dad."

Clearly, dark fears were hidden by the cavalier attitude that has been bred into generations of Royal Navy Fighter Pilots.

Dedication and sacrifice have been the hallmark of British naval aviation since before World War II. The many thousands of aviators and flight deck crewmen that have died during the conduct of their aviation duties at sea in war and peace deserve to be acknowledged and celebrated by their Mother Service and by the Nation as a whole. Fully worthy of memory and mention, for instance, are the Sea Harrier pilot combat losses in the Falklands Conflict:

- Lieut. Nick Taylor, 800 Squadron–shot down by ground fire when attacking Goose Green at very low level.

- Lieut. Alan Curtis and Lieut. John Eyton-Jones, 801 Squadron–missing in action when prosecuting a fast-moving target [an Étendard armed with the Exocet sea-skimming missile] that was threatening the Battle Group at very low level over the sea in bad weather.

- Lieut. Gordon Batt DSC, 800 Squadron–died when hitting the sea after launching from HMS Hermes at night for a ground attack mission after a long day of flying.

Whenever a naval fighter pilot colleague and friend dies through accident or enemy fire, it is a watershed moment for his peers and is never easy to rationalise. The Squadron still has a job to do and that has to be the focus of all the aircrew and engineers.

Remembering the departed with pride rather than desolation is the key to maintaining morale and fighting effectiveness.

It was therefore with considerable surprise and disappointment that I and my family toured the Fleet Air Arm Museum in April, just before Kris' Memorial, and found that the high points of British naval aviation history and gallantry were not being adequately presented to the public. Indeed, I found it unfitting and of great concern that the only books available online from this Naval Museum celebrate RAF aviation icons from World War II and general military aviation – NO BOOKS about Fleet Air Arm aircraft and achievements. Books publicised for sale include 7 books on RAF aircraft–Vulcan (4), RAF Spitfire and RAF Mosquito (2).

A list of some of the books that should be publicised and available from the Museum is provided at Annex F.

The Museum does of course present many iconic fixed wing carrier aircraft and must be commended for the same. However, this does not in itself provide the public with any feel at all for the extraordinary global history of the Naval Service and of Royal Navy Strike Carrier success and commitment.

One of our guests at Kris' Memorial Event, a seasoned veteran of the First Battalion Scot's Guards, admitted to me that up until the Event he had never even known or realised that the Royal Navy Fleet Air Arm existed. The general public appear to be of the same mind.

This must be viewed as the tip of the iceberg of public ignorance about the under-resourced Naval Service (often referred to as the Silent Service) and the key role that it needs to continue to play to ensure our national security and well-being.

Significant players in the conduct of that role are Royal Navy Fighter Pilots, the most highly qualified of whom are the Air Warfare Instructors. Hollywood and the US Navy have christened these élite aircrew Top Guns.

Our Top Guns have served our nation with distinction for many decades. Each generation has passed on its expertise to the next; thereby ensuring that our Naval Service and our Carrier Battle Groups have the capability to project air power on a global basis successfully in support of our National interests. But to what end?

When Kris and his colleagues finally returned to the UK, their expertise, dedication and loyalty to the Crown was summarily dismissed and forgotten by a Whitehall establishment that lacked integrity and true air warfare expertise. In a direct rejection of the National Security Committee's recommendations in the 2010 Strategic Defence and Security Review, the Chief of the Defence Staff, Air Chief Marshal Sir Jock Stirrup persuaded the Prime Minister, David Cameron, in a private/secret meeting at RAF Brize Norton to withdraw our carrier-capable Close Air Support Harriers from service and to retain in service at much greater cost the obsolete Tornado GR4. This decision was a direct slap in the face for the Fleet Air Arm and Her Majesty's Naval Top Guns. Their career prospects as front-line pilots were destroyed in one fell swoop. And Britain no longer enjoyed the services of carrier-borne fighter aircraft.

Kris and his colleagues, many of whom were already suffering the torments of PTSD now had the burden of unjustified sacrifice by their masters in Whitehall. It was a heavy cross to bear and eventually contributed to my son's demise.

There is a direct link (which I shall demonstrate later) between this and many other acts of betrayal that resulted in the present inability of the Royal Navy to fulfil its traditional global National Security role effectively.

Figure 9. Whitehall madness.

For the record, most of the facts and figures presented in this book, especially those in later chapters, have stood up to scrutiny at the highest levels in Whitehall. Confirming this, First Sea Lord Admiral Sir George Zambellas(2013-2016) once confided to a mutual acquaintance, "Sharkey Ward's figures are uncannily accurate".

Let the story begin.

1

ATTITUDE (1992).

*"Yeah, though I walk through
the valley of the shadow of death,
I shall fear no challenge and confront all adversaries
with attitude and lethal force...."*

As you may already have noted from the Top Gun film, a brazen attitude can be of great assistance when you have to put yourself into harm's way–whether in the air or on the ground. It enables you to demonstrate to your peers and your adversary confidence, competence and fearlessness even though, in all logic, the odds may be stacked against you. This can mean the difference between life and death.

Before relating the formative events that eventually shaped me into one of Her Majesty's Top Guns, I believe it would be revealing to relate how my own brazen attitude probably saved my life a few years after voluntarily retiring from the Royal Navy in the mid-80's.

I had set up and had been running a small but moderately successful defence-related company based in the UK, Defence Analysts Limited. The Company employed up to 25 retired Special Boat Squadron and Special Air Service personnel and its main income was drawn from protecting oil tankers in the Arabian Gulf from destruction at the hands of Iraqi Exocet missile attacks during the Iran-Iraq war. We prevented the total loss of 12 oil tankers. When the war ended so did the income and a change in plan was necessary.

I decided that a new life in Turkey would be the thing and my bank in Whitehall, Holts, agreed to providing financial support for building a three-star hotel in Marmaris on the south coast. I moved there with my young and gorgeous Turkish wife, Semiha, to build the hotel and enjoy the Mediterranean environment. For various reasons, Semiha's parents believed wrongly that I was a multimillionaire and allowed me to marry her principally so that I could look after them in their dotage. Also, with my having employed so many retired Special Forces personnel in my small Company, the Turkish family connected the dots, again wrongly, and presumed that as well as being a moderately well-known fighter pilot I was also one of these fabled characters. This presumption was to serve me well.

Figure 10. Our Marmaris Apartment.

I kept myself very fit in Marmaris, running around the town and the Marina every day in the hot afternoon sun. Blue-eyed, with closely cropped hair and well-muscled, I was christened the 'Gestapo Man' by the locals. This gave me considerable respect and protection within what must be described as a rather dangerous society.

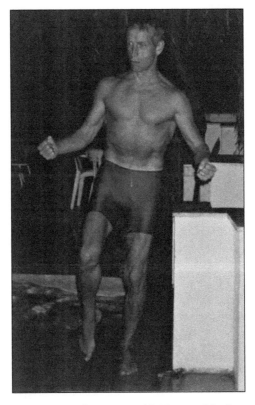

Figure 11. The 48-year-old "Gestapo Man".

Semiha's parents, Köksal and Ikbal, moved down to join us from Istanbul and her father persuaded me to lend him £10,000 for the purchase of a small Guest House, Imrem Pansion. They were from the Adana region of the country – famous for Turkey's spiciest food and where extreme violence both domestic and otherwise was a norm. Other regions of the country had developed an appropriate description for the males of that community, "Adana Bears".

3

And Köksal was one of the finest examples, beating his wife at the slightest excuse and maintaining a macho reign of terror within the home and in the local area. I learned with some dismay from the family that he used to be the executioner for a major Adana Mafia family. He was indeed a huge figure; more than 100 kilos, well over six feet tall, barrel-chested with a hooked nose and arms that appeared to stretch nearly to the floor–a true gorilla of a man. He had a clear propensity for violence, was as ignorant as a plank of wood and when enraged became more like a nightmare than a human being.

All went well until the Bank of England pulled the rug from under me in the mini depression of the late 80's/early 90's and called in the development loan for the hotel that I was building. I was up the creek without a paddle. Being in a financial bind, I was unable to continue regular financial help for Semiha's parents.

As soon as they realised the gravy train of my financial support was ending, all bets with the family were off. For the following two years and mainly behind my back they tried to persuade Semiha to leave me so they could marry her off to a rich family. As was their custom, they even invoked curses on our marriage which eventually appeared to have some effect. Throughout this process, Semiha was very resilient but the pressure was on.

In the end, they were so antagonistic that I decided to call in the loan that I had made to Köksal for setting up his Guest House. He told his daughter to tell me, "No way!"

But I was not prepared to let him off the hook so easily.

Eventually a meeting was set up in the Guest House and I prepared a written statement demanding repayment. Semiha acted as interpreter. It was to be a brief but exciting experience – akin to going into the lion's den.

4

As we entered, Köksal lounged in an armchair on the far side of the salon. He was smiling and full of himself. Ikbal hovered around nervously near the open plan kitchen. Another gentleman, a stranger, sat far to our left. We remained standing, about 25 feet away from Köksal. I had already emphasised to Semiha that she should translate everything I said as precisely as she could.

"Köksal, I have come for the money that you owe me."

He glowered and sat up straight. "I don't owe you any money. This is my accountant and he has confirmed that you owe me money." As he spoke, he became a little agitated, was clearly angry and the smile disappeared. He began drooling at the lip. I stared him in the eye and said to Semiha "Please, translate this exactly".

"Köksal, you are a liar and a thief. I want my money." Tact and diplomacy were not my middle names!

Absolute pandemonium broke out.

The accountant turned white as a sheet and nearly fainted. Ikbal started to scream uncontrollably knowing that extreme violence was about to follow. And, of most interest to yours truly, Köksal completely lost it. His huge frame rose up out of his chair into a fighting crouch and now he was not just drooling, he was literally foaming at the mouth as he ambled across the floor. Semiha was frozen to the ground in fear.

It didn't look good!

But I was completely calm and outwardly unperturbed as he approached: showing not a smidgen of concern as I stared into his bloodshot eyes. I knew that I had just one chance of survival–I would hit him in the throat with all my power as soon as he came within reach. If that didn't work; curtains!

Amidst the continuous screaming and much to my hidden relief, he stopped in front of me just out of reach. His eyes showed extreme confusion and I suddenly realised he was afraid. Continuing to stare at him with a vengeance, I slowly pulled the written demand for payment out of my pocket, threw it on the floor between his feet and said to Semiha, "Now translate this."

"Köksal, you are a coward as well as a liar and a thief." Which she duly did.

He was completely stunned but didn't approach one inch closer.

After a demonstrative pause and still staring directly into his eyes, I half-turned to Semiha and said, "I think we have outstayed our welcome. Let's go home."

I didn't get my money but I was on a high: very thankful to be still alive and fully realising that my reputation had been a successful weapon.

It's called attitude. And I shall continue this Turkish saga in Chapter 33, at the end of the book.

THE MAKING OF
THIS TOP GUN

2

EARLY DAYS AND MY LIFE
AT READING SCHOOL
(1943 – 1962).

M y father, Johnny, joined the Royal Air Force as a late teenager in 1939 and became an engine fitter specialising predominantly on the Merlin engine which powered our Spitfires
and Hurricanes. He was evacuated at Dunkirk after his Lysander
squadron was wiped out by the German blitzkrieg. He was then
posted to Medicine Hat in Alberta, Canada to assist in the training
of Canadian fighter pilots. It was there that my mother, Margery,
gave birth first to my brother Michael and then to me in 1943. We
all returned by sea to the UK safely in 1944, avoiding being sunk
by German U-boats.

Johnny was then posted to India as part of a crew to build the Dum
Dum airstrip outside Calcutta in an area that was virgin jungle. It
was used to fly supplies over 'the hump' (the Himalayas) to China
for the war effort against Japan.

He used to recall with great pleasure that one of his colleagues was
a concert violinist and would play the most beautiful music which
echoed round the green hills of Darjeeling. His pleasure was no
surprise. As a boy he was the No. 2 Soprano in all England. And as
an adult he had the most spectacular soft tenor voice which almost
rivalled that of the legendary Neapolitan tenor, Benjamino Gigli.

He was frequently asked to sing Arias at RAF Mess Dinners and I grew up in awe listening in our home to his remarkable voice. That is why I continue to adore such music–though my own singing voice is more of a croak.

In later years, returning to England after the war, Johnny went through Officer Training School and with the rank of Flight Lieutenant, was attached to the Royal Pakistan Air Force Base, outside Karachi, at Mauripur, in 1950.

In the interim I had contracted bronchiectasis – the illness that eventually claimed the life of King George VI. It was a desperately challenging time for my mother.

Following months of care in bed at home I was hospitalised for about a year. The doctors feared that I might have also contracted tuberculosis; this meant me being kept in isolation with no visitors– an extraordinarily lonely time for a six-year old kid. The prognosis was not good and the doctors wanted to operate (as they did with King George VI) – 'my only real chance of survival' they said. Fortunately my mother refused — and when father was posted to Pakistan the medical experts surmised that the dry heat there could indeed be the answer to such survival. They were correct.

My primary school education took place mainly in Bispham, Lancashire, at Karachi Grammar School and then finally at Shinfield Primary School near Reading, Berkshire.

I have very happy memories of Shinfield, of my schoolmaster, Mr. Green and the Headmaster, Mr. Jackson. They were special days: a three mile walk to and from school each day through the pastoral beauty of Berkshire farms and fields; daily wrestling matches at lunch-time with a punchy character, David Searle; leading the Morris dancing team and partnering my childhood

11

sweetheart, Hazel Clark in country dancing competitions; and of course lots of sport.

During these halcyon days and without the benefit of modern communications and the Internet, I didn't have a care in the world and was oblivious to the ongoing major international events that were to reshape the world's stage. And I was unaware of the vital role played by UK aircraft carriers in some of these events. These included the Korean War, 1950 – 53, and the Suez crisis in 1956.

In Korea, HMS Triumph joined the USS Valley Forge to strike at North Korean targets shortly after N Korea attacked the South in June 1950. The British aircraft carriers Triumph, Theseus, Glory and Ocean provided all the UK's tactical strike and fighter operations throughout the 3 years of the war. RAF involvement was limited to transport flights into safe airfields and some flying-boat Maritime patrols in the open ocean off Japan. RN carrier aircraft flew thousands of effective sorties.

Suez saw a combined assault on Egypt by British and French carrier-borne and land-based aircraft. In the British operations, the RN deployed 3 fixed-wing carriers, Eagle, Albion and Bulwark plus 2 helicopter carriers, Ocean and Theseus. Because of their ability to gain better position, the strike carriers reacted more quickly to calls for offensive air support than RAF aircraft in distant Cyprus and Malta. Despite only having one-third of the total British strike fighters, the RN flew two-thirds of the strike sorties and their aircraft spent longer over the target area. RAF aircraft had long transits from their bases, carried less weapons and could spend little time on task, most of that at high level to conserve fuel.

It would not be too long before I began to understand the implications of such events for our national security and global interests.

Life changed markedly for me on leaving primary school and going to Reading when my parents were posted to RAF Changi, Singapore. For the first term I was a dayboy and then joined East Wing House as a boarder. Initially, I was traumatised and extremely homesick. There was no privacy by day or night, there were no comforts of home. Nearly all the furniture in the common room was dilapidated and broken, mealtimes were a challenge without any home cooking and, worst of all, the other boys in my first year had already spent a term there–leaving me as the odd man out.

After a few weeks the homesickness subsided and I began to return to my normal self. This was made much easier by the careful understanding of my Housemaster, Frank Terry, his wife Doris and the Matron. Frank proved to be a wonderful role model – especially regarding integrity and loyalty.

It was not in my character to dwell on things past and so I soon put my heart and soul into this new adventure; indeed, it was a welcome challenge.

I found out that happiness and survival at boarding school depended on standing up for yourself with fisticuffs–something I was already very comfortable with from primary school days. I had no choice about being at the school and so I concentrated on making the best of it. That was not too difficult.

Academics were not my forte – adequate, one might say. I was more interested in sport. Our teachers were definitely old-school – dedicated, suspicious of everyone and not averse to corporal punishment and mild physical abuse. This was not enough reason to be afraid or well-behaved. On the contrary it was often the source of great amusement in the classroom. The main practitioners of the physical abuse were two delightful characters, Mr. Streatham, the chemistry master and 'Bonk' the geography teacher, who didn't suffer fools gladly. Mr. Streatham would say, "Stand up, boy, so I can knock you down!" Of course, one stood up and then got knocked down by a hay-maker round the ear. 'Bonk' on the other hand wouldn't give any verbal warning at all. He would approach one's desk, grunting unintelligibly with his fist at the ready – the middle finger knuckle standing proud to cause more pain. Then he would give you one! Or two if you tried to duck! I loved them both dearly.

Corporal punishment with a long bamboo cane was reserved to the Headmaster, Charles E Kemp Esq. , the three Boarding House Masters and the Captain of the School. I used to thank my lucky stars that I was not in West Wing where "Thug" Lindsay, a retired Army Major and sadist, would cane his boys with his military walking stick – it had a shiny brass knob at the business end. If the knob came off during the event, he would bend down, replace it and then continue–frequently drawing blood. He should have been locked up!

Such traditions were entirely in keeping with a School that had 800 pupils and an 800-year history. If you broke the rules you had to pay the consequences and to me that was fair enough. In my first two years, I became the most caned boy in the school – mostly for horseplay in the dormitory after lights-out. Punishment from Frank Terry was not unduly severe but was shrouded in theatrical fury.

It usually took place very early on a Sunday morning. Frank would burst into the dormitory, drag me by the hair from my bed in my pyjamas, down three flights of concrete stairways and into his study – where he would at last relinquish his grip on my hair. There was always a senior prefect present as a witness. "At it again, NDW!" he would sneer in his high-pitched tenor voice. "Bend over", as he carefully selected one of three canes, cracking each one in turn down on the top of his desk to create atmosphere. My punishment inevitably graduated as time went on from three light

strokes to six of the very best–no more than that was legal, fortunately. Occasionally I was near to tears but I never let it show.
Instead I would stand up after the caning and drive him crazy by
saying, "Thank you, Sir" with nary a tremor in my voice. This
used to amuse the School Captain, Buchanan when he stood as
witness and once outside the study he would whisper, "Well done!
I'm proud of you!"

That made it all worth-while as well as showing off my bruises to
my chums. Water off a duck's back!

The School had become a real home: my first experience of fully-fledged camaraderie and team spirit. It also represented the
second 'aspirational ladder' in my life: the first, wanting to be like
the RAF Black Arrow formation aerobatic team and the later ones
including Dartmouth College training, Flying Training and finally
Font Line Fighter Pilot training. Each ladder invited a desire to
succeed and to try to be the best – with plenty of role models to
admire further up each ladder.

The teaching staff provided an umbrella of genuine concern for
the care and advancement of all the boys, encouraging healthy
competition in the classroom and on the sports field. And when I
first looked up the ladder, I had two dreams; to be Captain of the
School and Captain of the 1st XV rugby team. It was not a com-
pulsive desire: just a rather fanciful target with the second dream
always appearing more attainable than the first.

All in all, it was a very happy and rewarding time. Taking cold
showers every morning at dawn supervised by our normally com-
passionate Matron was not exactly a highlight – particularly in
winter. But we only had to endure that bitter routine for the first
two years after which we were considered relatively human.

Having a set daily routine suited me well. On Sundays and after weekday breakfast, the whole school would attend morning prayers in our very becoming Chapel which seated all 800 boys– only 120 being boarders – the majority were dayboys. Our padre, Jack Newman was an excellent fellow. Short in stature (like me – barely 5 ft 9 ins) and afflicted with a permanent stoop, he encouraged the study of contemporary religions and lateral thinking with healthy discussions in the classroom and at the Debating Society: all of which I found fascinating.

Sundays apart, normal classes were held until 4 o'clock except for Wednesday and Saturday afternoons when much emphasis was placed on inter-school sports fixtures. These were my favourite days of the week especially during the autumn term when rugby ruled.

Weekday evenings were taken up with organised homework in a classroom or later, as one became more senior, in one's study, followed by Boarding House evening prayers–which always culminated in a rousing chorus of, "Jerusalem" – led by the fine tenor voice of Frank Terry.

By my early teens, a pecking order had been established that was mainly based on sporting prowess, whether intra-school or inter-school, and on fighting ability. Captaining the Colts XV on the rugby field brought me a lot of status with my peers as well as a little undesirable attention. To some of the older boys I represented 'a cocky young bastard' who needed sorting out. Since the age of twelve I had stood up for myself with fists against all-comers; no matter what their age or size. Various levels of bullying were the order of the day and, when I was the object, I would have none of it. This resulted in frequent physical confrontations with older boys – who at first didn't get it! I would literally see red, feel no pain and never give up. It was a natural formula that served me and my contemporaries (whom I protected) very well indeed.

By the age of about 15, my reputation had put me at some risk. It was a time when the homosexual instincts of various individuals came to the fore and they tended to prey on the weaker members of our community. I was oblivious to this regrettable trend until one day when I was warned by a very substantially built senior rugby player that if I didn't cool it, I was going to get a night visit by a team of guys who would sort me out! I immediately told him to get lost and that I wasn't afraid of him or his buddies.

Very soon afterwards when I was considering dabbling in music and wanted to buy a clarinet, another senior from a different boarding house approached me. Frank Harman was the son of a clergyman whose vicarage lay on the other side of the school's main playing field. "I have a clarinet for sale if you are interested" he said. "Come over to my father's place and take a look at it."

When we arrived in his room at the top of the vicarage, he came to the point. "You have a choice to make. Let me 'do you' now or you will get a night visit from several of my friends who will all do you!" I told him in very direct terms, "You must be F'ing joking!" Without any hesitation I stormed out of the vicarage, made a bee-line across the playing field, something that was forbidden except for school prefects and therefore attracted considerable attention, and immediately reported the incident to my Housemaster, Frank Terry. He was appalled and that same day Harman was expelled.

Word got around fast. Don't try it on with NDW.

It is true to say that I was very competitive in spirit, somewhat ambitious and unquestionably unruly at times. But my main driving force was general contentment with life and living only for today and for the next rugby match. I would always applaud and support those who were better than me–for example, a dayboy called Bob Towner who was by far the best all-round athlete in the school. He took training more seriously whereas I preferred an illicit cigarette behind the bicycle shed.

Early on in Junior school I must admit to a massive ego boost when Frank Terry let it slip that, one day, I would probably be School Captain – despite all the canings. This naturally gave me much self-confidence which I may not have done too much to hide. This was demonstrated not too long after the Harman incident. Frank popped his head into my room very late one evening and said, "NDW. Come down to my study, please." As I put on my dressing-gown I wondered whether another caning loomed – it had been ages since the last one.

"Come in, NDW, and take a seat. This is a very serious matter that I want to discuss. "I really thought I was in the poo again.

"One of our House Monitors, Brown, has run away and I gather from his parents that it is because of you! What have you got to say?"

I was completely taken aback. Brown was at least three years older than me. I respected him and liked him. I couldn't for the life of me work out how or why I had made him so insecure and unhappy and I related this to Frank.

"Well, he is coming back to us and I want you to make a special effort to be nice to him and make him feel at home. Understood? OK, you can go back to bed now."

It was a clear case of how I could offend people without really trying. But I soon forgot the incident and carried on as usual – albeit being extra nice to Brown.

At the end of my time as Colts Rugby XV captain I was more than delighted to be selected for the final 1st XV match of the season. To me this was as much the Holy Grail as later becoming a fighter pilot and was the precursor of a very rewarding last two-and-a-half years at Reading.

It was not all a journey of success, though. Yes, I became an early School Prefect, then Captain of the 1st XV and then, my ultimate dream; School Captain with my personal office in its own building with almost unlimited powers. Even the school masters were prohibited from entering this precious space without knocking. It had far more utility as a smoking room than the back of the bicycle sheds.

Figure 12. School Captain.

Through my own fault, I was less than successful and under-achieved on the academic front. This was a direct result of pure laziness and taking the easy way out. My main aptitude was for the sciences, maths and physics, but I didn't care for chemistry and I could see that taking other subjects at Advanced Level demanded far less work. So I opted for English Literature, History and Geography. That would have been OK if I had applied myself at least half-enthusiastically but I didn't. For English and just three weeks before the exam I had not even read some of the syllabus works: Shakespeare, Webster, Milton, Chaucer and Bacon's Essays. In English and European History, I concentrated on just the 30 Years War period instead of 300 years. It was a demanding time trying to catch up by revising in the hot summer weather, lying by the river Thames near Sonning and watching the girls go by. Miraculously, I passed all the exams but not well enough to get into Oxford where I had mistakenly thought my rugby ability would save the day.

My other notable 'failures' were not being successful at the South of England Rugby Trials and the South of England Springboard Diving trials – even though that was not through lack of effort.

Two of my main adopted roles as School Captain were to stamp out 'bullying' and encourage team spirit and youthful enterprise. Even in those days I was a firm advocate of the Nelsonian 'blind eye' and I had learned this from Frank Terry. For example, anti-smoking patrols by day and night were not my thing. But when truancy from classes in the senior school became something of a problem I did engage in appropriate action. This turned out to be fun.

The perpetrators were mainly at least 16 years old and would miss classes to go down to local public houses for a beer and a smoke. The ultimate punishment for this would be the cane at the hands of the Headmaster – a truly exceptional fellow who knew the value of delegation. This allowed us to keep him on a pedestal as a powerful and much respected leader – while we got on with running the school.

The Vice-Captain, Nick Staunton or another Prefect would accompany me on these pub patrols. Nick was a good friend and a very special all-rounder; academics, sport and an excellent role-model for all the youngsters. On entering a pub and finding miscreants there, we would make a big deal of it but without any drama: explaining that if they were caught again, they would have to deal with the Headmaster. "So, leave your beers and cigarettes on the table and get back to school!" Of course, we drank their beer and confiscated their cigarettes–and if we found nobody in the pub we would have a beer and a smoke anyway.

Attendance at morning Chapel was a focal point of school life and extremely enjoyable with more than 800 boys and teachers singing their hearts out each day with rousing hymns. It was surrounded by formality. First the boys would enter and be seated, then the prefects followed by the teachers in their gowns and mortar boards. A short pause later, the School Captain would walk down the aisle to take his raised seat, centre-left and then the Headmaster opposite him to the right. The Lesson Reader was always chosen by the School Captain and I reserved the best readings for myself, especially 1 Corinthians 13: "For now we see through a glass, darkly; but then face to face: now I know in part; but then shall I know even as also I am known." I shall always remember the sound of my steel-tipped shoes echoing around the hushed chapel as I approached the rostrum, watched intently by hundreds of my peers.

It was all good preparation for Dartmouth Naval College. But first I had to get in.

I hadn't performed well during my interviews and exams at Oxford University, enduring the whole week while coping with a devastating bout of flu. But the several days of Naval Cadetship Board interviews and tests went rather better.

I was surrounded and rather daunted by a team of hopeful candidates who were already fully Navy-oriented and knowledgeable. Many had received special coaching from their Schools and I began to feel like a fish out of water.

The leadership aptitude tests went very well but I was not so sure about the interview with the Board Psychologist. It lasted forty-five minutes and I was only asked one question, "Are you a selfish person?" Forty-five minutes later I finished my answer, following which the 'psycho' said quietly, "That will be all, thank you."

The main Board Interview in front of three Naval Captains was equally disconcerting but, with hindsight, amusing. I was fully relaxed and very direct as I tried to answer questions; lounging in an armchair in sports jacket and crimson waistcoat. It was abundantly clear that I knew very little about the Senior Service or about ships and the sea. One of the Captains pointed to a painting on the wall and said, "Can you tell me what that is?"

"Yes, sir. A sailing boat."

"Ah! But what kind?"

"A yacht."

With some impatience, "Yes, but is it a yawl or a ketch?"

"No idea, sir. I am joining the Navy to fly."

Something must have impressed them because just before Xmas I received two letters: one saying I had been turned down by Oxford and the other formally offering me a full Naval Cadetship at Britannia Royal Naval College, Dartmouth.

The open ocean and blue skies beckoned.

3

College life as a Naval Cadet (1962/3).

E ntering the impressive halls of Britannia Royal Naval College, Dartmouth was undoubtedly a shock to my system – down at the bottom of the ladder once more.

On leaving school I had been selected for an inaugural prize – spending a month in the United States with Thomas T Lenk, founder and President of the Garcia Fishing Corporation. He and his wife Mary, their two sons, Timmy and Eric and his mother made it the trip of a lifetime: frequenting top restaurants in New York such as the Four Seasons and the 21 Club and other prestigious establishments in Denver and San Francisco. After one special Wine Cellar extravaganza in the Golden Gate City we were strolling down the street after many Black Label Jack Daniel bourbons and copious amounts of vintage wine when we passed an extremely attractive young woman who was stark naked – carrying her clothes over her shoulder. I was learning a bit about the other side of the tracks.

The Lenks arranged for me to visit my birthplace, Medicine Hat, Alberta and two other cities, Phoenix and Dallas, where they had arranged for me to stay in the penthouse suite of the Hilton Hotel. I was being terribly spoiled!

Couple all that with having been at the top of the pile at Reading School and you will understand my feelings as I joined Dartmouth– well and truly at the bottom of the ladder again. Even worse, I knew very little about the Royal Navy having been brought up within the culture of the Royal Air Force. My accent was distinctly provincial and I found myself surrounded by very smooth-talking Naval Cadets, many of whom had generations of prestigious naval names in their family histories such as Hamilton, Freemantle, etc. During this baptism of fire I felt very much like a fish out of water.

It was somewhat fortunate therefore that the college staff con- sidered new cadets to have only half a brain and that they were going to provide the other half or in my case, three quarters. This levelled the playing field a little and made it much easier for me to adapt to my new regime.

The first term was used to knock us into shape: more like a boot- camp. The emphasis was on physical fitness, discipline and learning rudimentary skills of sailing, power boating and rowing (known as 'pulling' in naval-speak) on the River Dart below the College. There was no free time and cadets were forbidden at con- siderable peril to walk anywhere around the establishment – we had to double (run) everywhere: in steel-tipped boots that skidded mercilessly on the immaculate mahogany floors that infested the place.

Unlike former days with younger entries, there was no longer any corporal punishment for misdemeanours. The caning of cadets in front of the whole college was a thing of the past but an equally demeaning form of correction was available and it was rather more taxing. This was known as ROB (Required On Board) 'Charlie'. 'Bravo' and 'Alpha' were lesser punishments.

As far as I recall, 'Charlie' would be given for serious lapses in dis- cipline such as being late on morning parade. The miscreant would have to report to one of the College's Parade Ground Instructors in full military kit (gaiters, webbing belt, back-pack and Lee-Enfield rifle) at the top of the Sand Quay steps that led down to the river and by a steep part of the road known as Heart-Break Hill. The rifle weighed about 11 lbs (5 kilos) and during punishment had to be carried above the head in both hands. There were 365 steps from the College down to Sand Quay.

The routine was simple and, inevitably, everything had to be done at the double. Down to Sand Quay and back two or three times and then up and down Heart-Break Hill a few times. It tended to concentrate the mind more than a little. And indeed it all took place during the only free time of the day – late afternoon. (As far as I remember, Heart-Break Hill only claimed one fatality – yes, through heart failure!)

The silver lining to it was that we were all terribly fit from our boot-camp-style daily routine which started at 0600: down to Sand Quay for half an hour rowing a cutter; back up for breakfast followed by morning parade; at least three sessions of circuit training in the gym or swimming each morning; afternoon sports (for me, rugby) and classroom training each evening – not forgetting the assault course. There was no time to think – just to obey orders.

Strangely, you might think, I only had one session of ROB 'Charlie' and that was enough for me.

'Alpha' was a regular affair: very mild by comparison but still testing. It consisted of rig-changing. Our cadet's quarters (dormitories) were on the other side of the College from the Sub-Lieutenant's cabins and they were our tormentors. The slightest infraction, real or imagined, could result in 'Alpha': racing across to the Sub. Lt's cabin and being told to return in five minutes wearing a different rig. This could be rugby kit, evening dress, parade uniform, etc. Three or four rig-changes were the norm after which your bed space and locker had to be put in pristine condition before evening rounds – perhaps just 15 minutes later.

'Bravo' was the most fun if you can call it that. It usually resulted from infractions on the parade ground under the watchful eye of the College Gunnery Officer, Lieutenant Frank Trickey. Without question he was truly adored by all of us. An impressively tall and robust figure with a pervasive sense of humour and extraordinary language, his most remarkable attribute was his baritone voice. He rivalled Regimental Sergeant-Major Ronald Brittain, MBE, Coldstream Guards for the loudest voice in the land! He would stand on the ramparts overlooking the parade ground which was about the size of a running track and just whisper. We could hear every word. And when he yelled your name the whole parade ground shook. If you were lucky, when you became the focus of his critical eye your punishment would be standing at attention in front of one of the statuesque figures taken from famous galleons' bows and telling the figure, at the top of your voice and in the foulest language that you could think of, what a useless, miserable cadet that you were. This often occurred in the presence of the College Commanding Officer and his wife – both of whom would listen closely to all the epithets with considerable amusement.

If you were less fortunate, you would be required to run several times around the parade ground ramparts with the same old rifle above your head. Character forming or just learning a lesson?

After he left Dartmouth, Frank went to HMS Raleigh where ab-initio naval recruits were trained. Again, he was a huge success. One Sunday when all the Staff Officers and their wives were already seated and the young sailors were entering the Church, Frank espied one young lad who had forgotten to take his cap off. Frank's booming voice echoed around the place of worship: "Take your hat off in the house of the Lord, CUNT!" Not surprisingly it brought the house down with hysterical laughter.

My lack of maritime experience became fully evident on the river Dart: I was never going to represent England at sailing. There were a selection of different dinghies and I managed to capsize all of them regularly. To make up for this I was adept at power-boat handling.

I had joined up to fly – not to mess around in boats. But that was the price you paid for first becoming a career seaman officer on the General List rather than choosing a short-service commission as an aviator.

If boot-camp had been a shock to the system, it was nothing compared with the next part of training.

In January 1963, I embarked in HMS Wizard with the Dartmouth Training Squadron for three months in the West Indies (a W-class destroyer of the British Royal Navy that saw service during World War II and was later converted to a Type 15 frigate).

Figure 13. HMS Wizard before conversion.

This 'cruise' was to make us thoroughly familiar with the conditions that our sailors had to endure when at sea. In today's terms they were anachronistic to say the least and no special favours were forthcoming: which was entirely reasonable.

Our cadets' quarters for about 30 of us consisted of a cramped mess deck not much larger than the living room of an average modern home. We each had a small locker for our possessions and our beds were hammocks slung from the deck-head (ceiling). There was less than a foot between hammocks – certainly no room to swing a cat. Ventilation was limited to a small number of scuttles in the ship's side.

All that might have been bearable but for four things.

First, the whole ship perpetually stank of diesel fumes and fatty smells from the galley (kitchen).

Second, we spent the first week at sea in the English Channel and Bay of Biscay in very rough, wintry weather with the ship rolling and pitching constantly: it was snowing part of the time.

Third, the Foreign Nationals under training were grouped together in one corner of the mess deck by their own choice and would spill food, sauce and drink on the deck below their hammocks with gay abandon – and without cleaning it up. More smells!

Fourth, our duties included cleaning out the heads (toilets) on a daily basis.

Put that all together with a prolonged bout of seasickness and you can imagine how miserable I was. My only relief was going out on deck in freezing weather to scrape ice and snow from the superstructure. When we found out that our captain, Lt. Cdr. Jenks suffered from perpetual seasickness when afloat, it put things in some perspective.

Our lot could only get better and it did.

Soon we were in more tropical climes having sailed South before crossing the pond towards the Caribbean. Now the weather was balmy and we could spend a lot of time working on the upper deck: cleaning, paint-chipping and painting. Our sister ship, HMS Tenby, was in company and watching her ride slowly up and down the huge swells in mid-Atlantic like a toy boat provided me with my first real sense of the power of the sea.

More than half-way across the pond and in 5,000 feet of water, the Captain provided some welcome relaxation by ordering "Hands to bathe." Sailors with loaded rifles were positioned around the upper deck on shark-watch as we all dived into the flat calm sea. There was a lot of Sargasso-type seaweed floating on the surface and the sailors thought it would be fun to try to force the same down the cadets' throats. Good fellows.

Our time in the Caribbean remains a bit of a blur: very enjoyable but without any significant incident. My later visit as a Midshipman was to be far more memorable.

On our return to the UK we encountered a severe storm in the Bay of Biscay. HMS Wizard had no stabilizers and bounced around like a cork in the heavy seas: regularly rolling 45° one way and then 45° the other. By that stage we had all fully gained our sea-legs – except for our Captain who continued to suffer bravely without complaint. It was therefore pure excitement to experience the true power of the sea. Standing up without holding on to something was impossible.

Despite the storm, routines had to be followed as usual. This led to a scene that could have been taken from a Charlie Chaplin movie. One of our Astro-Navigation training lessons was to take place in the Charthouse which was configured with several chart tables and very tall stools. As the ship continued to roll heavily, every loose article was thrown violently backwards and forwards including books, the stools and ourselves. It was nearly impossible to keep a good footing.

Then through the doorway hatch came our Instructor with blood streaming down his face from broken nose and teeth. "I think we had better call it a day!" he burbled. He had obviously lost his footing.

Back at Dartmouth for the final term of the year, life was much more fun. We had more latitude and tons of sport, colloquially known as 'jock-strapping'. The most rigorous event was a 40-mile trek over the bleak terrain of Dartmoor followed by a 10-mile journey down the River Dart pulling (rowing) a heavy cutter: challenging but satisfying when over!

At the end of our Cadet year we were given the opportunity to opt for where we would like to spend our Midshipman year at sea. Each of us had to put forward three choices. It was a matter for great discussion and the competition was intense for the plumb appointments. I devoted a great deal of time and energy spreading the word that 'everyone was opting for the West Indies – so there was no point in trying for that'. The scam worked brilliantly. Only a handful opted for the Caribbean and I was one of the lucky ones.

4

A MIDSHIPMAN IN THE
WEST INDIES (1963/4).

W hen I joined the frigate HMS Tartar, F133, in Plymouth as a
Mid with Chris Samuel, I was full of optimism and excitement. That optimism was well-placed and fully justified. 365 days
of enjoyment and adventure beckoned as I realised quickly that I
was joining a very happy ship.

Figure 14. HMS Tartar.

Tartar had recently been commissioned as the first-of-class of the Royal Navy's new Type-15 anti-submarine frigates. On sailing, it was planned for her to deploy to Gibraltar and the Mediterranean Station but during the major NATO Exercise Riptide IV, in which we participated after leaving harbour, this was changed and we were off to Bermuda to join the West Indies Squadron for Bahamas Patrol duties.

Riptide was an outstanding opportunity to work with the US Carrier Battle Fleet in the Eastern Atlantic as just one part of a formidable striking force. The centrepiece of attention was the new nuclear-powered guided missile cruiser, USS Long Beach. Immensely powerful and well-armed, she had a top speed of more than 45 knots. And as I noted with some amusement in my journal, she had hidden uses:

> "The Americans use the size of their ships to full advantage: and in this they may be one step ahead of the Royal Navy–for they carry their Cadillacs and other high-powered automobiles around with them. From the look of things, the Captain of the Top on Long Beach has a job more like that of a garage owner and car-park attendant than a sailor."

Mids had to keep a weekly Journal and mine was supervised by our Training Officer, the ship's Navigator, Lieutenant Jim Dixon – a very impressive, tall Aussie. One had to be a little careful when making entries because Jim was a very formal, traditional naval officer and any implied criticism of the command was not welcomed–whether justified or not. After one trip north to Bermuda from the Caribbean, I wrote:

> "The passage was not a challenging one navigationally but we did find some difficulty in pinpointing our position at certain times. Our only aid to navigation was

using the sextant to measure our position from the sun and the stars. This was frequently impossible because of complete cloud cover."

Big Jim's comment was as follows:

"A scarcely valid 'dig' at the navigation department which is neither true nor appreciated."

This led to the use of not a little artistic license. Mids needed to know their place.

The tone of any ship's company's existence is always set by the Captain. Commander Brian Hutchings RN, an experienced submariner, became a role-model for me. He had a great sense of proportion and knew how to trust and look after his men. They returned that with loyalty and dedication.

I can't say that our deployment wasn't all fun – because it was. Mids were there to learn professionally and to bridge the gap between the lower deck and the Wardroom. We truly had the best of both worlds and we were given a genuine welcome by one and all.

Whatever the reason, I managed to develop a special albeit unusual relationship with the Captain. He had a very good sense of humour and, as it turned out, was very forgiving in nature. But if he addressed you as 'Snottie' rather than as 'Mid', it was a clear indicator that you were not in his good books.

'Snottie' was the uncomplimentary nickname given to Mids in the days of sail when they used to wipe their noses on their jacket sleeves. Buttons on the cuff were introduced to prevent this disgusting habit. The captain addressed me in this way on our first official port of call after we had welcomed guests onboard for a formal cocktail party. Music for the gathering was provided by our embarked Royal Marine contingent, some of whom proved to be adept musicians as well as Commandos. Shortly after the party started, I approached the best-looking woman there and asked her to dance. She was delighted to do so. Almost immediately, the next man on the floor dancing was the Captain and soon we were all having a less than formal wild time.

After the party was over, the skipper reverted to formality and told me, "Snottie, don't you dare start dancing again at one of my cocktail parties. Your leave is stopped." I didn't take him seriously and so on the following evening I went ashore to enjoy the pleasures of Caribbean nightlife, returning on board at about 1 o'clock in the morning. As I crossed the gangway, the boatswain's mate quietly advised me to go the long way around to my cabin. "The Captain is in the Wardroom, Mid, and all the other officers tend to avoid him at this time of night." The unspoken reason for this was obvious–the Captain liked to drink late into the night and enjoyed his officers' company. I declined to go the long way around, poked my head into the Wardroom and said, "Good evening, sir!"

Sitting alone, he looked up at me with a broad smile on his face and said, "Hello, Mid! Come and join me for a drink." He then added with another broad smile, "I thought I had stopped your leave."

"So you did, Sir. But I didn't think you meant it." He laughed and didn't mention it again. Three hours later I retired to bed a very inebriated and happy soul after countless whiskeys on the rocks.

This was to become a regular habit at each port of call – dancing at cocktail parties, stoppage of leave being ignored, followed by late night sessions with my leader. On one occasion our Wardroom session took place the night before leaving harbour and I retired to my cabin at 0500–as did the Captain. We were due to slip from alongside at 0800 when I was supposed to be taking charge of the lads on the forecastle. I was late on deck and looked up rather sheepishly to the bridge. Our First Lieutenant and Executive Officer, Lt. Cdr. William Willington Chatterton-Dickson, a very straight-laced professional, was incensed with rage – so much so that he threw off his cap and jumped up and down with fury. My drinking partner leaned over the open bridge wing, "Snottie, why are you late? Your leave is stopped!" Obviously, I had to learn that however hard you play, you must always get to work on time.

In today's Navy my behaviour would not have been tolerated and would have led to severe recrimination and, as it was repetitive in nature, to an indelible black mark on my record. But unlike conditions within the modern Service, there was a pervasive sense of humour and a good balance between work and play on the ship – even when at sea and on patrol. With hindsight I suspect that the other ship's officers were more than a little grateful to me for keeping the skipper happy during the midnight hours when in harbour.

Of the full year deployed, we spent only 100 days in harbour/ alongside and I made full use of the time ashore, enjoying all the exciting ports of call and local Caribbean entertainment. But conventional night life was not always on the cards.

Cartagena, Columbia was one of those places. By day it appeared dowdy and by night, uninviting. Alec Dumbreck, our Scottish doctor, and I were invited for a drink in the Chief's Mess late one evening. The Chief Shipwright and another Chief whose name escapes me decided to accompany us ashore in a last attempt to find some entertainment. We hailed a taxicab on the jetty and, with language being a problem, I used sign language to tell the driver that we were interested in women and music. With a big grin, he nodded furiously and off we set.

We soon found ourselves driving out into the jungle-covered hills surrounding the city and began to wonder whether we had made the right choice. After about twenty miles we arrived at a sprawling hacienda-style building with shutters on all the windows and a closed entrance door complete with metal studs and a small access grill that was also shut – could have been in a James Bond movie. It was all quite eerie but with encouragement from the taxi driver we knocked on the door. A face appeared behind the grill, briefly looked us over and then welcomed us inside. We were confronted by a long corridor with many closed rooms on each side, at the end of which was a large party room filled with the delights of the Caribbean. Music filled the air and about 50 good-looking hostesses were immediately attentive and demonstrating their wares. They appeared to have a strict dress code: high heels and a short see-through negligee but nothing else or, high heels and flimsy panties but nothing else. Yes, it was a brothel but the wares were very difficult to refuse.

As we sat at a table enjoying a beer or two, the young things were flocking around us wanting to dance. My older and wiser companions were unwilling to take any further initiative and so I said to Alec, "I want to go and enjoy myself. If I catch anything, will you look after me?" He said that of course he would.

She was very pretty but all did not go well. I was new at this game and once we were disrobed and on the bed I began fondling her and kissing her all over. This was not to her approval and she began yelling obscenities. I dressed quickly and returned to the party room. When I explained what had happened, the guys were very amused and told me, "Don't let that put you off, Mid. She must be a weirdo. Go and pick another one."

Soon I was back in another room with a dusky beauty who could actually speak some English. After having the time of my life and we were lying back on the bed, she whispered, "I think you are new at this, yes? Let us do it one more time." I didn't need a second invitation.

In the small hours of the morning, halfway back to the ship in another taxi, I suddenly realized that I had left my watch and tie in the girl's room. So we turned around, retrieved them and eventually made it back on board in the early morning. For the next three weeks of 'incubation' I was dreadfully worried about catching something. Queues of young stricken sailors were forming outside the sick bay as I was given the all clear by Alec. What a relief it was!

The routine for me at sea was regular and straightforward enough: the morning watch on the bridge from 0400 to 0800 and then the first-dog watch from 1600 to 1800. It was a good start to the day, watching the sun rise every morning at about 6 o'clock in the company of our veteran Gunnery Officer, Dougie. He had many stories to tell about the Battle of the Atlantic including being sunk twice by German U-boats.

Much of our time was spent in the balmy waters of the Bahamas patrolling from Cay Sal to the Turks and Caicos. Our task was to apprehend and hand over to the cutters of the United States Coast Guard any Cuban refugees fleeing from the oppression of the Castro regime, and to arrest freedom fighters whose passages might be taking them into or out of Cuba. It was also an important part of our job to prevent exploitation of the refugees by the owners of small fishing vessels who were demanding extortionate prices for the mean task of ferrying these victims of circumstance from Cuba to the nearby British territorial waters.

One important strength of our mission capability was the embarked contingent of Royal Marines led by a gentle, bronzed giant, Lt. Ben Herman. There could have been no better front-line representatives of the Naval Service than those young men.

Ben was the Navy tennis champion. His playing partner on board was Sub. Lt. Mike Moreland, a tall, freckled, go-get officer whom I was to serve with again later when we were both flying Phantoms from the deck of HMS Ark Royal in 892 Squadron.

Our frigate was not welcomed to the West Indies Station by sunshine, palm trees and golden beaches, far from it. On crossing the Atlantic, our first port of call was to be Bermuda but when we were still a few hundred miles away from the Island we found ourselves on a collision course with Category 3 hurricane Beulah with maximum sustained winds of 120 mph (195 km/h). The question facing us was whether to make passage more to the north and outrun the storm or to turn to the southwest and go behind it. As hurricanes tend to turn to the right, it was decided to take the northerly route and hope for the best. As fate would have it, it didn't turn to the right, maintaining its northerly heading and we found ourselves in the middle of it.

What an experience! We endured the storm for two days and in the middle of the night we passed just through the edge of the eye where the winds were at full strength and from directly behind us. Our ship had very effective stabilizers and these kept us on a relatively even keel despite the mountainous waves. For safety reasons, all hands were kept off the upper deck but the enclosed bridge proved to be an ideal platform for witnessing the strength of the ocean. The winds were so strong that they ripped the tops off the waves in great plumes of white fury.

After a brief reconnaissance of Bermuda Island which I found to be extremely expensive thanks to the presence of American tourists, we made passage south to Freeport, where we refuelled, and later, on to the turquoise waters of our main patrol area, the Grand Bahamas Bank. It was there that we officially took over the duties of patrol ship from HMS Ursa.

My first view of Freeport, on Grand Bahama Island, was a disappointment. I had mistakenly expected the coastline to be grandiose and impressive, instead of which it was flat and uninteresting. The new harbour was only half-constructed and the island was bare apart from a new casino-cum-hotel that was being built. Nassau on Grand Providence Island proved to be a very different kettle of fish. The coast was lined with attractive beaches and the hotels and brightly coloured houses looked as though they harboured a very prosperous community. It had all the indications of a very good place to visit. As we briefly lay at anchor there, the Senior Naval Officer West Indies, later to be Admiral of the Fleet Sir Edward Beckwith Ashmore, GCB, DSC, made an informal visit to the ship in anticipation of his cruise on board in March of the following year.

The Cays that we had to keep an eye on had names that could have been taken straight out of a piracy or James Bond novel such as Gun Cay, Dog Rocks and Hogsty Reef. For the most part, it was unnecessary to land a search party to look for Cubans because most of the islands were merely sun-baked heads of coral protruding from the sea – with no cover and capable of supporting only the basic forms of life, such as land crabs. When we did send a landing party ashore, it was either because we had seen something suspicious or because the whole island could not be examined in enough detail from our sea-boats or Gemini dinghies.

Landing parties were often the order of the day with midshipmen and sailors manning the sea-boats and Royal Marines in charge of the Geminis. Boarding parties led by Lieut. Gordon Harris (another very amenable and seasoned naval officer) were also employed to investigate the many small boats that were found in British territorial waters and to search for refugees and freedom fighters in illegal transit to or from Cuba.

The ship's most rewarding catch came at the start of our second patrol in late October 1963. Following a brief visit to Freeport, reports arrived from a U. S. Coast Guard aircraft that there were two suspicious looking boats lying in Cay Sal lagoon. We steamed south in great haste.

In a heavy sea swell our sea-boat stood off the entrance to the lagoon while our two Geminis went in with a landing party consisting of Naval and Royal Marine personnel. They found a group of unperturbed Cuban guerrillas just sitting there. The marines and sailors were wearing steel helmets and it was this headgear that had apparently convinced the little, armed band that we were Americans (so they presumed themselves safe, being in British territorial waters). Great was their surprise on being held at gunpoint, searched and arrested.

In the mistaken belief that we were the U. S. Navy, they had neglected to destroy any of their papers or charts which were duly found to be very incriminating. As for arms and ammunition, they had in their possession eight rifles, a submachine gun, 30 sticks of plastic explosive, three hand grenades and mountains of ammunition. The prisoners were bound and brought on board. Overnight, the Royal Marines searched the island for more arms and Cuban personnel. The next morning we made a quick passage to Nassau to land our prisoners.

We rescued many refugees from parlous circumstances and arrested more than a few freedom-fighters. From the refugees we learned much about the dreadful conditions they had left behind. The Cuban dictator, Castro, was maintaining his regime with a reign of terror. His forces were given full power to shoot or rape anyone they chose. A woman refugee that we rescued declared that 19 members of her family had been shot out of hand. Communism ruled in Cuba with the enduring assistance of Kruschev and the Cold War Eastern Bloc nations.

Another memorable occasion occurred when the Royal Marine boss, Ben Herman, was officer of the watch. He sighted a tiny dinghy, nothing larger than a small rowing boat in the deep blue waters south of Grand Bahama Bank. It was overloaded with 11 refugees and in danger of being swamped by the waves. As they were being brought on board it became clear that one of the survivors was a pregnant woman who had just gone into labour. She was rushed to the Sick Bay where the ship's doctor, Surgeon-Lieutenant Alec Dumbreck acted as midwife for the birth of a healthy baby girl. It was typical of Jolly-Jack's sense of humour that the Sick Bay attendant carried the afterbirth on an open tray through the sailors' dining room whilst they were enjoying their lunch. We later heard back from Miami that the very grateful mother had christened her daughter Benita–after the man who had saved her.

In parallel with these official duties, the Captain approved many informal excursions ashore for the ship's crew to deserted Cays so that the full beauty of the underwater corals and pristine beaches could be enjoyed. Snorkelling in the company of groupers, stingrays, barracudas and reef sharks was an amazing experience that may be commonplace now but in those days was a true adventure. Barracudas were very curious creatures and would follow you like a shadow as you swam around the coral banks, spear gun at the ready. There was no shortage of fish for beach BBQs or for taking back on board for dinner. But having a six-foot shark circling around you underwater was disturbing, to say the least. It usually meant a rapid exit from the water.

In the early 60s, the fish of the Bahamas had not yet been tainted by mercury poisoning from U. S. industrial waste and became a delicious, regular part of our diet onboard. Barracuda were the easiest to catch. Their habit of following a swimmer just a few feet behind the shoulder led to their rapid demise. We would swim into a rocky pool by the water's edge where an accomplice would be waiting with a small explosive scare-charge. As we left the water, the scare-charge would be dropped in, stunning the fish–not something that would be condoned today.

HMS Tartar's armaments needed to be kept fully functional and available for use–as with all warships at sea. Apart from small arms, these included two 4.5-inch guns, two 40mm Bofors guns and the Limbo, or Anti-Submarine Mortar Mark 10. The mortar weapon was linked to the sonar system of the ship, firing on command when the submarine target was in range. The rounds were projected so that they fell in a triangular pattern around the target. Limbo could fire in any direction around the ship and was very accurate. A salvo consisted of three rounds, each weighing 400 pounds of which 200 pounds were high explosives. To check full functionality, each weapon system had a practice allowance of live rounds for firing each year.

We fired the mortar in deep water on many occasions during the deployment. Two of them were with live munitions. The only targets available were shoals of fish which had been detected on the ship's sonar. After firing, one of the ship's sea-boats, a motor-cutter, was launched rapidly so that we could collect the dead fish for consumption on board. It proved to be a hopeless task. Our sea-boat was surrounded by dozens of sharks in a feeding frenzy and they attacked anything that we lowered into the water including the tip of an oar.

Another occasion for firing the mortar was when Admiral Ashmore relinquished his command of the West Indies Station. As we steamed past his frigate making our formal salute, we fired hundreds of toilet rolls which unfurled in the air and landed on target, festooning his ship–an old-fashioned send-off that was much appreciated.

Our ship's guns were fired regularly, whether on patrol or in Weapons Ranges off Key West and Trinidad. In the Bahamas we occasionally used them to destroy unmanned boats that had been used for smuggling people and contraband. The guns were very accurate but direct hits against such tiny targets were difficult to achieve. It sometimes proved impossible to sink these small craft with gunfire. On one occasion, we commenced firing the 4.5-inch gun at 4,000 yards and then opened up with the 40mm Bofors when in range. Although suffering severe damage, the small wooden craft would not sink until we sent the Royal Marines on board to lay plastic explosive around the engine mountings.

When off duty from Patrol, we visited many of the Windward and Leeward Islands. It all added up to a midshipman's paradise–an endless chain of working hard and playing hard.

During our time providing hurricane relief in Tobago following the impact of category 5 Hurricane Flora, I had to collect our Captain from inshore late at night in the ship's motor cutter. Alongside the jetty, the sea was very rough and a hidden concrete pylon under the water impacted the boat's propeller – bending its shaft. We suffered intense vibration all the way back to the ship. It was customary in those days that if he bent his boat, a Snottie's leave was automatically stopped until repairs had been completed. I decided to assist with the repairs that night. It had to be ready for early morning trips on the following day. Engine Room Artificer Holden and I worked on replacing the new propeller shaft in the boat from 2300 to 0230 and felt a real sense of achievement when the job was done. No sleep that night because I then had the morning anchor-watch from 0400 to 0800: a small price to pay for having perpetual fun.

A significant part of my time off-duty at sea was spent in the company of the ship's Coxswain, Sam Smythe who was the senior non-commissioned officer on board, and the Chief Petty Officers in that 'holy-of holy', the Chief's Mess. The daily rum ration for all members of the lower deck was still in place at that time. It was an institution that should never have been discontinued by Their Lordships, giving great pleasure to all ships' companies without adversely affecting operational readiness. The Senior Rates would receive their rum tot in neat form, straight from the barrel. Junior Ratings would receive theirs already mixed with two parts of water to one part of rum. This was so that they could not hoard it but had to drink it on the day of issue.

Supervising the rum ration issue each day was one of our duties as Midshipmen. In the heat of the tropics this demanded some special care. The rum barrels were stowed in a small compartment in the bowels of the ship which was filled with the exotic aroma of their contents. Too much exposure could lead to unconsciousness and much care was taken to avoid this as exact quantities of the fiery liquid were pumped by hand from the barrel for distribution to the mess decks.

As you might have guessed already, the Senior Rates were entrusted to save their neat rum for consumption at the time of their choosing and this allowed for generosity of spirit towards privileged guests in their Mess Deck. There was always an open welcome for midshipmen and I used to spend many hours with them knocking back a tot of rum with a beer chaser. I quickly developed a huge respect and admiration for these highly qualified and well-educated sailors–upon whom the efficient operational functioning of the ship depended. This respect was to serve me very well indeed when I eventually became a commanding officer – 'loyalty downwards' being the key words.

Lower deck hospitality could occasionally be taken too far and yours truly was a victim of this generosity when we spent Christmas alongside in Barbados. On Christmas Day it was the custom for the Captain and Officers to do rounds of the ship together, visiting each mess deck in turn and sharing the festive spirit. Brian Hutchings gave an explicit order to his Wardroom officers, "You are not to do independent rounds of the ship today". As a submariner, he knew too well the dangers of imbibing too much Navy Rum. I had no intention of disobeying his order but decided to make a short visit to the Coxswain just to wish him and his colleagues a personal happy Christmas. Mistake.

It was about 10 o'clock in the morning when the delighted Chiefs welcomed me into their mess deck, insisted that I should sit down and have a celebratory drink: Grog, of course. GROG, the nick-name for Navy rum, was so-called because of its origins. King George Rex received a regular shipment of rum from Grenada and, stamped on each side of the keg, the initials stood for George Rex On-board Grenada.

Not wishing to offend, I gave in and said, "Okay, just one to celebrate!" Our banter was very relaxing and so along came the second tot with beer chaser. Then another. Then another. As midday approached, I remembered there was to be a different celebration in the wardroom in honour of the birth of Ben Herman's daughter. I made my excuses and then somehow staggered along the passageways and up the ladders, entering the wardroom with a big smile on my face. I remember clearly standing with the other officers as Ben distributed the flutes of champagne. As I received my glass, it slowly slipped through my fingers and dropped to the deck. That is when my lights went out and I remember nothing more until 12 hours later.

Afterwards, I learned that the ship's Engineer Officer, Lt. Cdr. Stephenson and one other had carried me to my cabin, placed me in one of the two bunks and had taken it in turns to watch over me. Apparently, they initially thought that I was vomiting blood but they soon realized it was dark Navy rum.

The only good thing about it was that they had placed me in the wrong bunk–that belonging to my fellow midshipman, Chris Samuel. And what a mess it was! One Christmas Day completely ruined but a valuable lesson learned. I should have listened to the Captain.

A very important side of life onboard was sport and to my delight we had a keen ship's rugby team. There wasn't much time for practicing or training but unlimited enthusiasm made up for that and our games against local sides were always well fought. I hadn't realized that rugby was so popular throughout the Caribbean and we were often mesmerized by the skill, athleticism and strength of our opponents. During a two week visit to Bermuda we played five matches, winning some and losing some.

Two of our most memorable games were enjoyed in very different environments. The first was in Southern Trinidad when we anchored off Pointe à Pierre and were hosted generously by the Texaco Oil Refinery. The game was held on a rock-hard sandy pitch with very little grass. We emerged from the game covered in bloody grazes but we had surprised the host team by winning 6 – 0. The beer went down well afterwards.

The second was in mid-winter when we travelled by coach to Boston during our official visit to Washington DC. The pitch was covered with 3 inches of snow over 3 inches of mud and our opponents were huge American-football athletes. I started the game at scrum half and soon was unable to pick up the ball, never-mind pass it; thoroughly drenched from head to foot in icy mud and frozen to the core. I ended up playing on the wing as we were well-beaten.

One of the major events of our year was the visit to Washington DC to show off our new first of class frigate to our U. S. Allies. It was bitterly cold as we steamed through Chesapeake Bay and up the Potomac River and we spent many hours on deck chipping away a blanket of ice. A very grandiose welcoming party awaited us on the dockside with several bands and a host of top-level dignitaries from the U. S. Navy and the Pentagon. The timing of our arrival presented some ship-handling problems.

The flow of the Potomac River is governed by the state of the tide. With an incoming tide, which it was, the flow was upstream rather than downstream. But to get alongside at our berth which was port (left) side-to and between two jetties, we had to turn sharp left out of the stream giving the stern of the ship strong momentum to the right. At the same time, we would have to go astern on the ship's engines to take the way off the ship. When going astern, Tartar's single propeller rotated clockwise and the paddlewheel effect of this gave the stern further momentum to the right.

Big Jim Dixon, our Navigator or 'pilot', was fully aware of all this and recommended to the Captain in the strongest terms that we should use the tugboat that was provided in order to control the swing of the stern away from the jetty. His advice was ignored. As we were going slow astern on the main engines and the bow rope was attached to a jetty bollard, despite full use of the ship's rudder the stern continued to swing to the right until we found ourselves ignominiously parked across the two jetties. The tug was then used to pull the stern properly alongside. The atmosphere on the bridge was electric. There was embarrassment all round. With hindsight, if we had proceeded upstream, turned around and entered our berth in a right-hand turn, all might have been well.

But our less than impressive arrival was soon forgotten and we were wined and dined in very gracious style by our U. S. hosts. Many visitors came on board to see the ship, being welcomed by frozen midshipmen on the gangway. In the evenings, cocktail parties ashore abounded and I spent one very late memorable evening on the couch in an Admiral's home with his very understanding daughter: the highlight of my visit.

Figure 15. Cocktail Party ashore.

I was sad when my Midshipman's year had to come to an end but as it did so the Captain put some special icing on the cake. We were transiting the Bay of Biscay towards UK by night in fog and there were many fishing fleets and other shipping spread across the ocean ahead. It was a time for extreme caution. As I entered the bridge just before 0400 for the morning watch, Commander Hutchings was sitting relaxed in his chair. There was no sign of any other officer of the watch. He didn't say much.

"Midshipman, there is a lot of traffic around tonight. Make sure you steer clear of fishermen's nets. If in doubt, call me. I shall be in my cabin. You have the Watch!"

There could have been no higher compliment. It was a moment I shall always treasure. He retired to bed having given me a confidence boost like no other. With great care we threaded our way through the fog and the innumerable radar contacts and, no, I didn't need to call him. Like any exceptional leader, he refrained from looking over my shoulder and slept peacefully until dawn.

It had been a most rewarding and enjoyable year but now I had to turn my attention to new challenges at Dartmouth College.

5

SUB-LIEUTENANT'S YEAR AT COLLEGE (1964/5).

The return to Dartmouth, newly promoted with a shiny gold ring on my arm, heralded a quantum change from my sea time in HMS Tartar but proved to be no less rewarding. It was a happy reunion with old friends from our initial Cadet year but we now had some status and, with it, responsibility. Apart from continuing with our professional learning, our most important task was setting a good example to the new entry Cadets. This was made easier by the fact that we were already placed on a pedestal with some experience from sea and enjoying comparatively ritzy, college living conditions. We each had a private cabin and our dining took place in the College Gun Room, a most impressive environment by any standards mirroring the beauty of Greenwich College's famous Painted Hall and a major change from the cadet canteens.

Highlights of my year were three-fold: flying the Tiger Moth bi-plane, rugby and, of greatest satisfaction and import, being in-charge of a Division of cadets.

I cover the Tiger Moth flying in Chapter 7.

Figure 16. The Gun Room, Dartmouth Naval College.

The college had several rugby union teams and much to my delight I progressed rapidly from the 3rd XV to the 1st Team: playing at the position of inside-centre-three-quarter. Our fixtures included games against the other two Service Colleges (Sandhurst and Cranwell), Manadon Naval Engineering College and many local civilian teams. The latter could be extremely physical encounters, putting it mildly. When we played Newton-Abbott I found this to my cost. I was nowhere near the ball when I suddenly found myself half-throttled in a headlock by a huge forward who proceeded to pound my face with his free fist. A penalty was awarded as I found myself half-conscious on the ground with my nose re-positioned an inch or so across my cheek. The College Surgeon Commander was on the touchline as I staggered off in a daze.

"Put your head between my legs" he ordered. I did so, was firmly gripped by his knees and then received a hammer blow to the nose with his fist. That solved the problem: the nose was back in place. After a few minutes of recuperation, I was back playing on the pitch – seeking my revenge.

Our team was privileged to have the services, as a player and coach, of one of the best-ever England Rugby Team second-row forwards, Instructor-Lieutenant Mike Davis. It was quite an experience when he arranged for a team of Internationals to play against us. The England fly-half, Richard Sharpe, ran rings around me.

For the second of the three annual terms, I was surprised and delighted to be appointed as the Exmouth Divisional Sub-Lieutenant in charge of first year Cadets. There were four other Divisions and competition between all of them was intense.

I vacated my cabin in the Sub-Lieutenant's quarters and moved into a cabin integrated with the Cadets' dormitory. The power behind the throne in the Division was Chief Petty Officer White, a very senior gentleman who provided continuity for the supervision and training of the Cadets. He never interfered but was always available with good advice and assistance. I ran the Division in the same manner that I later ran my Sea Harrier squadrons and this bore considerable fruit.

Right at the very start, I explained to my Cadets that they were going to be trusted entirely with making our Division the best in the college, that they knew and must abide by the rules and that I would be giving individuals responsibility for organising all competitive events and extra-curricular activities. Only their efforts would make us the best and I would not be looking over their shoulder. I told them I would always be on hand if and when they were in doubt. It was a magic formula.

The Exmouth Cadets rose to the challenge impressively. They won all eight of the inter-divisional competitions with me hardly raising a finger. And their discipline was impeccable; except for our two Libyan Navy cadets.

One day an incident took place in the queue for lunch in the cadets' canteen. The Libyans tried to jump the queue and were told to get lost. They responded by head-butting two of the other cadets and starting an affray. The first thing I knew about it was a knock on my cabin door. The two miscreants stood there crying their hearts out, wringing their hands with tears streaming down their cheeks, telling me that it wasn't their fault and they had been punished unfairly. I told them to cut it out. As if by magic, the tears stopped and were replaced by big ingratiating smiles. It didn't work! I told them to f***k off and accept their punishment like a man. I also confiscated their monthly cigarette ration.

In today's world of political correctness they might well have got away with their unacceptable behaviour. What is it that they say about political correctness? "It is tantamount to picking up a turd (excrement) with one's fingers at the cleanest end."

Later, it did appear to have a part to play in the Sub-Lieutenant's Gun Room at a formal Mess Dinner. I was sitting next to a tall, very charming colleague, Perry Cope. Across the mahogany table sat one of Nkrumah's nephews from Ghana. Perry said something quite harmless that obviously upset the Ghanaian. He leaped up on the table, picked up a silver candelabra and smashed it over Perry's head. Then he proceeded to rant and rave whilst doing some sort of war-dance on the table. Perry didn't blink an eye but watched the performance with amazement as did the rest of us. Eventually the Ghanaian sat down but he was not asked to leave the dinner or punished for his extraordinary actions. It would have been a different story if a UK Sub-Lieutenant had behaved in the same way.

The year produced a litany of very happy memories.

When the James Bond movie, "Goldfinger" premiered in Plymouth it was a must see for all of us. My very close friend, Jeremy Parkes and I drove the 50 miles into the town only to find a huge queue which fully encircled the Odeon cinema. It was just 15 minutes before the film started. Jerry and I walked up to near the front where a group of Dartmouth sub-lieutenants were already in line. They told us to go to the back of the queue. More than disappointed, I told Jerry to follow me and we went across the road to a gas station. I politely asked the proprietor if I could use his phone and then made a call to the Odeon cinema itself, asking to speak to the Manager.

> "Good evening. This is the duty Lieutenant-Commander of Dartmouth College. We have a military emergency on our hands. Would you please be good enough to put a message on your cinema screen saying that there is a military emergency and all officers under training from Dartmouth College and Manadon College are required to return to base immediately."

Within minutes, hordes of cadets and sub-lieutenants rushed out of the cinema and the queue outside virtually disappeared. Gleefully, Jerry and I bought our tickets and thoroughly enjoyed the film. The next day at college, all hell broke loose but the ensuing witch-hunt failed to identify the culprits.

At the end of the very rewarding year and as was the custom, a formal Mess Dinner was planned to say farewell to us all. Unfortunately and very sadly our most famous Prime Minister, Sir Winston Churchill passed away and out of respect the dinner was cancelled. John Ford, our excellent College Commander and Executive Officer would have presided at the dinner and he was generous enough to tell me privately how he had planned to sum up my year at the college:

> "Never has a Division been run so well from a horizontal position!"

6

AN ADVENTURE IN HONG KONG (1965/6).

The fourth year of Dartmouth training was spent embarked in sea-going warships where all Seaman Officers under training had to earn their Bridge Watchkeeping and Ocean Navigation Certificates. This sojourn could either be spent in the less than exciting waters around the UK or in exotic and tropical billets around the globe. There was intense competition for the latter and each Sub-Lieutenant had to present three choices of where he would like to go. I used the same trick that I had employed in my earlier choice of the West Indies Station. This time I spent a lot of energy spreading the word that everyone was opting for the Hong Kong station and so it was better to choose somewhere else. The ruse worked brilliantly yet again; I was appointed to the HMS Penston and later, Woolaston, 8th Minesweeper Squadron at HMS Tamar, Hong Kong. The other lucky guy, Paddy McKnight was appointed to a sister ship.

At the time of selection, the Borneo crisis was ongoing and represented an opportunity to see some 'action'.

Figure 17. HMS Woolaston, 1967.

In the Confrontation with Indonesia 1963-66, Britain and the Commonwealth supported the Malaysian Government against Indonesian aggression and deployed forces from all 3 Services. The Far East Fleet provided a considerable deterrent against Indonesian escalation and the presence of its strike carriers posed a threat that Indonesia could not counter. Carrier and air group transits of high-visibility international waters such as the Sunda Strait added to the deterrence value.

A decisive role in support of the Royal Marines and Army was played by the Navy's Commando Helicopters flying several thousands of hours operating from Albion and Bulwark in succession and mostly from Forward Air Bases ashore in unusually demanding conditions over a period of 4-5 years.

Penston was due to deploy to the combat theatre. It was going to be exciting. Then, sadly from my point of view, the crisis was resolved before I reached the ship and the deployment was cancelled. A huge disappointment, to say the least.

But I did get the opportunity to witness some action on my flights out to join the ship. At Singapore I took off in an RAF Beverly for the hop to Hong Kong. We had to refuel in Saigon at a US Air Force base amidst the turmoil of the Vietnam War. F-105 Thunderchiefs and other aircraft laden with bombs were operating from both runways on their missions of war – I had heard much about the Red River Valley and this was more than impressive. Then, sometime after we took off, I looked down and happened to see the shock-waves of bombs detonating in the jungle below. I wouldn't have missed it for the world.

A more personal adventure awaited me in Hong Kong.

It was there that I met Francesca Maria Gill; one of the most beautiful young women in the world. She had been brought up in Africa by an English father who was a prison governor by trade and by her mother, a petite and charming raven-haired Spanish Lady.

Francesca worked in a boutique, was a photographic model and lit up every room that she entered, whether it was a private lounge or a public nightclub. Her startling looks came mainly from her mother's side. She had a dusky skin, dark brown eyes, the most kissable full lips, an incredible figure, raven black hair and a smile that would rival that of Helen of Troy. She indeed had a face that could launch a thousand ships and when I first saw her I fell deeply in love with her.

This first meeting took place on the Peak of Victoria Island in Hong Kong. There was a party, a large party in a big house at the top of the Peak and my friend Robert Wallace or Bob, as I like to call him, escorted me. He was a young trainee manager of the Hong Kong and Shanghai Banking Corporation: later to rise to the top layer of management of that organisation.

We had known each other well at our school in Reading – we were both in the same boarding house. His father was Group Captain Bertie Wallace, a Royal Air Force navigator, and his mother was a lovely lady who used to make wonderful cakes for Bob to bring back to school after a weekend at home. Occasionally, I would go with him to their beautiful house in Ascot and I always remember the gracious way they would look after me.

I knew that Bob was in Hong Kong before arriving there and very soon after I arrived I contacted him and we got together. He was quite a racy fellow, shorter than me in stature and very much taken with the ladies. He knew of every eligible or available girl in the colony of Hong Kong – including about 400 Philippino girls at the bank.

As we drove up the winding, steep road of the Peak in the TR2 sports car that I had hired, he assured me that there would be lots of young ladies available for partying at our destination. As we walked in through the door to the main lounge area, there amid perhaps 100 guests stood a girl who took my breath away as soon as I saw her. She wasn't looking at me. She was just enjoying the party. Bob noticed my intense stare and said, "Nigel, you have no chance there! All my friends and I have tried it but no one can get near Francesca Maria Gill–she is untouchable!"

It wasn't so much a challenge to me although I did like challenges. I simply had no choice whatsoever but to talk to her, get to know her and to make her my girl.

I remember little of the party itself but what I do remember very well is that I escorted Francesca Maria Gill away from the party and took her home to her apartment in my car in a very drunken state; falling unceremoniously out of the car as I relieved myself halfway down the hill. She didn't appear to mind such ungentlemanly behaviour. It was the start of the most wonderfully romantic relationship.

To say that I was wildly, madly, passionately in love with her was an understatement. She filled my mind completely every waking minute of the day. Whenever off-duty I would go to her boutique, take her swimming in the Tamar pool and generally 'hang out' together. She told me many stories of her time growing up in Africa – especially her fear of snakes. Very soon, she was the most important part of my life.

I did, of course, have other priorities to attend to as well; the principal one of which being my duties on board HMS Penston, the minesweeper. I learned very rapidly that the Captain, Bob Edward was a very impulsive no-holds-barred type of commanding officer. A Buccaneer pilot and Air Warfare Instructor, he didn't pander to his officers and men. He expected them to know their job and to do it well and there were no excuses if you failed in your duty professionally. I came up to his mark as the Navigating Officer, Gunnery Officer, Correspondence Officer and Wardroom Wine Caterer without any question. But unfortunately, following my wonderful earlier sea time in HMS Tartar as a Midshipman and my obsession with Francesca, my social habits of intense and hard playing in the evening and overnight did tend to conflict with the way I appeared to conduct some of my duties on board.

Socially, I had still not progressed or matured much from the time of being a Midshipman. I enjoyed my drink and going ashore and having a wild time on the dancefloors of nightclubs – with, of course, generous amounts of alcohol. I mistakenly thought that Bob Edward being an aviator would understand this age-old affliction that was a hallmark of the Fleet Air Arm.

The Army Garrison officers based in the New Territories on the Kowloon side of Hong Kong harbour were certainly in tune with such behaviour. They were real brothers in arms and invited me to one of their formal Mess Dinners. It was a splendid occasion in full dress uniform and I was treated royally as their only guest. After a wonderful meal and copious amounts of alcohol I was obliged to take part in their traditional army mess-games: a time to let off steam. It was all a lot of fun including mess rugby where two teams face each other and attempt to move the ball, an empty waste-paper basket, to the opponent's end of the Mess – always a complete rough house. The only problem facing me was that they decided to have an Army versus Navy game – but not in the style of Twickenham Rugby Ground. It was one naval officer against thirty or more Irish Guards. They all lined up at one end of the Mess with yours truly at the other and very graciously allowed me to start proceedings with the ball in hand. Not to be deterred by numbers, I charged at them like a lunatic and in seconds was drowned under a large pile of very drunk, gleeful opponents. I sus-pect it had all started off as something of a joke – testing out the Navy – but there were no holds barred and I eventually emerged from the carnage with my dress uniform literally torn to shreds. A little bruised and battered, I was amazed to see that one of their number had a broken nose and one, a broken arm. What an evening.

Getting back over the harbour to Victoria Island at 3 o'clock in the morning became a trial. The only means of transport was by very small water-taxis whose drivers took one look at the appa-rition on the dockside before moving on: I did indeed look like a scarecrow. Eventually I persuaded one of them to carry me over but couldn't possibly enter HMS Tamar dockyard looking like a tramp. The only solution was to clean up and spend the night at Francesca's apartment.

Sadly, I was not a man of private means. During the deployment my Midland Bank Manager would write to me first in black type, then alternating lines of black and red and finally all in red. But he was a good soul and never bounced one of my cheques. My only income was that earned by me from the Navy but my desire to be with and to please Francesca meant that I entertained her like a princess. We rapidly got to know each other well and inevitably I would stay the night in her apartment and come back to the ship early in the morning ready to change into my uniform and get on with the job—which in most circumstances meant going to sea for the day on patrol, or sometimes for a few days at a time.

It wasn't very long before I began to get an inkling of why the Fleet Air Arm had christened my Captain, Bob Edward, with a less than complimentary nick-name. A Buccaneer fighter pilot, he was also an Air Warfare Instructor and was very forceful in his manner. Unpredictable, very impulsive and he asked his new Navigator, yours truly, to do some quite extraordinary things. He would not allow me to take things slowly and to approach my new responsibility as Navigator with sensible caution. A fine example of this was the first night that we took our sweeper through a narrow entrance less than 80 yards wide into one of the tiny rocky bays on the mainland coast.

Neither he nor I had been into the bay before by day or night, and it was a very black night. During the day I had prepared a plan for entering the bay and anchoring the minesweeper and showed it to him. This included a slow approach through the narrows into the main part of the bay then a sensible further reduction in speed prior to taking way off the ship for anchoring. He looked at my plan and said, "That is nonsense. The way that you are going to do it is as follows. We shall enter the bay with engines at half ahead with revolutions to give us 12 knots. You will then give just two orders, one of which will be 'Stop main engines' and the second will be 'Half astern main engines'. We shall wait until the way is off the ship and then we shall drop the anchor. Is that understood?"

I did not procrastinate about the matter because I could see in his eyes, which had a glint of amusement but a very great deal of certainty in them, that he meant what he said. However I did think to myself, 'what an Idiot'.

There were no lights in the little bay. The entrance was very rocky and there was absolutely no moon that night. This meant that I had to take the ship in using the radar alone for positioning and trust that my radar offsets and transit lines were correct. Otherwise, quite simply, we would either run aground on the rocks or the shoreline.

The anchorage went as planned. We came hurtling into the bay at far too high a speed for my liking. I ordered 'Stop main engines' and then 'Half astern main engines' when we were half a cable (100 yards) from our anchor point. We dropped the anchor and, as we gathered way astern, I stopped main engines. We remained there for the night.

It was my first real lesson on the unpredictability of my Captain. Perhaps I should say he was predictably unpredictable and it was my good fortune that I proved adequate as a navigator, never letting him down. Whatever the task and however difficult it was, I managed to succeed in doing it properly and safely. This was a good thing because Bob Edward did not appreciate the times when my social habits tended to impinge upon my duties on board.

Francesca and I normally frequented the Italian nightclub in the basement of the Hilton hotel on Victoria Island. It was our regular night stop and we enjoyed dancing together, drinking together and simply falling in love with each other. Whenever we entered, the place would stop for a moment as all the guests admired my lovely lady. Testament to her remarkable charisma was when Elizabeth Taylor and Richard Burton made an entrance at the Club one evening – and, no, the place did not stop – Francesca remained the centre of attention.

Regularly I would run out of money and would then go to see my Chinese tailor, San Cheong in Wan Chai for more cash so that we could continue to enjoy the evening. That money transaction often took place as late as one or two o'clock in the morning. Whatever the time, San Cheong was always there in his shop, with his little Chinese workers at their machines sewing suits and shirts, and he would always greet me with great charm and courtesy, "Come in! Come in! Do sit down and do have a brandy."

Having a brandy with him meant a tumbler full of the fiery brown liquid and whilst I was enjoying this courtesy, I would write my cheque. Then it was back to the Hilton for more fun with Francesca before retiring to her apartment where we would sleep together in a manner that was anything but platonic until dawn awoke us.

Occasionally, the dawn didn't awake me quite early enough and it would be a mad scramble in a rather crumpled suit of civilian clothes to get back down to the Naval Dockyard, rush on board the ship, change into uniform and appear on the bridge prior to the ship's planned sailing time. As time went by my return on board got later and later until the fateful day when I had to leap across the Senior Officer's minesweeper and jump the yawning gap to my own ship, Penston, as she was pulling away from the senior vessel. I raced up to the bridge and in a very chirpy way addressed the Captain. "I have the con, Sir!".

It was not a good move.

His face was twisted with rage and he said to me with complete distaste in his voice, "No you don't! How dare you come to my bridge dressed like that! Go and change into uniform immediately. "Something told me at that stage that I was in serious trouble. I raced to my cabin, rapidly showered, changed into my clean pressed whites and calf skin shoes and returned to the bridge. He wouldn't let me take the con for going out through the Harbour, which would be my normal duty. When we got well away from Victoria Island out to sea, he spoke for the first time: "Sub-Lieutenant, your leave is stopped."

Now this was not the same order of leave stoppage that I used to receive from Captain Brian Hutchings as a Midshipman. This was unquestionably a far more serious matter. I said to him, "Yes, sir. For how long?" To my horror he replied with some venom, "For three weeks." My heart sank. I would not be able to see my gorgeous Francesca for three weeks. I would not be able to lie in her arms overnight, or go to the nightclub with her, or do anything with her. It was a tragedy in my life, a major one.

But I did sneak ashore a couple of times without getting caught.

Having put that episode behind me, I was treated to a real demonstration of the Captain's intransigence. We were conducting a week-long, twenty-four hours a day minesweeping exercise out at sea. Our crew consisted of five officers: the Captain; Terry Brogan, First-Lieutenant and in charge of the sweeping equipment operation; two Midshipmen, Paul and Abu Bakir (Malayan); and me.

Throughout the week we ran four-hour watches , four on and four off, and I was paired with the Captain for bridge watch keeping. Our set routine was to wake-up/call our relief using the boatswain's mate in time for him to be up on the bridge five minutes before the hour. About mid-week and in the middle of the night, the Captain forgot to call me. By chance I awoke just in time to get to the bridge right on the hour: five minutes late. He did not apologise. Quite the contrary.

I was utterly flabbergasted when he told me, "You are late! Your leave is stopped forever." The true nature of the man was revealing itself. And he meant it.

A couple of miserable weeks later, I had the opportunity to turn the situation on its head.

A rather smarmy Captain approached me in my cabin. "Nigel, I have a close friend visiting for a few days with nowhere to stay. Would you mind him using your bunk?If you say yes, I shall temporarily give you your leave back while he is here and you can go and stay with Francesca." I couldn't believe my ears.

"Sorry, that isn't going to wash. Give me my leave back for good or no deal, Sir." He left the cabin in a fury.

Very quickly I got together with the other ship's officers – explaining the sad situation and asking for their support. They gladly agreed to refuse to give up their own bunks – they had been horrified by the Captain's precipitous decision to stop my leave. They were as good as their word.

A day later, the Captain visited my cabin once more – a disingenuous smile on his face. "OK, Nigel, if you give up your bunk for my friend's visit you can have your leave back – period." I smiled sweetly, "All right, Sir. You have a deal."

The next time we crossed swords, it was entirely my own fault. We sailed in company with the other two minesweepers for a month's visit to Singapore where we were to exchange the Penston for the Woolaston. Over the previous couple of weeks I had had a fun time ashore with very little sleep – and was dramatically hung-over. So much so that on leaving harbour I went to the quarter-deck, vomited over the stern and then retired to my cabin for 36 hours. Guess who was not amused? My 'friend', Bob.

After having surfaced from my cabin, I received the inevitable bollocking and was told, "You have a lot of ground to make up if you are to receive your Ocean Navigation ticket. Make no mistake about that." Was the man softening?

En route south we were navigating using sun and star sights with the sextant – and I was very rusty at that. Worse, throughout our transit of the South China Sea there was complete cloud cover for most of the time – preventing any useful astro-navigation. Eventually there were breaks in the cloud one sunset and I managed to get three good stars: establishing an accurate position fix. For a change, Bob Edward seemed pleased – until the positions recorded by the squadron navigator and Paddy McKnight in the other two ships came in. They agreed on one position which was 30 nautical miles behind my own fix. Bob beamed and said, "What do you say to that?"

Quick as a flash I replied, "They are wrong, Sir. My fix is good. That will be confirmed when we see the land ahead on radar in four hours at a range of 80 miles."

To give him his due, Bob smiled and said, "OK. If you are correct you will get your Ocean Nav Ticket – as well as a bottle of champagne from me. If not, you get neither."

The radar fix on the land ahead materialised as forecast and Bob was as good as his word. We shared the bottle of champagne in the Wardroom. "Why were they so wrong?" he asked.

"I believe they were both estimating their position because they didn't get an adequate star-sight. I guess they forgot to consider the current running down the South China sea and so their dead-reckoning fix was out by a long way. And indeed, I suspect that Paddy may have copied the squadron navigator's position fix."

Our four weeks in Singapore were hectic, transferring from one ship to another. It meant lots of paperwork for yours truly.

During the visit I took the Ship's Diver course, qualifying despite broken metatarsals in my left foot. I had already broken the same foot playing rugby at Dartmouth. All Navy Diver Courses include a lot of 'jock-strapping' – keeping fit – which in Singapore dock-yard meant pounding round a selection of wooden walkways that were criss-crossed with 2 inch-by-1-inch wooden battens. Landing on one of those too energetically broke my foot. But it was a ques-tion of carrying on as usual with a strong strapping in place. Being the only officer on the course meant setting an example and I had to keep up with the young sailors.

Two parts of the course are worthy of mention.

There was the mothballed aircraft carrier, HMS Triumph moored in the Strait and we had to learn how to leap off the 50-foot flight deck without injury. Feet first with legs angled forwards was the order of the day – worked like a charm.

The other part was much scarier – 40-minute night dives along the muddy bottom of the Dockyard. The dives consisted of feeling one's way along an elaborate array of ropes that were anchored to the sea-bed. It was pitch-black and any undue movement caused the mud to rise up in thick swirls limiting any visibility to almost zero. Nobody told us that the ropes had been laid over a colony of poisonous sea-snakes. As I felt my way along the ropes on my first night dive, I felt something slippery run through my fingers – and saw a trail of phosphorescence speeding away into the dark-ness: a sea snake. It was quite unnerving but we all got used to it and nobody was bitten.

When we arrived back in Hong Kong in our new ship, all went better than usual onboard. No scrapes and no stoppage of leave.

But our extrovert Captain still insisted on treating the ship like a speed boat. One day on entering the small naval harbour he came in with a flourish, was going too fast, cut it too fine and rammed the bow of the ship into the jetty – causing considerable damage to the hull and forcing some of the smart wooden decking on the forecastle to spring loose. The Commodore happened to be watching from his office overlooking the dockyard and that resulted in a Swords and Medals invitation for Bob to present himself for a major bollocking.

I am proud to say that as his Navigator I protected him from worse evils. But my relief, Ian Hughes, was not so fortunate. Within six months of my leaving the ship, the Captain ran HMS Woolaston aground twice.

During my time oboard I was promoted to Lieutenant and, with huge delight, received my appointment to begin flying training. But well before I left there was a much more momentous occasion.

Sitting in the Hilton Night Club I proposed to Francesca and amazingly she said "yes"! I was over the moon, but utterly penniless as usual. Refusing to accept anything other than a champagne celebration I informed the other guests that my beautiful girlfriend and I had just got engaged and hinted that some champagne would be welcomed. In very quick time, several bottles arrived on our table and we all had a mega celebration.

All my colleagues had fallen in love with Francesca and one of them was my favourite, Midshipman Ashton Shuttleworth from a sister minesweeper. His brothers Ian and Richard were in my year at Dartmouth and had become good friends – so I was rather like an uncle to Ashton who was the perfect young gentleman and officer. Soon after our engagement Ashton approached me and asked nervously but very politely, "Can I have your permission to invite Francesca out to dinner?" I was taken aback but couldn't help laughing and admiring him. "Of course, you may – go and ask her." She was delighted to accept and thoroughly enjoyed the evening.

Like the rest of my life, my departure from the ship was fraught with incident. I had to hand over all my jobs to my relief and during this process I found a couple of problems – with the Wardroom Wine Account and with the Classified Navigation Charts. I thought I had been meticulous in the running and care of both.

The Wine Account was short of about HK$2,000. This worried me not a little for days until I realised that on the dockside by the ship was a huge pile of crates containing returnable bottles. "Dockyard Jenny" would collect and pay for them at irregular intervals. After checking the empties the $2,000 became fully accounted for.

The other problem could have been much more serious. Some of the classified charts could not be found anywhere. Captain Bob appeared to take delight in informing me that I would not be allowed to return to the UK until the charts were found–without which a Board of Inquiry loomed. My navigator's assistant and I had searched the charthouse and the lockable chart cabinet several times to no avail. On the last day, I had a brainwave (yes, it's not impossible) and we dismantled the chart desk to find that the missing ones had slipped over the back of the drawer and were totally hidden from view.

Hong Kong had been an exceptional experience. Little did I know as I flew home that I would have to suffer the dubious attentions of Bob Edward again in the not so distant future. But before that, the lovely Francesca flew back to England and I started flying training. Life was looking good.

FLYING MEMORIES – THE LONG ROAD UP THE LADDER.

The following 14 chapters recount the challenging journey facing any aspiring Navy Fighter Pilot. It is a journey that the majority of aspirants are unable to complete. The long selection process begins with hundreds if not thousands of hopefuls applying for flying training in the Navy or the RAF. Aptitude tests, medical exams and leadership tests remove the majority of candidates at the first hurdle. The flying training pipeline then places each candidate under a microscope to establish what level of military flying he or she can achieve, if any, without putting themselves or others into danger.

From this pro-active selection process the different levels of potential, airmanship and competence are established. At each level of training, student pilots who have reached the limit of their potential are graded out of the fast-jet system and may be offered continued training on helicopters, transport aircraft or as fast-jet Observers/ Navigators/Radar Intercept Officers.

The surviving fast-jet military pilots are then graded once more in relation to their final potential. In the RAF, for example, the very best would have gone to the Harrier rather than Typhoon or Tornado. In the Royal Navy, only the very best pilots are accepted for carrier-borne fast-jet aviation: the most demanding flying job in the world. And the most aggressive of these later become Air Warfare Instructors (AWIs) and Top Guns.

7

THE TIGER MOTH – MY
FIRST TASTE OF 'FREEDOM'.

Tiger Moth flying was an early and fun look at aptitude – to see if one has the necessary basic skills. But the meat of the learning process really began with Basic Flying Training and continued, almost without pause, until one qualified by day and night in the front-line.

At the age of fifteen, the brilliantly fresh autumn air brushed past my face buffeting my cheeks as I threw the tiny aircraft around the sky with gay abandon. Above me the blue autumn sky and the fluffy, cotton-wool cumulus clouds infected my soul and magnified my sense of freedom. The silver canvas, stretched taut over the wings of the Tiger Moth biplane, shivered and matched the sun's reflections in the waters below as I looked down and searched for prey.

Close by, the other student pilot, Tony Glover, was also enjoying being set free. We were Boarders from the same school in Reading, Berkshire: steeped in 800 years of tradition and history. Both of us were aficionados of sport, particularly rugby and gymnastics. The great fighter pilot in the sky had been kind to us, enabling us to win Flying Scholarships and we now had 30 incredible days on the Gower peninsular in South Wales at a small grass-strip airfield, Fairwood Common to learn a little about flying and, hopefully, to gain a Private Pilot's Licence. My elder brother, Michael, had already taken his own course the year before at Thruxton and had passed with flying colours.

For two, new and enthusiastic students it had been a quick and relatively easy transition from being earthbound mortals to being set free by our rather uncompromising but very capable instructor, Mrs Ashton. We had taken off in the flying club's two Tiger Moth aircraft for a fun trip together in the local area.

Cocky as ever, we had completed our first solo flights a couple of days before. It was normal for there to be a least six flights before an instructor would send a student solo. But on the fourth flight and after a particularly heated exchange in the air between Mrs. Ashton and yours truly, I was told, "if you think you are so bloody clever then get airborne and fly it yourself!" Which I duly did.

A few days later and far below me, horses and carts were spreading out over the glistening sands of Bully Inlet in their daily search for cockles as the morning tide ebbed.

I throttled back the noisy engine, dipped my left-wing and side-slipped smoothly down towards the golden beaches. As I passed through about 100 feet I applied power to the engine and skimmed across the sands between the carts and their astonished drivers. My close friend, Tony, followed me at a distance and couldn't believe his eyes when I throttled back once more and made a rather bumpy rolling touch-down close to one of the carts. The horse was not amused. It reared up and then set off across the sands at a horrendous pace with its little Welsh driver in his flat cap attempting to maintain some decorum as he emulated one of the better Giles cartoons.

Whilst I was laughing my socks off, it suddenly dawned on me that if I didn't get out of there fast I could be really in the 'poo'. Mrs Ashton was going to give me rocks if I allowed her aircraft to be bogged down in the sands as the tide engulfed it – not to mention the problem of making an unauthorised landing on the beach during my third solo flight in the aircraft. I immediately applied full power and in doing so, with the aircraft rotating sharply nose-down around its wheels, nearly planted the propeller into the sands that I now so dearly wished to escape. But I kept the power on, controlled the aircraft's attitude with the elevator and slowly but surely accelerated through the clinging sand to flying speed. As I lifted off and climbed out towards the open sea and the clouds a huge sense of relief settled over me and the adrenalin rush that had persuaded me to act like a complete idiot subsided. I smiled ruefully to myself as it dawned on me that I might well have lost the aircraft in the estuary's unpredictable sands. That would probably have been the end of my private pilot's licence and of any future flying career. Dodged the bullet there!

Down below, the little Welshman had regained control of his horse and cart but could still not quite believe what he had seen– an antique aeroplane overtaking his cart on the beach. He didn't know whether to be angry or to wave farewell to the little biplane that was soon to become just a small dot in the distance. So he raised a rather uncertain fist in the air and I could just imagine his colleagues gathering around him making helpful remarks such as, "What's up with your old nag, boyo? Can't you control it anymore?"

Later, on my solo cross-country/land-away flight from Swansea to Bristol I learned another lesson. I was flying over the Cardiff area at 3,000 feet and against all reason, as I sat strapped into the open cockpit of the small plane, I tried to light a cigarette. It took several attempts with the final one succeeding because I bent down low over the control stick to get out of the wind. But as soon as I sat up I noted with some alarm that I was now down to 1,000 feet and the tip of the cigarette blew away immediately.

In the years to come, I would find myself in the 'poo' at my own instigation on many occasions and it was only through large helpings of the luck-of-the-Irish coupled with a certain amount of ability that one day I would achieve my dream of becoming a fully-fledged Royal Navy fighter pilot.

Before that was realised, I was fortunate enough to have more fun with the Tiger Moth at Dartmouth and later at Yeovilton.

The third year of the Dartmouth General List Course concentrated on professional knowledge and training, academics, sport, fitness training and, for the lucky few, flying the Tiger Moth out of Roborough Airfield near Plymouth. We had six of the vintage aircraft and those of us who had already elected or were going to elect to be naval aviators as our future sub-specialisation became members of the Club. Most of the Club's work was checking out the aptitude and flying skills of Short Service Commissioned Aviators who spent just a few short months of initial Naval training at the College. They spent a lot of time at the airfield during the working week. One of these was a close friend from Cheltenham who had been humorously christened Ivan Orgee by his parents. His father, John was an experienced rally driver who had passed on his love for speed to his son.

Already having my Private Pilot's Licence, I was privileged to be appointed Sub-Lieutenant-in-Charge of the Flying Club and we were all overseen by two stalwarts of the Front-Line Fleet Air Arm Buccaneer world; Lt-Cdrs Lyn Middleton, a South African, and David Mears. A small team of naval pilots at Roborough, both retired and serving, made up the Instructing Staff and were a joy to work with.

Dartmouth itself was exciting, demanding and satisfying: The Flying Club was the icing on the cake.

It was a 50-mile drive to the airfield through the very narrow, winding Devon lanes and concentration was crucial for survival. There was often no room for two cars to pass on the road and one had to use specially enlarged passing points to allow the passage of oncoming traffic. Hairy, because we always used to drive too fast, but lots of fun.

In the air I spent most of my time throwing the bi-plane around and trying to perfect my aerobatics – with a lot of excellent guidance from the staff during duel sorties. They rapidly taught me the limits of the aeroplane and, especially, how to recover when going beyond the limits. I had two favourite manoeuvres: a high 'g' stall into a spin and a stall-turn. I would practice them incessantly on my solo flights over the countryside around Plymouth. All of it was good groundwork for the Real McCoy to come.

One of the highlights of my third year at Dartmouth was taking all six aircraft on a flying camp expedition to Montpellier in the South of France. With the Tiger Moth having very limited range, we had to hop from one grass airfield to another on the way there and back. The weather was very kind to us throughout and I shall never forget crossing the Channel in brilliant afternoon sunshine with the light grey canvas of the wings matching the high cirrus cloud and the rippled waters below. Lyn Middleton and David Mears accompanied us – always sitting in the front passenger cockpit.

On one leg of the journey I flew with Lyn in my front seat and couldn't help but notice his head jerking slightly to the side every 30 seconds or so. It was a little confusing but I ignored it until after landing. When I mentioned it to David Mears, he sensibly advised me to say nothing but told me that the head movement was involuntary and was caused by Lyn's earlier traumatic experiences when flying from carriers. The behaviour was a nervous condition known colloquially within the Navy as being 'twitched'.

Lyn had survived two separate incidents when, after being launched from the catapult off the deck of his aircraft carrier, he crashed into the sea ahead of the ship and was run over by the carrier. He escaped from each sinking aircraft and was fortunate enough not to be shredded into pieces by the ship's powerful screws. Such events would have deterred many from further operational carrier-borne flying but Lyn would not think of hanging up his flying boots and he carried on regardless. An extremely brave fellow whom I gladly served under later in the Naval Staff.

He was quite definitely a rule-book fanatic which I found out to my cost during the week at Montpellier. I had flown a general handling sortie with him, demonstrating my aerobatic skills. When we landed, he told me in his inimitable Yarpee accent, "OK Sharkey. Go and practice your aeros but no stall-turns." I asked him why and he replied, "Because they are too steep!" Not to be outdone and thinking to myself 'how absurd, stall-turns are supposed to be vertical manoeuvres and cannot be too steep', I flew away from the airfield about 15 miles, a safe distance so I thought, and happily practiced my full aerobatics routine – including stall-turns.

When I landed, Lyn was incensed. He had been watching me with binoculars. He gave me a five-star bollocking in front of all the pilots and grounded me for the remainder of the camp. Whilst he was ranting on, Robin Gainsford was humorously standing behind him pretending to clock him with a wine bottle. What fun days and one time that I didn't dodge the bullet.

For the last night in Montpellier we had to sleep rough in the old Customs Shed – on smooth concrete counters, 3 feet off the ground. During the night, I rolled over in my sleep and fell like a zombie to the concrete floor. The crack as my head hit the deck woke everyone up – proving how hard-headed I was and probably adding yet another concussion to my rugby repertoire.

Many years later in 1980 when I was running the Sea Harrier Headquarters Squadron, I was privileged to be able to take on the fun task of Tiger Moth display pilot. Our Historic Flight had some former front-line aircraft such as the Sea Fury and the Swordfish, as well as an old Tiger.

After flying the Hunter, Phantom and Sea Harrier, it was an amazing feeling strapping into the old biplane once more, leather helmet and all, and taking to the air. Flying it to its limits and doing perfect three-point landings brought back many happy memories. Very quickly I worked out an aerobatic display that I felt would please the crowds.

But it wasn't all smooth sailing!

One day when I wanted to practice, the wind over the airfield was 40 knots–just about the same speed required for a normal take-off. With a sailor on each wing tip holding the aircraft down, we positioned it into wind on the grass in front of the control tower and I applied full power. The sailors let go and it was an amazing feeling doing a vertical take-off in something other than a Harrier.

I flew off in the direction of Castle Cary, a peaceful country town just a few miles away to the north-east and began practicing my routine over some empty fields. The end of the display consisted of three loops with the final loop merging into a landing. My aircraft did not have a fuel system that allowed inverted flight and so I had to be careful not to apply negative G.

All went well until I was upside down at 1200 feet over the edge of the town in the third loop. I had failed to pull enough positive G and the engine failed – starved of fuel. But fortune smiled on the brave: I rolled my wings level and looked around for somewhere to land. I was lucky. There were several fields below me and I chose one of them for my forced landing. But as I glided down into the wind, I hadn't taken its unusual strength into full account and found myself touching down safely but in a very small field surrounded by tall trees—well short of the field that I had been aiming at.

As I sat there rather relieved in the cockpit deciding my next step and calling Yeovilton on the radio, a farmer arrived on his tractor, looked at me in a very bemused way and said in a broad Somerset accent. "Arrr! You must be filming that new TV series on World War I."

I apologised for landing in his field and told him I would soon be gone – explaining that a helicopter would be arriving to start me up and allow me to take off. He just said, "Arrr!" and drove away.

With the strong wind it was an easy matter clearing the trees after take-off and soon I was back at Yeovilton, landing almost vertically on the patch of green in front of the tower.

8

Basic Flying Training – RAF Linton-on-Ouse (1967).

B y the time I joined 136 Fixed Wing Course at No 1 Flying Training School, RAF Linton-on-Ouse, Yorkshire, I was almost delirious with excitement.

The airfield reminded me very much of the historic World War II past with dowdy looking Nissen Huts for accommodation and large, dark green Hangars that had seen better days. Our Squadron Boss was a thoroughly engaging character, Squadron Leader Sid Edward and he was supported brilliantly by a team of Navy and RAF Instructors. All were extremely friendly and approachable on the ground and in the air and they regularly entertained us in their homes. We also had the strong and necessary support of a quite extraordinary character; the Senior Naval Officer, Commander Derek Monsell who occasionally provided a much-needed buffer between RAF pomposity and Naval tradition. This proved necessary just days after we joined and, as the appointed Course Leader, it was my distinct pleasure to deal with it.

Our senior Ground-School Instructor (as opposed to Flying Instructor) was an archetypical Flight-Sergeant and he was lumbered by what were to me unacceptable local Station Rules concerning the place and deportment of Students. We crossed swords straight away when he told us that "when on duty around the air base we were to salute RAF Sergeants – especially when marching as a squad between classes". I immediately informed him that such irregularity by commissioned Naval Officers was not under any circumstances going to happen – come hell or high water. It was my first brush with Crab wishful thinking (Crab being the generic nickname for RAF personnel – as is 'Pongo' for the Army). Despite lofty, misplaced rhetoric from the Station Command, I won that first battle – and a few more to come.

Ground School was vital to understanding everything about the aircraft that we were going to fly, the Jet Provost Mk 3 and 4, and for learning all the Aviation Rules associated with Military Flying (not always my strong point).

Flying the Jet Provost at Linton for several months was a thoroughly exciting and satisfying experience. The more we learned, the more there was to learn. And the whole time we were being assessed constantly to see whether we had the aptitude and aircraft handling ability to continue to Advanced Flying Training. For some, being under the microscope was extremely stressful and their performance suffered accordingly – leading to an early exit from the Course and a return to other naval duties. This was all part of establishing aptitude and airmanship–which are essential for the maintenance of flight safety and survival in the air – a key factor.

It would be remiss of me not to emphasise that our Instructors were totally dedicated to their task and would share equal regret and disappointment whenever one of the Course fell by the wayside. They provided unremitting encouragement to us all, striving to turn enthusiastic students into material fit for operational flying.

When a close Dartmouth colleague, Philip Unwin was chopped (slang for failing the course) from the senior course, he was heartbroken with an indescribable feeling of failure. I consoled him with my youthful wisdom:

"Philip, you are not in any way a failure. We are all no different from monkeys when it comes to natural aptitude. Whilst we may not have an aptitude for military flying, there are other areas where we can be first class and where others might fail. It is just the luck of the draw!"

We were most fortunate to have Flt. Lt. Mike Merrett RAF and Lt. Roger Seymour RN as our own 'lead instructors'; not forgetting a lot of moral support from Lt. Mike Jermy and others. (Roger's son, Kevin, became a top gun in his own right flying the Sea Harrier and then the Harrier GR 7/9 in Afghanistan where he was my son's commanding officer.) This moral support and the camaraderie of all the students made Linton a golden era in my misty past. Friendships were forged that followed us through training, into the front-line and beyond. I was especially taken by Sub. Lieutenant Robin S G Kent who was revoltingly good-looking, always impeccably dressed (he was nick-named Snapper because of this) and a totally kindred spirit in the squadron, on the sports field and in the bar. Our career paths crossed many times leading ultimately to us both heading up 801 Squadron in the Falklands War.

There are so many special memories to recall both in the air and on the ground.

My first solo in the Jet Provost took me in a climb to 25,000 feet above the wintry Yorkshire Moors. As I looked down from the little jet to the snow-laden ground far below, I went through a water-shed moment. "What the hell am I doing up here? All alone in an aluminium tube high above the earth on a cold winter's day." It was one of the few times that I have felt rather insecure in the air. But I got over it.

The learning curve was high and included various notable incidents that were well worth remembering for later life-saving reference.

I was up one day on a dual training sortie with Flt. Lt. Plummer at 20,000 feet returning to base. The weather was somewhat inclement with a few cumulo-nimbus thunderheads dotted around and we were in and out of the clouds. By chance we flew from some light cloud straight into a thunderhead. Very rapidly the air darkened around us in heavy turbulence and then our instruments appeared to be going haywire – although the attitude indicator showed we were still straight and level, the altimeter showed that we were descending very rapidly. Plummer said very calmly, "Just keep us straight and level. Don't try to climb! We are in a major downdraft and will eventually fly out of it." The altimeter plunged from 20,000 feet to 12,000 feet before we exited the cloud system. It was a bit unnerving.

Recently, I considered that the loss of the Indonesian AirAsia Flight 8501 from Surabaya, Indonesia, to Singapore on 28 December 2014 over the Java Sea was probably caused by the aircraft entering a huge thunder-head and being dragged down whilst in level flight. I would suggest that the aircrew had no prior experience of such matters and apparently failed to recognise properly what was happening. They probably raised the nose to stop the indicated rate of descent and subsequently the aircraft stalled during an abnormally steep climb and was unable to recover.

Later in our course, we had the student aerobatic competition. I had been watching the experienced Station display pilot going through his practice routine which included a 'square loop' and a 'hammerhead stall-turn with inverted push-out recovery'. Somewhat optimistically, I decided to incorporate these into my own routine and, during the competition with Flt Lt Plummer beside me I nearly came to grief during the latter. In this manoeuvre the aircraft is flown vertically upwards until there is no speed on the clock. It is then allowed to pitch forward until going vertically downwards. Then, instead of pulling back the stick to recover to normal level flight with positive 'g' one pushes the stick forward and uses negative 'g' to recover to inverted level flight. This takes up more height than using positive 'g'.

In my solo practice sessions I had used a base height of 3000 feet but during the competition the base height was 1000 feet–much less of a safety margin. After hammer-heading, starting to push the stick and accelerating earthwards, I realised that there was not enough height to push out–as did the instructor. Change of plan and nearly a change of trousers! As Flt Lt Plummer was quickly pointing out without taking the controls, "You'll never make it", I had already rolled the wings, pulled back hard on the stick and managed to recover only a little below base height. Dodged the bullet twice that day because I still won the competition.

As training progressed, my course was moved on to a second squadron of instructors who did not have a leader with the pro-Navy friendliness of Sid Edwards. Squadron Leader Bob Turner appeared to dislike us all and me in particular. As an example of the friction between us, one day he passed down a message to me saying that the flower borders outside the hangar needed weeding and my Course was to get out there and do the job. I couldn't believe it. I went to his office, looked at the RAF airmen lounging and playing football on the lawn outside his window and said, "See those guys, Sir? Those are your gardeners: my officers will not be involved in that." He was apoplectic and, as we could not agree, I stormed out of his office and called on Derek Monsell, the Senior Naval Officer. He had a quiet word with Turner telling him to wind his neck in. This did not bode well for my course and we were continuously harassed by the gentleman. To me, it was just water off a duck's back.

By the end of the course, our relationship had not improved and a final confrontation occurred during the Course Passing Out Ball in the Officers' Mess.

That morning, our Pilot's Wings had been formally presented to us on parade by the visiting Fleet Air Arm VIP, Captain Chilton RN. But even that was a close call.

During the very early hours of the night before, my course had followed the Fleet Air Arm tradition of leaving 'our mark' on the air station. '136 FW' was plastered all over – on the Nissen hut roofs, in large day-glow letters high up on the control tower and in huge white letters painted on the runway that were legible from 30,000 feet. This might not have been too unacceptable but the airman who stood on the rapidly erected scaffolding getting ready to remove the day-glow strips from the control tower stepped backwards to admire our handiwork, fell off and broke his leg. To make matters worse, we had soaked the Air Commodore's flag with glue and despite a fresh breeze it hung limp and unimpressive at the top of his flagpole when he arrived for work. This had the result of severely pissing him off. Disrespect!

A hastily configured meeting was immediately held by the Top Brass to decide whether we should all be sacked and the Passing Out Parade cancelled. Where was the sense of humour?Totally absent; as in the RAF funny-joke book – a lot of empty pages.

Fortunately, common sense prevailed, the Wing's Parade was held and we all moved on to the white-tie Ball where I gave my fare-well speech standing and walking on the long mahogany dining tables, thanking all the instructors but taking the mickey out of Turner. This of course went down like a lead balloon with him and his wife.

Figure 18. Back Row: Robin Kent, David Law, Don Thompson.
Front Row: Fred Hatton, self, Derek Holley.

At about one in the morning, I was standing with my pint of beer in the ante-room surrounded by all the pilots when Mrs. Turner, resplendent in her ball gown, stormed into the group carrying a large jug filled with ice cubes and confronted me. Without any warning she reached out, grabbed my wing collar and ripped it open with studs flying everywhere from my stiff shirt. She proceeded to pour the ice cubes down inside my ruined shirt-front and then spent a few seconds pummelling them into my chest with her fists. "That will teach you to be unkind to my husband!"

Somewhat bemused by all this, I still had my full pint of beer in my hand and, when she had finished, I decided to pour it over her head, hair-do and all with a smile. She ran off like a scalded cat.

Whilst at Linton my engagement to the lovely Francesca came to a most ignominious end – all because of my complete lack of understanding that others may have a completely different way of looking at things – particularly women and I say that as a criticism of yours truly, not the other way around. This very sad episode has haunted me ever since.

Francesca had followed me to England from Hong Kong to stay in her mother's first-floor apartment overlooking the wicket at Sussex County Cricket ground. I used to write to her from Yorkshire practically every day and see her occasionally at weekends. Then, with my Midland bank manager's assistance and generous spirit I bought a smart second-hand Cortina GT with a few Lotus modifications.

This was when I made one of the biggest and most regretful mistakes of my life – for which I shall always be ashamed. As I write, I still cannot come to terms with my actions. In one of my letters to Francesca which were always full of love, I was gauche enough to suggest that we sold her engagement ring to pay for new tyres on the car – and then I would buy her an even nicer one. I thought she would see it as a practical measure. She didn't understand – and at last it dawned on me how much I must have hurt her. Too late, young man. Too late. I was devastated and deservedly so.

Eventually, she was to marry a more understanding Israeli Intelligence Officer.

My final memory just before leaving Linton was standing next to Sid Edwards on the tarmac watching a fly-past display of the brand-new Navy F-4K Phantom jet fighter with Lt. Mike Moreland at the controls: we had been together in HMS Tartar and I was later to serve with him in 892 Squadron. All of us were awe-struck by the deafening power being shown off. Sid turned to me and said, "Nigel, one day soon you will have your name painted in gold letters on the side of one of those."

Figure 19. The dream was to come true. Launching from Ark Royal.

There could have been no better encouragement from a truly decent fellow.

9

ADVANCED FLYING
TRAINING – 759 NAVAL AIR
SQUADRON (1968).

L ife was, as they say, a 'bundle of cherries' as I drove my
newly acquired, British-Racing-Green Cortina GT along the
narrow, beautiful winding coast road of the Pembrokeshire peninsula between Haverfordwest and Royal Naval Air Station, Brawdy.
Entering the gates in bright sunshine with those cherished gold
wings on my uniform sleeve, I didn't have a care in the world.
There were no clouds on the horizon, just optimism and excitement at the thought of flying my first fast jet swept wing aircraft,
the Hunter; the aircraft flown by Roger Topp's fabled Black Arrow
formation team.

My Course, 136 Fixed Wing congregated in the Wardroom Bar
after throwing our gear into the modern cabins which were to be
our homes for the next few months. We met the members of the
senior course and welcomed Nigel Charles into our own course –
a truly brilliant aviator in the making.

I was immediately impressed with the senior course high spirits
and devil-may-care attitude to life. With hindsight, there were
three main reasons for this new and electrifying approach to continued flying training.

Figure 20. Nigel Charles, Robin Kent, David Law, self, Mike Blisset and Derek Holley.

The first was that 135 FW course was already halfway through the Advanced syllabus, had left the Hunter conversion squadron, 759 Naval Air Squadron and were commencing the Tactical Flying Course with 738 Squadron. This meant that they had shown themselves to have the right aptitude for Fast-Jet operational flying and had demonstrated the necessary basic skills for handling the aircraft. In other words, they had achieved a lot, had avoided being chopped and could now look forward to learning how to use tactics and weapons effectively in combat. Any thoughts of failure were receding fast.

The second reason for high spirits was the Staff. The Instructors were front-line naval aviators, most of whom were either Qualified Flying Instructors (QFIs) or, rather more excitingly for the students, Air Warfare Instructors (AWIs). The QFI staff were centred mainly on 759 Squadron whereas 738 Squadron was crawling with AWIs. As always, the former displayed an abundance of aerodynamic knowledge and smooth handling skills; the latter were punchy, aggressive ("spelt with 5 'g's and don't you bloody forget it!!!!"), extrovert and ready to "kick arse" at any time of the day or night. However, common denominators between the two dissimilar specialisations of Instructor were that most of them were keen to help you through the course, expected 100% effort at work and play and clearly loved the Fleet Air Arm and its way of flying. They always demanded perpetual and overriding attention to Flight Safety which might quite wrongly be perceived as an unusual partner to aggressive flying. Their attitude was highly contagious.

The third and final reason for levity was that Brawdy was a good fun place to be. Yes, it was a bit out in the sticks and was built on the edge of the cliffs with a runway surface rather akin to a roller coaster, but the camaraderie was truly invigorating and we students began to feel that we belonged to the military air world: a very proud feeling.

759 Squadron converted us from the slow, straight-winged Jet Provost to the swept wing, supersonic-capable Hunter, considered by many to rank alongside the Super Sabre as the nicest-handling jet of its time – a 'pilot's aircraft'.

It was a major step forward and a very different class of flying. Flight Safety reared its head on a flight-by-flight basis because if you didn't fly the aircraft within its approved operational envelope it was very likely to turn around and bite you, sometimes resulting in the loss of the aircraft and, ultimately, your life. There were many "do's and don'ts" and there was no excuse for not knowing them or not abiding by them. We were involved in a steep and very demanding learning curve towards professionalism and, as we progressed, it was fundamental to understand that making a mistake could endanger the lives of others as well as our own.

Brawdy existence represented a strange combination of sober discipline and attention to detail in the squadron and in the air, coupled with somewhat excessive fun and high-living when off duty. There was also plenty of sport available and I used to get my exercise playing rugby for the Air Station; getting to know the locals' viewpoint and trying to avoid getting mauled to death by Welsh Miners. Inevitably, the two contrasting styles of our daily routine would conflict and bring the wrath of the Staff down on our shoulders.

The locals tolerated us but were also very wary of us. They were particularly protective of their women–more so than I could have imagined. One Friday, our course spent the evening in a public house in Haverfordwest. We were having a wonderful time and the pub was packed. Then, in through the door slinked a gorgeous girl accompanied by a rather handy-looking young Welshman. One of my major faults is something I cannot control and is the unfortunate attribute of allowing my facial expressions to broadcast what I'm feeling–whether distaste, cynicism or in this case, adoration. I couldn't take my eyes off her. Quick as a flash, her escort got right in my face demanding why I was looking at his girlfriend. My instant reply was, "Because she is gorgeous. What of it?" He wasn't at all pleased: "Better step outside then, boyo!"

With such a kind invitation, what could one do? I led him out to the dark courtyard behind the pub and turned to face him with my back against an old stone wall. It was with some consternation that I saw two of his hulking buddies follow us outside and stand just behind him. Things didn't look too good for a moment. Then, with some relief that I didn't show I said with considerable disdain, "Before we get started, you better look behind you, Boyo!" Four of my Course, led by Derek Holley, had lined themselves up in the rear and were ready for action. The bravado immediately left the Welshman's face and, as he and his buddies retreated to the pub door, he retorted rather weakly, "Okay then, just keep your eyes off my girlfriend!" We all chuckled and went back to our beer. Dodged the bullet again.

Commander Carl Davies was the boss of 759 Squadron and remained in command until the outfit was disbanded on 24 December 1969. His background was flying fighter-bombers and, in particular, the Buccaneer which as we fighter jocks say, "Fuccaneer flies". Probably the best handling low-level aircraft ever built including today's selection, the Buccaneer represented the navy's Over-The-Horizon nuclear strike and attack capability and its crews tended to get vertigo when operating at more than 50 feet above the deck over land or sea.

Early on in the course, Carl made the point of flying with each student in the twin-seat Hunter T8. The cockpit ejection seats were side by side; ideal for the instructor to monitor his student's habits and actions. I remember my first flight with the Boss very well indeed. It was my initial low-level sortie in the Hunter. The Jet Provost low level speed had been 180 knots (210 mph); the Hunter was flown for training at 360 knots (414 mph) and theoretically at the same height as the JP in the overland training areas i.e. 250 feet above ground level. The main point of the trip was to map-read one's way safely and professionally along a pre-planned route through the valleys and over the hills of Wales, remaining on track and on time throughout. Visual observation was used to check the accuracy of one's position and corrections had to be made in heading and speed to arrive at the end of the low-level route within 200 yards of the designated track and within three seconds of the planned time. The planned time en route for my flight was 45 minutes, hence the route length was 270 nautical miles or 310 statute miles.

Sitting in the left-hand seat next to the man who had final control over my future as a pilot was initially slightly unnerving. That he was a low-level expert did not reduce the butterflies. As in most walks of life, first impressions were very important and I didn't want to let myself down in front of the Boss.

But the flight turned out to be 100% enjoyment, albeit hard work keeping track of the ground which would be flashing by underneath us at a rate of 6 miles per minute. The weather was perfect with blue skies and no low cloud as we descended into the scenic beauty of the Welsh countryside, full of gently winding valleys and green hillsides. One essential trick to safe low-level flight is to anticipate the approach of steep hills, pulling up early but preventing the aircraft from ballooning above the crest of the terrain. In combat, one needed to avoid being detected by 'enemy' radars.

Naturally, on this training flight and on all others we had to avoid annoying towns and villages and did so by popping up/climbing or diverging from the track. But away from population centres there were plenty of farmers in the fields to give us a friendly wave if they were quick enough–or an angry fist–who can tell? Sheep would scatter as we crested over ridges and green hilltops and the navigation task proved not as difficult as I had imagined. I had more fun than I'd ever had in my life before and all too soon the flight was over and we were landing back at Brawdy.

On the ground, my nerves returned. In the air it had been easy to forget that one was being continuously monitored but the real meat of the flight was always discussed in detail at a post-flight debrief. This was where one learned most from the Instructor about one's inadequacies and/or talents.

Sitting in the Boss's office with a coffee, I had no idea whether I had performed adequately or not: as a student, 'adequately' usually meant 'well' because the staff never handed out bouquets gratuitously.

"OK, Sharkey," my new nickname[3] was catching on fast, "how do you think that went?"

It was pointless trying to bullshit so I said, "Pretty well on the whole, Sir. We were on track at the end of the route but my time-keeping was a little dodgy." We had been more than 5 seconds out at the end of the track.

"Agreed! I enjoyed the flight and didn't feel scared or in doubt at any stage. But what do you estimate your height over the ground to have been and what should it have been?"

"It should have been not less than 250 feet, Sir." I retorted guardedly. "Maybe it was a bit less in places?"

"And the rest! You hardly ever reached more than 40 feet above the deck! That is too low! But your flying was perfectly safe so don't worry: just make sure you get it right next time."

Relief.

My next low level flight was a solo (no instructor) but with a chase aircraft, followed by a solo with no chase. At least it was theoretically "no chase" but the staff would often follow you secretly from a distance to see if you played according to the rules. My solo with "no chase" was an unmitigated disaster in many ways but a hell of a lot of fun and fortunately no-one was spying on me.

After taking off and clearing the airfield at about 2,000 feet, it was normal practice to broadcast a radio transmission to say where you were entering the national low-level system, for how long

---

[3] Sharkey is a generic navy nickname for those with the family name, Ward. Its origin was in the days of the Barbary Coast Pirates when there were two Sharkey Wards – one a true pirate and one a disgraced Naval Officer.

and where you would exit the system. This would allow other aircraft in the same low flying area to keep an eye open for you. I made the call but failed to complete the post take-off check that the airbrake was working properly. The airbrake switch was on the throttle lever and on its operation the fuselage mounted airbrake would swing down and a doll's eye in the cockpit would show white. Place the switch forward and the airbrake would swing in, the doll's eye returning to black. If the operation showed a mal-function then one would return to base to get it fixed.

My mistake was that I had only completed the first half of the check and so descended into the low-level area at 360 knots with a glaring white doll's eye that I didn't notice and a lot of power on the engine to maintain speed. It should have felt all wrong to me and I should have noticed the doll's eye; but I was so keen to get on with the fun part of the trip that I noticed nothing.

After about 20 minutes of exhilarating flying, I checked the fuel and found to my horror that I was running very short. I knew I would have to return to base immediately and anyone watching from outside my cockpit would have seen a huge question mark hovering over my helmeted head. Suddenly the penny dropped, "Oh, F***! The airbrake!"

With the airbrake properly housed, I still had to return to base but had enough fuel to fly direct and remain at low level where fuel consumption was higher. From where I was, this route took me straight down the Bristol Channel and I intended to make the most of it. Beating up ships had been talked about by my peers occasionally in the bar so I thought I would try it for myself. This predilection for annoying people on the deck was later to get me into serious trouble. I raced down the channel, picked out a small boat several miles ahead and made a beeline for it. The water was flat-calm and it was difficult to gain any perspective of height or distance. Just as I was thinking that the boat should be growing larger in size, I whistled over the top of it at about 10 feet–it wasn't a boat at all. It was a navigation buoy.

Continuing homewards, this didn't worry me until I noticed that the windscreen was absolutely plastered with dead flies. How the hell was I going to explain that away? Flies at 250 feet, Sharkey– you must be joking. I could hear the recriminations before I landed.

Strangely, my very early return to base was not remarked on by anyone at all and the aircraft ground crew had cleaned the windscreen before I had to ask. I therefore escaped the expected wrath of the staff and dodged the bullet; but felt very small and very unprofessional. As they say in the flying world, I learned a lot from that.

Our course flying syllabus included all the domestic aspects of flying: aerobatics, close formation, instrument flying which was very hard work for ab-initio's, handling in the circuit with different styles of take-off and landing, a lot of low-level flying and some work on basic fighter combat manoeuvres.

We all learned our most important lessons the hard way, doing rather than listening. Robin Kent nearly joined the brown-trouser club on a solo low level. He found that aileron rolls at less than 50 feet can bring you down to earth literally–fortunately without a big bang in his case. But it was a very close call because after the flight the ground crew found grass compressed into his aircraft's under-fuselage airbrake. 'Porcelain Features', as I jealously liked to call him, lost the rosiness in his cheeks for a few hours and we all eagerly shared his experience with him over a beer. It was an honest, if unbriefed, mistake and he was lucky to be alive–not that low-level aileron rolls are difficult–they are just dodgy if you get them wrong.

Before passing out of 759 Squadron, two incidents nearly spoiled my future. The first was following a memorable mess dinner, before which my course had been promised that there would be no flying the next day. Beware of Instructional Staff bearing false witness about good news! All of us had let our hair down to the N'th degree. I retired to my sack (bed) at about 0430, pissed as a newt and happy. At 0730, I was shaken by an irate QFI who said, "Come on! You're flying with me on a general handling sortie. Get your kit on!"

Protestations and curses had no effect. Before I knew it, I was in the cockpit and airborne with a less than sympathetic Colin Crowther, if I remember correctly. Despite my heavily inebriated condition, the flight went adequately until we returned to the landing circuit. I attempted several approaches to land and each time my air speed was too high; despite increasingly careful throttle handling. The QFI was highly amused by my ignorance and poor handling of the jet–and totally unhelpful. On the final approach he said, with intense sarcasm, "You will find it much easier if you use the flaps."

I had failed to touch the flaps and had failed to recognise the obvious result of attempting a higher speed flapless landing. To put it mildly, I was furious; with myself, with the bloody Instructor and with having to get airborne when I was in no fit state to fly.

On the deck, this lunatic QFI who, in my opinion then and now, was more suited to a leading role in a Tom Sharpe novel than to supervising and training pilots, proceeded to castigate me and then filed a very bad report on my abilities in the air. It never registered with him that the sortie was completely out of character and should not have been flown under any circumstances. As it was, the threat of the chopping block was held over me for the last few flights on the squadron. This led to a very nervous course leader getting airborne for his final handling check with the Air Station's Chief Flying Instructor, Commander Chris Cummins.

Chris was a real gent. Friendly, balanced and able to put you completely at your ease. The day was a blustery one with heavy rain and about 25 knots of wind, gusting 40 knots. The wind was down the short runway and we took off, climbing through the heavy clouds into bright sunshine and went through all the disciplines of aerobatics and emergencies before returning to the airfield circuit. All went well until the final stages of the last approach when we were committed to land and when it was too late to go around again.

Just before touchdown, a line-squall swept across the runway threshold causing the wind direction to veer to the right through 90°. In an instant we were faced with a 40-knot crosswind, with the aircraft cocked so far into wind so that the view of the runway was obscured by the heavy rain on the cockpit quarter-light. Our windscreen wipers were only fitted to the front panel.

But we were committed to the landing and so I kicked the jet straight with rudder before setting her down firmly on the half-flooded surface. Decision required. Stream the braking parachute or not? If I did, the crosswind could pull us off the runway; if I didn't, the wet surface of the short runway would inevitably cause us to over-run the runway and end up in the grass or off the cliff into the sea. I streamed the chute and immediately felt the aircraft pivot round towards the relative wind, about 15°. I was working like the proverbial one-armed paperhanger to keep us on the runway as both main tyres burst and we juddered violently to a halt. Chris said nothing. I shut down the engine and waited in lonely silence for the crash truck to come and tow us in.

The Chief Flying Instructor left the jet first. I just sat in the cockpit for about ten minutes wondering what he was going to make of that. Was it the end of the line for Sharkey Ward?

When I eventually joined him in his office with some hot coffee, he smiled and said, "Well done, Ward. You handled that very well and the flight wasn't at all bad either. You've made it!"

I still did not leave 759 smelling of roses. Carl Davies was very fair in his summing up. He referred to my earlier 'bad' sortie and said, "Whatever the reasons behind it, that was not good enough and it puts doubts in my mind as to whether you are going to be able to cope with 738 Squadron and operational training. However, in everything else you have done well so I am going to let you continue."

Thank goodness for that. My lowest point was past-history and I was determined not to drink and fly again. It was, at least, a good resolution. . .

10

Tactical Flying Training – 738 Naval Air Squadron (1968/9).

Figure 21. A new beginning with the Hunter GA-11.

The rubber really hit the road in 738 Squadron – commanded by a much-lauded Navy AWI, 'Knobby' Hall. Our learning curve got steeper, there was no room for silly mistakes and, for most flights, we students flew the single-seat Hunter GA-11 – 'GA' standing for Ground Attack. This was akin to the excitement of riding a high-powered racing motorbike – only more so and with a new, exhilarating dimension – the open sky.

The key to our progress lay in what we could learn from our very talented front-line Air Warfare Instructor (AWI) Staff. They set the standard, didn't suffer fools gladly and took no prisoners. This was the last filter before Operational Flying Training in the Fleet's Fighter and Strike jet aircraft – we were getting near to the Holy Grail.

I cannot emphasise sufficiently how privileged we were to be surrounded by these proven practitioners of Naval Air Warfare. The expertise of decades had been passed down to them through the medium of a succession of legendary AWIs whose own talents and knowledge had benefited from their predecessors. During this prestigious carrier-borne Naval Air Warfare history many precious lives had been taken by the Grim Reaper as the peace-time Navy continually pushed the limits hard to be fully ready for combat and conflict at any time.

The constant pressure put on the students acted as a microscope– examining in great detail their suitability for safe, multi-role, all-weather fighter/strike operations by day and night from aircraft carriers. A genuine airborne multi-tasking capability would be essential in the front-line. Somehow this pressure had to be compensated for by letting off steam – and this was strongly encouraged, if not always totally condoned, by the squadron staff. This was best exemplified by an extraordinary Mess Dinner celebrating the Battle of Taranto – when string-bag Swordfish aircraft flying from our carriers torpedoed and sank the Italian Fleet in World War II.

A re-run of the Battle was to be staged after a Mess Dinner in the Brawdy Wardroom with satisfied and very noisy diners looking on. Expectedly, two of our extrovert and most accomplished Staff

AWIs, Fred de Labillière and Neil Rankin, were to represent the attacking Swordfish. We students (Nigel Charles and I) were to man the plywood Italian warship on the carpet. Both parties eagerly prepared their aircraft and ship models. Fred and Neil constructed a two seat Swordfish which was suspended from the Wardroom ceiling and had ominous wires tracking down to our warship model – about 20 feet away. Nigel Charles looked hilarious/devastating in a white and blue striped T shirt with two massive balloons giving him a very realistic Italian trans-gender look. I was more modestly attired. For ship's armament, our warship had 4. 5-inch brass shell casings from which we fired cabbages loaded with explosives that subsequently went off and covered all and sundry with thousands of bits of green shrapnel. We also had aluminium bowls from the galley filled with water which we dotted around our warship and into which we dropped thunder-flashes to simulate bomb bursts. Additionally, we had several flour bombs powered again by thunder-flashes which we rolled under the heavy mahogany dinner tables to explode and simulate the fog of war.

Fred and Neil had outgunned us though – by some margin! They had prepared a cluster of five Coast Guard rockets armed with powerful Maroon explosives to hurtle down the wires and destroy our ship. To say it was all a bit of an overkill would be a gross understatement.

Battle commenced.

The metal bowls of water were ripped apart by the thunder-flashes into flat flower shapes and the water was vaporised–no plumes of water but good noise. The Swordfish crew in their World War II leather helmets and goggles lit the rockets and their torpedo raced down towards us at lightning speed – completely destroying our warship as the Maroons went off. Meanwhile we were firing salvoes of cabbage bombs and delivering the flour bombs under the tables. It was a magnificent sight, cheered on by all present and deafeningly loud.

As each bomb went off under the tables, they were lifted off the carpet by about six inches and all the crystal glasses and decanters destroyed. Very quickly, visibility in the Wardroom dropped to near zero thanks to the flour and all present rapidly vacated the area to re-assemble in the ante-room bar for more relaxed drinking.

It was a huge success; applauded by all and with no injuries. But, as always, there was a price to pay the next day. The Wardroom carpet had been ruined and needed replacing, the ceiling of the wine cellar below had been cracked by the explosions, crystal-ware had to be replaced and every inch of the walls and furniture was covered in tiny pieces of blasted cabbage. It was expected and no surprise that the Taranto Battle participants' monthly bar-bills were charged for the repairs. Such is life in a dark blue suit.

In the air it was no less exciting. We were introduced to the bombing and rocketing of surface targets on a local weapons range. Competition for the best results was keen, healthy and closely monitored. Continued progress in formation and instrument flying was made. But the meat of the learning curve concentrated on air combat tactics and leading low-level formations of attack aircraft as well as providing fighter escort for the same. It was all challenging and utterly satisfying. We had started the process of being turned from proficient pilots into Fighter Pilots.

One less than praiseworthy incident did interrupt this progress for Robin and me and nearly put us both deep in the 'poo' – or worse (I related this story in my book on the Falklands Air War – apologies for repeating myself).

It was a Sunday and the Squadron Senior Pilot, Fred de LaBillière, and his wife Sue had thrown a party at their home for all the squadron aircrew, including the students. Drinks at lunchtime extended all afternoon and as it was getting dark Robin suddenly remembered that we both had an invitation for a strawberry and cream tea and to watch Tom and Jerry cartoons at Fred Hatton's house in Haverfordwest, some 10 miles distant. Neither Robin nor I could walk without assistance thanks to Fred de La Bill's more than liberal hospitality, and so amid much merriment we were carried to my Cortina and set off erratically down the winding coast road in the dark at ever-increasing speed.

That would not have been too bad but I decided we should share the driving; with me on the pedals and Robin on the wheel – a bit like flying together.

Shortly after flashing past a flathatted grockle (local) with wife and kid bouncing along in their little Austin A35, I jokingly said to Robin, "You have control.", and took my hands off the wheel. Mistake!

All the lights went out. This was probably a result of the car hitting the nearside banking, which then threw it across the road and head on into another vertical mud and stone bank at about 85 mph. At that moment, we both lost our own lights as well. I woke up lying on the road gazing in awe at my pride and joy, which was sitting inverted on the tarmac in a very crumpled condition. Both front wheels had been pushed back under the rear seats and the only car panel that was in one piece was the boot lid.

The sad condition of the car occupied my befuddled brain for a minute or so before I thought of Robin. I had been through the windscreen, but where was my dear old pal? I remember staggering around the remains of the car through the stench of leaking petrol and eventually espied my codriver lying unconscious inside the cockpit on the inverted roof. He looked remarkably peaceful and unmarked, but the first threads of full sobriety and fear struck me as I wondered whether he had gone to join the Big Fighter Pilot in the sky. I crawled into the wreck in a panic, switched off the ignition and after a couple of rough shakes awoke my partner from his beauty sleep. If we had been using unleaded petrol Robin would have been dead burnt to a cinder.

'Hi, Sharks. Gosh you look terrible!'

This wounded me not a little when I realised that my face was indeed a mess and Robin's extraordinary good looks remained unimpaired. And as I was pulling him out of the car through the side window, streams of blood from my face dripped all over the new suede waistcoat that I had lent to Robin for the party. It just wasn't my day. But at least we were alive and in one piece.

In what appeared to be no time at all a car pulled up next to us in the dark. It was Nigel Charles. He had recognised the wreck from the red Chinese tapestry cushion lying on the road that I always kept on the rear seat.

'I think you two need a lift to the Sick Bay, don't you? You'd better get in.'

'But I'm bleeding like a stuck pig. It will ruin your back seat.'

'Never mind that. Get in quickly before the police arrive.'

At the Sick Bay, I realised the extent of the damage. My scalp had been torn apart at the eyebrows and pushed an inch or so up over my forehead. There was blood everywhere as the young Surgeon Lieutenant placed me on the operating table and started to stitch. I felt no pain but immediately fell in love with the nurse who held my hand throughout the sewing lesson. My overtures of boozedup passion did not get a result from the young lady, though, and soon it was Robin's turn on the table.

He had only received a clothlike tear in the back of his scalp, but whether because he wasn't quite so drunk or for other reasons his stitching hurt like hell. It was some consolation for me as I sat listening to his muffled groans with delight.

The police arrived before the Doc had finished with Robin and I was instructed by the medical staff to hold my breath throughout the short interview and to feign total shock. This I did and the police rapidly gave up trying to solicit a statement from me. Soon we were both on our way to the Haverfordwest Hospital for over-night observation.

When we returned to the Air Station the next day after a second suitably unproductive interview with the police, it was evident that trouble was brewing; our accident had not gone unnoticed. Self-inflicted injury during flying training is deemed a sin by Their Lordships because it wastes the taxpayers' money and slows down the flow of aircrew to the front-line. Even broken limbs sustained whilst 'jockstrapping', playing rugby for the Air Station for instance, are severely frowned on and incapacitation from alcohol-induced car prangs is considered over the top.

A very officious and soberfaced Fred de LaBillière trooped us into the office of the Commander 'Air' who began our formal bollocking. He asked how we had managed to get so drunk and act so irresponsibly during flying training. Didn't we know the rules? What the hell was going on?

'Actually, Sir,' replied Robin, 'we were invited to a drinks session which turned into a party. I'm afraid we got legless.'

'That's just not good enough! You're supposed to be big boys now, not fucking Girl Guides. You've got to learn to control your drink or there's no place for you in the Fleet Air Arm. I'm now seriously considering your position on this flying course.' It was a real threat, but underneath both offenders hoped that the Commander was just enjoying frightening them. After pausing for breath, he continued, 'By the way, whose party was that?' He glowered in impressive style.

'Well, you were there, Sir. At our Senior Pilot's house.'

It was time for more bullshit as they both realised their part in the incident. After much posturing, swearing and threatening, Fred waved his great hairy arm as a sign of dismissal. That was the end of the interview and no more was said.

Others on our course were not so fortunate.

The first casualty, being chopped, was Derek Holley. He had been a little at odds with David Law in the crew room following one of their early close formation sorties. David had been very concerned at the way Derek had moved from one formation position to another–such as from the starboard or right wing of the leader to line-astern. With three or more aircraft in very close proximity in the sky, any changes of formation position must be conducted in a very disciplined and standard way. An unpredictable move spells collision and possible loss of life.

After his next formation flight with Holley, David entered the crew room as white as a sheet, threw his helmet down on the deck and sat with his head in his hands, furious, waiting for Holley to enter. I was watching with some interest, not only because I was the appointed Course Leader but because I remembered well the last occasion that David had been so annoyed. It was during Basic Flying Training.

We had been on a pub run near Linton-on-Ouse and had graduated from pints of beer to drinking the fabled "Yard of ale". Done properly, the 2.5 pints of beer from this trumpet-shaped receptacle must be consumed all in one go, without pause. All of us had managed our yard of ale when some bright spark suggested a yard of Guinness! It was a question of leader to the front and I was the first to try. I was never a fast drinker and the Guinness went down slowly but surely. I successfully coped with the air bubble from the bulbous base and was quaffing the last half-pint of the treasured liquid when young David chirped, "I'll give you a hand!" and, putting his hand under the base of the yard, levered it upwards. This broke my concentration, covered me with Guinness, made me as mad as a hatter and resulted in me giving him a belt in the face. He didn't like that and immediately implanted his healthy young teeth in my shoulder, returning my gesture with interest. Pandemonium broke loose with a pile of bodies on the floor trying to separate us. No more yards of Guinness were drunk that night.

Back to the crew room at Brawdy, where we were waiting to see what would happen when Holley walked in.

"You F***ing Idiot!" cried Law, with intense venom. "You nearly killed me! I'll never fly with you again!" It was serious. "Come to that, I think I'll jack my hand in from this lot with arse-holes like you in the sky!"

Holley appeared bemused and half surprised. He made a weak attempt to defend his conduct in the air then carried on as if nothing had happened. But the incident had not gone unnoticed.

That evening I was standing in the Wardroom at the bar when Derek came in. "Like a beer, Sharkey?" he beamed. "Thanks, Derek." He then turned to the staff instructor next to me and said, "Beer, Sir?"

"I don't know what the hell you're doing in the bar, Holley. You're chopped. I would have thought you'd be packing your things by now." And so it was; a very surprised and disappointed Holley joined the clan of the unwanted and departed our company. His fault had not just been a dangerous manoeuvre. All of us are capable of that once. Repeating the same error was unforgiveable. This was compounded by his lack of recognition of what he had done in the air and his unwillingness to accept the fault. I was sorry to see him go, but not surprised.

David Law sadly taught us all the ultimate lesson as far as mistakes in the air are concerned. He had overcome his scrape with Holley and was doing fine on course until his last close-formation sortie. After a four-ship (four aircraft) stream take-off, David, who was last off the deck, had to join the other aircraft in close formation as they circled over the bay near the airfield. He was joining them from below at about 400 knots and, looking up and sideways at the leader, he forgot about the water below, pulled wide and impacted the sea. Tragedy and reality struck home! Many Fleet Air Arm pilots died each year at sea but this was our first exposure to the horror of it happening to a friend. He died instantly and the force of impact ripped him out of the cockpit and his seat. When we watched his floating body being lifted by the Search and Rescue helicopter his arms slipped through the strop like string – all the bones smashed – and he disappeared under the waves for good.

This tragic event could have had a totally demoralising effect on us all. For those never faced with day-to-day mortal risk it may be difficult to understand the proven Fleet Air Arm response that we followed. The best way of overcoming such disasters was to gather in the bar, drink to the health of the departed and remember the many others that have died through the medium of a good Fleet Air Arm singsong. Crying into one's beer didn't help and it is not the fighter pilot's way.

We were soon to finish at Brawdy and ready to join our respective Operational Flying Training Squadrons. Sadly the team parted ways, Robin and Mike Blisset went off to Royal Naval Air Station,

Lossiemouth to fly Buccaneers and Fred Hatton went off to fly the Gannet at Culdrose. Nigel and I were off to Yeovilton to fly the Sea Vixen.

11

Operational Flying
Training at 766 Naval
Air Fighter Squadron
(5 March to 21 July 1969).

A t Yeovilton a whole new world beckoned. The Holy Grail
was in sight. This was the last major challenge before joining
the élite: those front-line gladiators that had made an indelible
impression upon me so many years ago in Penang. It was now
March 1969 and a momentous year lay ahead.

Nigel, or 'Tubes' as he was affectionately known, and I were joined
on course by Sub. Lt. Ian Sutton and Flying Officer David Webb
RAF who had just completed their Observer Training. Known in
the RAF as Navigators and in the USAF as RIOs (Radar Intercept
Officers), RN Observers were a key element in the operation of the
Sea Vixen Fighter weapon system: particularly the Air Intercept
(AI) Radar. And this meant that we had to learn how to cooperate
with each other, cockpit-to-cockpit – not just for weaponeering
but also for flight safety, deck-landing and fighter combat – 'dogfighting'. It was a special relationship of trust and reliance from
which I learned an immense amount in the coming years – our
back-seaters were the best of the best; guardian angels you might
say. Naval Aviators as Angels? That's a new one.

Within days of arriving on the Squadron we had learned the aircraft systems, cockpit drills and emergency drills and were ready to get airborne – there was no simulator available for dummy-runs. My first impressions of the Sea Vixen were mixed. It was huge (55-foot wingspan) and the pilot's cockpit was equally vast – especially compared with the Hunter GA-11 that fitted around you like a glove. This made me feel somewhat uncomfortable initially but, of much greater import, the back seat of the jet was a real nightmare for Observers. Nick-named the 'coal-hole', it was accessed via a metal panel in the 'roof', was of cramped proportions and enjoyed just one small side-window for viewing the outside world. It also had a sinister reputation for trapping Observers inside when they needed to eject – with tragic results. The death rate for Vixen aircrew was greater than that of the infamous Luftwaffe 'Flying Coffin' – the F-104 Starfighter.

None of this was in my mind as I took off for my first familiarisation flight with Lt. Bob Woolgar in the 'hole'. As we accelerated rapidly down the runway and lifted off effortlessly a dramatic change in the weather suddenly set in. Low grey cloud rolled over the airfield from the west accompanied by heavy rain – well below limits for unrated new pilots. The remedy was to land as quickly as possible without getting caught in the clag. Following Bob's instructions, I kept under the cloud and having eventually found the Fuel Jettison lever in the cockpit, ditched most of our fuel load into the air over the surrounding green fields of Somerset– most of it would evaporate before reaching the ground. We kept the airfield in sight and when our weight was sufficiently down carried out a low-level circuit and landing without incident. But there had been a lot to take in and I particularly recall the unusual need to raise the Vixen nose very high after touchdown to cause drag and help the aircraft braking system – we had no parachute to stream as had been the case with the Hunter. Total flight time was just 25 minutes.

The aircraft proved to be a joy to fly and very quickly Nigel and I were immersed in exciting operational tactics and procedures, including the art of Air Interception which was the Vixen's main role. This conveniently led into fully developed dogfighting which was later to become my favourite pastime – even surpassing low level jollies.

The staff of 766 were a truly impressive team of pilots and observers that provided us with yet more of a 'feel' for front-line operations. Although still students on paper, we were treated more as junior members of the squadron – still with much to learn but having demonstrated the right ability to go forward. There was no room for complacency though. If you couldn't hack every part of the syllabus there was always the danger of being chopped. This nearly happened to Dudley Davenport on the course ahead of us. (Two courses went through 766 at the same time.)He could not quite get the full feel of the aircraft during landing. As mentioned earlier, part of the Vixen's runway braking routine was lifting the nose high to create extra drag and Dudley simply could not prevent over-rotating and dragging the twin tail booms of the aircraft along the runway surface. Eventually, he made it through to 893 Squadron in HMS Hermes.

Nigel and I continued to enjoy and progress – taking care to steer clear of any major no-no's – particularly the aircraft's propensity to depart from normal flight into a spin if pushed too hard. There was plenty of front-line experience to show that a Vixen could not be recovered from a fully developed spin – usually occurring during fighter combat.

One day we were sitting in the crew room waiting to fly when a flamboyant staff pilot, 'Fingers' Rothwell and his observer walked in. They were cheerful enough and had just been picked up by helicopter from the fields of Devon after ejecting from their spinning aircraft. Too much 'g' at too low a speed had caused a high 'g' stall, wing drop and loss of control. It was the talking point in the bar that evening.

Amazingly, the next day 'Fingers' took off for more combat training and the same thing happened. One more spin and one more aircraft lost. Pushing it too hard can bite you.

Sadly, our course then suffered a tragedy. Tubes took off with Ian Sutton in the coal hole for an air combat training sortie and the manoeuvring was going well. He was pulling maximum 'g' for the airspeed – which created heavy buffeting over the wings, shaking the whole aircraft. A natural pilot, he was fully in control and nowhere near 'g'-stalling the aircraft. As bad luck would have it, both long slim 'pitot head' probes, one on each wing that sense airspeed and altitude sheared off simultaneously – a result of the heavy buffet. Tubes had his head looking out of the cockpit – completely engaged in the dogfight and therefore had no inkling of the failures.

In the coal hole, Ian was suddenly faced with an altimeter that was erroneously indicating a rapid and horrendous loss in height. This coupled with the heavy buffeting and 'Fingers' Rothwell's recent accidents must have persuaded him that the aircraft was in a spin and there was no time to lose. He pulled the seat handle and ejected from the aircraft. The first thing Tubes heard was the bang as the seat cartridges fired and as he looked round he could see the tell-tale, empty seat rail sticking up out of the coal hole. He immediately made an emergency call for the rescue helicopter to scramble to his location and flew the jet home safely without any air speed or height information.

We were all desperately sad to hear later that the chopper had found Ian – but he had landed with a broken arm in a large pond, couldn't clear himself from the parachute that descended over him and was drowned.

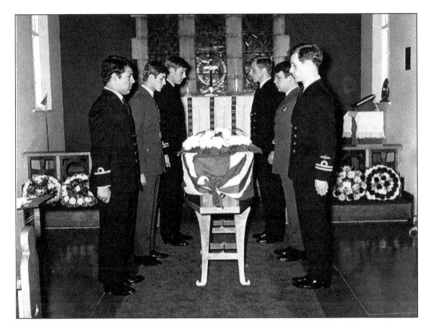

Figure 22. Saying goodbye to Ian.

As ever, after he was buried at the Naval Chapel in Yeovilton village, it was back to business as usual – but with heavy hearts and long-lasting regrets.

Our Passing Out Parade was held on 21 July. It was the Holy Grail that all of us had striven for: Certificate of Qualification as a Naval Fighter Pilot presented by the Commanding Officer of HMS Heron (RNAS Yeovilton), Captain C V Cunningham.

I was also privileged to receive the Kelly Memorial Trophy and Admiral Sir Dudley Pound Prize for the year's Best Operational Flying Training Student from Lady Kelly who was accompanied by Admiral Sir Derek Empson GBE KCB.

The parade and presentation were followed by a suitable Course celebration in the Lamb and Lark public house in Yeovilton village – a much-favoured watering hole.

My mother and sister, Anne (who was then the gorgeous Miss Harlech) had driven down from Gloucestershire to join the party and Anne rapidly became the centre of attention.

Figure 23. Miss Harlech.

My 766 Squadron boss, Dunbar Dempsey was particularly taken and after many champagnes he persuaded her to take a ride with him in his very smart Alfa Romeo convertible – much to every-one's amusement. It wasn't too long before the car returned. Anne had vomited all over the rear seat and was completely non-com-pos-mentis – a huge source of merriment except for the boss!

At the end of the Course, Tubes went straight to a front-line Sea Vixen squadron still at the tender age of 19 years and was soon flying from the deck at sea. I was fortunate to be appointed to 767 Naval Air Squadron and 892 Naval Air Squadron in continuation to fly the new Phantom F-4K but I had to wait for a couple of months before joining the new outfit.

890 Squadron existed to provide continuation flying for front-line Sea Vixen aircrew between appointments. Whilst there, I was very much the new boy surrounded by seasoned aviators. I was a 'nugget' pilot straight out of Operational Flying Training–still completely in awe of the gladiatorial naval and marine aviators who have flown from our carriers and ships for more than 100 years. I thoroughly enjoyed the relaxed atmosphere and getting to know new faces. Neddy Bateman was the boss and set the tone for a very happy small squadron.

It was during this holdover that my invigorating low-level flight along the beaches of Cornwall and Devon with Bernie Steed took place.

Bernie and I planned a low level "jolly" starting at Land's End and finishing near to the Lilstock Nuclear Plant in the Bristol Channel. What led me to select this route was one of my last flights in 738 Naval Air Squadron from Royal Naval Air Station, Brawdy in South Wales. On 5 February 1969, I was leading eight Hunter aircraft on a practice low-level strike mission against a disused airfield near Chivenor. Fellow students from 136 Flying Course were on the mission and included 'gung-ho' pilots such as Robin Kent and Nigel Charles. The mission also included several Staff Air Warfare Instructors who were monitoring our every move and providing fighter opposition to our strike.

Crossing the Western Approaches to the Bristol Channel at very low level, we hurtled in over the beach at Chivenor at 480 knots and approximately 50 feet. Unfortunately, as we approached the target, I wrongly believed we were off-track by a few hundred yards and so I adjusted our heading. I was mistaken and when we pulled up sharply to dive on the target, a market garden warehouse

on a disused airfield, we were too close and nearly in the overhead. Not wishing to let this spoil the party, I rolled over and led
the four attack Hunters (the other four were fighter escorts) into
a very steep dive, 60° instead of 20°; something of which the
Stukas of World War II would have been proud. Pulling out of the
dive without hitting Terra Firma was very hairy – nearly brown
trousers time!

When we returned to base, all our four attack Hunters were found
to have exceeded their maximum 'G' limit by some margin (up
to 11g recorded) and many rivets were missing from the wing-
tips of each aircraft. At the debrief, the head-up display camera
film taken from the cockpit of each strike aircraft made exciting
viewing (suicidal would be a reasonable description) and Frank
Cox, the mission Instructor, told me to destroy all the film before
Neil Rankin, the Senior AWI, had any chance of seeing it.

Later that same year, Bernie and I set off in the Sea Vixen over
the sea along the coast from Land's End. The many sun-drenched
beaches of Cornwall and Devon beckoned like a magnet and we
decided to visit as many of them as possible. Mistake.

I still remember with Technicolor clarity running in to one such
beach filled with tourists. Piling on the power of the two Avon
engines, I descended to almost zero feet over the waves and accelerated to 550 knots. There was a small valley running up and away
from the beach and so I chose this as my exit point. Nearing the
beach I had to pull up slightly to avoid a man in a kayak!

As we crossed the beach and pulled up sharply through the
valley, the noise from the 55 ft wingspan jet must have been truly
horrendous.

Figure 24. A little bit low.

Looping up and over above the beach I remarked to Bernie that "the 'grockels' are waving at us; we should give them another show." And we did.

Another mistake. The 'grockels' had not been waving – they had been shaking their fists.

Blissfully unaware of having caused the brave British public considerable distress and with adrenalin in full flow, we continued our 'jolly' up the coast 'visiting' several beaches in similar style until I spied a merchant vessel being towed by an ocean-going tug near to the Island of Lundy. Another visit beckoned. On the open sea, if you approach a vessel and keep a part of the vessel aligned with the horizon then, as simple physics dictates, you will fly past the vessel at the height of the chosen 'part'. I chose half-way up the bow of the merchantman. After we passed under the tow-rope Bernie let rip one or two expletives as we turned back up the Channel and eventually returned to Yeovilton.

This somewhat cavalier flight did not go unnoticed by the public or indeed by Naval Air Command. There were going to be penalties to pay. But it wasn't until I had already joined 767 Phantom Conversion Squadron that the fruits of my labours came home to roost.

12

767 Phantom Conversion Unit (September – November 1969).

O nly a few days after joining my new squadron and when I was totally immersed in learning about my new aircraft, the past caught up with me. I was told to report to Commander Air, Derek Monsell in the control tower. He knew me well from Linton flying training days. Bernie Steed also received the same invitation but it later became clear that I was the main focus of attention.

"Remember that flight that you two made on the 24th July?" Derek was scratching his arse as he spoke: a sign that this was not good news.

"Yes, sir." I immediately knew it had to be our extended low-level jolly. Not good news!

"Both of you go away and independently provide me with the track your aircraft took and all flight details: no later than 1400, today." The poo-warning bells were ringing loudly. We went away and did as instructed. The next day I was again summoned to the control tower – alone this time.

More arse-scratching. "Bad news, I'm afraid, Ward. Despite recommendations to the contrary from Captain Cunningham, the

Admiral has decided you are to be Court-Martialled for low-flying. He says it won't do you any harm: might even help your career. Make yourself available in the Captain's office at 1400. Oh, and by the way, before you landed that day, we had already had 17 complaints from the public!" Ouch!

Things moved very fast from there. The Captain was clearly sympathetic as I paraded before him. He read out four separate charges of illegal low-flying i. e. flying below 2,000 feet within three miles of the coast. Four beaches were marked on a map which I was allowed to scrutinise.

"How do you plead?"

"Guilty of the first three, sir, but not the fourth."

"May I ask why?"

"That is the wrong beach. It was the one next door."

He then formally charged me on three counts, placed me under house-arrest and advised me to choose a prisoner's friend to accompany me until the Court convened: which was to be in a matter of days. My best friend from Dartmouth, Jeremy Parkes of 892 Squadron gleefully agreed to be my 'friend'.

All my peers thought it was a huge joke, especially Jeremy, but I was not completely of the same mind. The maximum penalty for the charges was two-years in jail. The only silver lining to this dark cloud that had descended over my future was that the Wardroom was my home – so Jerry and I had full access to the bar.

The Court-Martial Board consisted of four Fleet Air Arm Naval Captains presided over by Tony Casdagli, an extremely popular and experienced aviator. I was marched in ceremoniously by

Jerry without my cap and surrendered my ceremonial sword to the Court. During the relatively brief proceedings, Derek Monsell and Neddy Bateman (CO of 890 Vixen Squadron) gave glowing character statements. Much to my astonishment, I learned later that Derek had spent several days religiously learning by heart his two-page testimony on my behalf. Something I shall never forget. It was then my turn to speak.

"Lieutenant Ward, do you have anything to say in mitigation of your guilty plea?"

At some length, I explained that I had indeed been properly instructed on the Regulations in AP(N)76 under which I was being charged. But that had been a long time ago during basic flying training. Since then and particularly during advanced flying training, I had been accustomed to flying well below 2000 feet within 3 miles of the coast on training flights under the close super-vision and leadership of various experienced Staff Pilots. These flights had erased from my memory the Regulation in question.

The Board ordered me to retire whilst they considered their verdict and any penalty. It wasn't very long before Jerry again ushered me into the court. My eyes went straight to my sword which, as expected, was pointing towards me: the verdict was guilty.

Much to my eternal relief, Captain Casdagli addressed me as follows: "Lieut. Ward, we the Board find you guilty as charged. However, in the light of Witness' statements and your own miti-gation plea, you are hereby Reprimanded."

A suitably alcoholic celebration followed in the bar but, much to the horror and shame of my parents, the following morning national newspapers contained reports on the proceedings with headlines such as, "Terror pilot frightens children" (Telegraph).

It was no surprise to us all that the event signalled some changes to the flying training system. The aftermath also included a flow of letters from the general public to yours truly berating me and suggesting various impossible physical acts. As Christmas approached, I jokingly suggested to my peers in the bar that I was going to send an appropriate Christmas card to each of the complainants. It wasn't long before Derek Monsell called me on the phone saying, "Don't you dare!" And of course I didn't.

Although my flying training was now complete and I had been appointed to fly front-line Phantoms, I had no illusions about the challenges that still faced me. There remained an awful lot for me to learn before I could feel at home with my boyhood idols. Full qualification as a Royal Navy All Weather Fighter Pilot by Day and Night was still a distant goal that would depend on personal performance when embarked. Success in the flying training pipeline was now nothing but a treasured memory as I was surrounded by the exceptional expertise of those I desired to emulate. The challenge was there but although my self-confidence remained high, my natural cockiness had to be put away in the shadows. This was not difficult as, once more, I found myself at the bottom of the ladder.

767 Operational Conversion Squadron, commanded by Peter Marshall, was staffed by some of the best fighter pilots and observers in the world. Indeed, they included members of the team that had been responsible for assisting in the creation of the Top Gun Academy of the United States Navy at Miramar, San Diego e.g. Doug Borrowman (AWI), Peter Goddard, Nick Childs and Paul Waterhouse. It was a privilege to be trained by these outstanding exponents of twin-seat Air Intercept and Fighter Combat.

Figure 25. Phantom F-4K of 767 Squadron.

In May 1969, these top guns had participated in and won the Daily Mail Trans-Atlantic Air Race, focusing full attention on the Fleet Air Arm and commemorating the 50th Anniversary of the first trans-Atlantic crossing by John Alcock and Arthur Brown. As reported by Wikipedia:

"Organised by the Daily Mail newspaper, the race was actually a race of individuals between the top of the Post Office Tower in London to the top of the Empire State Building in New York and vice versa. Each of the individuals or "Runners" had to use some form of air transport.

The shortest overall time between London and New York was by Squadron Leader Tom Lecky-Thompson flying a Royal Air Force Hawker Siddeley Harrier in 6 hours 11 minutes. The shortest time between New York and London was by Lieutenant Commander Peter Goddard, an Observer in a Royal Navy McDonnell Douglas Phantom in 5 hours 11 minutes. The Royal

Navy entered three "runners" each to be flown across the Atlantic in a Phantom. The navy runners flew from the Floyd Bennet Naval Air Station to Wisley Aerodrome and were refuelled by Handley Page Victor aerial tankers over the Atlantic.

On 11 May 1969 a Royal Navy Phantom of 892 Naval Air Squadron set a new world air speed record between New York and London in 4 hours and 46 minutes.

The Vickers Alcock and Brown trophy was awarded to Lieutenant Commander Peter Goddard for his 5-hour 11-minute crossing[4]."

Al Hickling (AWI) of 892 Squadron was Peter's pilot. Half-way across the Atlantic at 40,000 feet, supersonic and miles from any-where, Al decided to make the flight more than interesting. He raised an object in his hand up to near the canopy so that Peter, in the rear cockpit, could see it.

"Hey Pete, did you know how easy it is to dismantle the top of the joystick?" There it was in his hand and without it being in its proper place, the aircraft was uncontrollable! A superb sense of humour but he knew exactly what he was doing.

The Navy's victory was recognised by Rolls-Royce who provided the Spey 201/2 engines for the UK Phantom. They presented 982 Squadron with a brand-new, crimson Rolls-Royce Silver Cloud to be used as a squadron runabout.

---

[4] This time included racing down The Empire State building and up the GPO Tower.

Being surrounded by such expertise and publicity was rather over-whelming for yours truly but I was soon to understand that encour-agement rather than criticism was the order of the day.

Getting airborne in the new Phantom F-4K was almost the culmi-nation of a life-long dream (I had yet to land the aircraft onboard HMS Ark Royal). It was an utterly exhilarating experience – sit-ting in an aluminium tube with 42,000 lbs of angry thrust which kicked you in the back hard when you selected afterburner (reheat).

My first flight in the F-4K was with Lt. Cdr. Peter Rickard in the rear cockpit as my Observer and guardian angel. The sense of anticipation and excitement was intense as we taxied onto the centreline of runway 27 at Yeovilton. Checks complete, we were cleared for take-off. Wheel brakes fully on via the rudder pedals, I pushed the throttle levers to full military power. A quick check of engine temperatures–they were okay–then I released the brakes and selected full afterburner. It took a few seconds before the afterburner kicked in and with it the tremendous acceleration that forced me back in my seat. In no time at all, we lifted off the runway at about 150 knots. Undercarriage and flaps up before we hit 250 knots and then we were climbing away at 400 knots over the end of the runway and Ilchester Village into the heavens. Such power inevitably took me by surprise. It was almost like being left behind by the aircraft.

The atmosphere in the crew-room was totally conducive to learning; including learning from one's own mistakes without unnecessary recrimination. This came fully home to me after one of my early landings.

Our new aircraft was itself undergoing minor teething troubles, one of which was that the maxarettes which prevented the wheel-brakes locking-up (like the ABS system in cars) were not yet func-tioning. If you more than touched the brakes on landing at about

140 knots, the brakes would seize solid with disastrous conse-quences for the tyres and undercarriage. We were all well-briefed on this, "Wait until the aircraft braking parachute has the speed well under control before applying the wheel-brakes".

Unfortunately, the wheel-brakes were applied via the rudder pedals used for keeping the aircraft straight on the runway and full concentration was needed to prevent the brakes from acti-vating. I got it wrong!

As we touched down, my toe pressure on the rudder pedals engaged the brakes. Disaster! Immediately, the brakes locked on, the tyres burst and the whole jet shook violently as we hurtled down the runway, raw metal on concrete. We stayed on the runway but the undercarriage bore the brunt of the landing. It was written off at considerable cost. As I entered the crew-room I felt mortified but Brian Davies, Boss of 892 Squadron came to my rescue.

"Don't feel too bad about that, Sharkey. It can happen to anyone and it happened to me when landing on the trans-Atlantic air race." Somewhat comforted, I made sure it didn't happen again.

Like the Sea Vixen, the Phantom had become a true multi-role, all weather aircraft requiring expertise in Air Intercept, Fighter Combat, Ground Attack and Surface Attack against ships. Initially, it had been designed purely for the ground and surface attack roles but its performance and versatility ensured that it was transformed by its users into a world beating Fighter.

The state-of-the-art technology in the 60s made it essential to have two aircrew to cope with the workload of flying the aircraft to its limits (the pilot) and operating its advanced radar and weapon system to full advantage (the observer). Communication and trust between the cockpits was essential and had many benefits. One of these was having four eyes instead of two during air combat manoeuvring. Another most significant advantage was that experienced observers could provide inexperienced pilots with valuable airborne training and vice versa.

And with the Phantom came the dimension of supersonic flight which provided many tactical benefits for air intercept and air combat. The jet could be moved rapidly around the sky to an optimum position for intercepting enemy aircraft and, in air combat, the full power of the engines could be used to maintain maximum manoeuvrability and energy. However, over-use of the afterburner could very quickly drain the fuel tanks to empty. In full afterburner and at low level, the two Spey engines could consume up to 1,800 pounds of fuel (225 gallons) per minute. Injudicious use was therefore self-defeating.

During an equally balanced dogfight, a useful Phantom manoeuvre would be to exit the fight at the right moment, when aircraft positioning meant it was safe to do so, accelerate to high-speed and then return to the fight with maximum 'g' and energy. Peter Goddard first guided me through this tactic in bright sunshine off the coast of North Cornwall during combat training against F-8 Crusaders from the French Navy. When the Crusader was pointing directly away from our aircraft, Peter yelled, "Full burner! Unload!" Unload meant taking all the 'g' off the aircraft resulting in minimum drag and best acceleration. It was a new and exhilarating experience for me taking the jet to Mach 1. 8 (about 1000 knots) in a gentle, curved descent. "Now pull back hard through the vertical!" As we did so at maximum 'g', the aircraft soared to the heavens. "Cancel burner!" As we rolled wings level over the top, we were now pointing at the Crusader with a distinct height/ energy advantage.

If you got this manoeuvre wrong, you would expose your tail to a missile shot which is exactly what happened to the F-15's when our Sea Harriers were fighting them at Yeovilton and at Decimomannu in 1981. (as described in Chapter 21.)

Having learned an enormous amount from the Top Guns of 767 Squadron, it was time at last to join the Front-line. Deck-landing and healthy competition awaited.

13

892 NAVAL AIR SQUADRON (DECEMBER 1969 – OCTOBER 1971).

Figure 26. The 892 Squadron F-4K Phantom All Weather Fighter.

For my first seven months in 892 Squadron, we continued to be based at Yeovilton under the instructive command of Brian Davies. I had to wait until 14 June 1970 for my first deck landing and embarkation in HMS Ark Royal: a major milestone in my flying career. Prophetically, 14 June also signalled the last milestone in my flying career twelve years later: the end of the Falklands War in 1982.

The front-line atmosphere lived up to all my expectations and the initial time ashore represented a relatively gentle introduction to the real McCoy.

As you may already have noted, although everyone worked as a closely-knit team, there was always healthy competition between the crews to see who was best: who was Top Gun. I was still a long way from that lofty position.

At that time Royal Naval Air Station Yeovilton, HMS Heron, was one of the busiest military airfields in the world with several Sea Vixen squadrons, a Hunter support squadron, Search and Rescue helicopters and the Phantom squadrons. The Buccaneer Squadrons were based at Lossiemouth. Whilst ashore, day flying and night flying were the norm for five days a week with most weekends off for aircrew unless you were Station Duty Officer. Ground crews and particularly squadron engineer personnel would often work the weekends as well.

One Sunday, I happened to be the Station Duty Officer when the lads had just finished working on one of the Phantom's engines. An engine function test was required. I taxied out to the main runway with a Petty Officer Engineer in the rear cockpit. "Have you ever experienced full afterburner in this jet?" I asked. He replied, no. "OK, then, I'll give you a quick demo." It was not a particularly clever move but there was plenty of runway ahead of us and I had already cleared the engine-test run with the Duty Air Traffic Controller in the tower.

I checked the engine performance at full military power before releasing the brakes and selecting afterburner. The Petty Officer loved it. After a few seconds I closed the throttles and started to brake but we were already travelling very fast down the runway. Ahead of me, a Navy car had decided to cross the runway. I braked harder and had slowed to a walking pace as the car disappeared towards the Station Church in Yeovilton village. My passenger had enjoyed the treat but the tower immediately called me up with not a little indignation, "Were you aware that the First Sea Lord was in that car?" I certainly was not and thankfully heard no more about it.

Whether flying from Yeovilton or from the deck of HMS Ark Royal, I found that all the lessons that I had learned or tried to learn during training and conversion slowly but surely began to knit together during this my first front-line tour. There was an awful lot to take in if I was to catch up with my more experienced squadron colleagues. But this was made much easier thanks to the example set by the other pilots and the exceptional knowledge and assistance of the observers. The latter were to prove my right arm in the air, especially for deck landing, air intercept work, fighter combat and of course instrument flying in heavy cloud and/ or at night.

It was in fighter combat that a much-cherished relationship was born. Doug MacDonald, an Observer and fully qualified AWI, frequently took good charge of me during fighter combat exercises. He knew far more about the tactical handling of the Phantom than I did and would yell from the back seat, "Pull harder. Reverse now. Keep rolling. Don't stop, I said keep rolling!" His advice was always spot on and rapidly earned my respect.

Our relationship was extremely combative. We were both very aggressive characters with large egos and this was to come to a head during my second tour in the squadron. But during the second half of this, my first tour, we flew together a lot and this gave me a head start towards eventual AWI selection and qualification.

Probably the best piece of advice I ever received concerning fighter combat (dogfighting) came from Taylor Scott, a very accomplished AWI top gun if ever there was one: one of the greats. The aim of the game during a dogfight is to get behind your opponent and bring your weapons to point at him–no easy matter. Taylor's advice was earth-shatteringly simple but intuitive.

> "Sharkey, as you well know, during any form of flight the lift vector from the wings is always pointing vertically upwards from the airplane. This remains true in heavy manoeuvring, no matter what the attitude of the aircraft is; pulling 'g', rolling horizontally or in the vertical, etc. What you must never forget during a dogfight is to try to keep your lift vector pointing at the 6 o'clock of the other aircraft. Do this successfully and you will always end up in his 6 o'clock."

That, along with Dougie's airborne help, was a turning point that signalled a major improvement in my combat performance.

Alongside Dougie, my two greatest mentors in the rear cockpit were Leo Gallagher and, in my second tour, Desmond Hughes; both of them Irish and brilliant tacticians and weapon system operators. Leo could probably have played rugby for Ireland if he hadn't joined the Navy. Desmond, although as small as me in stature and a very modest character, was someone you wouldn't want to mess with physically – he was dynamite when provoked and very cool with it.

Like its sister capital warships, HMS Ark Royal had a well-rounded Air Group with which to satisfy the Air Defence and Strike/Attack Roles of the Fleet: 12 Phantoms with 14 crews; 14 nuclear-capable Buccaneer low-level Fighter-Bombers with 16 crews (also providing Air-to-Air Refuelling); 5 Airborne Early Warning Gannets and 3 Search and Rescue Helicopters.

Figure 27. HMS Ark Royal Air Group.

The Commander 'Air', known as the CAG in the US Navy, was responsible to the Captain for the Operational Readiness and Flight Safety of the Air Group and was usually to be found in Flyco: part of the bridge superstructure overlooking the whole flight deck. He was supported by Lieutenant-Commander Flying

(Little 'f') who controlled domestic flying operations in proximity to the ship and on the deck.

Fixed wing aircraft relied upon catapults and arrestor wires for launch and recovery and this meant that all flying operations had to be conducted in cycles: with 1 hour and 40 minutes between each cycle. A typical cycle would include the launch and recovery of 4 Phantoms, 4 Buccaneers and 1 Gannet; with a helicopter air-borne as a plane guard – ready to pick downed aircrew out of the sea. One hour and 40 minutes later, a further launch and recovery cycle would start.

The flight deck was, therefore, frightfully busy and congested and was no place for the faint-hearted. Its smooth operation required exceptionally precise and detailed organisation and for-ward planning.

The ultimate challenge for the flight deck crews was to con-duct these operations in bad weather and heavy seas: when the deck was slippery and the ship was rolling, pitching, yawing and heaving. Such ship movement could impart dangerous momentum to the heavy, 25-ton aircraft on deck and there was always a need to be moving them around for launch, recovery or maintenance. Unless they were chained down to ringbolts in the deck they could have a mind of their own. On one occasion, it took about 30 flight deck and aircraft handlers to prevent unwanted movement of my aircraft readying for launch.

For aircrew, landing in such conditions was a nightmare.

The good balance of the Air Group provided for continuous, excel-lent air-borne training opportunities: especially for Air Intercept and dissimilar fighter combat e. g. Buccaneers against Phantoms under Airborne Early Warning Gannet control. The Buccaneer aircrew were no push-over. They too had experienced AWIs who kept them up to the mark.

During my front-line baptism, Leo Gallagher and I were partners in crime; that is, for the most part, we generally flew together. He had the questionable privilege of taking me for my first deck landing. This was a moment I had always dreamed about. And it required 100% concentration and very smooth, accurate flying.

We had prepared for this moment with numerous Mirror Assisted Dummy Deck Landings on a marked-out section of the main runway at Yeovilton. The landing-sight (known as the Mirror) gave cues to the pilot for staying precisely on the necessary glide path to the deck. But the difference on land is that there is always a ground-cushion effect from the air trapped under the aircraft just before touchdown which causes the aircraft to flare and reduce the rate of descent slightly. This does not occur on a carrier – the air cushion is dissipated over the sides of the ship. The end result is that the aircraft touches down on deck very firmly indeed – more of a 'heavy landing' than a smooth arrival. (See Annex A for a rather technical and detailed explanation of this and of other carrier deck-landing idiosyncrasies.)

On an approach in the Phantom and with the undercarriage, hook and flaps down, the optimum angle of attack of the aircraft, which defines the precise required speed of the aircraft, was signalled to the aircrew in our headphones. A steady tone indicated the right angle of attack – on speed. A lower beeping tone indicated that you were low on speed/power, probably leading to a sink below the glide path–an extremely dangerous condition with the steel stern of the ship beckoning. A high beeping tone indicated that you were too fast and could either rise above the glide path and miss an arrestor-wire or much worse, break the wire with catastrophic consequences.

From a downwind position abeam of the ship, Ark Royal looked uninvitingly small. Having carried out all the landing checks, my adrenaline was in full flow and as we entered the final turn with the undercarriage and arrestor hook down, I called, "Finals, four greens". There was a low, slow beeping tone in the headphones which I knew would become a steady tone when we rolled out on the approach centreline. As we did so at about half-a-mile from touch-down, the deck looked even smaller as the stabilised landing-sight came into view. In order to stay safely on the glide path, I had to keep the bright white meat-ball in line with the two, horizontal green datums.

"On sight!", I called rather breathlessly. The Landing-Sight Officer (LSO) replied. "Roger! You are on the centreline and on the glide path." Leo was continuing to give me information on my speed, angle of attack and power setting. There was an awful lot of information to take in from different quarters but I was very grateful for all of it. The ship started to loom large but the edges of the narrow, angled runway were lined with obstacles – aircraft to the right and the landing sight to the left. There was no room for error. The LSO continued:

"Roger. Roger. You are going slightly high." It was all happening very quickly. A small reduction in power and fractionally lower the nose.

"Roger. Back on the glide path. Roger."

"You are going slightly low. A little power." The LSO had an urgent tone to his voice. Low was dangerous. We were almost there but I applied too much power.

"You are fast and going high!"

A resounding thump as we hit the deck very hard and, thinking we had landed safely, I immediately started to throttle back. Big mistake!

"BOLTER, BOLTER, BOLTER. POWER, POWER, POWER. FULL REHEAT!" came the screams from the bridge and Flyco[5]. We had missed the wires. I slammed the throttles into full reheat but it took time for the engines to wind up and the burners didn't light until we had hurtled past all the parked aircraft and left the deck.

Everyone held their breath as we disappeared from sight below the bow.

At that moment, I was mentally well behind the aircraft and thinking more about the indignity of missing the wires than hitting the sea. Then, a welcome surge of power from the afterburners hit us in the back as we floated towards the water and stopped our descent in the nick of time. A huge plume of spray from the jet exhausts arose behind us as we hurtled back into sight above the bow, rising like a Phoenix out of the ashes. Big cheers from the many 'goofers' (members of the ship's company) watching from the ship's superstructure! And intense relief in my cockpit!

Leo was a total star. Completely calm, he continued as if nothing had happened – reassuring and professional, he encouraged me as we turned downwind for a second go. My next approach was much better and we caught a wire. One of my boyhood dreams had at last become a reality – celebrated of course by a few beers in the bar.

---

[5] Flyco is situated alongside the bridge and is where the Commander 'Air' (the Air Group Commander) and his deputy, Lieutenant-Commander Flying (known as Little 'f') oversee flight deck and local air operations. Squadron Duty Officers are frequently in attendance – especially during special occasions such as first deck landings by day and night.

The following day, Leo accompanied me on my first catapult launch. This proved to be more straight-forward but no less exhilarating.

We taxied onto the waist catapult under direction from the Flight Deck Chief. As we did so the water-cooled blast deflectors were raised behind us, the nose wheel was extended, the steel hold-back was connected to the aircraft and the thick, steel-wire catapult strop was attached. The Flight Deck Officer gave us the wind-up signal. Checks completed, I selected full military power and then full afterburner. At full power, the noise on deck reached 150 decibels – enough to cause physical damage to personnel who got too close. In the cockpit, it remained relatively quiet.

Adrenaline pumping through my veins, I braced my right arm behind the control column after signalling that we were ready to go. Down went the green flag and moments later the catapult took over, shattering the steel hold-back as it did so. The huge acceleration pinned us back in our seats as we rattled over the uneven deck and off the bow of the ship.

Airborne and thoroughly excited. Leo reminded me to raise undercarriage and flap as we soared easily away from the deck and cancelled the burners. What a way to get airborne!

Much later-on, when Her Majesty the Queen visited us in Portsmouth Harbour, I was one of the very lucky ones to be introduced to her in the welcoming ceremony on the quarterdeck. I was second in line and could hardly contain myself. Our brief was to shake her hand without gripping it, address her first as "Your Majesty" and from then on, "Ma'am". After a short chat of no more than 20 seconds, she would push one's hand away and move on to the next in line. It did not go entirely as planned.

Figure 28. Intense excitement in the cockpit.

"And what do you do on board?" she asked.

"Well, Your Majesty, I'm a Phantom fighter pilot."

"Really?" Her eyes lit up. "Is that exciting? Tell me more."

"Oh, yes, Ma'am. Very exciting. Launching from the catapult is even better than an ejaculation!" I couldn't believe what I had said. The Duke of Edinburgh, the Admiral and the Captain were all standing behind her and I could hear them grinding their teeth as they visibly winced.

She didn't move on. Instead her eyes sparkled and she laughed. "My goodness! You must tell me all about it." I did so and four minutes later she reluctantly pushed my hand away and moved on to the next in line. Her sense of humour had saved my day!

It was not all smooth sailing, though. Hiccups would regularly occur and nobody was immune.

Although that first squadron embarkation was to be relatively short, only a few weeks, it was full of intensive flying in the North Sea and the Western Approaches and even more satisfying and enjoyable than I could have imagined. We were continuously practicing all the aircraft's roles including air-to-surface rocketing and bombing on the splash target towed behind the ship, a quick diversion ashore with a bomb that failed to release from the aircraft and, most impressive of all, my first live missile firing on Aberporth Range in Cardigan Bay. It was a beautiful sunny day with clear skies as Leo guided me through the launch of an AIM-7E Sparrow III medium-range missile against a high-flying target drone.

After Leo had acquired the target on radar at long range and positioned us for an in-range head-on shot, I pressed the firing button and as the missile was ejected downwards from its flush fuselage mounting, I called "Fox One away!"[6] The rocket motor immediately ignited and propelled the missile at lightning speed up and away from the aircraft leaving a long trail of white smoke behind it. After motor burn-out, the smoke disappeared and the missile was lost from sight against the clear blue sky as it glided its supersonic path to the target.

"Splash one drone!" The kill was confirmed by the range telemetry system operators on the ground.

During our next few weeks ashore, flying continued apace mixed with much-needed, relaxing social releases from stress at local

---

[6] "Fox One" indicated the release of a missile against a head-on or distant target. "Fox Two" indicated the release of a short range missile from behind a target. "Fox Three" indicated a guns kill on a target. (Our Phantom was not fitted with guns/cannon.)

public houses and in the Wardroom Mess. On 1 September 1970, Command of the Squadron was handed over from Brian Davies to Nick Kerr who had a distinctly bullish and aggressive exterior which masked a remarkably wise and understanding leader. One couldn't help but adore and respect him.

To my delight, Brian Davies wrote in my Pilots Flying Log Book:

"A keen pilot who flies with zest. Carrier Operations: Good. Armament: Average. Instrument Flying: Reliable."

I could wish for no more than that.

Just a couple of days before we re-embarked, tragedy occurred. Alec Stuart, the squadron staff officer, and Pip Coombes were flying a low-level air intercept sortie over the English Channel in very difficult 'fish-bowl' conditions. The sea was flat calm and although there was bright sunshine, a thick haze obscured the horizon – there was no visible delineation between sky and sea. Alec and Pip never returned – they went down without trace.

It was a real downer – but we had to get over it. As we sat mulling it over in the crew-room, my new Boss suddenly addressed me. "Ward, you are just the man I need. We need a new Squadron Staff Officer and, as of now, you are it!"

Although I may have been an obvious choice with my background as a career officer and one-time ship's correspondence officer, I was less that elated: dumbfounded would have been more to the point. "Yes, sir!" We were to embark the following day and all I could think about was a daily routine that now included hours spent in the bowels of the ship looking after the mountains of squadron paperwork including formal returns, correspondence, daily orders, flying programmes, etc. But it proved to be not as bad as I feared. We had a superb Leading-Writer in the office who took care of most of the work. Delegation and trust were the key.

Nick Kerr knew how to delegate but he was also a master of 'taking-the-piss' and testing out his officers. My most important test came the same evening that we embarked. The Wardroom bar was bedlam; packed solid with aviators and ship's officers quaffing a few ales. I was standing having a beer or two near the back of the Wardroom renewing acquaintances with Buccaneer chums and the Airborne Early Warning Gannet boys when a booming voice filled the air.

"Staffie, get me a drink!" It was the boss, Nick, at the bar.

I didn't move and everybody stared at me. "Sharkey, that's your boss! Aren't you going?" one exclaimed. A deafening silence was settling over the gathering. I carried on drinking my pint.

"Staffie, get me a fucking drink!" He sounded furious and ferocious. I thought fast – this can't become a habit – I was nobody's push-over. At the top of my voice, I shouted, "Get your own fucking drink!" and got on with my beer.

The Wardroom assembly gasped! But Nick Kerr just grinned and let it go. I had made the right move – a good working relationship had been established and I could get on with my flying.

A few days later the ship was way up in the North Sea flying air defence and strike missions in a NATO exercise, Northern Wedding. We were a long way from land and there were no diversion airfields available within range. Our only landing place was the deck of HMS Ark Royal: in other words we had nowhere else to go if the deck became unusable. I was airborne with my long-term friend, Jerry Parkes, in the rear cockpit. He normally flew with Al Hickling, one of our fabled AWI Top Guns. We were the only aircraft airborne and it was getting very close to land-on time. Flyco called us up. "Conserve your fuel! We have a problem on deck!"

Our fuel state was about 3400 lbs – just about down to land-on weight. Doing as instructed, we cruised around at medium height and best endurance speed – saving fuel.

Flyco: "We have no wires available for land-on. Will keep you informed." OK! It was a beautiful, crisp and clear day. There was nothing to be concerned about. So we thought.

As our fuel state dropped towards 2400 lbs, I began to think about having to eject from the aircraft and getting wet. Jerry was still unmoved and bubbling with confidence, "Al and I have landed-on with low fuel many times. Not a problem, Sharkey."

On-board, the flight deck engineers were working flat out to get arrestor-wires available. Up in Flyco and the bridge, serious discussions were taking place between the Captain, Ray Lygo and my old friend Commander 'Air', Derek Monsell. Should the crash barrier be rigged? Crash barriers take time to rig and have been known to decapitate pilots. The Carrier Command was between a rock and a hard place and, as very interested parties, we were kept well-informed in the air.

As our fuel state dropped below 2000 lbs, reactions in the air and on the ship changed noticeably. Jerry was now also realising that getting wet was more likely than not. On-board, Derek Monsell scratched his arse, as was his wont, and told Ray Lygo that he 'needed a shit'.

Crunch-time came as our fuel state dropped to 1200 lbs. One wire as opposed to four had just been made serviceable on deck. The crash barrier would not be rigged and we were to take our chances trying to catch the single wire. If we didn't catch it, the aircraft would be lost and we would have a first ride in our rocket-powered ejection seats!

It was tension all-round as we turned in for our approach with 700 lbs of fuel remaining – a second approach would not be possible. Jerry was no longer chuckling as we levelled out on the centreline and on the glide path – but he was keeping the right information flowing. If we missed the wire, we would have to eject and lose the aircraft. Getting wet was a minor thought by comparison. The Search and Rescue helicopter would pull us out of the sea very quickly.

There was very little deck movement ahead of us and that was a huge bonus.

It was a perfect approach until we were a short distance from the ship's stern. My sub-conscious then took over. I allowed us to sink a fraction low before hitting the deck to ensure that our hook caught the wire. Although that wasn't the best decision, good fortune came to the rescue. The hook bounced on the deck near the stern but came down again just in time to catch the lone wire. We had recovered safely on board. It was an immense relief for all concerned and deserved a few beers in the bar – especially as it was my birthday the following day.

As with all first-tourists (a new boy on board), my progress was carefully but discreetly monitored by the squadron command. This process was not intrusive in any way and I was allowed to show my true colours both in the air and within the ship/the air station. I didn't need any encouragement and was just very happy learning my trade from the old and the bold. 'Old' is perhaps the wrong adjective. Some of my short-service peers were younger than me but had been flying in the front-line gaining experience and expertise for four years whilst I was still undergoing career Seaman training through Dartmouth College. All were fully proven and well-qualified.

Occasionally, my career background and associated 'maturity' proved to be a rationale that led to me being selected for other events.

After our exercise in the North Sea, we deployed directly to the Mediterranean where our multi-role training at sea continued 24/7 and our brief time spent in Malta proved to be remarkably good fun – a very wild run ashore.

As we were operating to the southwest of Crete, the need arose to get our Lt. Cdr. Flying, Peter Marshall, my old boss in 767 Phantom Conversion Unit to England to attend the Man of the Year Dinner. He was so honoured after having guided a stricken airliner down to a safe landing after it had been struck by lightning and had suffered the drastic loss of critical flight information. He needed to be flown to RAF Luqa in Malta, 400 nautical miles away to the West, in the backseat of a Phantom.

The stable young career officer, yours truly, was chosen to be his chauffeur!

When briefing the sortie, I suggested that we might make the trip short and interesting. "What I plan, Sir, is a supersonic climb out from the ship and to transit to Malta at Mach 1. 6 at 40,000 feet. En route, perhaps you can flash up the radar in case we need it at the other end." Peter, a highly experienced Phantom pilot, happily agreed.

We blasted off the catapult and stayed in full afterburner in the climb, pushing over at 14,000 feet, accelerating to supersonic speed and continuing the climb. As we were very quickly passing

35,000 feet, the ship's air controller called. "Anoxia, anoxia, anoxia. Check your oxygen."

We checked. "Our oxygen is fine. What is the problem?"

"The problem is you are heading towards Israel rather than Malta. You have joined the 180° Club!"

Cursing myself and feeling not a little embarrassed, I banked the aircraft hard to the right and, using up a lot of sky to the south because of my speed, turned back towards Malta. As a result of my mistake, we were now many miles south of our launch position and had consumed quite a lot of fuel. I didn't account for this and stuck to my game plan. It was a beautiful day without a cloud in sight as we hurtled along above the deep blue sea, 40,000 feet below.

With an estimated 60 nautical miles to run, I asked Peter in the rear cockpit to go to radar mapping mode and to confirm the position of our destination. There was no such thing as GPS in those days. The radar saw nothing ahead, just the empty sea. Consternation in my cockpit and Peter said nothing. We appeared to be up the creek without a paddle. I feverishly looked around the hazy horizon for any sight of land.

Way off to the right I saw a brown smudge on the horizon. That had to be it! But our problems were not over. Still at Mach 1. 6, I turned hard right towards what I hoped was the Island, cancelled the afterburner and noted with dismay that our fuel state was down to 1200 lbs. Fuck!

"Pan. Pan. Pan. Luqa this is Omega Leader approaching you from the South from high level in cruise descent. I am nearly out of fuel. Request straight-in approach to land. I repeat, I am nearly out of fuel." Peter remained calm and silent as the Island rapidly came into view.

"Roger, Omega leader, understood. You are clear straight-in behind the Hercules at 3 miles on finals." I could see the Hercules but knew that any delay in putting my aircraft down could be cata-strophic. Our fuel state was indicating less than 400 lbs. With the undercarriage on the way down, I turned very hard in front of the Hercules and slammed the aircraft down on the runway. Parachute streamed and hard breaking brought us down to taxing speed as we turned off the runway with the fuel gauges on zero.

Waves of relief flooded over me. As he climbed out of the cockpit, Peter Marshall made a simple comment: "That was not your best trip, was it?"

"No, Sir. Indeed it wasn't!" To say that I learned from that fiasco is an understatement.

A few days later, a significant and very proud step forward for me occurred. The Boss and Commander 'Air' signed the following on 25 November 1970:

> "Certified that Lt. N D Ward has carried out 68 hours and 51 Deck Landings since embarked in HMS Ark Royal and I now consider him to be proficient in the Phantom All Weather Fighter role by Day."

This proficiency included all aspects of the aircraft's roles and carrier-based operations including Air Intercept, Fighter Combat, Air-to-Surface and Air-to-Ground weaponry, Close Air Support and Instrument Flying.

Two days later, I carried out my first night deck-landing. Once more, Leo had drawn the short straw and was in the rear cockpit. This was an entirely different kettle of fish from daylight operations.

It was viewed as something of a black art by not a few of our front-line pilots – a result of many crashes and fatalities over recent decades, especially at night. Up to the early sixties, it was usual for each embarked fast-jet squadron to lose up to two crews during every commission. The Grim Reaper had always been lurking. Although refined procedures, aids and training had reduced this dreadful toll, it remained at the forefront of some pilots' minds as they prepared for a night launch.

As a new boy onboard, my first understanding of this came one evening in the bar. Two aviators entered the Wardroom in full flying kit – absolutely against the Mess Rules but nobody complained. They needed a beer and a cigarette before getting airborne. One of them was so twitched and was trembling so much that he couldn't light his own cigarette – sympathetic hands obliged. The amazing thing was that he then went out on deck, got airborne and returned on board with an impeccable landing. I was more than impressed with their courage.

Night flying at sea has two opposite faces. One, a clear bright night under the moon and the stars with a clearly visible horizon and a calm sea. The other, pitch-blackness in clag with no horizon and a rough sea. All pilots therefore need to be highly proficient at Instrument Flying, i. e. flying and fighting the aircraft without any outside visual references. A great emphasis was placed on this capability with regular training and check-flights when disembarked.

It was with all this in mind that I approached the deck for the first time at night. It was bright and clear with a good visible horizon as we started our Carrier Controlled Approach some 12 miles from the deck. All I could see ahead of me was one small bright light – that was the ship. From there on in, it was a question of smooth instrument flying and mind-over-matter until we got close to the ship. By that stage we were already maintaining a steady controlled descent on the glide path and on centreline.

My concentration was far higher than by day and I was breathing rather more heavily. As the bright light expanded into a multitude of dim lights, the runway outline appeared and the landing-sight became clearly visible. It was now a question of taking in all the normal cues, visual, verbal and audio, and obeying them accurately.

As we got in very close, the key was not to 'fly the deck' but to rely on the landing-sight and to keep straight. Before I knew it, we had thumped down on the deck, caught the target three wire and were being marshalled away from the runway. Another milestone safely past. It hadn't been so difficult and the whole experience sowed seeds in my mind for the future.

As Christmas, 1970 approached, the ship returned to the UK and 892 Squadron disembarked off Gibraltar for return to Yeovilton. Some icing on the cake awaited me. Nick Kerr assessed me as follows:

> "A young pilot who has done well to fly from the deck at night on his first tour. Carrier Operations: Steady and Safe. Armament: Good. Night/Instrument Flying: Progressing Well."

And then, to my complete surprise he informed me that I was to take a Course and become an Instrument Rating Instructor (IRI). I was totally flabbergasted but tried not to show it. Here I was, half-way through my first tour and surrounded by squadron pilots with far more experience – indeed, some of the best in the world.

And I was to become the Squadron IRI – carrying out Instrument Rating Tests on those aviators that I still thought could eat me for breakfast. My flight hours were well short of the normally accepted level for IRI qualification.

I didn't dwell on it too much. It was a development that I didn't even try to interpret until much later. With hindsight, I suspect that the Boss and the Senior Pilot were more than content with my instrument flying and thought the new challenge would do me good. I passed the Course before the end of January 1971.

The new year took my learning curve to a new level. Whether ashore or afloat the squadron engaged in the continuing practice of all its operational roles by day and night; both defensive, air inter-cept and fighter combat, and offensive, surface attack against ship targets and ground attack/Close Air Support. Rather than being just the new boy, I felt I had become one of a very professional team and when ashore at Yeovilton I flew with all the squadron observers, learning a few new tricks from each of them.

When embarked, it was usual as well as sensible practice to be teamed up with a single observer so that we knew each other like the back of our hands. This was good for general combat training but its main value was in being prepared for the unexpected and for the often-dangerous challenges that are the hallmark of deck operations.

Just before re-embarking in April, I was teamed up with Doug MacDonald. Although I was sad to be parted from Leo, the new relationship had many advantages for me. Doug was a very tal-ented AWI with all associated attributes: aggression, a will to win and a not-unreasonable bent for taking charge. He also had an abrasive sense of humour in the air and on the deck and didn't suffer fools gladly. With two like-minded aviators in the same aircraft we proved to be a great team albeit with many arguments over points of detail. I was the aircraft captain but most of the experience was in the rear cockpit. One of Doug's exceptional qualities was that he could take it just as easily as he could dish it out and he rapidly earned my full respect, although sometimes I tended not to show it. I would go to war with Dougal, as I like to call him, any day of the week.

At the beginning of June, we deployed to the Eastern Seaboard of the United States for more war-fighting training with our American counterparts. During the deployment our Squadron enjoyed a brief working detachment to Naval Air Station Cecil Field near Jacksonville, Florida. It was a good opportunity to bond with US Navy aviators in the air and on the ground.

Hospitality was exceptional and the Boss, Dougal and I spent a very special evening having dinner at the Station Commander's home. He was a very tall, fit, old and bold four-ring Captain and fighter pilot with the same instincts as ourselves. After dinner and not a few drinks, he was keen to play a few mess-games and suggested arm-wrestling. I was the first to take up the challenge and beat him resoundingly three times in a row. Not to be outdone, he immediately challenged me to leg-wrestling – lying on the floor with one leg vertical and inter-twined with the opponent's leg. It was no-contest. I found myself flying through the air and crashing down with my knee on his coffee table, which disintegrated. All square and with my leg being temporarily out of action, I sat on the floor by his armchair while he patted me on the head and told me that his wife was leaving him because he was not going to be promoted to Rear-Admiral! In order to lighten the mood, I suggested we all tried drinking a Blue Blazer. The key to this game is to take a liqueur-glass filled to the brim with Grand Marnier, light the fiery liquid and then drink the whole glass down without putting out the flame or getting burned in the process. It was one of my favourite party-tricks. Unfortunately, we were drinking out of small plastic cups, not glasses, and so my demo went awry. I drank the liqueur but the cup caught on fire and had to be doused in an ashtray. No more Blue Blazers that night.

Back at sea again on leaving Cecil Field, I remember most vividly the seven Close Air Support sorties we flew on the Vieques ground-attack range to the East of Puerto Rico; three of them by night. The latter entailed very demanding flying, was extremely exciting and laid the groundwork for conducting the same type of missions in the single-seat Sea Harrier during the Falklands War.

We approached Vieques from the South at 450 knots and low-level over the sea; armed with Lepus Flares and two pods of live 2-inch rockets, 36 rockets to each pod. Dougal handled the precise navigation to the target on a very black but clear night. Running in to Vieques, I selected the Lepus Flare on my weapons control panel.

Dougal: "Standby, standby. Now!" We had reached the pull-up point at 1. 6 nautical miles from the target. Curving smoothly up away from the waves and pulling 4 'g', I prepared to launch the flare.

"Standby, standby. Now!" A gentle thud as the flare was released. It would soon burst into life over the target with 3 million-candle-power of light. There was only about 20 seconds before it did so. In the cockpits we were both concentrating hard on our flight instruments as I rolled nearly inverted and pulled another 4 'g' – offsetting our line of attack by 45° and killing our rate of ascent. We rolled level at 2,000 feet, still in pitch darkness and with the target still unseen to our left. Change the switches to select the Rocket pods: Arming Switch on.

As the flare burst into life, our target, a disused, beached landing craft was clearly visible under the unearthly glow. Dougal had got it exactly right. Another 4 'g' as we turned hard left and pulled the nose down into a 20° dive. I put the crosshairs of my sight onto the target, pressed and held the firing button. What I experienced in the next few seconds was totally out-of-this-world.

Streams of rockets left the pods, their motor-burn briefly lighting up the aircraft before they smoked their way down to the target like so many arrows. It was eerie and distracting as we flew down a virtual tunnel of smoke trails. I was fascinated. But it was not a time to be fixated on the target – failing to pull out in good time had killed too many aviators in the past. I ceased firing at 1200 yards and pulled another 4 to 5 'g' up and away from the exploding rocket warheads. A Direct Hit on the landing craft could be seen before the flare slowly settled under its parachute and extinguished. Once again, we were cloaked in darkness and fully back on instruments as we turned away from the range and headed home.

Enervating would be an under-statement.

At the end of July, Nick Kerr signed my Log Book and certified that I was now "proficient in the PHANTOM All Weather Fighter Role by day and night": another treasured milestone.

Before leaving the Squadron, the ship was operating to seaward of the Firth of Forth, Scotland. Dougal and I were airborne at night on an air defence sortie against a low-level Buccaneer strike. We gained radar contact too late for any head-on Sparrow shot and had to turn in astern of the strike. The Buccaneers were in-bound doing about 550 knots. It was pitch-black as Doug tried to acquire them on our radar.

"Faster, faster!" Doug was yelling in his inimitable Scottish brogue.

I engaged full afterburner and very quickly we were supersonic just 500 feet above the waves.

"Faster, faster!" came the call. But no luck on radar.

We flew over the ship at Mach 1. 2, delivering a major shock wave/sonic boom as we did so. As I cancelled the burners and climbed away, Doug was chuckling to himself in the rear cockpit. "Sharkey, you have just exceeded the centreline fuel tank speed limit by some margin. And," he gleefully continued, "you have just boomed the ship and the whole of the Firth of Forth!"

It wasn't long before our Squadron Direction Officer, Harry O'Grady, came up on the air and said, "We heard you, Sharkey!" Nothing more.

On-board the ship, chaos reigned. The massive shockwave had produced a bang like a crash on deck. Decades of dust had been released from the air-conditioning system, pictures had fallen off bulkheads, as well as other carnage. Nick Kerr had leaped from his cabin fearing the worst – crash on deck? In the air, I had that dreadful feeling of being in the poo once more.

After a safe land-on, I unstrapped, climbed out of the aircraft and looked at the centreline fuel tank. Its fairing close to the fuselage had been practically ripped off. Optimistically, I said to the Petty Officer of the Watch on Deck and the Plane Captain, "Can you fix that without telling the Boss?" They just shook their heads and grinned.

Amazingly, Nick Kerr didn't even mention the incident to me. He knew he didn't have to do so. What a character!

A treasured memory of my outstanding Boss was from the ship-at-tack exercise that had been arranged with the US Fleet off the Eastern Seaboard. Two large US Navy aircraft carriers were keen to demonstrate their air-to-surface power against a decommissioned destroyer target that had been filled with table-tennis balls to prevent it from sinking too easily. They agreed that Ark Royal could make the first air attack and that they would then finish the job. Nick got airborne with thirteen 500lb high explosive retard bombs, approached the target ship at 450 knots and 200 feet. He released all the bombs in a single salvo: a direct hit, massive explosions and the target sank. The two US carrier air groups just looked on with admiration.

He had been a very special Boss whose forbearance and understanding was ultimately demonstrated when he recommended me for the Air Warfare Instructor Course.

It is difficult to describe the complexity and intensity of operating three front-line squadrons with all their weaponry from a floating airfield the size of a couple of football pitches. Our carrier operations were made all the more important because of the continuing Cold War with the Soviets. Unseen by the public, Soviet aircraft and ships were constantly monitoring and shadowing our fleet units in the North Sea and the North Norwegian Cape area; preparing for any outbreak of hostilities. The same was true in the Mediterranean Sea, the southern flank of NATO.

Harassment of our flying operations appeared to be the main intent of Soviet warships and so our carrier was often accompanied by a Russian destroyer and/or a small trawler-sized Electronic Intelligence (ELINT) gathering vessel. The latter would be absolutely festooned with aerials and radar dishes and its role was to learn as much about Strike Carrier operations as possible. The Soviets had no such capital warships. We had an effective way of dealing with these ELINT shadows. We would fly over them at supersonic speed and very low level, just above their mast height. The resulting sonic boom/shockwaves would cause havoc with all the electronics and power supplies on board, rendering them out of action for considerable periods of time.

But having a Russian destroyer in company attempting to disrupt flying operations by day and night was not quite so easy to deal with. They would often attempt to prevent the carrier from turning onto a flying course for the launch and recovery of air-craft. They did this by physically putting their destroyer in the path of the carrier and then avoiding collision at the last minute by breaking away.

During the dark night before I flew Peter Marshall to Malta, the Captain of a Kirov Guided Missile Destroyer made a serious error. We were in the middle of launching aircraft when ship's radars showed the Kirov cutting across our bow hoping to disrupt the launch. A collision was imminent and our Captain, Ray Lygo, very calmly took charge of the situation. A 50,000-ton ship has immense momentum. It cannot stop or turn rapidly without due warning and there was no warning. Nor can the ship's main engines be slammed straight into "full astern" from "half ahead" when doing 30 knots through the water without causing serious damage.

As the Kirov continued its turn across our bow and loomed towards us out of the dark, the Captain ordered in a very measured way, "Slow ahead" then "Stop main engines" and after a pause, "Slow astern main engines". On deck there was a Phantom in full after-burner on the catapult about to be launched. It was Nick Kerr. Flyco cancelled the launch at the last minute thereby preventing the 50,000-pound jet from being catapulted into the superstruc-ture of the destroyer.

There was a resounding thud which reverberated through the ship as Ark Royal's bow impacted the Kirov amidships. The destroyer heeled over through 60° or more before its momentum allowed it to slide off our bow and down the port side of the ship. The Captain had saved the day.

While this was happening, I was in the wardroom bar in Mess Kit with a group of off-duty aviators enjoying a few drinks. The thud and vibration of the collision spelt some sort of disaster. Was it a crash on deck? We all rushed up to the flight deck with drinks in hand and found that all flying operations had been cancelled and the aircraft that were airborne had been diverted to Malta. Under a bright moon, we watched as our ship's boats were launched to rescue a handful of Russian sailors who had been washed overboard. After attention in the Sick Bay, they were all dressed in dry Royal Navy uniforms and returned to their ship. But they were not allowed on board their destroyer until they had stripped naked and thrown the uniforms into the sea.

There was only minor damage to our bow and so normal flying operations continued the following morning.

The problem of Soviet aircraft constantly monitoring and shadowing our fleet units in the North Sea and the North Norwegian Cape area was best deterred by carrier-based airpower. We were able to intercept and identify these aircraft well before they came within the range of UK's land-based Quick Reaction Alert fighters.

Many of these interceptions took place at night, usually against Bears or Badgers rounding the North Cape and detected by long range allied radar systems. The Soviet aircraft would operate without navigation or any other form of lights, dark grey aircraft on a pitch-black night. Our job was to intercept them: not a difficult task. But we also had to get close enough to read their identification number which was painted in small black letters on the tail fin. That meant getting really close – within feet.

The Soviet aircrew had a well-developed sense of humour. By day and at low speed and low level they would wait until we were in very close formation then manoeuvre sharply towards us, trying to fly us into the sea. By night, they would again wait until we were very close to their tail-plane and then shine a bright searchlight into our eyes, ruining our night vision and making us break away.

On one or two occasions, they would illuminate and display the centrefold of Playboy in the rear gunner's window.

All these games took place miles away from land and from the carrier over a very unwelcoming and turbulent sea. But that was par for the course.

14

764 NAVAL AIR SQUADRON
– AWI TRAINING (OCTOBER
1971 – MARCH 1972).

The next step towards Top Gun status now beckoned. As with the Instrument Rating Instructor Course earlier in the year, my total flight hours as a pilot-in-charge during training and in the front-line were well short of that normally needed to become an Air Warfare Instructor: I had just over 800 hours. But I was brimming with confidence and couldn't wait to get started.

The only possible cloud on the horizon was that the Boss of 764 Squadron was Bob Edward who had been my Commanding Officer in the Hong Kong Minesweeper Squadron. From my subjective point of view that had not been a totally harmonious relationship because he had displayed a different style of leadership to my other Bosses to date. But the lack of harmony had probably been more my own fault than his – a clash of personalities. At least I was now prepared and ready to toe the line – up to a point.

The first two months of the course were spent undergoing ground school training at Whale Island, Portsmouth: learning in detail about all the weapons in service with the Fleet Air Arm including missiles, bombs and rockets. It was essential for an AWI to have a full working knowledge of their construction, careful handling, ballistics, guidance, delivery parameters, etc.

Ground School was completed just before the Xmas break, 1971. I spent the latter getting married and going on a skiing honeymoon in Obergurgl, Austria. I had proposed to the young English Rose, Alison Gaye Taylor at Yeovilton and took her airborne in a twin-seat Hunter T-8. It was a magical flight: very low level over the green hills of Wales, a supersonic dive over the Bristol Channel and then aerobatics on the way home. She was delighted – but less so when she broke her ankle on the nursery slopes of the ski resort. Later, our union was to produce our lifetime pride and joy; our two amazing sons, Kristian Nigel and Ashton David.

Figure 29. The lovely Alison enjoyed her flight.

On reaching Royal Naval Air Station, Lossiemouth in early January, the pressure was on. There were three of us on the Course; David Berry from Buccaneers, Twiggy Hansom and me from the Phantom. Tim Gedge joined the staff of the squadron on hold-over from the front-line and did a limited amount of training – he was not an AWI candidate but a very accomplished Qualified Flying Instructor which demanded very different qualities.

The excellent Staff Instructors included some very experienced aviators, Lt. Nutty Walters (AWI), Lt. Neil Forrest (AWI) and Lt. Frank Cox, all of whom were dedicated to getting us through the Course successfully.

In order to qualify, one had to demonstrate rapid and effective response to the unexpected, a high quality of leadership and performance in the air plus fully competent sortie and tactical weapons briefing and de-briefing. The preparation for, briefing and conduct of all flights had to be meticulous; as did the de-brief. All of it had to be conducted with flight safety at the forefront of the mind.

Dave Berry and I were of very similar character and so competition between us was obvious, intense and healthy. Twiggy was a much more amenable soul but still an exceptional pilot.

The aircraft that we flew were single-seat GA-11 Hunters – as experienced during advanced flying training. It was a huge pleasure to fly them again: very manoeuvrable and forgiving. "Kicking the tyres, lighting the fires and getting airborne" was our *modus operandi.*

Course pressure was unremitting. Most sorties were very short owing to the proximity of two weapons delivery ranges, Tain at 20 miles to the West and Rosehearty at 40 miles to the East. Garvie, 80 miles to the North-West was also used. Free airspace

for air combat manoeuvring lay just off the airfield to seaward
and the north.

Every sortie was packed with action. In just 56 flying days I flew
117 sorties with a total flight time of just 85 hours and 10 minutes. Each of those sorties began with a detailed briefing starting
an hour before take-off and concluded with a debrief only a little
shorter. And before it all, the sortie leader would have to put very
neat and detailed briefing points up on blackboards with coloured
chalk. Each sortie of 45 minutes therefore entailed approximately
three hours work on the ground for the sortie leader.

The clear emphasis was on: a thorough briefing, being in full control of the debrief and being able to recount and critique the conduct of the sortie and of each pilot involved, and last but not least,
demonstrating good, safe leadership and control in the air.

There was hardly time to think during the long days. But it was no
more than I had expected. And as expected, I had the feeling that
I was not Bob Edward's favourite student. But I may well have
been mistaken. Nevertheless, I was watching my six o'clock at all
times and this added to the pressure and to my resolve.

The Course ran in phases, honing expertise already developed
in the front-line and covering: Air-to-Air gun tracking against a
weaving target, 2-inch Rocketing, Dive Bombing, Air Combat
Manoeuvring (one-on-one, two-on-one and two-on-two dogfights), Tactical Reconnaissance, Close Air Support with Forward
Air Control, Armed Reconnaissance, and Strike Progression. The
varied, multi-role content of this syllabus prepared students for
the final make-or-break tests: leading eight aircraft safely and
accurately at very low level through the picturesque Highlands
of Scotland to attack a specific target – four of the aircraft acting
as ground attack bombers and the other four providing fighter
escort for the bombers. Each strike mission was opposed by staff

pilots in 'bounce' aircraft, referred to by the strike as bogeys, who could and did attack the strike formation at any time attempting to cause chaos on the outbound and inbound legs and over the target. Complete and effective control had to be maintained at all times. On landing, the Strike Leader had to recall and critique in detail the movement and disposition of every aircraft.

The only aide-memoire available to the leader was the collection of notes he was able to scribble on his kneeboard during the mission: not easy to do during fully developed fighter combat at low-level.

Not a few students had failed the Course at the final hurdle through the poor leadership of their Strike Progression missions. Decision making and flight safety were an important part of these missions and, eventually, this brought me into direct and open conflict with the Boss.

The target on my planned final Strike Mission as Leader was close to the coast, South-East of Lossie mouth; near Forfar in the lowlands North of Aberdeen. The weather forecast for the whole of the transit route and the target area was abysmal: complete coverage of very low-level thick cloud. After our eight aircraft got airborne, the cloud was so low that we could not enter the low-flying area safely.

I transmitted, "We shall follow our planned route above the clouds. If there is any clearance we shall descend and continue the Strike as planned." When we reached the target area, there was still continuous low cloud coverage stretching to the horizon, far out over the North Sea. I considered the options. Penetrating the low cloud layer with eight fast-jets in zero visibility and without radar-altimeters was not a sensible option – even over the sea. I judged it was too hazardous and decided that Flight Safety had to come first.

I transmitted again. "This is Strike Leader. I am aborting this mission. I repeat, mission aborted. Remain in battle formation for recovery to base."

We entered the Crew-Room for the mission debrief.

Before I had said a word, Bob Edward stood up. The look on his face didn't augur well. But in accordance with good AWI practice, I cut him short. "Sir, this is my debrief. Please sit down until I am finished!" Reluctantly, he did as I had bid (I may have omitted the word, please). When I had finished, he took the floor.

There was no mention of flight safety or that the target area was clearly inaccessible. I recollect that his words were not sugar-coated and were approximately as follows. "That was a complete disgrace. You should have tried to get below the cloud over the sea and then tried to penetrate to the target. For your sake, tomorrow the Staff will demonstrate how a strike mission should be led and conducted. It will be led by Tim Gedge. Then you will lead another strike mission and pass or fail on the outcome. Understood?"

I looked him steadily in the eye. "Yes, Sir!" I couldn't really complain because it was a matter of subjective judgement and he was the Boss. But I was sure that if I had tried to take the strike formation down through the clag he would have been on my case in the air – condemning me for lack of flight-safety-awareness. Of course I didn't know exactly what he was thinking, only he knows that. But I was very sure that my decision had been correct. Later, I was informed by one of the Boss's old and bold contemporaries that when he was in the front line and leading a division of four Buccaneers at very low level in low-level-strike formation, he flew his wingman into the top of a pine tree. Fortunately, the Buccaneer was very strong and the pine tree-top very weak!

The next day, amidst much rather unnecessary bravado, the Staff strike was briefed. It was to be against Garvie range, near Cape Wrath; 80 miles to the North. Tim had not been selected for the Course; he was just holding over – a very strange choice for leading the demonstration strike. I suspected that the Boss, in his inimitable fashion, was playing the one-upmanship game – making a rather unnecessary point. But in the air, it all backfired.

Tim lost control of the Strike formation completely. The four fighter-escort Hunters became detached from the four fighter bombers and try as he did, Tim could not get them back together again. They returned to base totally independently – the Escort recovering from North of Tain Range and the Strike aircraft from the South. It really was a disaster that would have signalled certain failure for a true AWI candidate. But at the debrief and to my astonishment, Bob Edward displayed a complete lack of objectivity. He stood there smiling and congratulated Tim on a good strike mission! What on earth was he thinking?

The next day it was my turn. I had a point to prove.

Picture if you can, the steep hills, valleys and vales of the Highlands; sparsely populated but with wildlife often in evidence on the hilltops including herds of deer and magnificent stags displaying their antlers. My eight Hunters are winding their way to the North-west at about 50 feet and 420 knots along the floors of the valleys and occasional open spaces covered in heather. Where the terrain permits, the four strike-aircraft are in a widespread battle formation and when the valley narrows they move close in behind me into a relaxed echelon formation called Low Level Strike. The four fighter escort Hunters are split into two pairs behind us and on each flank of our strike aircraft – giving good cross-cover and watching our six o'clock.

Speed over the ground is seven miles per minute and terra firma is flashing by only 50 feet below. Huge granite hills all around obscure the horizon and hide the opposing threat of bounce aircraft, bogeys. Every pilot has his work cut out, watching for bogeys, staying in formation and avoiding the ground. All eyes are out of the cockpits, searching feverishly for the first sign of a pending attack. The bogeys know our route and can pounce at any time.

I detect a bounce aircraft coming over the hills and call, "Strike Leader, bogey in our right, four o'clock high. Escort, counter starboard." The four Hunters pull 4 'g' towards the bogey. Escort leader has it under control. The bogey turns away and disappears over the hills.

I call, "Escort resume!" The four Hunters reverse their hard turn and rapidly regain formation behind our strike aircraft. Intense lookout continues as the strike leaves the shelter of the valleys and progresses northwards towards Garvie Range. Then, all hell suddenly breaks loose.

One bogey approaches nearly head-on in our right, one o'clock. I turn the formation to meet it head-on and fly through. At the same time, a second bogey is detected approaching from the left, nine o'clock. Escort Leader counters his fighters to oppose the second threat. I call, "Escort three and four. Go high and reverse. Take out the first bogey." Two separate two-on-one dogfights develop and the bogeys are defeated – but are turning away for more attacks.

Meanwhile, I have countered my four strike-aircraft through 180°, back-tracking to stay in close touch with the Escort. Once together, I resume our track towards Garvie. I know that more bounces will be coming, especially over the weapons delivery range itself. I move the four strike-aircraft into Attack Echelon Starboard as we approach the pull-up point. We are still down in the weeds.

4 'g' on the clock as we pull up rapidly and then, before 2,000 feet, roll over and pull hard down over the cliffs into a 20° dive. The target is in our sights. Simultaneously, Escort Leader calls, "Two bogeys inbound! Right 3 o'clock! Engaging!" The escort is looking after our six as we dive on to the target and release weapons. I pull up hard to the right followed by the other three bombers – hiding our six from the bogey threat. The escort does a great job keeping the bogeys from attacking us. Aircraft are every-where in the sky as the bogeys retreat and we all descend to very low level in good formation for the return to base. Just one more attack to be repulsed successfully on the way home and soon we are landing in a stream of aircraft on the runway.

During the debrief, I carefully recount all mission details including the tactics used in each combat. There is no dissent from the floor – nor could there be. The sortie had been as near perfectly exe-cuted as possible: formation integrity maintained, target success-fully attacked and the bogeys' offensives repulsed. No adverse comment from the Boss who had flown with us. He was satisfied.

Dave, Twiggy and I had passed the Course and were now AWIs. But Bob Edward insisted on having the last word. After presenting us with our Certificates, and for reasons best known to himself, he presented an Honorary AWI Certificate to Tim Gedge.

My misgivings about Bob Edward had not been well-founded. The assessment he wrote in my Log Book was as follows:

"A competent and aggressive pilot whose ability has developed well on the A. W. I. Course."

But I was going to have to wait before flying again in the front-line. I had been posted to the Lieutenants Staff Course at Greenwich and then on to a NATO staff job in Norway.

15

Lieutenants Staff Course at Greenwich (1972).

G reenwich College with its famous painted ceiling and Queen Anne architecture was where young Lieutenants received their first formal grooming in service writing. (This was reinforced much later with in depth training at the fully-fledged Greenwich Staff College.) It was excellent preparation for one's first job as a Staff Officer; in my case, with NATO.

My own style of writing up to that point was rather flowery having studied Advanced Level English Literature at school. But I managed to adapt reasonably well, producing so I am told the best Staff Paper on the course ("How to maintain a presence East of Suez with six Frigates").

The brief 'sabbatical' was immense fun, all the more so because my close friend, Buccaneer Pilot Robin Kent was there with me.

There were good times in the bar as well as in the lecture hall where we were privileged to receive many VIP Lecturers. One of these was the Rt. Hon. Michael Foot. In question time I asked him, tongue in cheek, "Sir, have you ever considered becoming Minister of Defence?"

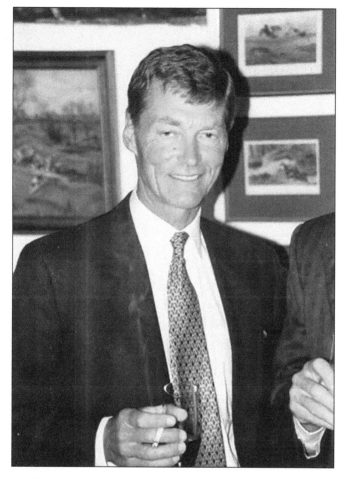

Figure 30. Dr. Commander Robin 'Snapper' Kent MiD DPhil.

He looked quite non-plussed and said briefly, "No! Why!"

"Well, Sir, it would make an impressive front-page headline in the national newspapers – "Foot Heads Arms Body"!

He didn't reply but it brought the house down.

16

NUCLEAR INTELLIGENCE OFFICER IN NATO (1972-74).

Although in a desk job rather than a flying appointment, my time at Headquarters Allied Forces Northern Europe (AFNORTH), Oslo, Norway advanced my general warfare knowledge considerably, particularly regarding the Cold War Soviet Threat. The Headquarters was run by General Sir Peter Whiteley, Royal Marines (himself a front-line fighter pilot) and my chain of command included Captain Graham Lowden RN and Major John Paul, a talented, career USAF Intelligence Officer who was my immediate boss. NATO has often been described as somewhat dysfunctional but I saw no evidence of that at AFNORTH. The ongoing threat of nuclear war ensured the full dedication of all Staff Officers no matter what their nationality.

There was perhaps one exception to dysfunctionality. When my friend Fred de Labillière was in a NATO post, he had a special Cosmic Top Secret Atomal identity card printed on which there was a photograph, not of himself, but of a gorilla. During two years with NATO, nobody ever challenged this special identification!

John Paul proved to be a leader that anyone would be happy working for. He knew the art of delegation and of measured oversight and had immense responsibility: running the Nuclear

Planning Cell which coordinated closely with Supreme Allied Commander Europe's team, planning all aspects of any nuclear conflict including the strategic targeting and deconfliction of all projected nuclear weapon strikes against Soviet and Warsaw Pact military targets. We worked in a nuclear-proof bunker in the heart of a granite mountain under very tight security.

The entrance to the bunker included a very long tunnel carved out of the rock and it was constantly patrolled by dog handlers with the most ferocious and aggressive Alsatians–to whom nobody was a friend. They would try to attack anybody and so one was always hoping that their handlers' restraints would not break.

Our tactical and strategic nuclear weapon training was provided at a dedicated Nuclear Training School in Oberammergau, Southern Germany where we learned all about Nuclear Weapon Effects against a full range of targets.

Details of our work are best left unsaid. However, my new status as an AWI had not gone unnoticed and was respected at all levels of the command. This led to me having two challenging remits in addition to my normal work. General Whiteley had observed two major gaps in AFNORTH's recognised warfare plans/knowledge.

The first was conventional rather than nuclear. Mine Warfare had raised its ugly head: there was no established Threat Assessment or Policy Statement on how to deal with it. It represented a key danger to the fjords, ports and trade routes of the Northern European Theatre and further afield. The Soviets had a huge stockpile of sophisticated, state-of-the-art mines that could be delivered by air or sea. Captain Lowden told the General, "I have just the man to deal with this. He's an AWI. I'll clear it with John Paul and get him working on it straight away."

After a lot of intensive research and weapon evaluation, I produced the required Mine Warfare Policy and Threat Paper which was subsequently formally adopted.

The second remit was directly related to my appointed nuclear work. A serious conventional threat to Northern Europe was the Amphibious Warfare capability of the Soviet Fleet. Should conflict break out, it had the potential for enabling the overwhelming invasion of all North European coastal States – including Norway and the UK. One of the last-ditch ways that this could be prevented was with the tactical use of nuclear weapons. Another Policy Paper was needed. The questions to be addressed included: what size of weapons, what disposition of ships and weapons, surface or sub-surface bursts, the effects of local topography, etc. My remit was to define the minimum number, size and deployment of weapons needed to destroy a Soviet Amphibious Task Force in a variety of environments: in-shore, off-shore, within Fjords, etc. Tactical rather than strategic size of weapons was the key.

The Oberammergau Training proved critical in arriving at the optimum solution and after weeks of work I was able to provide the Command with the answer–which was again adopted.

My third and most significant remit was decided by John Paul and me after many long internal discussions within our bunker. We were appalled at the existing Trip-Wire Policy that NATO had adopted.

Trip-Wire's basic message to the Soviets was: "The slightest invasion of NATO territory by the Soviets or the Warsaw Pact will result in an overwhelming nuclear offensive across the board." This would have triggered all-out nuclear war throughout the Western hemisphere and annihilation of all countries involved. Armageddon! It gave no room for manoeuvre or restraint.

We decided to make a formal recommendation to the Supreme Allied Commander, Europe (SACEUR) and did so in a highly classified Paper. In brief, the recommendation was as follows:

"1. The Trip-Wire Policy is misguided and prevents any form of Graduated Response which could deter escalation into all-out nuclear war.

2. It is therefore recommended that a new Policy of Graduated Response is adopted and clearly communicated to the Soviets. This Policy should be as follows:
   a. The slightest invasion of NATO territory by the Soviets or Warsaw Pact Forces will result in immediate but measured retaliation.
   b. That retaliation will be the destruction of a Soviet or Warsaw Pact military installation with a single nuclear weapon.
   c. If any invasion continues, further use of specifically-targeted nuclear weapons will result.

3. The launch of a single nuclear weapon would be a clear statement of intent and give time for the Soviets to rethink their invasion initiative."

It took several months before we received a reply. The good news was that SACEUR had welcomed our Paper and agreed that Graduated Response should indeed replace Trip-Wire. However, the bad news was that SACEUR's staff considered that a single nuclear weapon would not be a sufficient statement of intent and that 20 such weapons should be used instead. We were flabbergasted. The simultaneous use of 20 weapons could and probably would be seen as the first wave of an all-out nuclear offensive – resulting in disastrous all-out retaliation. Be that as it may, we had indeed got rid of the Trip-Wire policy. It was a step in the right direction.

Serving in AFNORTH had been a pleasure. My eldest son had been born and it was time to get back to the Front-line.

17

BACK IN THE SADDLE (1974).

B
efore re-joining 892 Squadron in the front-line I had to get back into decent flying practice after spending nearly two years behind a desk. The fast-jet elements of RNAS Yeovilton were being moved temporarily to RAF Leuchars, the home of 43 Squadron F-4s and the Phantom Training Flight, during runway repairs at Yeovilton.

Getting back in the saddle and ready for embarked operations took just a little time with two separate Courses. The first part of the refresher flying took two-and-a-half weeks and was conducted by Naval Flying Standards Flight using the twin-seat Hunter T-8. Aircraft handling skills came back very quickly. It was similar to riding a bike: once you know how, you never forget. It was a lot of fun and very satisfying.

The most exciting sortie was flying with Charles Manning, the Boss, on a low-level trip through the Scottish Highlands. It was December '74 and the North of Scotland was swept with gale-force winds. These caused extremely heavy turbulence across the glens and down the mountain sides. Despite the grey skies and intermittent showers the beauty of the highlands was staggering. As was my wont, we flew at 420 knots and very low level along the valleys and over the lochs and the whole time the aircraft was being shaken like a rattle by the turbulence. It was so severe that my helmet kept on banging sideways and uncontrollably against the cockpit canopy. But I felt that I was back home and fully in-synch with the aircraft.

In January I joined the Phantom Training Flight under the command of Sqd. Ldr. Andy Walker who conducted my first re-familiarisation flight in the F-4K. He was a very amenable character, albeit not without the odd tinge of inter-service rivalry and a predilection for sticking to the rules and regulations (see Chapter 20 for comment). This was decently balanced by the Naval aviators on his staff. One of these was Colin Griffin, a Senior Observer who had been part of the Top Gun training initiative at Miramar, San Diego.

I arrived at RAF Leuchars with Lt. David Braithwaite (AWI) just before a major Air Station security exercise was to take place. David and I were new to Leuchars and unknown to the majority of the Staff. We were therefore ideal candidates for attempting to penetrate airfield defences and cause havoc. It was all taken very seriously because of the high-level danger then posed by the IRA.

We decided it would be a good idea to kidnap the wife of the Station Commander, Group-Captain White and then the Groupie himself – with whom we would force access to the airfield. It all went to plan. David had his shotgun with him as we knocked on the door of the White's Residence which was outside the airfield perimeter. Mrs. White was absolutely charming and after hearing our plan was delighted to play the game. She invited us in and provided a welcome gin and tonic. She then called her husband:

"Darling, the IRA have taken me prisoner at home and want you to come here alone, or else!"

It didn't take long for the house to be surrounded at a distance by the RAF Regiment brandishing rifles and machine guns. Then the Group Captain's official car pulled up at the front door and out stepped an officer wearing the Groupie's epaulettes. But we had done our homework and knew it wasn't White. I let him in through the door and was engaging him in some unfriendly conversation when the real Groupie burst into the lounge from the rear of the house with shotgun raised at the ready. It was a bit unnerving staring down the twin barrels of a loaded shotgun – but the gin and tonic helped!

"I'd put that down if I were you" David said. Simultaneously, he prodded the Groupie in the back with his own shotgun and we were in charge once more. In order to defuse the situation, I explained who we really were and asked the Groupie if he was willing to play our game. Very graciously, he agreed but balked at offering us another gin and tonic.

"Okay, then. This is what you are to do. Tell the Regiment guys outside that this is not an exercise and they have to bugger off. When they have done so, you will be taken in the front seat of your car with me driving and with David in the back seat with his shotgun clearly visible and pointing at the back of your head to the Main Gate. There you will instruct all armed defenders to back off and allow us entry to the airfield. We shall then proceed to the Air Traffic Control Tower where we shall simulate its destruction. Is that all clear?"

The Station Commander followed the instructions precisely and very soon we were parked by the front entrance to the Tower. Counter to our instructions, several shooters/snipers surrounded the area. As I carefully got out of the car, an RAF Regiment Flight-Lieutenant approached me on the Tower steps. He was brandishing a 9mm Browning pistol.

I ordered him to back off and take his men with him. He was unmoved. As we learned later, he had just returned from operations against the IRA in Northern Ireland and was deadly serious.

In a very measured voice he said, "No chance. You are to release the Group Captain immediately and surrender or I will shoot you in the stomach. I am not joking." To prove his point he ejected a live round from the pistol and prepared to fire. "Oh, dear!" I said to myself, feeling extremely vulnerable.

Group Captain White sprang into action and in a very loud voice shouted, "All of you put your guns down. This is an exercise. John, I repeat this is an exercise and it is over." Reluctantly the Flight-Lieutenant lowered his gun and made it safe. I was not a little relieved. David and I disappeared to the bar for a very welcome beer.

The Phantom Refresher Course covered all the roles of the aircraft and after just eight sorties I was getting well back in the groove and was programmed to lead six Phantoms on a Strike Progression exercise culminating in a first-run, practice bombing attack on Pembrey range, on the South Wales coast – shades of the AWI Course. Colin Griffin was my observer. The mission was to launch from Leuchars, transit at medium to high level to the Irish Sea, let down to low level on entering the North Wales Coast and stay at low level throughout Wales before pulling up and attacking the target. En route we were scheduled to be bounced by a variety of 'enemy' aircraft acting as bogeys: Hunters, Lightnings and Phantoms.

My job as Strike Leader was to control the safe execution of the mission to a successful conclusion. Our division of four bombers flew in battle formation; two loose pairs half-a-mile apart on each other's beam. Escort Leader and his wingman stationed themselves about half-a-mile astern, one on each side of the strike and spread a little wider. This overall formation allowed good visual cross-cover for all aircraft – vital for watching the six o'clock when expecting to be attacked.

The rolling green hills of Wales are nothing like the Highlands of Scotland and present fewer opportunities for undetected ambush. I therefore kept the formation very low, skimming the terrain and hilltops at about 50 feet. This did not go down well with Andy Walker who was flying as the Escort wingman.

"Strike Leader, you are too low. Move it up!" I didn't respond.

"Strike Leader, I say again, you are too low. Move it up."

I replied. "Escort 2. Roger your last. Continuing the Strike."

Ignoring his instruction, we stayed low and successfully denied the bounce aircraft any kills.

Colin had the navigation spot-on. As we neared our pull-up point I called, "Strike, attack echelon port, go." After pull-up we were to break hard starboard into the dive, track the target and release our practice bombs. It all worked perfectly. After dropping our bombs and pulling 4 'g' upwards over the target I started to turn to the right, inland.

Colin immediately over-rode my intention and told me to come hard left. I didn't argue – he was older and wiser than me and a Staff Instructor. But turning left took our six Phantoms straight into a civilian airway – taboo for military aircraft without appropriate clearance. So we continued a very hard turn left in the climb, exiting the airway to the North as rapidly as we could and joining up in formation for the journey home.

Although he said nothing at the debrief, which I ran in typical AWI style ("I'm in charge and you better believe it!"), Andy was furious and afterwards he privately stated his intention to convene a Board of Inquiry and possibly a Court Martial for "entering controlled airspace without air traffic permission" – with me as the accused.

Colin gallantly came to my rescue. "You can't do that, Boss. It was on my order that Sharkey turned to the left. He was going to turn right but I insisted on the left turn. I, as a senior staff instructor, was therefore responsible." A really good man! No more was said and I progressed back to the front-line.

18

892 SQUADRON UNDER BILL PEPPÉ (MARCH TO NOVEMBER 1975).

As far as aircrew are concerned, the hierarchy in a twin-seat fighter squadron has two main elements under the Commanding Officer; pilots and observers. The Senior Pilot and the Senior Observer are appointed as Executive Officers overseeing their specialist elements and are responsible for the performance, conduct and operational training of those aviators.

The Senior Pilot is also responsible for running the daily flying programme, dictating who will fly on which sortie with whom and works with the ship's Air Operations team to define that programme. Operating a multi-role fighter effectively demands continuation training in all roles and the Senior Pilot is given vital support for all weapons training by the Squadron AWI. The latter provides sortie briefs and phase briefs for each role including weapons delivery, tactics and flight safety. Air Intercept training is the province of the Senior Observer. Good liaison between Phantom, Buccaneer and Airborne Early Warning Gannet squadrons in Ark Royal was vital and combined briefings were often the order of the day.

Each sortie was usually a composite one. For example, Air Intercept usually terminating in Air Combat combined with Rocketing on the splash-target towed behind the ship prior to land-on. Deck landings were always critically scrutinised, graded and monitored by a squadron representative in Flyco and by the ship's Landing-Sight Officer.

A vital part of the hierarchy was the Squadron Air Engineer Officer who ensured that there were aircraft available for each sortie on deck, in the right configuration and with the right weapons loaded. He worked closely with the Senior Pilot and the ship's Hangar Control Officer and Flight Deck Officer to prepare for this before a flying programme was decided.

Seamless cooperation between all ship's Air Departments was a pre-requisite for successful flying programmes and for the operational readiness of the carrier.

It was a huge surprise for me, still a Lieutenant, to be appointed Senior Pilot of the Phantom Squadron after returning from my NATO job. I was to take over from Tim Gedge. Although I was now an AWI, initially and unusually I was going to have to demonstrate authority over some much more experienced aviators. I didn't consider it an ego boost; more a serious challenge.

Up to that point, I had learned a lot about leadership in the air and on the ground. Nearly all my previous bosses and superiors had demonstrated good leadership but they had not sought to be put on a pedestal. They earned respect through performance, consideration and loyalty downwards. This resulted in dedicated and happy squadron teams.

At first, it was business as usual under the firm, lively and open-minded command of Bill Peppé. Small in stature and blessed with a cavalier sense of humour he never sought to be put on a pedestal. He didn't need to because he was adored by all his team. He welcomed me to the squadron and immediately told me that he

understood the delicacy of my position as a Lieutenant and graciously wished me a fair wind with my early progress. He didn't
need to tell me that he would be watching me carefully until I took
over from Tim to ensure I was up to the job.

I had something of a private agenda in my head when taking up
my appointment. Apart from the usual fighter-pilot desire to be
top gun at everything, I wanted to put to bed the idea that night-
deck-landing was a black art and I wanted to improve the air
combat performance of all my pilots – me included. I was to have
six excellent RAF pilots in my team, all of whom were enjoying
their first experience of flying from a carrier. This fitted well with
my agenda.

Most of our time was to be spent at sea on various short deployments during which HMS Ark Royal was honed to a level of complete operational readiness. Exciting times lay ahead.

Bill Peppé was made from the same mould as Nick Kerr, a typical
Top Gun who knew how to delegate and at the same time retain
full control. His sense of humour prevailed even in the air.

Not long after returning to the squadron, I was airborne at night
engaged in Low Level Air Intercept training over the North Sea
with Greg Aldred in the rear cockpit: Greg, who had also been a
part of the Miramar Top Gun initiative, and I were now a set crew.
The Boss was flying the other aircraft. As was often the case, it
was a pitch-black night.

We had just completed an intercept and were preparing for the
next one. It was all relaxed in our cockpits as we proceeded to
separate at 500 feet, 420 knots with no visual outside references.
The cockpit was eerily quiet with just the hum of the avionics and
air-conditioning in the background. The Boss was supposed to be
miles away readying to turn in for the next intercept.

187

Suddenly there was a loud bang, the whole aircraft shook and a blinding light filled the windscreen. "What the…?" Greg grinned in the rear cockpit.

"That was the Boss!" he chortled and indeed it was.

He had flown directly underneath us at supersonic speed in full afterburner and then pulled up and away just ahead of us. All he said over the radio was, "Haw, haw, haw!" A frivolous welcome for the Senior Pilot-designate.

One very good thing about the Boss was that he could take it as well as dish it out. His night deck-landings occasionally provoked a little teasing, especially from observers. 'More like a crash on deck' was occasionally mooted. After one particularly close call, Desmond Hughes impolitely joked, "T'is time to hang up your flying boots, Boss!" Bill took it in good heart and responded with his favourite riposte, "Shave orff, Desmond!"

All of us could have an off-day during night deck-landing. Mine came when in the North Sea, about 120 miles from Leuchars. It was a dark night but it wasn't dreadful weather and the ship movement in the moderate sea was minimal. Our first approach appeared to be just routine but I let the aircraft ride slightly high as we crossed the stern.

"Bolter, bolter, bolter" came the call from Flyco as we missed the wires and hurtled off the bow. Eight challenging approaches later we finally caught a wire after having refuelled twice from the air-borne Buccaneer tanker flown by Davey Owen. As our approaches to the deck slowly grew in number, so did the frustration and my over-controlling in the cockpit. Not surprisingly I was very on edge as we plugged into the Buccaneer's refuelling hose for a second time. We were in and out of low cloud which didn't help keeping very close formation on the tanker. My concentration was intense as we closed to within just a few feet of the tail – right next to my cockpit. Suddenly and quite unexpectedly, the Buccaneer's tail hook slammed down – almost close enough to touch – causing me to withdraw rapidly from the hose basket in mild shock. Davey Owen, an AWI, just chuckled over the radio. After finally catching a wire and climbing out of the aircraft, Greg and I were totally soaked in sweat from head to foot. Greg didn't speak to me or to anyone else until the next morning: when it was business as usual. I just consoled myself with a beer in the night-bar.

Off-days happen. The answer was, "Get over it!" That was the only occasion I missed the wires and bolted at night.

All went well for the nine months under Bill Peppé. Our first deployment was to the Eastern seaboard of the USA where we conducted air-to-ground and air-to surface weapons training at Vieques Island and on the Atlantic Fleet Weapons Range off Puerto Rico. It was there that I had the pleasure of firing my second Sparrow AIM-7E radar-guided missile and this time it was a short-range shoot against a surface target, a Septar radio-controlled power boat drone. The seas were rough and my observer for the day was Bernie Steed, with whom I had managed to get myself court-martialled.

Bernie achieved a good radar lock which was essential for missile guidance and, indeed, we could see the target visually. Firing a missile from an aircraft is always a very impressive event as the motor ignites and speeds away from the aircraft like a bullet leaving a long trail of white smoke. In peacetime and because of the high cost of such missiles, only a few can be fired every year. So I was fortunate having this second firing and was to have a third when we returned to the Puerto Rico area the following year.

189

The missile didn't hit the Septar drone which had a very low profile. It passed just over the top. But it would have hit a frigate or destroyer fair and square.

We then moved on to a short disembarkation at U. S. Naval Air Station Oceana, near Virginia Beach, where we were hosted very generously by our U. S. Navy counterparts. Getting to know them was not just a pleasure, it was a form of bonding for when we operated at sea together which was often. During the detachment, three crews were lucky enough to fly across the United States to visit the home of Top Gun at Naval Air Station Miramar, San Diego for a long weekend. I was one of the lucky ones as was Tim Gedge. After that, I was to take over from him as Senior Pilot.

The hospitality at Miramar was outstanding. On climbing out of my aircraft, I was met by Phantom pilot Steve Letter who handed me the keys to a sports car and the keys to his buddy, Smoots's private apartment which included a waterbed covered in black silk sheets. The deal was to enjoy but to leave the girlfriend alone. We got on well together in the Bachelor Officers' Club bar and decided to fly together the next day.

I rode in the rear cockpit of Steve's Phantom F-4J for an air combat sortie and then took him up in my F-4K to demonstrate the increased power that we had. Jerry Kinch, our Senior Observer and Tim Gedge, the retiring Senior Pilot refused to authorize my flight, "Not me, Chief!" So I said, "Okay then, I shall authorize myself!" I certainly did not want to let Steve down.

As soon as our wheels left the ground, I kept it low on the runway and then, as we were racing through 400 knots, pulled the aircraft straight up into the vertical through 12,000 feet. Steve was duly impressed but not so the Captain of Miramar. As soon as we landed, we were carpeted in front of the irate Commanding Officer.

"Today the San Diego Noise Abatement Society is monitoring excessive noise from this airfield. Your performance take-off nearly broke all their instruments and set good relations back years! You are grounded until you depart my air station! Now get out of here." He was definitely not a happy bunny!

How to ruffle feathers without really trying!

Back at Oceana, Bill Peppé didn't even mention my faux pas at Miramar and I settled in as Senior Pilot with an intensive flying programme that continued through November when Bill left the Squadron.

Before leaving the USA, we were allowed to utilise the air-to-ground weapons ranges in the Florida area and on one sortie from Oceana I planned a four-aircraft first-run- practice-bomb-attack against a target positioned in the centre of a small lake in Dare County. The target itself consisted of a selection of white poles radiating symmetrically from the target centre. As we pulled up from low level I called, "Right, one o'clock. The blue buoy in the centre is your target."

Four Phantoms raced down the dive delivering their practice bombs, each one of which released a puff of white smoke on impact around the blue buoy. As we pulled off the target and looked back down to monitor the fall of shot, the blue buoy started its outboard and sped off to the side of the lake. It was a local fisherman trespassing on the declared firing range! Luckily for him, there were no direct hits.

Back in home waters and amidst continued intense operational flying, two memorable events took place. The first was when Her Majesty Queen Elizabeth the Queen Mother came on board to meet our sailors. It was my distinct honour to meet her personally – she had the most extraordinarily beautiful violet eyes – and then participate in a special flying display demonstrating weapons fire-power and aircraft performance.

I launched from the bow catapult very light on fuel, stayed in full afterburner and pulled up into the vertical, continuously jetti-soning fuel and rolling the aircraft like a corkscrew straight up to 20,000 feet. Then it was down to the sea surface behind the ship, running in at deck level and high speed, firing 144 rockets in a 5 'g' turn as I passed close to the bridge. The rockets self-destructed in an impressive fireworks display that filled the sky ahead of the ship. One more high-speed pass over the deck in front of the bridge, just tens of feet away, and then it was time to land on.

The second event was a 'blow-out' Squadron Mess Dinner in Ark Royal's Wardroom Annex. Aircrew at sea in a conventional air-craft carrier live on the edge. The operational flying that they carry out by day and by night involves high levels of stress and concen-tration. This accumulated stress has to be relieved somehow and that is best achieved when gathered together in the Wardroom off duty. Such gatherings allow for very informal contact between superiors and subordinates and this allows messages to be got across in both directions, usually by subordinates who wish to have their say. It is a great leveller.

Dining-out Bill Peppé before he left the squadron was an extraor-dinary example of this. What began as a five-course, five-star formal dinner after many drinks in the bar expectedly deteriorated into amusing and out-of-hand bedlam after the Queen's Toast and when the port was passed. Cheeky misbehaviour resulted in the culprit being fined a round of port by the Boss. Each time the port was passed meant another full glass of the tawny liquid for one and all. By the end of the dinner in the small hours of the morning, it had been passed more than twenty times. I remember very clearly Badger Bolton, one of our RAF officers, standing at the boss's shoulder as the latter lost complete control of the evening. Badger was ceremoniously eating his wine glass, grinning shamelessly as a trickle of blood flowed down from the corner of his mouth. Various missiles starting with bread rolls and escalating to harder objects whistled passed the boss's head as he proudly watched his war-fighters relaxing.

During this mayhem, six aircrew from 809 Buccaneer Squadron burst through the Annex side door with a firehose in hand intending to spoil the party. They never got the chance to turn on the water. Desmond Hughes leapt from the table in full attack mode defending the honour of the squadron. In frighteningly quick time three of the Buccaneer boys were dispatched to the Sick Bay and the other three ran off like scalded cats.

There was no question that the morale of the squadron and the air group was very high.

During my tenure as the new Senior Pilot I was wary of upsetting the established order of things. The necessary operational expertise was already available in the squadron and it was my job to ensure that it was continued and, where possible, increased.

What I had found during my first tour in the squadron was that events in the air were not always accurately discussed during sortie debriefs. This was particularly so with fighter combat. Some of the old and bold leading such sorties would misrepresent the conduct and result of an individual combat to suit their own egos. This did not help with the learning curve of the younger aircrew.

I was assisted in my quest to change this practice by the arrival on the squadron of David Poole who had just completed the Empire Test Pilot course. Known as Pooligan the Hooligan because he never flew in a straight line, David returned with a complete knowledge of Phantom handling characteristics and he knew

193

exactly where the limits to controlled flight were to be found. Going beyond these limits could spell disaster.

As Senior Pilot, I led him on his first refresher air combat sortie and he beat me all ends up! When we landed, I didn't contest the combat results in any way – much to the amazement of others sitting in on the debrief. My reputation had been rather dented.

"David, that was truly remarkable. I want to learn precisely where I went wrong and later, I want you to explain the same to a gathering of all squadron aircrew."

David explained that he knew the aircraft's handling limits better than I did, especially in the very low speed regime and that was where he had won each combat.

I immediately introduced a flying program of learning based on David's expertise. This was centred mainly on the conduct of air combat sorties against the Buccaneer but without the Phantom being allowed to use after-burner. The low-level, low-speed fighter combat expertise of all aircrew increased significantly and I used the whole exercise to impress on my pilots the importance of being honest in a debrief. It was a major step forward.

It was sad that Bill Peppé eventually had to move on and a Change of Command of 892 Squadron took place.

19

SENIOR PILOT OF 892 NAVAL
AIR SQUADRON (1975/6).

With the arrival of the new boss in the squadron, there was a distinct change in atmosphere. Usually, Naval Squadron Bosses were Lieutenant-Commanders but now we had a fully-fledged Commander, Hugh Drake who was also an observer as opposed to a pilot.

He was definitely a true professional. However, the cavalier leadership and sense of humour of Nick Kerr and Bill Peppé appeared to be a thing of the past. At the same time my own attitude as Senior Pilot and AWI remained the same: I was going to work hard, play hard, look after my pilots and push them to the limit, come what may.

As well as the new Boss, we also had a new Senior Observer, Doug MacDonald who had proved to be an outstanding airborne mentor to me during my first tour in the front-line. I had learned a lot from him and he had earned my full respect as an observer and a seasoned AWI.

Very quickly, a buddy-buddy relationship blossomed between Hugh and Dougal, after all, they were old friends from Miramar days. But with it a detectable and unfortunate divide at the top of the squadron materialized – between them and me. This was not in any way attributable to the professional conduct and performance of my pilots or myself. At no stage during the coming year was this called into question. But there was indeed a personality clash between Mohammed (me, the Senior Pilot) and the mountain (the new Boss) – and the mountain was not going to budge. I do not presume to know what was going on in his head–I can only relate a subjective view of our relationship.

Hugh Drake was very tall and, from my point of view, very patronizing–playing much on his Senior Officer status. My sense of humour and directness did not go down well with him. Further, I am told that my facial expressions often display my feelings and this may well have been one cause of dis-harmony.

My opening gambit may not have been very wise. I christened him the Munster and asked him how his bolt was (the one in the neck). Definitely not amused! Eventually I came to the view that he liked being put on a pedestal: happy to dish it out but not happy to take it.

The initial *moment critique* in our relationship was probably when I took him on his first night Air Intercept sortie from Leuchars after he had taken command. He was a very experienced Phantom Observer and I was very keen for him to see the level of expertise and aggression that we had already achieved. One of the best pilots in the squadron was in the other aircraft, Lt. John Dixon (JD), who always played hard, worked hard and flew with great flare. I briefed the sortie which was to conduct radar-controlled air intercepts on each other at medium level with a view to obtaining a kill. The designated target aircraft for each intercept was to attempt to avoid being shot down by manoeuvring as well as changes in height – and try to gain his own kill.

It was a fairly bright night with a lot of tall cumulus cloud around. JD, the other night pilots and I had developed these night intercepts into what may only be described as fully-fledged night dogfighting; using a lot of afterburner and sky in the process. One had to make full use of the radar as well as keeping a mental plot of the other aircraft's position in the sky and of where he could possibly go to next. This was made much easier when the target used afterburner and could be visually tracked. But the vertical manoeuvring made the observer's task of illuminating the target with radar especially demanding.

On completion of each intercept 'the game was on' and we were barrelling around the sky and the clouds at high 'g' trying to either get an advantage or to escape. Hugh Drake didn't say much during these dogfights which were all part and parcel of our operational learning curve. It was immense fun for JD and me and I mistakenly thought that the Boss would be impressed and enjoy it too.

After we landed and reached the briefing room, he remained quiet until I had covered all the relevant learning points from the sortie. He then took the stage and gave me a severe bollocking, roughly as follows.

"I cannot say how furious I am. That was not the type of sortie that would allow me to get back in the saddle. It was a disgrace and you will reschedule it tomorrow night when there better be more appropriate flying." And he stormed out of the briefing room.

I had rather expected him to admit that he was definitely a little bit rusty but would catch up in no time. Disappointed, I thought his reaction was totally uncalled-for but said nothing, retiring to the night bar with JD.

A sense of humour and being one of the boys when in the air did not appear to be evident and I began to see that I was not the Boss's favourite bunny. Was it a pilot/observer thing or was it just me, I wondered?

Whatever it was, Dougal found it all very amusing and made a point of cosying up to the Boss at my expense whenever the opportunity arose. This didn't happen often because I did my best to avoid confrontation and concentrated on the development of my younger pilots – especially the first tour RAF exchange pilots who took to embarked operations like a duck to water. Their entrenched procedures from land-based flying were soon forgotten in spite of many bleats from one or two about "When I was on Lightnings". We christened them WeeWOLS!

All were or became very proficient fighter pilots and the youngest of them, Chris Hurst, managed to night-qualify from the deck before the end of the year. Much credit for this must go to the Commander 'Air', Bob Northard and his immediate predecessors for establishing the healthy ethos of putting Flight Safety at the top of the agenda. They cultivated an atmosphere which enabled the "Black Art" associated with night deck landing to be a thing of the past.

On his first night approach to the ship Chris found himself almost 40° off the centre-line at three-quarters-of-a-mile to run. Before Flyco could wave him off and divert him to Gibraltar, he somehow managed to get back on centre-line, on speed and on the glide-path before taking the wires. Quite remarkable! When he left the Squadron as an above average pilot, I recommended him success-fully for the Red Arrows.

Most of 1976 was spent embarked with deployments to the Eastern Seaboard and to the Mediterranean. Throughout, I was crewed-up with Desmond Hughes, occasionally flying with others.

Figure 31. Self and Desmond, 1975.

In early February we sailed for the Atlantic Fleet Weapons Range and made full use of the Vieques air-to-ground facility. By late March we needed a break and the squadron disembarked to Cecil Field near Jacksonville for some relaxation and some continuation flying. It was there that a second *moment critique* raised its head. My observer, Desmond, disappeared from the base for five days without a by-your-leave – obviously having a good time. I wrote the flying programme around his absence but quite understandably the Boss was not amused. On his return, I was summoned to the Boss's office along with Dougal.

This was clearly an Observer matter which I thought would be handled by either the Senior Observer, Dougal or the Boss – the former being responsible for Observers' conduct. But the two of them were in cahoots. The Boss addressed the matter:

"Senior Pilot, I want to know where Hughes has been. You are to find out and punish him."

I immediately retorted, "Surely that is not my place, Sir. He is an observer under Dougal's jurisdiction. If he were a pilot I would indeed need to get to the bottom of it. As you know, there has been no occasion where pilot discipline has been in question."

"But you fly with him, so this is your problem!" Dougal chimed in.

"Get on with it!" The Boss dismissed me forthwith with a look that appeared to hide a less than balanced agenda.

I found the situation somewhat reprehensible, even childish, but went through the motions as instructed.

"Desmond, welcome back! Where the hell have you been? I don't need to tell you that the Boss is pissed off and has asked me to deal with you."

His Irish brogue was delightful, "I was having a really good time, Senior Pilot. Apologies for causing any trouble."

I grinned. "Well, consider yourself reprimanded!" I could have stopped his leave or even formally Logged his behaviour but refrained from doing so.

Hugh Drake was not at all pleased but to me that was water-off-a-duck's back.

After Cecil Field and a short visit to NAS Oceana, Virginia, we returned to the Atlantic Fleet Weapons Range off Puerto Rico in May for some live missile firings against drone targets supplied by the US. The first event was to be the supersonic firing of a Sparrow AIM-7E missile head-on against a supersonic drone flying at 60,000 feet. There were too few opportunities for such live exercises and so we had to get it right. It took place in clear blue skies directly over the ship so that all could witness the track of the missile to the target.

As a safeguard, we launched two Phantoms – a designated shooter plus a back-up. Desmond and I were the former and JD flew the back-up.

Desmond acquired the distant drone on his radar and we accelerated to supersonic speed, achieving Mach 1. 2 in the climb as we passed 40,000 feet. The Range Safety Controllers gave us clearance to fire as we passed 42,000 feet. With the radar locked onto the target, I pressed the firing button. There was a short pause before missile motor ignition as the weapon dropped away from the fuselage housing. Then there was a loud bang, the sky was briefly obscured with missile exhaust smoke and we heard both engines winding down – we had a double flame-out on our hands. The missile was a rogue and we were fully aware that one such missile had once fired directly up through an American Phantom cockpit, killing the pilot. We had had a narrow escape but our troubles were not yet over.

While JD was successfully firing his back-up missile at the drone, there was feverish activity in our cockpits for a few seconds. The aircraft was deadly silent and without power: no electrics – just a 20-ton aluminium tube streaking through the sky under its own

201

momentum. Desmond yelled to me, "RAT. Stream the RAT". The Ram Air Turbine was there to provide emergency electrical power, without which it would be impossible to relight our engines. I had already pulled the RAT extension lever before we realised that we were still well over the design extension speed. Would it break up and fail? If so, we were going to get wet! It didn't fail and we were able to use our radios again.

We were too high for any attempt to relight the engines and so we set the aircraft up for a gliding subsonic descent over the ship. Other thoughts then began to come to the fore. The film, Jaws, had just had its premier and below us the sea was infested with very large sharks that followed the ship around hoping for a tit-bit, perhaps a downed aviator or two.

JD, elated with his successful missile shoot, was fully aware of this and used his radio to bring a little humour and balance to the situation. "Sharkey, what is your Bar Number?" It was custom for the passing of an aviator to be celebrated in the bar with all drinks being paid for by the deceased. I happily gave him my number.

As we descended through 25,000 feet, we attempted to relight the engines although we knew we were still too high. But at 18,000 feet we tried again and felt the welcome surge of engine power. Crisis over! A few exhilarating full-afterburner aerobatics and then a safe landing on board.

Three days later, another challenge arose – possibly indicating another *moment critique*. This time Desmond and I were launching for a live Sidewinder shoot. As we left the catapult, I tried to raise the undercarriage but found myself with three red warning lights. The undercarriage had failed to retract properly. Rapidly throttling back to keep the speed below 250 knots, I called Flyco to report the problem and then flew past the ship for a visual inspection. "Yes, you have a problem. Your Sidewinder has come off its rails and is trapped by the main undercarriage door. Conserve fuel and wait instruction. "

Then, "Try selecting undercarriage down and see if you get three greens". I did so, got three greens and flew past for a second inspection.

"The missile is now hanging from its launch rail and pointing up under the wing. Await further instruction." We flew around at slow speed while Flyco got its act together. They would decide what actions to take. From inside the cockpit we knew that there was a choice of options: jettison the missile and launch rail over the sea; land on board with the hanging missile in place; or divert to Naval Air Station Roosevelt Rhodes, Puerto Rico and carry out a gentle landing. It was all simple enough but it turned into something of a pantomime.

Commander 'Air', Bob Northard was very much a book man. Quite rightly he wanted to review the Controller Aircraft's Release document, the bible on emergency actions, to ensure that all his decisions were properly sanctioned. And for the next 45 minutes he began to fire questions at me about the precise instructions given in the CA Release which was quite a large document. I have no doubt that Hugh Drake was at his shoulder, egging him on with farcical questions, such as:

"Senior Pilot. What does it say at the bottom of page 23 of the CA Release?" Desmond and I were mesmerised; dumbfounded would be a better word.

"Warning!" I replied. I was guessing, of course. I was familiar with the CA Release but not word-for-word. Who would be?

Commander 'Air': "Very good. But what does the warning say?"

Guessing again, I replied, "It states that the jettisoning of mis-fitted ordnance hanging under the wing may result in collision with the aircraft".

"Very good, Senior Pilot. What else does it say?"

"That such jettisoning is not recommended."

More questions followed. It was proving to be more like a Television Quiz Game. But my less than perfect recall of the CA Release's words eventually satisfied Flyco. At last, the obvious decision was made, "You are to divert to Roosie Rhodes and download the missile".

Desmond and I were not at all impressed with the charade. We carried out an ultra-smooth landing on the 12,000-foot long diversion runway, hoping that the Sidewinder would remain in place – which it did. At the end of the runway, the US Ordnance Crew removed the missile, man-handled it to a burning pile and uncer-emoniously cut it in pieces with a chain saw. Then while we were refuelling some distance away, they burned it!

Intensive flying operations continued into July with all the pilots progressing well, especially in fighter combat. So much so that I introduced a new standard procedure. Whenever two Phantoms were returning to the deck in the usual battle formation, about half-a-mile apart, the Number 2 had to attack the Leader without warning and conduct a dogfight to a safe conclusion. Aircraft limits had to be strictly obeyed, particularly at low level. Subsequently, air combat expertise rose to another level.

1976 was of course the bi-Centennial of the US Declaration of Independence and Ark Royal marked the occasion with an offi-cial visit to Fort Lauderdale for July 4th celebrations. Our aviator

Admiral, Sir John Treacher embarked with his young Lady wife and presided over two Ceremonies.

The first was at lunchtime when he presented the Annual Trophy to the best US Operational Flying Training student. After the presentation there were drinks on the rear aircraft lift followed by lunch in the Admiral's suite for a chosen few. I was one of the lucky ones. At the drinks session, I did my best to chat up one of the guests – a beautiful young woman. She very pleasantly declined my amorous overtures and then it was time for lunch. The Admiral was a very good-natured man and welcomed each guest warmly. "Sharkey, let me introduce my wife. Darling, this is the Senior Pilot of the Phantom squadron." Rather abruptly she looked at me twice and said, "Oh, we have already met – at the drinks party!" Immediately, Sir John laughed out loud understanding what had taken place and ushered me in for a drink.

In the evening, a formal cocktail party was held on the flight deck. The centrepiece was a gleaming Phantom with the following inscription in large gold letters on its side:

"Royal Navy: 976 – 1976".

Our engineer's sense of humour had come to the fore.

The party was a huge success, culminating with the Admiral saluting the White Ensign whilst the Royal Marine Band marched immaculately up and down to "A life on the Ocean Wave" – before disappearing down the after-lift on the stroke of sunset. During the respectful silence that followed an elderly Fort Lauderdale guest in a red trouser suit covered in sequins, or maybe diamonds, shrieked out at the top of her voice, "Good old Queenie!" Then the applause erupted.

In mid-July, the Squadron dis-embarked for seven weeks to RAF Leuchars for some much-needed family time, during which a further *moment critique* took place. Flying continued on a less intense basis and I shared an office with Dougal. One morning I returned from attending the Station Daily Briefing and went to retrieve my papers and documents from our safe. I couldn't open it.

"Dougal, what's happened to the safe?"

"Oh, I have had the combination changed."

"Okay. Let me have it, please, so I can get on with my work."

"Sorry, Sharkey. It is need to know!" I really couldn't believe my ears. If this was a joke it was in very poor taste. No matter what I said, Dougal would not relent. Eventually after about half-an-hour, I walked into the adjoining Boss's office and explained the situation. There was no glimmer of friendly amusement on his face as Hugh Drake said with obvious distaste, "Senior Pilot. Go and sort out your own problems with the Senior Observer. It's not my problem!"

So I sat twiddling my thumbs, unable to carry out my appointed tasks for nearly the whole morning until sanity returned. Very reluctantly, Dougal gave me the new combination.

The various *moments critique* were steadily mounting up. I no longer had any doubt that the Boss had it in for me. Minor incidents contributed to the increasing divide. One day we had been sitting around in the Wardroom on board and the Boss was holding court with the younger aircrew. A miniscule pay rise had just been announced in London. Hugh Drake proceeded to praise the review saying how well-paid and fortunate we all were – his audience being made up of junior married officers who could hardly make ends meet. I remarked, "That's OK if you are a Commander, Boss, but these guys have wives and kids and hardly have a penny to their name." It wasn't the most tactful comment – nor was it received well.

My final embarkation in HMS Ark Royal began in early September and lasted until late October. Once again it was a very busy flying period on deployment to the Mediterranean and included one more major and final *moment critique.*

We were in Lisbon where one of Hugh Drake's elderly relatives/ friends lived. Our wives were visiting from the UK and for some strange reason he asked me to pick up his charming relation from her apartment and escort her to dinner at his hotel – along with my wife, Alison. I was pleased to oblige. When we arrived at her apartment in good time, she absolutely insisted that we have a drink with her first. It would have been rude to refuse her. As a result, we arrived at the hotel just twenty minutes later than planned. My apologies for the short delay were not welcomed. The Boss was incensed and proceeded to sit with his back to my wife throughout the evening, ignoring us both.

The next morning, back on board, he summoned me to his cabin.

"How dare you keep me and my wife waiting? I don't want any silly excuses like being invited in for a drink. That isn't going to wash. Do you understand me? And by the way I am in the pro-cess of writing your annual report so I would have expected better behaviour." Had it all been a set-up, I wondered.

After his rant and before leaving his cabin, I returned his venom, "One more thing for you to chew on. If you are ever again as rude to my wife as you were last night, I shall deck you. Is that understood?"

Needless to say, although he didn't read out to me my confidential report as he was obliged to do, I gather that it was not a good one. Surprise, surprise! I didn't dodge that well-aimed bullet.

The mountain apart, it had been a most exciting and professionally rewarding year.

Before I left the Squadron, one of my most experienced pilots came up to me on the flight deck and said, "Sharkey, you might be a little crazy but if we had to go to war, I'd like it to be with you."

Whatever Hugh Drake thought about me, that compliment was the cherished icing on the cake!

SEA HARRIER DESK OFFICER
IN THE NAVAL STAFF
(1976-79).

M y head-on clash of personality with Hugh Drake did not serve me well on leaving 892 Squadron. During the early part of my subsequent appointment to Whitehall as the Sea Harrier Desk Officer in the Naval Staff, it came home to haunt me and threaten my career prospects (as fully described in my book, Sea Harrier Over the Falklands).

It was not a question of having failed to get the job done. As the Senior Pilot, I had personally ensured that my pilots were in all respects ready for combat operations by day and night. Then, as the Sea Harrier Desk Officer in the Ministry of Defence, Whitehall, (the direct equivalent of the U. S. Department of Defense) I maintained strict control over the final development and production of the new aircraft and its weapon system. My welcoming brief from the Director of Naval Air Warfare was short and to the point. Captain John de Winton instructed me as follows:

> "Sharkey, the Sea Harrier Project is now all yours.
> If you need to spend any additional money you are
> clear to authorise the same up to a limit of £5 million.
> Beyond that you should clear it with me."

As it turned out, I didn't have to go back to him for such clearance. I kept costs down and capability up. As the formal representative of the Naval Staff and First Sea Lord at the numerous and regular Sea Harrier Program development meetings, I insisted on deadlines being set and recorded for all actions undertaken by the various entities present. This was anathema to the Civil Servants and resulted in confrontation. The subsequent first deadline had been agreed but had not been actioned by a Procurement Executive civil servant. I made a major fuss about it. After the meeting at British Aerospace (BAe), Kingston I immediately went to the office of the delinquent civil servant. In his presence but without a 'by your leave', I went straight to his Pending Tray and pulled out the document at the bottom of the pile. It was the remit for action from our earlier meeting and scrawled across it in felt-tip pen was, "THIS CAN WAIT". I revealed my findings at the next meeting in very strong terms! As a result all further deadlines were respected and met.

Limiting additional costs was also a matter demanding close attention – even for those items that are relatively small and therefore might slip through without diligent scrutiny. For example, the seven switches of the aircraft's radar hand-controller (controlled by the pilot's left hand) were being tested at BAe Dunsfold and needed to be mounted on a simple plywood box for convenience. BAe announced that this would add £8,000 to project costs: just for a plywood box, 6 inches by 12 inches by 2 inches! On behalf of the First Sea Lord I formally objected in no uncertain terms. That unjustifiable cost increase was not agreed.

As a result of such good housekeeping, the Sea Harrier was the first jet fighter ever produced by UK Limited to be on cost and on time. It was also fully up to its specified Naval Staff Requirement. I am very proud of the part I played in that.

It is pertinent to record that while there was just one Naval Desk Officer (me) running the Sea Harrier Project including oversight and direction of weapon systems such as the new P3T air-launched anti-ship missile, the RAF had approximately 15 officers running their Harrier aircraft Project alone– Squadron Leaders, Wing Commanders and Group Captains. Some workload, you might say.

But that was not all. My remit also included drafting formal Staff Papers commenting on all fixed wing aircraft proposals emanating from other parts of the Ministry. This provided me with valuable insight into the questionable manner in which fast jet aircraft and associated weapon systems and their costs were justified, if at all, and approved by Ministers. To put my own Staff Papers and their logical arguments into full context, they were written well enough to impress élite desk officers from the Directorate of Naval Plans who occasionally sent their own formal Papers to me personally for scrutiny and correction before being circulated within the Ministry.

Rightly or wrongly I had left Hugh Drake with a very poor impression of yours truly. In my own defence, his opinion was subjective rather than objective and was in direct contrast to the officially reported opinions of all my previous bosses during flying training and in the front-line. With hindsight, I believe there was a spill-over from Hugh Drake to those who initially surrounded me in the Naval Staff. My new boss and my desk predecessor (who gave me a truly inadequate hand-over of the Sea Harrier Project) were his old colleagues and unquestionably he had their ear.

In spite of there being no criticism at all of the manner in which I was running the project, my first confidential annual report from the Directorate of Naval Air Warfare was never shown to me as it should have been and proved to be the worst report in Naval Staff history. It was fiercely contested by the Naval Appointers who collect and collate such reports as part of the promotion process. One

Moment Critique is probably worth remembering and, I suspect, contributed significantly to the bad report.

For the first six months of my appointment, I had studiously commuted an hour each way into my bleak, grey office from North London arriving well before 0800 and leaving no earlier than 1900. My wife Alison, two boys and I lived in Married Quarters in Hendon and we had employed the services of a Norwegian au pair girl. One night, she arrived home in the early hours of the morning, staggering and in a very poor condition. She managed to get across to us that she had walked into a lamp post! I immediately rushed her to the hospital where, over the course of a few hours, she was diagnosed with a fractured skull. As 8 o'clock approached I telephoned my Assistant Director's office and spoke to his secretary, Grace, explaining the situation and that I would be in to work as soon as possible.

When I arrived in midmorning, other desk officers gleefully informed me that I was in deep shit. It did not take long for a summons to see the Assistant Director, Captain Chris Isaacs, immediately. On entering his office, I was given the bollocking of my life. "How dare you arrive late for work? Etc. , etc. , etc." I tried to explain the situation and told him that I had called his secretary about the matter. But it was like talking to a brick wall. His malice continued. "You don't call my secretary on such important matters," he yelled, "you call me! Is that understood?"

There was I running a £100 million plus project successfully and I was being castigated for being a couple of hours late and with good reason. I had had enough. I was enraged.

"I do not accept your bollocking, Sir!!!" And without more ado I stormed out of his office and slammed the door.

The bright side of this difficult time in my service life was that if I had arrived in the Naval Staff smelling of roses, I may well have been promoted earlier and would then have missed the opportunity to become Mr. Sea Harrier and to prepare the aircraft and aircrew for war.

And I did so with attitude.

Before briefly relating the final steps on my ladder towards becoming Her Majesty's Top Gun, I believe that my general attitude towards Ministry of Defence bureaucracy deserves some explanation and description.

The following anecdote taken from Christie McLean's web-site is symptomatic of the bureaucratic control and associated counter-productive developments or lack thereof that I was averse to within Whitehall and within individual Services:

"Wallace the Mule refused permission to compete in Dressage.

Figure 32. Wallace the Mule.

A rider whose mule was refused permission to compete in top dressage events hopes to rewrite the rule book.

Fed up with horses on her team going lame, Christie Mclean, from Stroud, Gloucestershire, asked British Dressage if she could enter her mule Wallace the Great instead.

But to her surprise the organisation said only horses and ponies could ride.

She said: "Other than the enormous ears in front of me, there's really no difference to riding a horse. He has an incredible brain, is so very willing and such a pleasure."

"I don't think it's a case of equine racism but more a case of the rule book being very out of date."

Wallace is fortunate. There may be hope on the horizon for mules.

Sadly, no such hope has been sustained by modern fixed wing naval aviators. No matter what their talents, experience and expertise, over recent decades Their Lordships have demonstrated a profound aversion to promoting them to beyond one-star rank. Covertly, most senior positions in the Naval Staff and the Fleet have been reserved for submariners and surface warship practitioners. Many of these must arguably be classified as 'career officers who are bereft of any experience or knowledge of maritime air warfare'. Such bias does not augur well for the Government's statement that "Our new carriers are at the heart of our Strategic Policy".

I am watching this space.

Our three Services have followed the convention of Political Correctness and have fallen in love with 'ticking the box' rather than crediting an officer with war-fighting capability and performance in command in the front-line. If you don't 'stand on your head' or 'jump from the mast-head' when so ordered, you are considered a maverick: proven leadership and expertise in the front-line appears to count for very little. But it is leadership in combat whether in exercise or war that is the most precious commodity of our Military.

With just one string to their bow, the RAF ethos is even more plagued by the 'tick in the box/control' mentality than the Naval Staff. Stalinistic oversight of front-line squadrons and aircrew has been imposed for decades. Administrative Command staff officers maintain draconian control of aircrew and squadrons with Command Operational Orders strictly controlling even the tactics to be used in combat. This has severely eroded the application of initiative and hard-earned expertise despite the excellent basic quality of their front-line aircrew.

I recall a direct example of this: one of our many Air Combat Training exercises between my Navy Phantom Squadron, 892, and the Air Force Phantom Squadron, 43 squadron "Fighting Cocks" led by Wing Commander Hank Martin, at RAF Leuchars in the mid-70's. Two sorties of four-against-four Phantoms were flown and on each sortie three combats took place. In each of the six combats, the Fighting Cocks were thoroughly thrashed. When debriefing the first sortie, we explained how and why we had won. In the briefest of terms, the division of four Navy fighters had split into four individual units whereas the Air Force fighters had split into only two units of two aircraft. This meant that the combat was four fighting units against two fighting units – hence, the main reason for our success. Hank Martin explained to us that RAF Strike Command Standing Orders had to be followed religiously and they dictated that "a section of two fighters must remain together during combat". The 43 Squadron aircraft used the same tactics in the second sortie with the same result. Being seen to disobey Strike Command Orders would have been a career-ending event.

Boards of Inquiry and Court-Martials proliferated under this regime with infractions by pilots resulting in the pilot and the squadron commander being prosecuted and the air station commander being removed. This stymied the latent capability of all talented front-line RAF aircrew and the combat effectiveness of the Service itself.

Fortunately for me in 1979, such Stalinistic control of naval squadrons and aviators did not exist. The fact that I had not taken Squadron Command Exams was ignored when, with the strong support of my new Director, Captain Lynley E. Middleton, I was chosen to command the Sea Harrier Intensive Flying Trials Unit.

Already established in the Naval Staff Sea Harrier desk and much to my surprise, I was directed personally to write the Defence Council Instruction (DCI) that formally laid out my mission and responsibilities. I made it very short. The published DCI instructed me with the following remit (not word perfect):

> "Prepare the Sea Harrier for front-line service including the provision of Training Procedures, Standard Operating Procedures, Squadron Standing Orders, Tactical Procedures and all supporting Engineering Procedures and Manuals."

My book, "Sea Harrier over the Falklands" provides detail of the execution of this mission by the dedicated aircrew and ground crew of the new Squadron, 700A.

Suffice it to say here that by April 1982 our two front-line Sea Harrier squadrons were ready to go to war.

There was of course oversight of the Trials Unit and follow-on Squadrons by Flag Officer Naval Air Command and by the Naval Staff in Whitehall but it was supportive rather than counterproductive. The only signal I received from the Director of Naval Air Warfare in London was a firm suggestion that I was 'programming too much fighter-combat training (dog-fighting) and should concentrate on air-interception trials and training forthwith'. Much to the horror of my very loyal and outstanding Staff Officer, Lt. Charlie Sterling, I instructed him to send the following reply:

"If you don't like the way I am running this Squadron, then replace me."

Perhaps I was pushing my luck but there were no more signals from our Ministry of Defence – just the strongest possible support and encouragement from Admiral Sir Henry Leach, our First Sea Lord.

I have little trust in the process of being quizzed about paperwork forms, returns and regulations as a pre-requisite to taking Command of either a Fighter Squadron or a Warship. Having won all the Fleet Air Arm awards for Operational Efficiency and Flight Safety with my three Sea Harrier Squadron Commands as well as successful service in the Falklands Air War, I am persuaded that such exams are not always necessary. Front-line experience in Squadrons and the demonstration of professional aptitude, qualification and capability within the chain of command is a far better measure of Command potential.

In so far as Ship Command Exams are concerned, yes, some hands-on experience at sea and appropriate qualification for Bridge Watch-keeping and Ocean Navigation is essential. This was part of my Dartmouth College career training. During such experience, ship handling capability can easily be established. It is no 'black art' and seasoned aviators take to it like a duck to water.

War-fighting preparation and capability is the lifeblood of Naval Aviators who gain valuable experience in all aspects of naval warfare when embarked as an integral part of a Task Force or Carrier Battle Group. Such broad war-fighting knowledge is not available to every surface warship practitioner – as became clear during the build up to the Falklands War. Unfortunately, there is no 'tick in the box' required for the demonstration of such experience and knowledge when considering an officer for Ship Command. Arguably it is far more important than just ship-handling and knowing by heart bureaucratic paper regulations.

The covert but well-known discrimination against aviators within the Navy is based on ludicrous logic:

"We surface navy practitioners are not allowed to command fighter squadrons so why should aviators be allowed to drive ships?"

The simple answer is that career naval aviators have demonstrated all the multi-tasking aptitude and expertise for successful command of a multi-role war-fighting unit within a naval task force. For career officers who become aviators, up to four years of intensive flying training and selection follows four years of seaman officer training – a combination to which surface navy specialists are not able to aspire. The end-result is that most career aviators have a more rounded war-fighting capability than many of their seaman counterparts and are well prepared for both squadron and ship command in combat. That is why the US Navy generally prefers Naval Aviators for the command of their strike carriers.

Later, in 1983, having proved myself as a war-fighter and then achieving equal first place on the level playing field of the Greenwich Naval Staff Course, receiving the Director's Prize, I presumed entirely wrongly that my track record had some merit. I deplored the discrimination against aviators that ignored such merit and refused to pander to the bureaucratic 'tick-the-box' mentality which was destroying the Fleet Air Arm. The consequences of my 'attitude' came home to roost when I was not appointed as the Commander 'Air' of the Navy's new carrier, HMS Illustrious. Contrary to the general expectations of all the Fleet Air Arm, the appointment went to an Admiral's protégé who had 'ticked all the recognised boxes'. But those 'boxes' did not include the essential understanding of all elements of the Air Group (Sea Harriers and Sea King ASW helicopters) and carrier operations. The officer was relieved of his post after just nine months. "Proof of this entire pudding" one might say.

Following this 'snub' I retired voluntarily from the Service. The Second Sea Lord Admiral Sir Simon Cassels KCB CBE then wrote a much appreciated letter to me saying that he was shocked that I had not been persuaded to stay and that my departure was a great loss to the Service. He asked why I had decided to leave. Sincerely grateful for his concern and loyalty downwards I replied with a long letter in the context of my remarks above. He circulated it around the Ministry of Defence and later, Admiral Sir Jeremy Black let me know it had "caused serious shock waves for about six months".

The letter by John Lehman at Annex B does much to support my viewpoint, and indeed my attitude.

21

SEA HARRIER OVER THE
FALKLANDS, 1982.

Figure 32. Author: dedicated and ready.

S itting alone at night, strapped into a little single-seat jet
fighter above the tempestuous and freezing South Atlantic
sea, not so far from Cape Horn, and awaiting the arrival of enemy

fighter aircraft was a novel experience. It was the early hours of 1 May 1982 and hostilities had broken out between the UK and Argentina after the latter invaded first South Georgia and then the Falkland Islands.

Above me shone a million stars and, below, parts of East Falkland and Port Stanley town were obscured by cloud. My ship, HMS Invincible, was about 100 miles away to the East. All I could hear was the gentle whine of the aircraft's avionics systems and my steady breathing through the oxygen mask. It was a moment that I had always dreamed about – being airborne and ready for combat.

As I searched the dark skies to the West on my radar, I reflected with some amusement on the last words I had heard on deck before I closed my canopy ready for launch. It was a Freudian slip from my squadron's exceptional Air Engineer Officer, Dick Goodenough, "Goodbye Boss!"

I had no fear of combat by day or night. I was ready. My only desire was to put my fifteen years of training for war into successful practice. My squadron was ready to wreak havoc with the enemy.

The tension throughout the fleet was electric. We were awaiting the arrival of a Vulcan bomber from Ascension Island whose task it was to attempt to disable Port Stanley airfield with twenty-one 1000 lb bombs (four carrier-borne Sea Harriers could have delivered these bombs without all the fuss and expense). Our masters in London had given strict instructions that during the time the Vulcan was in the area, our ships' weapons systems were to be shut down: the fleet was not allowed to engage any target in the skies and was therefore vulnerable to any attack. What on earth was London thinking?

The chances of our Carrier Battle Group mistaking the Vulcan for an enemy aircraft as it approached from the north were close to zero, whereas the chances of an enemy air attack on the fleet were much more significant: putting at risk the lives of thousands of sailors. But this was typical of the current RAF ethos: "We shall only commit our aircraft into action against an enemy if the safety and survivability of our aircraft is guaranteed." In the modern era, except for Desert Storm in 1991 when eight ground attack Tornadoes were lost, RAF aircraft have only been committed in action against undefended targets.

It didn't bother me at all that I might have to engage enemy fighters in combat by night to protect the Vulcan mission. That was my job, what I was trained for and I was champing at the bit, ready for action. All my training and experience were ready for the ultimate test and I was deadly calm.

As the Vulcan approached the target area, I broke radio silence, "Good morning, Black Buck." Apparently, this caused consternation in the Vulcan cockpit. No reply.

"Good morning, Black Buck. This is your fighter escort. The skies are clear over your target." Still no reply.

The Vulcan came and went. Its bombs failed to disrupt flying operations from Port Stanley airfield even for a day, with just one bomb impacting the side of the runway. My own mission was complete–no sign of enemy fighters. Whilst the Vulcan returned home to Ascension on a memorably long flight, I turned my attention to getting back on board Invincible.

The Carrier Battle Group was completely darkened – that is to say, no lights anywhere. I descended to very low level over the uninviting sea to hide my position and that of Invincible from enemy land-based radars and cruised in 70 nautical miles to where

I hoped the ship would be – one of about 40 Battle Group contacts on my little radar screen. My navigation computer was working perfectly and I was relying on my Captain, JJ Black to ensure that Invincible was precisely where he promised it would be. (He always got it right!)

Having selected the contact that I hoped was Invincible, I used my radar to set up a silent approach to landing. Prior to hostilities, night deck landings had already become routine for my squadron pilots with the ship's deck and superstructure well lit. Now, 8,000 miles from home where my family were fast asleep, there was nothing but blackness ahead of me as I descended down the glide slope at 160 knots. The aircraft was buffeting gently in the turbulent wind – but not enough to be a problem. At a quarter of a mile to go to the ship, I lowered my nozzles to the hover-stop and called, "Lights!"

Bingo! The dimly lit outline of the deck and the superstructure filled my windscreen. I came to the hover alongside the ship, moved sideways over the deck and put the Sea Harrier safely down on board.

But there was no time to relax. My squadron pilots were all well prepared for the long day ahead. Two were about to launch in the dark to provide fighter cover for a dawn airfield attack by eight Sea Harriers from HMS Hermes. And in the daylight hours that followed we were on constant air patrol, stamping our authority over the Argentine fighter and fighter bomber aircraft in successful air combat. The first kill of the war was not long in coming:

> "… Very quickly the Mirage III was in Paul Barton's sights. The Sidewinder missile growled its acquisition in his earphones and was rapidly locked onto the reheated exhaust from the Mirage's jet engine. He pickled on the firing button and called "Fox Two away!"

The missile thundered off the rails like an express train and left a brilliant white smoke trail as it curved up towards the blue heavens, chasing after the Mirage which was now making for the stars, very nose high. Paul was mesmerised as the deadly missile closed with its target. When the Sidewinder hit the Mirage, the Argentine jet exploded in a vivid ball of yellow and red flame. It broke its back on missile impact and then disintegrated before its blackened smoking remains twisted their way down to the white cloud tops and stormy sea below.

'Splash one Mirage!' called the excited Sea Harrier pilot. Then the incredible moment was over and he looked around hurriedly for his leader and the other Mirage. 'Where are you, Steve?'"

A detailed account of the next six and a half weeks of intense combat flying operations is fully recorded in my book, Sea Harrier over the Falklands. It is a story of dedication, fatigue, frustration and the establishment of air superiority over enemy air forces that initially outnumbered us by 10 to 1.

Deterrence and our proven combat expertise ruled the skies over the Islands.

Deterrence through strength is the ultimate weapon for preventing conflict and war. The nuclear deterrent continues to dissuade global powers from entering a major war that nobody can win. That aside, lower levels of conventional armed conflict are commonplace. Nations that divest themselves of meaningful military conventional power lay the door open for their national interests offshore to be plundered. Such unwise reduction in military/Naval power had commenced in Britain in the sixties and seventies.

Then, in the 1981 Defence Review, John Nott, the Defence Secretary, described plans to withdraw HMS Endurance, Britain's only naval asset in the South Atlantic. Navy Chief Admiral Sir Henry Leach warned that this made the UK appear unwilling to defend its territories.

The text of a note below sent by Mr Nott expressing his views on the size of the RN and its role illustrates his strategic myopia in that he actually believed that all we needed to bother about was out to 40 miles off our coast.

Defence Minister John Nott to Michael Heseltine (from the Thatcher Archives at Churchill College, Cambridge.)

(Sent before the invasion of the Falkland Islands, April 1982)

"I was determined that the Navy was not going to have a greater share of the Defence cake and he (Leach) was equally determined that the plans, which were over ambitious on the Naval side, should be retained.

I had been accused of wishing to ruin the Royal Navy. This charge was totally untrue. Changes that I pro- posed were best for the Royal Navy. They were just my whim but I really didn't believe that Naval gun- fire support was all that valuable... Now for another decade until the gun seems redundant, although, again, you come back to the central question of strategy, are we to have a Navy which is appropriately designed to fight low-level wars against the Hottentots and a Navy which is to be appropriate if need be for invading the uninhabited islands like Anguilla, or are we to have a Navy which is actually designed to meet the main threat of the British people… Which is principally 35 – 40 miles off the coast of Britain and the nation's flank from Soviet threat."

His views were testament to very muddled thinking.

Later that year and almost in the same breath, Mrs. Thatcher announced the quite extraordinary plan to sell our new Sea Harrier Carrier, HMS Invincible to Australia. These misguided public plans were a welcome green flag to Galtieri in Argentina. Without carrier-based air power, Britain would not be able to prevent an invasion of the Falkland Islands or retake the Islands. And so, in April 1982 the invasion took place.

In the rapidly convened War Cabinet, Mr Nott further revealed his ignorance of maritime warfare capability. He asked the Chief of the Air Staff and then the Chief of the General Staff to present options for the recovery of the Islands. Both admitted that there was nothing that they could do. Nott then tried to move on without comment from the Chief of Naval Staff but Mrs Thatcher insisted on hearing from Admiral Sir Henry Leach – much to the disapproval of her Defence Minister. And much to Mrs Thatcher's relief and delight, Sir Henry immediately stated that he could form a Task Force and retake the Islands.

The Fleet including the Royal Marine-led Amphibious Brigade was despatched towards the South Atlantic within days.

Fortunately, Argentina got its timing wrong. Had the invasion taken place a year later, Britain would have been powerless to intervene – unable to deter the territorial aggrandisement of the South American Nation.

On relinquishing his tenure as Defence Secretary, Mr Nott sent the following note to new Defence Minister, Michael Heseltine:

"I wish you all the best for your reforms but of course all my plans were mucked up by the damn Falklands War."

So much for Mr Nott's understanding of our global maritime defence needs.

The value of deterrence remained vital to Operation Corporate, our campaign to recover the Islands. We still enjoyed a powerful surface fleet of warships including an amphibious landing force for getting our troops ashore. Our Hunter-Killer nuclear submarines could wreak havoc with the Argentine Navy. The only major question surrounding our capability was whether or not we had sufficient air power to prevent annihilation of our surface and ground forces by enemy air. As the world now knows, the odds were not in our favour: initially just twenty Sea Harriers against two hundred enemy aircraft.

Deterrence proved to be the answer – inextricably linked to fighter combat expertise.

During the previous three years of introduction to service and operational development, my Sea Harrier Squadrons had taken full advantage of the expertise passed down by generations of AWIs/ Top Guns. Several AWIs had passed on this legacy to our Sea Harrier squadron pilots and in doing so had laid the groundwork for a reputation of fighter combat success that was unmatched. How did we achieve this?

I had applied the AWI ethos to the Sea Harrier world from the moment that the little 'jump-jet' was introduced to service. The Ministry of Defence Naval Staff had appointed me in command and had given me a completely free hand to direct and control all the flying trials, all pilot training and to develop all front-line operational procedures and tactics. It was definitely my baby as

"Mr. Sea Harrier" and the end result had to be right. The Royal Navy needed potent all-weather fighter aircraft at sea in its carriers.

Figure 34. The Argies christened us 'The Black Death'.

The operational development of our little jump jet from a ground attack Harrier relied on the aircrew and engineers of 700A Trials Unit, 899 Headquarters Squadron and 801 Naval Air Squadron and they were an absolutely superb team.

Their expertise, dedication, loyalty and effort provided a platform for exceptional success and I acknowledged this with unstinting loyalty downwards and complete trust. This was a magic formula and it allowed me to concentrate on my highest priority: we all had to learn how to fly the aircraft to and beyond its limits and apply that knowledge to fighter combat training, tactics and all other combat roles. That was Royal Navy Fleet Air Arm AWI business.

Figure 34. Dick Goodenough with some of his outstanding 801 Engineers.

In order to provide assurance of good domestic flying practices and flight safety (the Harrier breed could easily bite you hard if you treated it like any other non-VSTOL conventional aircraft), our team received outstanding support and advice from a handful of experienced ground-attack RAF Harrier pilots whose VSTOL advice was essential for the safe conduct of our task. With their help and against most expectations, we were able to develop our little jet into a world-class air combat fighter. And of particular note, the Sea Harrier Squadrons under my command achieved the all-time best flight safety record of any fast jet aircraft entering service.

Not long after Trials Unit formation I had received an invitation from the USAF Aggressor Squadron at Alconbury to visit them for some mutually beneficial air combat training. The word had got around that we had something different and special to offer. It was an opportunity not to be missed. Flt. Lt. Ian Mortimer (an RAF Qualified Weapons Instructor on exchange with us), Lt. David Braithwaite (an experienced Navy AWI) and I took three of our shiny new jets to Alconbury.

Figure 35. 801 young sailors enjoy the Bambara Trophy.

In a detailed welcoming briefing, we exchanged full details about our aircraft. Sea Harrier was subsonic and had a poor turning circle. The Freedom Fighter F-5E was supersonic and had a very tight turning circle – a clear advantage. But the very-slow-speed handling of the Sea Harrier was marginally superior and we also had the benefit of Vectoring In Forward Flight (VIFF) – moving our four thrust nozzles down. This allowed us to decelerate the jet instantly. When selecting 'full-breaking-stop' (nozzles fully down and slightly forward) at say, 400 knots, it felt like hitting a brick wall. No conventional jet fighter could match that.

To the bemusement if not astonishment of the Aggressor pilots, I volunteered to demonstrate this capability in the air before any full air combat sorties were flown.

"I shall set up each demonstration combat at 400 knots with your F-5 in a starting position about half a mile behind me, slightly higher and slightly offset [a position known as 'the perch']. At commencement of combat and from this advantageous position you will attack, trying to achieve a guns' kill on me. That won't happen. Before you know it, I shall be behind you in your six [o'clock]."

They were not convinced.

We got airborne and set up the demonstration as briefed. As I called "Commence" I saw the nose of the F-5 lower and he began to accelerate towards my six o'clock from behind and above me. Applying full power, I waited until he was approaching guns range then heaved fully back on the stick, pulling maximum 'g', rotating the nose rapidly upwards and preventing any possible guns tracking. As soon as my jet hit the vertical, I slammed the nozzles down to full-braking-stop, applied full aileron and kept the stick fully back. The aircraft bucked and shuddered but responded impeccably as it rolled, decelerated and skewed upside down. As I watched the F-5 pass underneath me I centralised the controls, slammed the nozzle lever forward and rolled down into his 6 o'clock as he tried to escape. Two further combats were enough to demonstrate the point convincingly.

We then entered a program of one-against-one (1v1) and two-against-two (2v2) air combat sorties and, bearing in mind we were operating against the best fighter pilots of the USAF, the results were compelling. Out of twelve sorties each, Ian scored nine kills, David scored six kills and I scored eleven kills (the Aggressor squadron boss got me when I made a mistake on the last 1v1 combat in a very slow-speed fight) – a kill ratio of 26 to 10 in our favour. Both our squadrons learned much from the detachment and the Aggressors were wonderful hosts – a superb example of honesty and integrity in the air and on the ground. I wrote a detailed report and sent it to them and to the Ministry of Defence.

A few days later the Aggressor Colonel called me. "Hey, Sharkey! I just had a visit from an indignant RAF Air-Vice Marshal from Whitehall who clearly hated your report. I told him that it was a very good and accurate account of proceedings. He departed a rather deflated bunny. Well done you."

The Air-Vice Marshal was a member of the Air Staff that had strongly opposed the introduction of the Sea Harrier to service. We had taken the ground attack Harrier and turned it into an out-standing dogfighting fighter that was much more capable at air combat than any of the RAF fighters. The AVM couldn't stand the truth.

Then, not long after the Alconbury detachment, I received a phone call from Bitburg, Germany. It was the boss of the F-15 Eagle Fighter Squadron.

"Hello Sharkey, we have heard about your successful training session with the Aggressor squadron and we would very much like to visit your base with two jets for some air combat training and evaluation."

The word was getting around and I was delighted. A couple of days later, two of the magnificent fighters landed at Royal Naval Air Station, Yeovilton.

Ian Mortimer and I flew two sorties of 2v2 against them. They had air-to-air radar and simulated a full weapons war-load of medi-um-range Sparrow missiles, short-range, heat-seeking Sidewinder missiles and guns. In addition they had extraordinary power and a far better turning circle than our little subsonic jet. We still had no radar fitted and we simulated just Sidewinder and guns. In order to even things up, Lt. Harry O'Grady, a brilliant Direction Officer from my time flying the Phantom F-4 K in HMS Ark

Royal, provided us with air intercept control from the ground keeping us informed of the precise relative position of the F-15's.

Each of the four combats began with us being 40 miles apart. We knew from UK Phantom experience just how to prevent successful, long-range Sparrow shots against us and so it all came down to within visual range combat/dogfighting. Having a small jet with a smoke-free exhaust was a great advantage, whereas the F-15 Eagle's large size and smoky exhaust enabled us to see them and keep track of them much more easily. Our plan was to drag them down to our height at fairly low altitude and then to use our excellent very slow speed manoeuvrability to keep them off our tails and win the fight. Their plan, as we observed it, was to approach us from about 20,000 feet above and to loop down behind us into our 6 o'clock like avenging angels.

Combat rapidly developed into separate 1v1 dogfights: with heavy breathing, maximum 'g' and adrenalin in full flow. We couldn't afford any mistakes or the Eagles would tear us to pieces.

It was easy to spot them visually as they hurtled down from the heavens and we had enough time to turn hard and be pointing straight at them, head on, before we passed each other. As we did so, they engaged full after-burner (reheat) and soared away into the heavens again out of range of our missiles for a second try at the same tactic. This time we again met them head on but at slow enough speed to be able to rotate the Sea Harrier vertically on its tail very rapidly through 180° just before we passed each other. Bingo! We were pointing at them in their six o'clock before they could accelerate away. The sidewinder missile growled loudly as we claimed a simulated 'kill' and called, "Fox Two. Splash one F-15!"

Every combat differed slightly and was hall-marked by ultra-aggressive flying. There were some very hairy moments of near-collision that kept the adrenaline flowing. But the hugely satisfying result that we all agreed to in the debrief was seven kills to the Sea Harrier and one kill to the Eagles.

Not long after these encounters, blue skies and December temperatures heralded an exciting day of dissimilar fighter combat over the Mediterranean Sea; 60 miles to the west of Aeroporto Militaire Decimomannu, Cagliari on the Italian Island of Sardinia. We had flown our Sea Harriers down across France from the UK to participate in tri-national fighter combat training against the best of the US and Italian Air Forces. It was a terrific training opportunity – even though the Italian pilots never turned up in the air to fight (but they did wear flashy flying suits).

We had already fought against our US Air Force adversaries, the fabled F-15 Eagle Fighters from their base in Germany and the Air Combat Instructor "Aggressor" squadron of F-5E Freedom Fighters and knew that they deserved the highest respect. It was a privilege to share the skies with them once more and benefit from their expertise.

For 801 Squadron, the unique attraction of the detachment was the state-of-the-art range in which combat was to be conducted: an Air Combat Manoeuvring Installation. Each aircraft carried a special telemetry pod that was monitored and recorded in real time by a ring of sensor stations encircling the combat area. The pod transmitted accurate information about each aircraft's relative position, heading, speed, attitude, angle of attack, 'g' and height. This information was collated by powerful computers on the ground and resulted in a complete three-dimensional recording of each combat which could be displayed on a large screen in the debriefing room – with freeze and replay options instantly available–just like a videogame. The real time view from each cockpit was available on demand and very realistic. The simulated release of missiles and the firing of guns was measured precisely to establish whether a 'kill' had been achieved, i. e. within range, missile acquired, gun tracking on target, etc. Spurious claims of 'kills' would be summarily discounted and disputed claims of combat success could be fairly and accurately adjudicated. In other words, one could not cheat and 'win the fight in the debrief rather than in the air'.

Critically, and during each sortie debrief, a pilot could see his tactical aircraft-handling mistakes at any part of the combat and could learn from them as they were pointed out by experienced Instructors. I was fortunate to be one of those – a fully qualified Air Warfare Instructor (AWI) trained by the élite aircrew of 764 Naval Air Squadron at Naval Air Station Lossiemouth, Scotland.

After getting used to the Decimomanu range facilities with private squadron sorties, the real business began against the F-15's and the F-5E's. Our little Sea Harrier jump jet more than held its own against these two superb fighter aircraft which could fly faster and turn much tighter. To the uninitiated, this should have meant a one-sided contest that we would always lose. But not so.

My squadron pilots approached the air combat detachment with a high level of confidence. Our earlier successes against the F-5E's and the F-15's had not been forgotten by our opponents. They treated us with a great deal of respect on the ground and, importantly, in the air. This proved to be to our considerable advantage. The real time recording of every engagement ensured that what had happened in the air was properly and correctly recognized afterwards in the debrief.

All 801 pilots acquitted themselves very well indeed, winning some and losing some. The icing on the cake for me came when I was programmed to fly alone against two F-15's and two F-5E's in a 1v2v2 combat mission. I had the major advantage of Desmond Hughes, my observer from Phantom days, providing me with a running commentary on the positions of the other four aircraft. It was a totally exhilarating fight which included a horrendous, near-head-on collision with one of the F-15's. Nearly time for brown trousers and far better than any video game!

In one brief skirmish with the pair of F-15's, Desmond had guided me in to intercept them from their left-hand side. They were in relatively close attack formation and didn't see me until I was racing in on their beam at 600 knots. They were less than a mile away crossing right to left at about 450 knots when they saw me and decided to take evasive action. Because of the need to conserve fuel they could only use reheat/afterburner and their supersonic capability when engaged in actual combat manoeuvring. But instead of breaking hard towards me and splitting up to give me two targets to cope with, which is what I expected, they decided to try to outrun me and deny me a missile shot. Applying full reheat, they both tried to run but it was too late. As I turned hard-left close behind them, I simulated the release of two Sidewinders at very short range. "Fox Two. Fox Two! Splash two F-15's". Why they chose to run rather than fight is still beyond me. Probably it was a result of our earlier close-in engagements.

During that electrifying combat sortie I claimed a total of seven kills – a mixture of Eagles and Freedom Fighters – with no kills against me. Back on the ground and when we reviewed each combat on the screen in the debrief, my claims were fully justified. This was too much for one of the F-15 pilots who tried to say it was all wrong. But the Aggressor pilots, bless their honesty, told him he had been well beaten and should take it like a professional – as they did themselves.

My two young first-tour pilots Charlie Cantan and Steve Thomas made remarkable progress during the detachment, understanding at last the tactical lessons that we had been trying to teach them verbally but without access to such digital technology. In fully developed fighter combat, a fraction of a second delay in decision-making is all it takes to make the difference between winning and losing your life. There are many nuances to this process of tactical thought. Anticipation, experience and knowing your adversary's capabilities, intent and future position can only be properly acquired in the air. This learning process usually takes a lot of time. As a result during training at our home base, I had been able to 'shoot down' Charlie and/or Steve within a minute of commencing combat. Following the 'Deci' detachment those days were now over – the penny had dropped and it took rather longer for me to achieve the same result.

Our successes had rocked the fighter world. We had built a reputation that was to have a major impact on the conduct of the Air War in the Falklands just a few months later.

This reputation proved to be a major deterrent to our Argentine adversaries and it was relevant and convenient that representatives of the UK's press were embarked in Invincible, including the Times, the Telegraph, the Sun, the Daily Mail and the Star.

As our Task Force journeyed to the South, world attention was focussed on our 8,000-mile deployment. Pundits of all nations anticipated failure. The Russian General in Berlin "expected that we would get our bottom smacked!" I had no such illusion. My Captain allowed our pilots to give daily interviews to the journalists and, being the Boss, I was given a free hand, leading the parade and able to transmit our supreme confidence to the British public and to our adversaries. The clear message sent was that we were going to thrash the living daylights out of the Argentine Air Forces.

This did not go unnoticed by the Argentine High Command and day one of hostilities gave real meaning to our reputation. Sea Harriers shot down a handful of enemy aircraft including two

Mirage III Fighters, a Mirage V Ground-Attack Fighter and at least one Canberra. No Sea Harrier losses were suffered then, or in any other air-to-air confrontation throughout the war.

The message understood and followed by Argentina was, "Don't mess with the Black Death (as they had christened us). Avoid contact at all costs." This proved to be critical to the conduct and eventual outcome of the air war and allowed our ground forces led by the Royal Marines to win a momentous victory.

Figure 36. HMS Invincible shows her paces.

The trust between JJ Black (our Captain), Dusty Milner (our Commander 'Air') and the squadron was immense and played a vital role in the war. My AWIs had drawn up plans for how we would win the air war including a night-time, low level coordinated attack on Port Stanley airfield on commencement of hostilities. We had six pilots fully ready for this. When we proposed this to the Air Group and the Admiral's Staff in HMS Hermes at the War Planning Meeting when en route south, the Hermes team derided the claim as 'impossible'. They had no pilots qualified for such a night operation and openly questioned my squadron's ability to conduct the same. JJ quickly interceded and proudly announced, "Sharkey Ward may be as mad as a hatter but if he says he can do something, you better believe it!"

Even though our plans were then somewhat grudgingly accepted by the Flag Captain and his team, the latter proved to have reservations about the Sea Harrier's night attack capability and decided on a dawn raid instead – rather predictable from the enemy's point of view.

Eventually, the decision was made that Invincible and 801 Squadron would be in control of the Air-to-Air War whilst the larger number of Hermes' 800 Squadron Sea Harriers would bear the brunt of Air-to-Ground operations – whilst still contributing to Combat Air Patrol, the outer layer of our air defence.

This decision was regularly ignored by certain members of Admiral Woodward's Staff who, without the knowledge or blessing of the Admiral himself, sent out a continuous stream of ill-advised directives to Invincible. The most inept of these was, "Sea Harriers are not to use their radars when on Combat Air Patrol defending Task Force Units."

The trust factor within Invincible came to the rescue. Whenever such directives were received, I would discuss them directly with JJ and Dusty at the daily Command Briefing, explaining the pro's and con's and what actions we should take. Inevitably, I would sum it up saying, "We must ignore this directive, Sir, and do it my way". Almost without fail, the Captain agreed, "OK, Sharkey. Make it so. We do it your way." (In days gone by, I might well have been shot on charges of mutiny.)

Had there not been such trust, it is probable that the Air War would have been lost leading to failure of the Campaign.

Enemy attack fighters always approached the Amphibious Beachhead in San Carlos Water or the Carrier Battle Group at sea at very low level. Invincible had been appointed the Anti-Air Warfare Control ship (AAWC), responsible for the control and disposition of all Sea Harrier Combat Air Patrols (CAP) from both Hermes and Invincible. Our plan was to maintain three continuous low-level CAP stations comprising two aircraft each in the threat directions: North West, West and South West.

Enemy fighters would have to penetrate through these CAP stations to deliver weapons against our ships and ground forces. There was not a little risk associated with the conduct of very low-level Patrols. The Western station in particular was all over the land–enemy held territory. And flying at endurance speed (rather than fighting speed) made us all the more vulnerable to ground small-arms fire. But as far as my pilots were concerned, doing so was a 'no-brainer' – effective defence of the San Carlos beachhead was not negotiable.

At all times, CAP aircraft were to use their radar – even though the radar could not see targets looking down over land. The logic behind this was that the Mirage V Daggers and A-4 Skyhawks would detect the presence of Sea Harrier radar with their Electronic Warning equipment supported by land-based radars and abort their planned attacks. Official Argentine sources admitted after the war that this tactic was very successful. More than 450 attack missions were aborted, saving many lives and many ships. This probably was the root-enabler of eventual Task Force success along with the 25 Sea Harrier air-to-air kills.

On one occasion when four Mirage Daggers did try to penetrate the low-level CAP screen en route to San Carlos, Steve Thomas and I shot three of them down. One Mirage got through. Steve was hit by ground fire immediately after that combat but was able to return safely to the ship.

However, against Invincible's explicit orders, some low-level CAP stations were often left vacant on the interfering instruction of Hermes, whose aircraft remained at 20,000 feet giving enemy fighter-bombers a free passage into the San Carlos beachhead and/or targets at sea. This mis-guided disregard of established CAP stations resulted directly in the demise of several warships including HMS Antelope, HMS Ardent, HMS Coventry and HMS Sheffield.

The Task Force's victorious recovery of the Islands was a cause for national celebration and international admiration. It was unquestionable proof that the Fleet Weapon System[7] and our Ground Forces had justified their existence and had lived up to their illustrious record of war fighting and intervention. The conduct of the air war was vital to its success and had depended upon the legacy passed down from decades of Air Warfare Instructors and Top Guns.

My team had done well. I was so proud of them.

After the war was over and some years later, one of my squadron engineers emailed me to say, "Sharkey, we would willingly have died for you." It was a two-way street.

---

[7] This phrase refers to the fully integrated capability of all Fleet units, Sub-surface, Surface, Air and the Royal Fleet Auxiliary support vessels.

22

The Origins of the US Navy "Top Gun".

I t was such pride, expertise and earlier achievement that paved the way for a select team of Royal Navy fighter pilots to contribute to the formation of the U. S. Navy Top Gun School.

The original blockbuster film, "Top Gun" gave the world an insight into the psyche of naval fighter pilots whose qualities and capabilities reflect the challenges of the most demanding flying job in the world: carrier-borne aviation and combat in all weathers by day and by night.

The term Top Gun has an exciting ring to it and, arguably, it is seen to describe the aviators who are demonstrably at the top of the ladder in the aggressive leadership and execution of combat training and operations.

The United States Navy Top Gun Élite had their origins in VF121 Squadron at Miramar Naval Air Station, San Diego during the Vietnam War in the early 60s. Highly manoeuvrable Russian MiG-15/17 and MiG-21 fighters were overwhelming carrier-borne US F-4 Phantoms and F-8 Crusaders in live combat – resulting in major losses. The F-8 was somewhat more successful than the F-4: being more manoeuvrable and, critically, being armed with an internal cannon whereas the F-4 was armed only with less reliable early-generation Sparrow and Sidewinder air-to-air missiles.

At that time it was the US Department of Defense's misguided view that all-missile armament (no gun/cannon) was the way to go for new fighter aircraft such as the F-4.

The release parameters for the early Sidewinder missile were limited to close range firings from the six o'clock of (behind) the target – and for that to be realised, the F-4 needed to use tactics, supersonics and the advantages endowed by its radar to out-manoeuvre the MiGs. This depended upon close cooperation between the Radar Intercept Officer/Observer in the rear cockpit and the pilot as well as, importantly, accumulated expertise.

In the UK, the Royal Navy Air Warfare Instructor Squadron, 764, was already in existence and had developed a wealth of talent and expertise in the art of twin-seat multi-aircraft dogfighting and radar-assisted fighter combat – with the Sea Venom and Sea Vixen fighters.

By chance, also in the 60s, it had been arranged for Royal Navy crews to serve on VF121 to obtain operational experience on the Phantom pending the delivery of the F-4K variant to the UK in 1969. It was a timely coincidence that 3 out of 4 UK exchange pilots were Air Warfare Instructors (AWI's) whose expertise was just what was needed to help develop effective Phantom air combat tactics.

A succession of our best Royal Navy AWIs and their Observers/ Radar Intercept Officers set off for the USA and the VF121 Phantom F-4A/B/J Training Squadron at Naval Air Station Miramar, San Diego. Their task was to learn all about Phantom operations and in return they were able to pass on their knowledge of operating a twin-seat fighter aircraft fitted with Air Intercept radar – the Pilot and Observer both contributing significantly and in harmony to successful air intercept and air combat manoeuvring (dog-fighting).

Royal Navy pilots and observers had gained much experience flying from carriers as closely-knit teams in twin-seat fighter aircraft whereas US Navy aviators of the time had only been flying single-seat fast jets such as the Crusader without a true all-weather Air Intercept capability. This valuable twin-seat experience had been incorporated into the AWI ethos which covered all other combat roles as well, such as air-to-ground attack (land targets) and air-to surface attack (sea targets) by day and by night.

This ethos was not laid down or passed on through the medium of written manuals or Command Orders, although the former had been introduced for background reading. On the contrary, it was the result of generations of experience and expertise being passed on personally within front-line squadrons – the old and bold guiding the development of the younger aircrew.

But AWIs did not just jump out of the woodwork. They were trained by a select team of experienced AWIs in UK's 764 Naval Air Squadron at Lossie mouth (see Chapter 14, above).

Selection for this prestigious course was not a routine matter and was considered the holy grail by self-respecting young naval aviators – all of whom had already proven themselves to be talented enough to carry out front-line combat operations from the decks of aircraft carriers in all-weather by day and by night–no mean feat in itself. Key qualities required to demonstrate AWI potential were manifold, including: Leadership, A marked aptitude for all combat operations, A desire to be the best (top gun), Supreme self-confidence (not over-confidence) and An appropriately aggressive nature. (There is no place in war for pussy-cats.)

Aggression was indeed the key but, of vital importance, an AWI had to demonstrate an acute understanding and oversight of tactics, weapon system knowledge and Flight Safety. When pushing the limits the latter meant the difference between life and death.

Being selected for AWI training depended on performance in the front-line and character. It was not a question of being a volunteer but of being seen to be made of the right stuff. And that 'stuff' included 'attitude' which often proved to be counter-productive with respect to career advancement in a straight-laced Royal Navy.

The Course itself was challenging but that was not a problem for the lucky few. One had to demonstrate excellent leadership in the air and on the ground; without which respect and loyalty from one's peers and superiors could not be attained. Intense pressure was applied to all candidates.

The Royal Navy crews who were initially despatched to Miramar during the 60s were the best that Britain had to offer. Some of them were legends in their own lifetime and I was extremely privileged to fly with many of them and to learn from them during my operational flying tours in HMS Ark Royal, 1969–1976.

The expertise that they were able to pass on was a significant enabler towards the Miramar Fighter Pilots radically changing the course of the air war in Vietnam, reigning supreme over the MiGs and creating the US Navy Top Gun School.

The new Top Gun Course was based on what had already been achieved by 764 Squadron at Lossiemouth. The driving force behind the Miramar Course's creation was Dick Lord; a legendary AWI within the Royal Navy's Fleet Air Arm and undoubtedly a supreme Top Gun of our Service. Without him and his team developing and demonstrating effective air-intercept and fighter combat tactics for the Phantom, it would have been much harder to turn the tide against the Vietnam MiGs.

The Royal Navy AWIs immediately saw how to minimise the disadvantage of the Phantom's relatively poor turning manoeuvrability and how to take effective advantage of the aircraft's supersonic capability for the development of a successful radar-controlled air intercept leading to the downing of adversaries.

Initially, Dick's major contribution was recognised formally in the upgraded US F-4 Tactics Manual but this appears to have been forgotten by follow-on generations.

The British crews who contribute to this remarkable transformation have not all been adequately recognised[8].

A further significant contribution to the mission success and the generation of US Standard Operating Procedures was made by Neville Featherstone, a much-revered Qualified Flying Instructor (QFI). QFI's are highly qualified aviators whose mission is to oversee squadron pilots for the maintenance of safe domestic flying practices and standards.

Warfighting, combat oversight and training remained the domain of the AWI and that was convincingly proven at Miramar. (Top Gun School moved from NAS Miramar near San Diego to the Naval Strike and Air Warfare Center, NAS Fallon, Nevada in 1996.)

It was directly thanks to the expertise of these dedicated Royal Navy air warfare practitioners and of their colleagues and predecessors, so many of whom paid the ultimate sacrifice during service, that the air war over the Falklands was won so convincingly by Royal Navy's Fleet Air Arm Sea Harrier pilots.

---

[8] In order of appearance on the Miramar stage from 1963 onward, they included; Jeff Hunt and Peter Goddard, Doug Borrowman and John Ellis, Dick Lord and Hugh Drake, Al Hickling and Keith Brown, Bob Jones and Nick Childs, Neville Featherstone and Paul Waterhouse, Dick Moody and Colin Griffiths, Dave Braithwaite and Doug MacDonald, Nick Harris and Tony Bull, Dave Allen and Desmond Hughes, Peter Jago and Taff Davis. Significant contributions were also made from home-base by AWIs such as Mike Layard and Bob Northard.

These legends deserve our Nation's eternal gratitude.

Hollywood has embraced the élan and flair of the embarked Top Gun. But the film is not about land-based pilots, the majority of whom have never been asked to put themselves in harm's way.

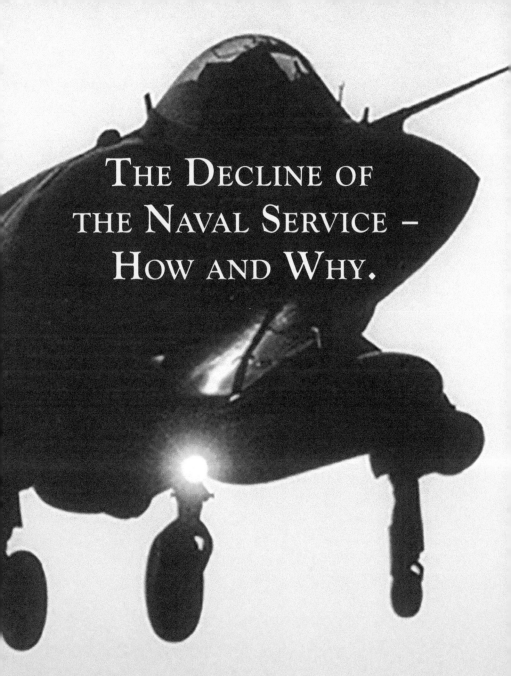

THE DECLINE OF
THE NAVAL SERVICE –
HOW AND WHY.

23

AIRCRAFT CARRIER BATTLE GROUPS – "THE TIP OF THE SPEAR"

Over recent decades and despite the many lessons learned during and since World War II, successive Governments have failed to recognise the continuing need for the robust naval power projection capability that used to guarantee the security of our overseas interests and safe passage on our global trade and energy supply routes. Instead, our Whitehall masters have listened to the misguided land-based-air viewpoint that "the RAF rather than the Naval Service can provide such security and safe passage". The Falklands War of 1982, the aggressive posture of the Chinese in the South China Sea and the recent stand-off with Iran in the Hormuz Strait have clearly demonstrated how fallacious that viewpoint has proven to be.

In order to begin to understand this failure and the effect it has had on our Naval Service, the reader should first be aware of the actual track record of global British Carrier Task Force operations since World War II.

Annex C briefly records 19 crises, conflicts and deterrence operations in which fixed-wing Aircraft Carrier Battle Groups were deployed in support of UK Government policy since 1948. These demonstrate that the availability of sea-based tactical aviation adds immensely to the nation's overall strategic deterrent capability. On several occasions no other form of intervention or deterrence was initially possible. More significant is the inability of potential aggressors to deter the deployment of aircraft carriers into areas supposedly dominated by land-based aircraft. The myth of vulnerability is belied by experience.

Although the RAF would have politicians believe that it is a globally mobile force, there are many examples of where it could not have deployed aircraft, aircrew and maintainers into conflict zones without the support of aircraft carriers.

> *"Strange as it may seem, the Air Force, except in the air, is the least mobile of all the Services. A squadron can reach its destination in a few hours, but its establishments, depots, fuel, spare parts, and workshops take many weeks, and even months, to develop."*
>
> W. Churchill. *"The Second World War."*
> Vol. 11, page 384.

Once deployed, the RAF then relied on sea-borne bulk supplies of fuel and ammunition which, in turn, needed the Royal Navy to maintain control of the sea supply routes–with its aircraft carriers playing a prominent role. Annex D provides examples.

More than 80% of all effective Air Power Projections since World War II have been conducted by the aircraft of British and United States Carrier Battle Groups. The absence of land-based fighters in the deterrence of those that would harm our National interests away from the NATO area is not a surprise. Unlike Aircraft Carriers, airfields on land cannot be relocated in response to an emergency. Nor can effective numbers of the land-based fighters that they serve be easily repositioned and/or fully supported – except by massive logistic air-bridges that are vulnerable to international overflight and basing rights. The proven cost-effective, rapid response alternative is the deployment of Naval Service warships and Royal Fleet Auxiliaries that enjoy the freedom of the seas. The simple laws of physics and international law indicate that this is not likely to change in the foreseeable future.

The decline of our Naval Service in recent times has been a direct result of politicians, Whitehall Military Staffs and associated Civil Servants failing to recognise these incontrovertible facts. Instead, spin, misguidance and neglect have shaped our Governments' lack of understanding of the military value of a robust, well-equipped navy. Things could have been very different if common sense had been deployed along the lines of Ronald Reagan's famous quote: "Trust, but verify". No such verification or justification of RAF claims of effective global reach has been made.

At the time of writing, there may be some hope on the horizon with the appointment of our new First Sea Lord, Admiral Tony Radakin. In his speech to Defence and Security Equipment International, 11 September 2019, he made the following commitment:

"My second priority [*after North Atlantic antisubmarine warfare*] is Carrier Strike. We are enormously grateful for the investment by successive governments and the nation. My task now is to deliver on this, increase and magnify the value of that investment. We need to shift the whole Navy to being a Carrier Task Group Navy. This will allow us to project our power around the world. And at a level alongside our American and French allies."

The Admiral's words are strongly supported by Dr Anthony Wells who is British by birth and a U. S. citizen. In 1982, as Head of Special Programs in one of the United Kingdom's intelligence directorates, he was actively involved in some of the most sensitive aspects of the South Atlantic Falklands campaign. He opines that

"Somewhere, somehow, amongst all the Brexit sound and fury, the U. K. must awaken to the intrinsic strategic imbalance in its force structure".

The closing pages of his 2017 USNI Press book, "A Tale of Two Navies: Geopolitics, Technology, and Strategy in the United States Navy and the Royal Navy, 1960-2015" support this viewpoint and are provided at Annex E. He expressly calls for:

"… a resolute statement of joint [UK and US] national resolve to use the sea and naval forces as "the primary means" to secure the vital national interests of the United States and the United Kingdom."

And he opines that:

"The substance of strategic expeditionary naval diplomacy and warfare, its core characteristic value, is its ability to signal, influence, deter, and, at worst case, provide the full range of measured force to meet all known and projected military-political-economic contingencies. This is the key lesson of naval history, and grand strategy."

Major General Julian Thompson CB OBE, Amphibious Brigade Commander in the Falklands War and one of UK's premier Military Historians has been researching the life of Admiral Marc Mitscher USN who commanded the Fast Carrier Force in the Pacific war. After the war the Admiral wrote the following:

"Japan is beaten, and carrier supremacy defeated her. Carrier supremacy destroyed her army and navy air forces. Carrier supremacy destroyed her fleet. Carrier supremacy gave us bases adjacent to her home islands, and carrier supremacy finally left her exposed to the most devastating sky attack – the atomic fission bomb – that man has suffered.

When I say carrier supremacy defeated Japan, I do not mean air power in itself won the Battle of the Pacific. We exercised our carrier supremacy as part of a balanced, integrated air-surface-ground team, in which all hands may be proud of the roles assigned them and the way in which their duties were discharged. This could not have been done by a separate air force, exclusively based ashore, or by one not under Navy control. "

The logic of this last sentence is telling in the light of the present decline in our own Naval Service.

So let us look at how and why this decline has taken place.

24

WHITEHALL NEGLECT AND MISMANAGEMENT.

Having put my all into learning from my Air Warfare Instructor predecessors, many of whom sacrificed their lives at sea earning the Queen's shilling and whose legacy of defending the nation merits deep respect, I wish to pay tribute to that legacy by recording below how and why our Naval Service has been allowed to decline to its present parlous state.

Prolonged periods of peace, for which we should of course be grateful, always bring negative pressure on public support for careful investment in National Security and Defence, particularly the Armed Forces.

It would be naïve to expect a fundamental change in this phenomenon or in the structure of the Ministry of Defence and of its oversight by the Government. But some adjustment in the conduct of that oversight might well reverse the current trend of not getting a decent bang for the buck. There should be no need for the much-vaunted Black Hole in defence spending. A relatively simple solution is offered at Annex G. It proposes the need for the full operational and cost justification of weapon systems present and future against the perceived threat. Roles and size of each armed service also require formal justification in the light of that threat.

Before presenting the history of the state-of-the-art in Whitehall and the part I played in it, I wish to make something clear. My father was an officer in the Royal Air Force (RAF)–hence my early Navy nickname, "Son-of-a-Crab[9]" – of which I was very proud. I was brought up within the fold of our Royal Air Force and developed a very high regard for that Service and for all the personnel and pilots therein. I have served under the command of RAF officers and have had the honour of commanding RAF fighter pilots in combat in the front-line. I remain thoroughly convinced that these front-line aviators are a professional breed and continue to be a real credit to the UK.

Just as my son, Kris, developed an early and long-lasting ambition to become a fighter pilot, my own real baptism came in my early teens.

It was during school holidays with my parents and siblings at RAF North Luffenham in Rutland that the guiding light to my future began to emerge. We lived in an idyllic setting across the valley from the air station in a charming farmhouse near Empingham Village, complete with egg-laying chicken runs, rabbit hutches et al. I recall with much pleasure our family dog, a Staffordshire Bull Terrier named Patch. He was just wonderful! It was a very rustic setting surrounded by endless fields of wheat and pasture.

In the summer holidays, my brother and I would work for the local farmers baling hay to earn some pocket money – watching with amazement as all the field mice and rabbits ran for their lives. And yes, I did have a girlfriend but our frolics in the haystacks were verging on total innocence because at eleven years old and for many years to come I really didn't know what 'it' was for.

---

[9] "Crab" is the nickname based on the sideways landing technique of RAF pilots as well as the colour of their uniform.

During weekdays (the RAF does not work at weekends), Squadron Leader Roger Topp would lead his famous Black Arrow Hunter formation team through their stunning aerobatic displays over the valley below our farmhouse. The sight of these twelve, jet aircraft in very close and immaculate formation doing loops and barrel rolls in the clear blue skies created a fervent desire in both my brother and me to become RAF pilots. I didn't realise at that stage that becoming a competent frontline fighter pilot entailed much more than daily jollies over the Rutland countryside. Nevertheless, I had been firmly smitten by an urge that would never go away until it was fully consummated.

A few years later in Penang, Malaya I accompanied my father and family to a cocktail party on board one of Her Majesty's Aircraft Carriers–possibly HMS Albion, but I am not sure. It was like entering a new, exciting world: a ceremonial welcome at the gangway to access the quarterdeck followed by a maze of passageways and ladders leading to the flight deck. In the vernacular, I was 'gob-smacked'. Legions of sun-bronzed Naval Officers and Fleet Air Arm fighter pilots in their immaculate white sharkskin shirts with gold epaulets and shorts plied us with drinks and gracious, warm hospitality. As if that was not enough, several magnificent jet fighters were parked around the cocktail party area. The evening ended with my first live experience of a Royal Marine Band marching up and down and playing "A Life on the Ocean Wave" and as the sun went down the White Ensign was lowered as the Captain took the salute. An incredible scene.

That was it. I no longer wanted to join the Air Force. From that moment I was immovably set on becoming a Navy fighter pilot. That is not to say I had lost my respect and regard for the RAF but the choice was clear. I couldn't imagine how these huge jets could land on such a small ship and I knew that this was what I wanted to do.

For the record and largely unbeknown to the public, Britain has three Air Forces:

- The Army Air Corps who provide essential air support for our gallant ground forces in combat;

- The Fleet Air Arm (which includes Royal Marine battlefield support helicopters) embarked in our warships that provide fighter jet and helicopter offensive and defensive air support for power projection operations around the globe, and;

- The land-based RAF whose prime roles are the defence of United Kingdom airspace, the logistic air support of the other two Services and the support of European NATO operations.

The Royal Navy's Fleet Air Arm is an integral part of the Fleet Weapons System, i. e. the maritime force that has successfully defended our Global National Interests and deterred our enemies for centuries. The demise of this Naval Air Force threatens not only the lives of our sailors at sea, Merchant Marine and Military, but also the effective defence of our global interests and, in turn, the UK's economic prosperity.

A strong Fleet Air Arm and Naval Service is not a threat to the proper functioning of the other two Services. But there needs to be a sensible balance of investment based on justified and demonstrated capability. That balance does not exist at present.

As one of a proud breed of Naval Aviators, I have watched with dismay as our Whitehall masters have disregarded military history and now appear to pay lip-service to declared Government Policy as described by Secretary of State for Defence, the Rt. Hon.

Philip Hammond: "Our new strike carriers are at the heart of UK Strategic Policy".

The progress of this 'disregard' is laid out below and explains the causes and effect of the pressure now felt by our Military Budget and of Britain's decline as a Maritime Nation.

Facts and figures provided in Chapters 25 to 32 are all in the public domain but as far as I am aware their relationship to each other has not yet been presented in a manner which allows the public and our politicians to 'see the wood for the trees'.

I accept that it is easy to forget the many constraints that are faced by our political masters and that, through no fault of their own, there is a dearth of rounded military expertise and knowledge within Parliament. Our Government therefore has no other choice under our present system but to rely upon the filtered advice that is presented to it by the Ministry of Defence.

The Secretary of State for Defence has the remit for arguing the case for overall military expenditure and, especially in peacetime, this is a difficult and unrewarding task. There are many other Ministries fighting for their share of the Budget and, not surprisingly, the electorate and the Treasury find it easy to put National Security and Defence well down the pecking order in peacetime. That is the inevitable result of our democratic system and the progressive leanings of the modern world.

It behoves us therefore to ensure that the military funding that is available is effectively spent to counter perceived threats to our economic lifeblood and prosperity.

This has proven to be nigh impossible to achieve for the following reasons:

- Abdication of detailed Ministerial Oversight, with funding disconnected from Strategy.

- Arbitrary Equal Funding for each of the Armed Services without due reference to the perceived threat.

- Partisan infighting between the Armed Services and the provision of misleading advice to Ministers.

At a Tri-Service Conference following the Falklands War, the then Minister of Defence, Sir John Nott stated, "It is my job to allocate funding to the Armed Services but it is up to them how they spend it." As a guest speaker, I challenged this alarming statement and was strongly applauded by all attendees. The Defence minister just grinned sheepishly – possibly remembering his own lack of support for a strong Navy as discussed earlier in Chapter 21 under 'Deterrence'! His rather surprising statement revealed the attitude of Defence Ministers stretching into the twenty-first century – cut the cake into three parts and let them get on with it, irrespective of the consequences.

Individual Services do of course have to put forward formal Staff Requirements for new weapon systems for signature by the Minister but this often tends to be a rubber-stamping exercise provided there are adequate funds within that Service's Budget. These Staff Requirements do not have to be subjected to a full justification process, i. e. the analysis of the associated perceived threat and the demonstrated ability of the proposed weapon system and Service to effectively counter that threat. This leaves the door open for the loudest voice to prevail and for some weapon systems to be procured in quantities that have little relationship to the global threats facing UK's interests.

Not unnaturally, it is up to each Service to fight its own cause and where mutual interests are at stake this has often led to obfuscation and misrepresentation. Unsurprisingly, within this less than satis-factory system it is the loudest voice that has typically prevailed. In support of this view, I received the following comment from a very senior Military associate:

"Honest answers from Whitehall, what a hope; that will happen when pigs are seen flying in formation round Big Ben."

If one Service publicises and celebrates its historical combat suc-cesses and a second Service fails to do so/refuses to do so, the first Service will naturally garner public and political recognition and sympathy – and, of particular importance, will have a louder voice in Whitehall and will receive often unjustifiable and dispro-portionate Government funding, irrespective of the commendable track record of the second Service.

In this context of public relations, the land-based Royal Air Force has done its job well. They have sponsored a proliferation of Land-Based-Air-Warfare Academics[10] who have the ear of senior Civil Servants and Ministers – an initiative not understood or matched by the Royal Navy. Clever PR has hidden the fact that there have been relatively few significant military achievements by the RAF since World War II and this lack of visible military success has been disguised by unfulfilled promises of capability and global reach and by constant reminders of the Battle of Britain and the Dam Busters' operations: whose contribution to our World War II victory is itself exaggerated.

---

[10] These Academics have no experience of maritime operations or Naval Air Warfare but their advice carries considerable weight with Cabinet Ministers and Parliamentary Committees. They perpetuate the myth that land-based air can protect the Fleet and our trade routes throughout the oceans of the world.

A new book by Max Hastings, "Chastise" has been reviewed by Patrick Bishop[11] and puts the Dam Busters raids and the bomber offensive over Germany into more realistic context. He discovers how the Second World War raids were not the brilliant success that we were all told.

Here are his comments:

"The Dams Raid of May 1943 was the most celebrated event of the bomber war, immortalised in music, book and movie, and firing the imaginations of millions of post-war schoolboys, among them the young Max Hastings.

Glorifying Bomber Command was a hard sell, given that most of their work consisted of incinerating cities, dealing death to hundreds of thousands of civilians in the process.

Chastise, the operation to destroy the dams of the Ruhr, whose water and hydroelectricity kept Hitler's war factories humming, seemed at first sight a morally unambiguous triumph.

But as Hastings explains … the glow of success masked some bleak truths. The raid was nowhere near as devastating as those who promoted it predicted. Nor was it victim-free. More civilians died that night than on any single Bomber Command operation to date. Half were not even Germans, but Polish and Russian women slave workers.

---

[11] https://www.telegraph.co.uk/books/non-fiction/bleak-truths-behind-dambusters/

That said, the Dams Raid was undoubtedly an amazing feat of arms, requiring great skill and enormous courage. Nineteen Lancasters, crewed mostly by men barely out of boyhood, flew in moonlight at treetop height dodging flak and power lines for an attack of surgical accuracy.

They were armed with an ingenious weapon that seemed to offer proof that Britain could hold its own in the war of technologies that always shaped the course of the actual fighting – the famous Barnes Wallis bouncing bomb.

And they were led by a glossy young hero, 24-year-old Guy Gibson, who in the hands of the Government propagandists proved as effective at PR as he was at dropping bombs.

It was no wonder that after 44 months of a struggle that had so far provided endless setbacks and little sign of sustained success, the Dambusters won a permanent niche in the nation's pantheon.

Over the years the gilding on the legend has chipped a bit, and this book rubs away more of the gloss.

... The raid was a test bed for two conflicting beliefs about what big bombers – the main weapon in Britain's offensive armoury since early 1941 – were for. The prevailing view, championed with savage eloquence by Bomber Command's chief Arthur Harris, was that their job was to smash up cities and break Germany's will to continue the war. Others, including his boss "Peter" Portal, felt that with ever-improving navigational and aiming technologies, the time for "area bombing" was over and the emphasis should shift to assaults on undeniably military targets.

Harris … moved swiftly and cynically to claim a generous helping of the glory. Nonetheless, his granite self-belief remained untouched and he stayed wedded to a policy of mass destruction until the end. Such was the power of his brutish personality that neither Portal nor Churchill dared to sack him, even after the appalling losses of the failed "Battle of Berlin" he launched in the winter of 1943.

Although the raid did not do major lasting damage to Ruhr industry, disruption could have been compounded by continued conventional attacks as the Germans struggled to rebuild. But Harris's intransigence ensured there was no follow-up and the initial success was unexploited.

Thus, contrary to the impression created by propaganda and the post-war film and books, the Dams Raid was a curiously inconclusive military event.

… In his memoir Enemy Coast Ahead, written not long before his death in September 1944, Gibson described his unease about the breaching of the Möhne dam which left 1,400 civilians dead. "The fact that they might drown had not occurred to us… Nobody liked mass slaughter, and we did not like being the authors of it. Besides, it brought us in line with Himmler and his boys." None of his superior officers showed such feelings.

This is a fine book combining great storytelling with a deep appreciation of the melancholy and waste that march in step with glory."

Much time has passed since World War II but the disingenuous and misguided propaganda persists.

British Carrier Power success has not been acknowledged or celebrated publicly by the Royal Navy. As a result, the public and many politicians have very little maritime awareness and the RAF has taken full advantage.

WHITEHALL AND "THE ENEMY WITHIN".

The story of Naval Service decline began in earnest in the 60's when false Air Staff claims of a global air defence capability were believed by Ministers and were inadequately countered by a Naval Staff that wrongly believed that they understood internal Whitehall politics. They seriously underestimated the persuasive if misguided influence of the well-prepared Air Staff whose lack of candour was brilliantly disguised by spin – and supported by sponsored, well-trained/brainwashed Air Power Academics.

It is probable that the Naval Staff believed that the unquestionable success of the Fleet in World War II and in subsequent conflicts/interventions (as iterated at Annex C) would be remembered by the public and our politicians – and that any associated PR initiative was unnecessary. In the face of a growing tsunami of RAF propaganda this was a grave error of judgement.

The events following the Falklands War confirmed this.

As the then First Sea Lord, Admiral Sir Henry Leach proclaimed, the Falklands Conflict victory could not have been achieved without the air war being won by a small number of Naval Sea Harrier fighter aircraft flying from HMS Invincible and HMS Hermes against great odds.

Even the Battle of Britain Association was persuaded to send the following signal to my Squadron, 801 Naval Air Squadron in Invincible, just after the Argentine surrender:

"From the Few to the Very Few. Congratulations on a job well done."

Maggie Thatcher and the British public basked in the aftermath of this success. Britain's military reputation and standing around the world was enhanced. But what was Their Lordships' response to the Fleet Air Arm success and to the limited contribution of the RAF?

It was a resounding silence that has echoed through the corridors of power ever since.

When the victorious Commander of the naval Carrier Battle Group, then Rear-Admiral 'Sandy' Woodward (author of "100 Days"), returned by air to the UK he was met by the Commander-in-Chief Fleet, Admiral Sir John Fieldhouse who–just before becoming First Sea Lord–made clear to Woodward on the tarmac of Brize Norton that the RN should not 'trumpet its Falklands achievement', saying that the victorious naval campaign including its air success should be kept low key: that is to say, played down.

This extraordinary instruction was reinforced when the Commander of the successful Amphibious Task Group, Commodore Mike Clapp CB was not even met when he returned to the UK. In stark contrast, Army Generals stood in line at aircraft steps to welcome home their gallant soldiers. Later and well after the Conflict was over and in true propaganda style, RAF Air Marshals also stood in line to welcome Phantom pilots home whose wives had produced babies in the single month that they were down south. (Where were these Phantoms when we needed them?)

At a much lower level, when I returned home to my Squadron's base at Royal Naval Air Station, Yeovilton, the Station Commander—a helicopter pilot—asked to see me in his office (even though I was not then under his command). The interview was extremely unpleasant. There was no, "Welcome home, Sharkey. Do have a seat." Instead and to my astonishment, the Captain left me standing and berated me saying, "The last thing we all need around here is for cowboy Sea Harrier pilots going around telling everyone how they won the air war down South. Do you understand me?" I left his office completely dumbfounded and wondering what on earth had been going on whilst we were away fighting in the combat theatre.

Much worse was to come. The RAF celebrated their limited front-line contribution to the conflict with vigour. Their numerically superior staff in the Ministry of Defence used their excellent PR team to take the lead in arranging post-Falklands functions. They spread totally misleading propaganda throughout the nation, claiming a significant role in the victory over the Argentinians. Their misguided influence was manifold. The signal, "From the Few to the Very Few" was conveniently forgotten.

For example, the Falklands Memorial Service held in St. Paul's Cathedral was organized by the RAF and as a result the congregation was overwhelmed with uniformed RAF personnel – the vast majority of whom had played no active role in the combat theatre during hostilities. Sea Harrier commanding officers and personnel were not even on the invitation list: so my pilots, engineers and I were unable to attend. Commodore Clapp who had commanded the Amphibious Operation and was a Commander Task Group (like Rear-Admiral Woodward, Commander Carrier Battle Group and Major-General Moore, Commander Land Forces) was not invited until late. Luckily, he and his wife were met as they entered by Captain Fox of the Commander in Chief's Staff and a space was found about four rows from the front.

This snub was repeated at almost all other similar events.

It should be noted that there was just one RAF fatality during operations (a fine young helicopter pilot flying from HMS Hermes) – whereas 256 Royal Navy, Merchant Navy, Royal Marine and Army fatalities were suffered.

It was not very long before the nation was persuaded by persistent and arguably disgraceful propaganda that it was the RAF who had won the war over the Islands–despite land force domination and all 25 air-to-air combat victories being achieved by Fleet Air Arm Sea Harriers flying from aircraft carriers HMS Invincible and HMS Hermes–and 450 enemy bombing missions being turned away by low level Sea Harrier combat air patrols.

The level of deceit appeared to know no bounds. Formal celebratory dinners were convened annually to recognise the achievements of the RAF Regiment ground-to-air Rapier Missile Battery. The propaganda machine claimed 23 RAF Rapier kills and yet detailed post-Conflict Ministry of Defence analysis found that there was only one half of one kill credited to the Rapier system and that was achieved by T-33 Army Rapier Battery in defence of the San Carlos Amphibious landings. De facto, the RAF Rapier team did not achieve a single kill.

After the Falklands and before retiring voluntarily from the Service, I was appointed as the Air Warfare Adviser to the First Sea Lord. During this period of intense Air Staff propaganda, a very high-level Naval Staff meeting was arranged to discuss the air war in the Falklands and the future of our Sea Harriers and Invincible class carriers. Attendees were exclusively of Admiral rank or four-ring Captains–except for myself, a Commander.

I sat and listened patiently for about 1 1/2 hours to the views of these recently converted 'experts' in Naval Air Warfare. As the meeting was drawing to a close, I raised my hand.

"Ahh, Sharkey. I thought you would have something to say!" The First Sea Lord chuckled.

"Yes, Sir, indeed I do. I have listened patiently to the many views of this august gathering and I am surprised that nobody has raised the issue of the Royal Air Force. My question to you is this, 'When are you going to start to fight the Naval corner more strongly against their onslaught?'"

There was a stunned silence from all attendees.

First Sea Lord smiled and replied, "Well, Sharkey, as you know I am to become Chief of the Defence Staff in three months and before I take up that post, I don't wish to appear partisan in any way. But thank you for your question". His integrity cannot be questioned.

The Royal Navy remained silent as their Lordships failed to challenge the Air Staff's vigorous attempts to rewrite history.

Amazingly, just one year after the Conflict the RN Presentation Team touring the UK made much of the contribution of surface warships and submarines to the victory but there was not one mention of the fixed wing Fleet Air Arm Sea Harriers winning the air war. This seemed to be an intended omission by a Naval Staff that has proved itself to be generally averse to recognising the history and global importance of strike carrier operations.

From the perspective of the new generation of Fleet Air Arm Air Warfare Instructors/ Top Guns there appeared to be an "Enemy Within".

A moment that I value deeply did occur when Maggie Thatcher publicly announced the six most influential 'names' contributing to victory. I was on that list alongside Sir Sandy Woodward and Maj. Gen. Sir Jeremy Moore. As Mr. Sea Harrier I was very proud of that accolade but it was lost in the noise of the RAF propaganda onslaught.

For the record, my Squadron's contribution to the air victory in the Falklands was summed up as follows:

a. Admiral Sir Sandy Woodward. *"If Sharkey Ward had not disobeyed orders, we would have lost the Falklands War."*

b. Admiral Sir Jeremy Black (Captain of HMS Invincible). *"While everyone on board played a significant role, not least 820 squadron with nine Sea Kings–they flew the equivalent of once around the world often in appalling weather without the loss of an aircraft–it must be 801 Squadron, the Sea Harriers, who take the ship's honours for the campaign. This small body of men, under Lieutenant Commander 'Sharkey' Ward, faced the enemy at close range. They had been reinforced by some aircraft of 899 squadron. They shot down nine aircraft, of which Sharkey shot down three, including a Hercules transport."*

c. Rear-Admiral Derek Reffell, Flag Officer Flotilla 3, who signalled: *"No other ship has contributed so much to the success of the Task Force group operations [as Invincible]."*

By the early 90's and having watched with dismay as the Royal Air Force continued to rewrite history by claiming the air war victory for themselves, I was persuaded to write my book, "Sea Harrier over the Falklands". On publication, it did not fit well with the Ministry of Defence but at no time has it been able to find fault with my narrative of the air war.

Following publication, Admiral Sir Sandy Woodward, Commander of the Carrier Battle Group, wrote me a long letter in which he told me that "it was a pity that we were not serving in the same ship". In the same breath, he firmly criticized just one aspect of my work saying, "the only thing you got wrong, Sharkey, is that you presumed to know what I was thinking". He was quite right and I publicly apologized and revised the content of the book accordingly. During the later 90's, the book was on the required reading list for Staff College students.

As an aside and also in the late 90's, Amazon. com used to grade all the most popular books that they had on sale. The list was split into various categories including Fiction, non-Fiction, Adventure, etc. My book was publicised under Adventure and was graded nine out of ten. In the same listing, Tom Clancy's books were graded eight out of ten. My Pen & Sword editor, Toby Buchan, grandson of John Buchan (The Thirty Nine Steps), told me that "it was the best book of its kind I have ever read!"

When we finally met informally in the late 90's, Sandy and I became great friends and for the next two decades worked together through the medium of many formal and informal papers and direct contact with successive First Sea Lords and Defence Committees trying to right the sinking ship that was the fixed wing Fleet Air Arm and the Naval Service.

In parallel, the RAF continued its aggressive denial of Carrier Task Force success. In 2002, Falklands War anniversary celebrations included a prestigious banquet in London for all those decorated as a result of the Conflict. The event was of course arranged and run by the Royal Air Force–a Wing Commander of the RAF Regiment was organising the dinner. Several 'names' were omitted from the invitation list, Admiral Sir Sandy Woodward, Major-General Julian Thompson, Commodore Mike Clapp and me. Our initiative to try and correct the egregious, misleading propaganda of our land-based Air Force had obviously ruffled feathers.

Correcting the record has proven to be an extremely difficult task and to put it in perspective I feel it pertinent to record the general theme that has emanated recently from Whitehall and the Naval Staff. This is best exemplified by the remarks of First Sea Lord (2009-2013), Admiral Sir Mark Stanhope (a submariner) to the Joint Service Staff College at Shrivenham. He commended our new aircraft carriers as being "perfect for formal cocktail parties and also for carrying amphibious warfare troops and equipment". But he made no mention whatsoever of the future fixed wing air group or of the carriers' offensive and defensive military value for deterrence, power projection and warfighting. Even when Stanhope visited Royal Naval Air Station Culdrose, he never mentioned the Fleet Air Arm but proudly told the astonished ship's company that he had gained some nuclear submarines!

The public understanding of the inherent military value to our maritime nation of having strike carriers available was not enhanced by the appointment of Mrs. Ursula Brennan as the Permanent Secretary to the Ministry of Defence. Her background in the Departments of Health, Social Security and Works and Pensions could hardly be said to fit her well in an appointment where she was accountable to Parliament for the efficient and effective use of our military resources. With no experience of the latter, she found herself to be superior to the Chief of the Defence Staff and appeared to be more interested in gender equality than the fighting efficiency of our Forces: as was amply demonstrated when she appeared before the Public Accounts Committee discussing the role and future of our new carriers. Her given views could be said to mirror those expressed by Sir Mark Stanhope at Shrivenham. Arguably, she had very little grasp of the subject matter. Remarkably, this was at a time when the Secretary of State, the Right Hon. Philip Hammond was publicly declaring that "our new strike carriers are at the heart of our Strategic Defence Policy".

Why has the Royal Navy not embraced the fixed wing Fleet Air Arm more vigorously?

There are some obvious answers to this question as well as less than obvious ones.

 a. The Naval Service has more worldwide commitments than the other two Services combined. The status quo in 2011 exemplified this.

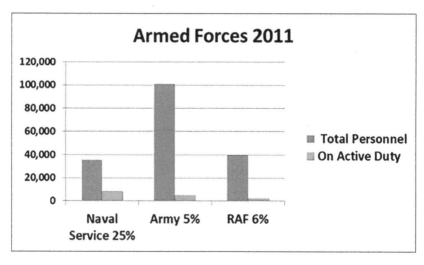

Figure 37. Active Duty ratios.

 b. Fulfilling those commitments and being able to support the defence and protection of our trade routes and overseas interests and the deterrence of those that would harm us requires more than just aircraft carriers.

c. Across the board, the Royal Navy is critically short of ships, submarines and aircraft with which to service its global commitments.

d. The three different factions within the Service (on the surface, under water, in the air) compete for resources. Despite its politically declared strategic importance, the carrier strike/air faction is the smallest in terms of size and influence.

e. As has been suggested by the RAF on many occasions, a large proportion of past Naval Staff Officers did not have in depth knowledge or understanding of naval air warfare and the utility of Carrier Battle Groups. Many of these senior naval officers (and civil servants/politicians) ignored the expertise and proven track record of the fixed wing Fleet Air Arm aviators and instead misguidedly relied on land-based RAF expertise in their decision-making processes. This has directly led to the build of our two new aircraft carriers in a configuration that does not support full Carrier Strike capability.

f. Extrovert personal qualities demonstrated by some true war-fighters (especially fighter pilots) do not gel well with Their Lordships, particularly in peacetime when being 'politically correct' and a 'yes man' is the order of the day. The latter qualities reflect widespread personal ambition within the Service rather than a dedication to war-fighting excellence and have ensured that many individuals have been promoted well above their level of competence as war-fighters and leaders. This has adversely affected the military decision-making process of Naval Staffs and, in turn, has prevented relevant maritime air warfare expertise being available for the guidance of our political masters.

g. Perhaps the biggest shortfall behind the Naval Staff's lack of appreciation for their aviators has been their misplaced belief that naval aviators and Top Guns "do not understand internal Ministry politics". This has led many of them to listen to the spin of the Air Staff and make quid pro quo deals with the latter. In general terms these 'deals' have resulted in the Air Staff getting what they want and the Navy getting nothing. It is not difficult to see who it was that did not understand internal Ministry politics: too many armchair Admirals.

The combination of the above factors has led to a malaise within the Service that has on too many occasions downplayed and/or failed to promote the strategic and tactical importance of fixed wing carrier-borne naval aviation. Notable exceptions to this malaise include Admiral of the Fleet Sir Henry Leach, Admiral Sir Raymond Lygo, Admiral of the Fleet Sir David Benjamin Bathurst, Admiral Sir "Jock" Slater, Admiral Lord West of Spithead, Admiral Sir George Zambellas and Rear-Admiral Linley Middleton.

This malaise appears to have spread to the Fleet Air Arm Museum itself where the proud history of Royal Navy Carrier Battle Groups is not being recorded satisfactorily. Instead, the British public is encouraged to buy books about a lone Vulcan raid on the Falkland Islands that had no material effect on the course of the war and about iconic RAF aircraft from World War II.

There are many Fleet Air Arm Carrier successes that the Royal Navy and the Museum should celebrate, especially those during World War II. These include:

- The disabling/sinking of the Bismark during the Battle of the Atlantic;
- The sinking of the Italian fleet in the Battle of Taranto.

- The Palembang raid that had the dramatic strategic effect of reducing the Japanese oil supply/war effort.

The Museum does not even acknowledge these major victories.

Surely, the Museum should, at minimum, have on display a Roll of Honour listing and celebrating these events/combat operations as well as more recent achievements (Annex C) – and should have books available to emphasise these (not books promoting Royal Air Force propaganda).

Some recommended books are listed at Annex F.

It would appear that something is amiss, to put it mildly. The commendable history of Royal Navy carriers and their embarked/ deployed fixed wing squadrons is being ignored and this is allowing the truly regrettable RAF public relations initiative to rewrite history in its own interest.

Further to the negligence, misinformation and lack of candour that has spread through Whitehall, other major factors that need to be addressed by the Government include:

- Inordinate costs being charged by British Defence Contractors for weapons platforms and weapons systems.
- Irresponsible Defence Contracts which do not demand value for money or a fully functional and effective end-product.
- Ongoing partisan advice provided by the loudest voice.

There needs to be robust and critical Justification of the charges made by the Defence Industry for new weapon systems and for the maintenance of current weapon systems/platforms. Immediate examples of lack of such justification spring to mind:

Frigates and Destroyers.

Direct Comparison–UK v Foreign Warship Costs	
UK Type 45 Daring–Guided Missile Destroyer*	£2 Billion
UK Type 26–Guided Missile Frigate (plus undeclared weapon system costs)	£1,23 Billion
US FFG(X)–new Guided Missile Frigate	£354 Million
French new Frigates	£585 Million

* The initial contract for 12 Daring Class Destroyers was at a declared cost of £12 billion. When the order was reduced to six ships in a government defence cut, we, the public, were informed that the Contractor would still receive the full £12 billion albeit for half the number of ships: i. e. £2 billion per vessel. Recent statements that each warship is costing the UK taxpayer £633 million must therefore be viewed as spin and lacking in candour.

The upkeep of the obsolete Tornado GR4 – more than £7 billion since Harrier withdrawal (figures by the National Audit Office); this is more than the cost of our two new aircraft carriers.

The continuing cost of collaborative Fighter Jet and supporting Aircraft Programs. For example, the Typhoon Fighter cannot be said to be effective in its primary role of defending the UK against the modern Russian threat (see Annex G) – and yet its overall program cost is now estimated to be more than £64 billion to date; possibly approaching £80 billion. This compares very unfavourably with the procurement cost of our two new and operationally flexible Aircraft Carriers at just over £6 billion.

If there is a root cause of the Black Hole in Defence Budget spending, that must surely be the extraordinary procurement costs of all our land-based Fighter Aircraft and their supporting establishments, aircraft and weapon systems. For detailed costs including Typhoon, see Annex J.

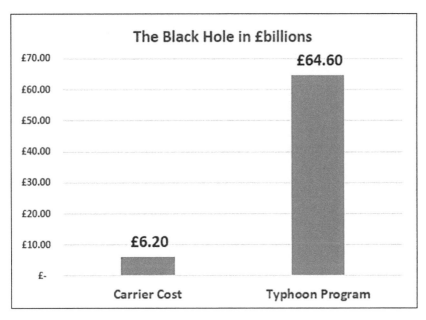

Figure 38. What caused the "Black Hole"?

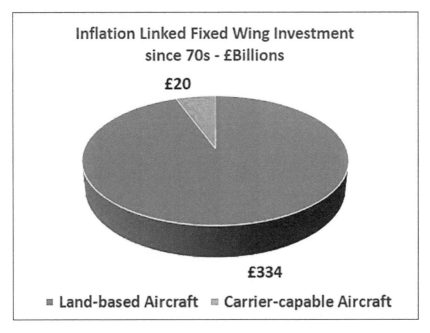

Figure 39. Royal Navy v RAF Investment Ratios.

We now hear a new idea from the retiring Chief of the Air Staff for absorbing large chunks of the defence budget without any chance of a useful return on investment.

He has proposed the development of a hypersonic fighter aircraft capable of up to five times the speed of sound that "would be able to safely penetrate enemy defences as a result of its high-speed". He suggests that such an aircraft would be extremely useful for operations from Cyprus against Syrian targets (mud huts and clapped-out pickup trucks). Does he not know that:

- Such an aircraft would be prohibitively expensive if built in Europe.
- Hypersonic missiles, whether land, sea or air launched would be the much cheaper, more versatile, more cost-effective and operationally effective option.
- Britain's trade, energy supply and overseas interests are global and not just limited to a small section of the eastern Mediterranean.

Current Defence Contractual Procedures have failed to protect the interest of the Armed Forces as end-customers – and the taxpayer. Notably:

- Allowing an arbitrary delay in build to double the cost of each Queen Elizabeth Class aircraft carrier (this extraordinary increase in cost has not been adequately explained or justified).
- Failing to ensure that the carrier Contractor was liable for configuring the carriers with a no-cost option for the fitting of Catapults and Arrestor Gear (as had been agreed in principle).
- If the end-product (e. g. Tornado Variants and Typhoon) doesn't function properly, the end-customer has to pay for fixing it – not the Contractor.

Whilst the size and effectiveness of the Naval Service dwindled, the loudest voice ensured that massive investment in land-based aircraft was achieved. But to what end other than "empire building"? Investment in land-based aircraft since the late 70's has been approximately £350 billion (at today's inflation-linked prices) whereas investment in carrier-based aircraft has been about £20 billion. Even foreign aid receives more funding than the spearhead of our strategic power projection capability.

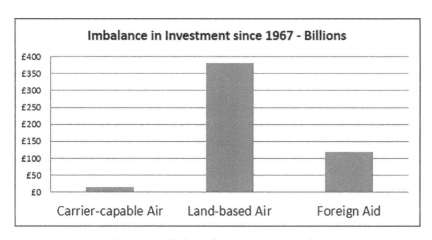

Figure 40. Imbalanced Investment cost us dear.

Yet with all that outlay of scarce Defence Budget funds, what is land-based air doing or what can it do, if anything, to protect our maritime trade transiting the Hormuz Strait? The same question must be asked concerning more distant choke points around the world including the Far East and the South China Sea.

The 2019 stand-off in the Strait of Hormuz has clearly demonstrated that our land-based Air Force cannot intercede to deter Iran or protect our shipping. The stationing of 3 (Fighter) Squadron of Typhoons in the Oman has done absolutely nothing to deter Iranian acts of aggression. For them to be at all effective they need to be conducting visible 24/7 combat air patrols over the Hormuz Strait whenever British merchant shipping is in transit. Even then, it is doubtful whether their limited weapon delivery capability would deter Iranian fast patrol boats from wreaking havoc.

The Chairman of the Defence Select Committee, Dr. Julian Lewis is correct. Britain's Naval Service has not been sustained at sufficient strength to safeguard our global maritime interests or to contribute significantly to those of our allies: too few ships with too few effective defensive weapons. Whitehall and our politicians now need to take the "peace-oriented" blinkers off and make appropriate provision for the protection of our trade and energy supply routes in the Gulf and elsewhere – particularly the South China Sea.

A massive land-based air force that does not have effective, sustainable global reach is not the answer. But, if properly equipped, the Naval Service can and would provide appropriate deterrence and defence of our maritime supply routes; just as it has always successfully accomplished.

This viewpoint sets the theme for what I have to say below: i. e. a relatively detailed exposure of the lies and deceit within Whitehall that have led to the emasculation of the Naval Service and the despair of Her Majesty's Top Guns past and present.

The very tip of the spear of our national capability to project military and political power and influence has been blunted in outrageous fashion.

26

"The Long-Term Plan".

There follows a detailed history of internal Ministry politics, of the "Tornado Mafia" and of misguided weapon system procurement over the last 50 years. It reveals support for a covert Long-Term Plan devised by the Loudest Voice to provide the RAF with a more convincing *raison d'être*.

That our successive Governments and our politicians have totally ignored military history, the tangible return on effective power projection investment in maritime force and, instead, listened to misguided statements/untruths from this Loudest Voice reflects extremely poor judgement and little common sense. This sorry state of affairs has directly resulted in a loss of strategic capability.

The UK has made some seriously bad decisions starting with Denis Healy cancelling the strike carrier replacement program (1967) and placing far too much emphasis on the deployment of the Army and the RAF in Germany where the United States armed forces already had the land-based Cold War threat covered.

The US saw the UK as a significant maritime power partner. They saw the cancellation of the fixed wing carrier replacement as a strategic error of huge proportions. Even after the Falklands, Thatcher failed to learn the key lessons regarding maritime strategy and still did not stop the downward slide of the Naval Service.

The chronology of events is telling.

In the 60s, the RAF could already see that the existence of the Royal Navy Fleet Air Arm and of flexible, globally-mobile UK Aircraft Carrier Strike Power stood in the way of justifying its own expansion – even its very existence. Successful intervention by UK Carrier Battle Groups in offshore crises such as the East African Mutinies 1964 and the Confrontation with Indonesia 1963-66 (see Annex C and D) as well as the ongoing demonstration of US Strike Carrier power off Vietnam left land-based air (other than strategic bombing) mainly powerless and in the shadows. Land-based air has its important functions but does not enjoy the freedom of the seas and the associated flexibility of rapid response.

Our Carriers therefore became priority 'targets' of the RAF. As it stands, the Long-Term Plan has been a successful one for the most part – but at major cost, financially and operationally.

I have monitored the progress of this Plan closely from inside and outside Whitehall (with the notable assistance and support of Admiral Sir Sandy Woodward and others) and I feel it is my duty to share my findings. Who else has the moral fibre to speak out? Very few, it would appear.

The Plan thrives on propaganda and is based on misinformation and deception.

In the briefest of terms, the chronological progress and key elements of the Plan have been as follows:

- Through misinformation and deception contrive the unwarranted demise of UK's Strike Carrier capability (beginning with the Healey carrier decision of 1967).

- Provide strong opposition to the introduction of the Invincible Class Harrier Carrier in the 70's (failed).
- Limit the size and scope of the Fleet Air Arm Sea Harrier Program–despite the fact that this small group of fighter aircraft provided victory in the air war over the Falkland Islands, 1982 in coordination with our surface warships.
- Claim against all demonstrable fact and logic that the RAF won the air war in the Falklands.
- Ignore and hide from the government and the public the costly operational failure of the collaborative Tornado Program.
- Use questionable Cold War arguments to gain approval for the equally costly Typhoon Program that has yet to demonstrate any realistic global Fleet Defence capability.
- Strongly oppose the UK's new Queen Elizabeth strike carrier program and, when the latter was approved, contrive:
  - The withdrawal from service of the Fleet Air Arm Sea Harrier,
  - The withdrawal from service of the carrier-capable Harrier GR7 and GR9,
  - The withdrawal from service of the Invincible Class carriers,
  - The delay in build and associated increase in cost of the new carriers,
  - The choice of flight deck configuration for the new carriers that inhibits true Strike Carrier capability–limiting the carrier Air Group to the relatively short-range F-35B STOVL Lightning II aircraft,
  - The planned joint embarkation of RAF and Naval F-35 squadrons in the new carriers and the take-over of Administrative Authority for all the Naval and RAF fast jet squadrons.
- Propose a new collaborative land-based Typhoon successor, the Tempest, to be realised by 2050, if approved.

Regular Strategic Defence Reviews have already stated unequiv-ocally that "air supremacy and air defence... is essential" for Expeditionary/Joint Task Force operations. Formal Review Policy requires rapidly deployable First Echelon forces "without pre-po-sitioning" [i. e. Maritime]. One of the principal reasons that we have carriers with an establishment of fixed wing fighters is that the Fleet has never been able to rely on "air defence by UK air-craft operating from ashore".

The consequence of the Long-Term Plan which pays little regard to the declared Strategic Defence Priority is now in sight. That is for the RAF to be able to suggest quite misguidedly that, to all intents and purposes, they have replaced the first echelon Fleet Air Arm's proven power projection capability with their own.

The very serious problems with this from a UK Defence and Security point of view are that:

- Since World War II land-based air has contributed little to the global projection of UK power and influence out-side the NATO-Europe area and has no experience of guarding the realm's maritime interests further offshore on a 24/7 basis.
- Thanks to the Plan, our new carriers do not have the nec-essary full Carrier Strike capability – as required by the Government's Strategic Policy;
- RAF personnel do not like going to sea and being away from home. They are used to a 9 to 5 weekends-off service environment which does not obtain at sea – and yet they own all our F-35B Lightning carrier-capable aircraft;
- The RAF has shown over the last 40 years that it is unwilling to commit aircraft into combat unless their survival is ensured either by third parties or through the medium of the substantial Defence Suppression of enemy air defence capabilities. Desert Storm, Iraq, 1991 was an

exception that proved the rule (see Chapter 28, "Tornado's In-Service Effectiveness").

- Our new carriers cannot embark such Defence Suppression capability because of the misguided flight deck configuration.

As you read on you will become aware of the many regrettable mistakes that have been made by successive Governments at the behest of the Loudest Voice. This is a problem that continues to develop.

The sustained campaign by land-based air aficionados against carrier air power has had the knock-on effect of reducing Government understanding and awareness of the continuing need for a robust fleet of surface warships and submarines.

27

THE LOUDEST VOICE AND THE UNPRODUCTIVE 'WAR OF WORDS'.

The expression, "The Pen is Mightier than the Sword" has proven to be correct regarding the inter-Service rivalries that have always occurred within our Whitehall Institutions. The Loudest Voice with the most flannel has held sway with politicians despite demonstrated incompetence and/or misrepresentation of capability.

In the modern era and since the 60's, the Loudest Voice has been that of the RAF. To their credit, they have achieved this first by recognising the important influence that Defence Staffs have with Ministers and, as a result, have placed a large number of Staff Officers within Whitehall, greatly outnumbering sister Services. Secondly, they have supported the strong growth of the number of Land-Based-Air-Power Academics within Whitehall circles where they have enormous influence at the highest levels, including the Cabinet Offices and Downing Street. The other two Services have been left behind and are suffering the consequences.

This has been compounded by the fact that during the last century Britain has experienced three phases of prolonged peace, leading to an extraordinary inability to recognise latent military threats to National Security during peacetime: Between the two World

Wars; Between World War II and the Falklands War, 1982; Since the end of the Cold War and the consequent Military Stagnation.

During these periods of peace, military reality and the expertise of proven war-fighters has been far too often ignored. The war-fighters will always justify spending on themselves and their like against perceived threats. But politicians and their civil servants must inevitably assess budget priorities, given peace prevailing, and engage in the ever-unpopular task of pruning.

The precise pruning of vital military assets has depended upon the ability of individual Services to fight their corner and the RAF were best prepared to do this. Through their own initiative, they do indeed have the Loudest Voice and have used it to the full to their own advantage.

28

THE FIRST
'MAJOR UNTRUTH'.

D uring the last ten years of the Cold War when Western
Europe and the USA lived under the threat of massive
Soviet conventional and nuclear attack, the people of the United
Kingdom trusted in the operational capability of the Royal Air
Force to protect the homeland base from air attack. Had war
broken out, regiments of Soviet Backfires, Blinders, Badgers and
Bears were poised to strike at the UK and its allies from the North
East and, in the uneasy peace, they regularly practiced doing so.
It is now understood that these attacks would have been conven-
tional rather than nuclear in nature.

According to ex-First Sea Lord, Admiral Lord Alan West, in the
Daily Mail of 13 November 2019, and since the collapse of the
Soviet Union, Britain's military planners have had absolute proof
of the effectiveness of our nuclear shield. Declassified plans
for a Soviet strike against Western Europe showed the Kremlin
was willing to use so-called 'tactical nuclear bombing' against
Germany, Holland and Belgium. According to the Supreme Allied
Commander Europe, the only land-based tactical air resources
available to him after 12 hours of such Soviet aggression would
have been a small number of Ground Attack Harriers operating
from unprepared dispersed sites.

But Lord West notes that the USSR was not prepared to fire nuclear missiles at France or Britain — because we had the power to strike back. Hence the massive conventional maritime Soviet offensive that was to be unleashed around the North Cape. There could be no more vivid illustration of how important it is for the UK to keep Trident.

With that background, the serious questions that I shall address are: Were the British public, Parliament and Britain's military partners right to place their trust in the ability of land-based military aircraft to oppose the Soviet threat? Could they sleep easy in their beds at night, knowing that they were indeed protected? They were told repeatedly by the UK Ministry of Defence Air Staff that the RAF was indeed capable of doing the job.

The true facts surrounding this matter of fundamental National/ NATO Security paint a very disturbing picture. It is a story of deception and inter-service jealousy that placed the United Kingdom in peril – and continues to do so today.

It is arguable that the fundamental causative factor for this deception lay in the remarks made long ago by Marshal of the Royal Air Force, Lord Trenchard, fondly referred to as the father of the RAF. When he heard about the possibility of a third new Service, Trenchard's first view was:

"a service beyond control of the Army and Navy would be very liable to lose its sense of proportion and be drawn towards the spectacular"

Trenchard predicted that, in the future, there would be no place for an independent Air Force. Instead it would be subsumed/amalgamated into the Army and the Navy who would direct their operations more efficiently by having full control over all supporting weapon systems.

This extraordinarily logical prediction struck fear into the hearts of Air Staff members in the UK Air Ministry and later the Ministry of Defence. By the late sixties this fear had reached the stage of paranoia. The underlying reason for this was the demonstrated lack of utility and efficiency of UK land-based aircraft in almost all crises, conflicts and deterrence operations since the end of World War II. It was sea-based tactical aviation that provided the nation's overall conventional deterrent capability. On many occasions no other form of intervention was initially possible.

To hide their general inability to respond to these crises, the RAF still revelled in the achievements of the Battle of Britain. They created an Air Staff and a Public Relations (PR) machine that continually reminds politicians and the public of that World War II event. Let us put it into context.

Notwithstanding the success of Air Force and of Naval and Commonwealth pilots over the Luftwaffe during the Battle of Britain, the war against the Third Reich was won principally on the land and at sea. The indiscriminate aerial bombardment of Germany by the RAF killed hundreds of thousands of civilians but did little to thwart the Third Reich's ability to fight back. It was the Allied Land Forces that secured final victory in mainland Europe and the Royal Navy that predominated in the Battle of the Atlantic.

Fully aware of all this, in 1967 the Air Staff had reached the point where they were willing to distort the truth to ensure their Service's future and sadly these untruths were believed by the Whitehall political establishment. To secure their position even more strongly, they introduced the term, "the indivisibility of air power" and through the widespread use of this meaningless phrase they convinced Ministers that it was their word on Air Warfare matters that should be listened to – not that of the more combat-experienced Royal Navy Fleet Air Arm and the Army Air Corps.

The subsequent Healey Carrier Decision of the late sixties did, to all intents and purposes, sound the death knell of the Royal Navy's Fixed Wing Fleet Air Arm. Despite the latter's proven utility and success, the Air Staff managed to convince Ministers that the RAF, rather than the Fleet Air Arm, could and should defend the Fleet at sea and British Interests in any part of the world.

Unfortunately for Britain, the Air Staff then totally ignored the long-established principle of *PACTA SUNT SERVANDA* ("agreements must be kept") and our Civil Servants and Politicians failed to demand a militarily sound justification of this claim. They trusted but did not verify.

This was the first Major Untruth.

No demonstration or recorded details of this promised capability were provided, such as the positioning of fighters overhead the Fleet for 24 hours a day. Instead an intentionally inaccurate, "modified" map of the world was used to show Ministers how the radius of action of a single land-based fighter supported by Air-to-Air Refuelling Tankers could reach the furthest point in any ocean in which the Fleet might be at risk. There was a problem, however. This was that the airbases in Australia were too far East for complete coverage of the Indian Ocean. So the Air Staff had a special map drawn up in which Australia was moved several hundred miles to the West. This was essential to their argument if they were to be able to convince gullible Ministers that the RAF could do the job.

Despite all common sense, basic physics, aerodynamics and mathematics (even a simpleton could see that during hostilities an air attack on the Fleet could happen at any time – when the land-based fighters were still ashore and many hours away from the Fleet), Ministers swallowed the lie. The RAF had said they could do the job. "We are the RAF. We are the experts in air warfare.

293

We do what we say we can do. "To divert attention away from Trenchard's prediction, they had succeeded in setting up the Royal Navy's Fixed Wing Fleet Air Arm as a sacrificial lamb. The fateful decision was made. Britain's aircraft carriers were to be withdrawn from service and the land-based Air Force would defend the Fleet and our overseas interests in their place.

How was this allowed to happen and why?

The simple answer is clear. The Naval Staff did not fight its corner adequately. Why? The antipathy of many Seaman desk officers towards aviators appears to have clouded the corporate judgment and initiative of the Naval Staff. I am quite certain that the experienced aviators in the Directorate of Naval Air Warfare (DNAW) presented papers in the late sixties that firmly demonstrated how fallacious and ridiculous was the RAF claim. I am equally certain that the other 5 Directorates in the Naval Staff refused to pass those papers upwards to Ministerial Level–shamefully, they believed the unjustifiable and far-fetched statements of the RAF rather than the more experienced and logical naval air warfare advice of their own Fleet Air Arm. Not for the last time, their Lordships shot themselves in the foot.

A stark reminder of the impotence of land-based air was presented in 1972. A show of strength by Buccaneers from HMS Ark Royal prevented a threatened invasion of British Honduras (Belize) by Guatemala. Land-based air was too far away and could do nothing to defend the UK interest.

But it was almost too late. In 1977, the last of the UK's conventional aircraft carriers, HMS Ark Royal, was decommissioned. The globally deployed Fleet at sea, our trade routes, energy supplies and UK's Overseas Territories were now to be protected by land-based air.

Then in the 70's and with the Cold War at its height, the Naval Air Staff managed to make it clear to Ministers that without its own carrier-borne All-Weather Fighters as a first line of air defence, the Fleet could do nothing to deter the approach of Soviet Reconnaissance aircraft such as the Bear towards UK airspace from the north-east. These were the aircraft used to locate and target British and Allied naval forces standing in the way of major Soviet air strikes. The RAF had already failed to demonstrate the ability to carry out this simple, relatively short-range task. These aircraft could now shadow the Fleet closely in peacetime or in tension without fear of retribution. The Soviets could keep an updated track of the Fleet and then strike at their pleasure.

Since the Healey decision, land-based fighters had never been seen in strength, or even as a token gesture, over the Fleet as promised by the Air Staff. This serious operational vulnerability convinced Ministers at last of the need for some level of Naval Fighter capability. It was agreed that the Sea Harrier should be procured for the sole task of neutralising Soviet shadowing aircraft.

Although the Healey Carrier Decision had decimated the rounded capabilities of the then Fixed Wing Fleet Air Arm with its Phantom F-4K Fighters, Buccaneer Bombers and Gannet Airborne Early Warning aircraft, the emergence of the Sea Harrier as the new Multi-Role Naval V/STOL (Vertical and Short Take Off and Landing) fighter and much later, of helicopter-borne Airborne Early Warning, gave back to the Fleet a small but important part of its earlier capability.

The Air Staff fought tooth and nail against the 1979 introduction to service of the Sea Harrier and the Invincible Class carriers; but to no avail. The sacrificial lamb had been reborn – at least for a time. However, the RAF continued to insist that they could defend the Fleet at sea and that this was still recognised as their role rather than that of the simple Sea Harrier. Improbable as it may now seem, the Major Untruth continued to be believed; with Ministers ignoring reality and relying totally on the land-based Air Warfare expertise and judgement of the Air Staff.

By the early eighties and after the introduction of the Tornado as the primary land-based RAF Fighter/Interceptor, the First Major Untruth led to a situation which threatened the very survivability of the UK if war did indeed break out against the Warsaw Pact. The absence of land-based fighter support during the South Atlantic Falklands Conflict in 1982 should have signalled a serious message to Ministers – but again, misleading propaganda ruled the day.

I was the MoD/Navy Sea Harrier desk officer in the late seventies when the Air Staff circulated formal Papers to Ministry of Defence Central Committees and to Ministers claiming that "the new Tornado Air Defence Vehicle would be able to mount continuous Combat Air Patrol missions over the Fleet at sea at up to 700 nautical miles from shore, thus providing the Fleet with a viable air defence". It was of note that they no longer claimed a comprehensive global capability, a fact that Ministers discreetly ignored. Nobody in Whitehall asked where these land-based aircraft would operate from in a time of tension East of Suez, in the Asia-Pacific region or in the South Atlantic.

It was part of my job as Sea Harrier Desk Officer in the Directorate of Naval Air Warfare to assess such claims and Papers formally and I drafted an appropriate and very detailed response for approval by the senior Naval Staff.

The message was logical and clear: even with the most unlikely but dedicated support of the whole UK Tanker Force, the Tornado could not provide effective air defence for the fleet even 400 nautical miles from the UK–and probably much less if required to operate from overseas bases. Further, it was clear that any such attempt to support the Fleet's needs would require all the air-to-air refuelling resources that were available and, as such, would completely negate the RAF's ability to provide other fixed-wing air effort (e. g. for defence of the UK mainland) should that too require tanker support.

The senior Naval Staff declined to pass this Paper on to Ministers; declaring that they did not want to rock the boat having just won the Sea Harrier debate. Arguably a major error of judgement.

This omission opened-up the playing field for the Air Staff who had done their work well. There was no critical/expert rationale presented to Ministers concerning the lack of military justification for the projected size and role of the Tornado Program.

The first Tornado Air Defence Vehicle (ADV) was flown in 1979 and subsequently entered service as the Tornado F2. The F2 was replaced by the F3 variant from July 1986. A total of 173 Tornado ADV aircraft were ordered for the RAF at an initial unit cost of £43 million each: £7. 5 billion. In today's money this equates to £40 billion plus an in-life cost of more than £60 billion –including many expensive upgrades. It is relevant that an alternative to the Tornado was an off-the-shelf buy of the F-18 Hornet with twice the capability and at less than half the cost. £50 billion could have been saved.

The upgrade of the F2 to the F3 included stretching the fuselage by 14 inches and the fitting of a new weapons system including replacement of the new Foxhunter Radar, developed by GEC-Marconi, a Company unfamiliar with air-to-air radar. The radar was several years late, 60 percent over-budget and still required successive upgrades to try to give the aircraft any of its required operational capability. In the mid-eighties, the retired Chief of the Air Staff, Air Chief Marshal Sir Keith Williamson, then the military air spokesman for Marconi, appeared on national television and admitted the bad news; that "the Tornado F3 might as well have concrete in its nose instead of the Foxhunter radar". Another upgrade was needed in the 90's and then, in the new millennium, an additional upgrade of the weapon system was found necessary – just to try to make the aircraft weapon system work.

Throughout this chain of events the Air Staff continued to advise Parliament formally that "the Tornado F3 was operational" – another major untruth. It could fly but without a functioning weapon system.

Was this investment worth-while? A look at Tornado's In-Service Effectiveness answers that question.

The Tornado aircraft project began as a collaborative Air Staff Target for a Multi-Role Combat Aircraft (MRCA). The proposed British Aerospace/Panavia design to meet this target could indeed have been a competent air defence fighter. Unfortunately and in addition to the severe radar problems, the partnership with Germany and Italy resulted in the MRCA design being modified to such an extent that the resulting Tornado ADV was smaller in size, had very short range and was much less manoeuvrable than originally planned. It was useless for within visual range air combat/dogfighting – so much so that it became a laughingstock within NATO.

When it entered service at the beginning of the eighties without a functional air-to-air radar it was unable to carry out autonomous interceptions of Soviet aircraft approaching UK airspace nor could it deploy radar-guided missiles against these threat aircraft. It had to rely on visual interception and attack and as such could only be considered a short-range and less than adequate day-fighter at best.

In contrast and although the Sea Harrier FRS (Fighter, Reconnaissance, Strike) Mk. 1 also had a relatively short radius of action, it proved to be a dominant dogfighting vehicle, beating all comers in visual air combat. It's restriction on radius of action was more than compensated for by the mobility and flexibility of the Invincible class aircraft carrier. Further, its small Blue Fox mono-pulse air intercept radar proved to have significant capabilities with contact ranges against Soviet bombers of approximately 80 nautical miles and contact ranges against small surface targets of 100 nautical miles.

As the following anecdote demonstrates, investment in the Sea Harrier provided rapid operational benefits for the Fleet:

> In 1981 HMS Invincible was operating with the powerful U. S. Navy nuclear strike carrier, USS Nimitz well to the north of the UK in exercise Alloy Express. My 801 squadron Sea Harriers were sharing the air defence role with the U. S. Navy F-14 Tomcat (of Top Gun fame). As usual, there was no sign of land-based fighter support from the UK, despite all the promises made to Ministers in Whitehall.

> I had just launched from Invincible for combat air patrol duties when the air defence radars in northern Norway reported a Soviet aircraft rounding the Northern Cape and heading towards our Carrier Battle Group. Invincible Direction Officers immediately advised me:

> "Sharkey. We have trade for you more than 200 miles to the northwest."

> "Roger. I'm on my way!"

> I lost radio contact with the Invincible as I disappeared over the horizon at about 150 miles. It was a strange feeling being alone in a tiny little jet at 35,000 feet, heading towards Arctic waters. But I was concentrating

on my radar and it wasn't long before I detected a firm contact ahead at about 60 nautical miles. The range to the target rapidly diminished and my clever little radar controlled the air intercept. At about 10 miles I became visual with the target and as I closed in, I could see it was a Bear reconnaissance aircraft. As I settled into formation on its wingtip, two Tomcats from the Nimitz arrived and joined me. To my delight and to their astonishment, the Sea Harrier had got there first at 240 nautical miles from Invincible. The American Admiral was most impressed and sent his congratulations to Invincible along with a photograph taken by one of the Tomcats.

Figure 41. Bear Intercept at North Cape.

He praised "the little jet with the big radar". As I returned to the ship, I was a very happy bunny.

At this time, the Cold War against the Soviet Bloc was at its height and the threat of air launched Soviet strikes against the UK mainland and its NATO allies was considered significant. Had the misguided Healey decision not been taken, the UK homeland base would at least have had the benefit of robust carrier-borne fighter

air defence. Now there was no effective land-based fighter protection of UK shores.

Despite all the evidence of the Tornado ADV's operational impotence in the years to come, the Air Staff continued to tell Parliament
that the RAF was capable of defending the Fleet at sea from Soviet
Bloc attack even when it could not even begin to carry out its own
primary task of defending the UK Island Base. Many billions of
pounds had been wasted.

As an aside, had Ministers accepted the Air Staff's apparent wish
to prevent the introduction of the Sea Harrier to Naval Service,
the Falklands Campaign could not have been fought let alone won.

When the Royal Navy Task Force sailed South in 1982 and unbeknown to the public, there was an atmosphere of fear and uncer-
tainty that could be seen in the eyes of almost every officer in my
ship, HMS Invincible. Most were willing to talk about it. The
entirely rational fear was of the Argentine Air Forces and the lat-
ters' overwhelming numerical superiority (200 aircraft) over the
handful of Sea Harriers available to the command (initially 20 aircraft). I was a lone voice in assuring all on board that despite the
odds, my 801 Squadron would be able to protect Task Force Units.
As the world knows, we succeeded but it was a very close call.

Why did it have to be so close a call?

Arguably it was because the UK Naval Staff had not fought the
Fleet Air Arm cause effectively or with genuine spirit during the
Healey Carrier Debate of the sixties.

Inevitably, the RAF proved incapable of providing air defence
fighter support for the Falklands Task Force *en route* South,
during the air war over the Islands or for four months afterwards–
until Port Stanley runway had been extended. Even then it was

courtesy of the ageing Phantom, not the Tornado, that land-based air defence became available from RAF sources – up to then it had been provided by Sea Harriers.

During the Conflict and despite the claims extant in Whitehall that the Tornado aircraft could provide Air Defence of the Fleet any-where in the world, the aircraft was conspicuously absent. Even if the laws of physics and flight endurance had enabled it to reach and to hold CAP over the Task Force, it did not have a working air-to-air radar and, unlike the Sea Harrier, already enjoyed a very poor reputation as a visual air combat fighter[12].

The Falklands air war was won by the Sea Harrier and surface war-ships alone. Tornado played no part. Land-based fighter support for the Fleet did not exist despite all the promises to the contrary.

However, one must note that the land-based RAF Tanker Force and Transport Aircraft did indeed play a recognisable role in the Falklands: supporting long range re-supply flights from Ascension Island with converted RAF Hercules aircraft – mainly after the cessation of hostilities. They also supported three long range, bomb delivery missions (dropping 21x1000lb bombs per mis-sion) and four anti-radar missile delivery missions by the Vulcan bomber (using the Shrike Anti-Radar Missile).

But these Vulcan attack missions, code word "Black Buck" depended upon:

•   Commander-in-Chief Fleet agreeing to a shameful Task Force "Weapons Tight" policy whenever the lone Vulcan

---

[12] The Tornado F2 entered service at the same time as the Sea Harrier FRS Mk1 (1979). Thanks to MoD(UK)Navy the Sea Harrier Project was on cost and on time. By 1982, the Sea Harrier was an effective weapons platform with an international reputation as a superb visual air combat vehicle. This was not so with the Tornado.

was over the target area. The RAF insisted on this policy – without it, the Vulcan would not have been deployed South of Ascension. This policy left the Task Force open to enemy attack during "Weapons Tight" periods.

• Sea Harriers providing the Vulcan with Fighter escort over the target area and activating ground-based enemy radars during Shrike anti-radar attack missions. Again, the RAF insisted on this policy as a prerequisite for the flights taking place.

In other words, without the presence of effective carrier-borne fighter cover over the target area none of these missions would have taken place.

Ascension lies approximately 3500 nautical miles from Port Stanley. The Air Staff calculated that in order to enable one Vulcan bomber to reach its target, a force of 10 to 15 Victor Air Refuelling Tankers would be needed. Vulcans and Victors were therefore flown down to Ascension and made ready for the initial attack on first of May 1982.

The RAF knew that they would need more than one mission to be sure to interdict the airfield runway. Their own estimates of the mission numbers required ranged from 3 to 25. However, it was soon clear that only one Vulcan at a time could be 'tanked' all the way to and from the target. This basic limitation severely reduced the justification and probability of success of this mission. The fact that it went ahead at all must, with hindsight, lead to a not unreasonable conclusion that the RAF wanted to become involved in Operation Corporate combat operations at any cost and initially this was their only means of doing so. They were clutching at straws.

The excellent book, "Vulcan 607" by Rowland White describes in great detail how two obsolete Vulcan bombers were modified and prepared for the Black Buck missions from Ascension. It was a mammoth effort to get the RAF into "the game". But post-war propaganda was diligently employed to claim that the only bomb on target on the side of the runway prevented enemy air operations from the airfield. This was a false claim. Just hours after the bomb was delivered, I was airborne on combat air patrol and intercepted three Mentor aircraft en route from Port Stanley to attack one of our anti-submarine frigates to the North of the airfield. I damaged one with cannon fire in cloud and then all three jettisoned their weapons and fled back to the airfield.

The suggestion that a Vulcan mission could have been used to attack Argentine mainland airfields beggars belief. There would have been no Weapons Tight policy and no fighter cover as demanded for the Black Buck raids.

It is a fact that 21 x 1000-pound bombs could have been delivered by just 5 Sea Harriers from the Task Force – and probably more accurately. The comparative fuel costs are instructive. The actual fuel cost of the first Vulcan sortie was approximately as given in Table 1 below.

Table 1. The cost in fuel of the first Black Buck mission.

First Vulcan Mission	No.	No. Tankers per mission	Give Away Gallons/ Tanker	Total Give away fuel gallons	Cost/ gallon	Total
	1	13	10,000	130,000	£4	**£520,000**

Details of conservative fuel cost estimates for all the Black Buck missions are given at Annex H. The 'bottom line' from this Annex shows:

Fuel cost per weapon delivered by the Vulcan from Ascension   £137,000

Fuel costs of each of only two[13] Vulcan weapons 'on target'   £4.7 Million

Fuel cost per bomb delivered by Sea Harrier from a carrier   £400

Table 2, below, demonstrates that the Black Buck Operation consumed more than twice the amount of fuel needed to support the 1500 combat missions flown by the Sea Harrier during the confrontation (average fuel consumption per Sea Harrier sortie was less than 750 gallons.).

Table 2. Fuel consumption Corporate – Black Buck and Sea Harrier.

	gallons
Black Buck–Total Fuel Spent (7 missions)	2,335,000
Sea Harrier Fuel–Total war consumption (1500 missions)	1,125,000

It is not unreasonable to ask:

• In the future, will the RAF place similar constraints on Task Force self-defence before deploying land-based RAF aircraft e. g. Air Refuelling Tankers in support of Queen Elizabeth Aircraft Carriers on Joint Task Force (JTF) operational missions?
• Was the achievement of one bomb on the side of the runway at Port Stanley out of 63 dropped a cost-effective result of these Vulcan missions and could this be classed

[13] One Bomb and one Shrike anti-radar missile.

305

as effective offensive support by Joint Task Force (JTF) Operations Out-of-Area?
- With such an insignificant combat air contribution to the Conflict how could the RAF go on to claim that they won the air war in the Falklands?

By the time the Kuwait crisis Desert Storm arose in 1991, attempts to provide the Tornado F3 with a working Beyond Visual Range[14] weapon system had been to no avail. The F3 was deployed from Saudi Arabia on Combat Air Patrol over the safe waters of the Arabian Gulf during the crisis but could not be committed to action over land against Iraqi fighters because it did not have a fully working weapon system. Further, the F3 airframe was limited in aerodynamic performance when configured in a war role and would have been unable to climb high or quickly enough to reach the anticipated threat aircraft. Operationally ineffective, it was kept in the rear by 'Stormin Norman Schwarzkopf', well clear of any action. This did not prevent F3 aircrew from receiving medals in the associated Honours List. More propaganda.

After Kuwait, the F3 was fitted at major expense to carry the AIM-120 AMRAAM missile. The updated F3 air-to-air radar was however not compatible with the missile. The radar could not "talk" to the missile to give it initial target information or to update the missile in flight to guide it towards the target during Beyond Visual Range firings. So the air force claimed that the missile was clever enough to be fired without radar guidance by just pointing it in the direction of a long-range threat. The demonstration of this reversionary bore-sight capability nearly had tragic results. When the missile was fired from the Tornado, the missile-head

---

[14] A Beyond Visual Range weapon system allows the fighter to engage enemy aircraft at long range, by day and night and in all weather. It is essential for the interception and destruction of incoming waves of enemy bombers and their escorts.

active radar side-lobes immediately locked on to the nearest target which happened to be an accompanying Tornado. The latter only escaped destruction because the very short-range turning circle of the intercept was too tight for the missile's aerodynamic design capability. No more bore-sight firings took place.

A further expensive improvement project was then approved to provide the F3 with a limited link between the radar and the AMRAAM. This might have enabled the F3 to conduct some all-weather Beyond Visual Range firings albeit with a lower probability of kill than other fully integrated systems.

The 147 Tornado ADV/F2/F3 had been procured at great expense to fulfil the need for the robust All-Weather Air Defence of the United Kingdom. Since its first entry into service and despite many costly upgrades it proved to be incapable of fulfilling this need. Nor had it ever been able to demonstrate or practice its vaunted capability in defence of the Fleet at sea or in defence of Task Force Operations world-wide.

The far from illustrious early days and in-service life of the F3 have been mirrored by the Ground Attack and Reconnaissance variant of the aircraft – the GR1/4. Its performance history and cost has also been shrouded in smoke, secrecy and unacceptable propaganda.

In the 70's, 138 Tornado GR (Ground Attack and Reconnaissance) aircraft were approved and then procured to carry out the role of low-level nuclear strikes against Warsaw Pact targets; specifically, military airfields and naval installations. During design and development of both Tornado variants, our European collaborative partners insisted upon a smaller aircraft than originally envisaged resulting in a much shorter fuselage–rather than conducting a professional redesign of the whole aircraft. The impact of this modification was highly detrimental to the air combat manoeuvrability and radius of action of both variants. The latter shortfall was to become another standing joke within other NATO air forces.

Further to fitting the Tornado Air Defence Vehicle with a radar and weapon system that did not work and that could not fulfil the operational requirement, the GR variant was initially built with completely different front and back-seat computer languages – so that the associated weapon control systems which were built by different Companies could not talk to each other. Major costs and delays were incurred remedying this extraordinary display of collaborative management incompetence.

Further Tornado delays, accidents and costs caused more embarrassment. During early service it was found that if the aircraft flew close to a strong radar emitter at low level, electronic interference with the engine computer control system resulted in the engines overheating and disintegrating causing the loss of the aircraft. Presumably, there had been no faraday-cage built in to protect such vulnerable systems. The Soviets made no such mistake with their jets. This did not bode well for low-level nuclear missions over Warsaw Pact territory.

Worse was yet to come.

In parallel with the decision to procure this aircraft, Ministers were persuaded to approve a Runway Denial Weapon, the JP233, at a staggering development cost of approximately £10 billion–100 times the cost of the initial Sea Harrier procurement. This weapon was to be deployed at high speed and very low level over Soviet airfield targets by day and night to crater a runway and make it unusable by enemy aircraft.

During the approval process I was still serving in the Directorate of Naval Air Warfare and wrote an official paper condemning the proposed way ahead. The essence of this paper was as follows:

- The military logic behind this aircraft/weapon program could not be justified;
- The low-level attack range of this weapons platform (Tornado) was so short that it could not even reach targets in Poland from West Germany without air-to-air refuelling;
- The Soviets had concentrated effective surface-to-air weapon systems all the way along its border with NATO at less than 100 metre intervals;
- In the face of such defences it was inconceivable that Tornado GR aircraft could safely refuel at low-level by day or night over Warsaw Pact territory from air-refuelling tankers at operational speeds of less than 250 knots–and without such tanking, they could not reach their targets.

Such military logic could not be challenged with factual argument and so the Armchair Air Marshals reverted to their only persuasive line with Ministers: "We are the Royal Air Force. We are the air power experts. If we say that we can do this, then we can!" This was utter nonsense and totally unjustifiable.

But the line deceived Ministers and was not contested by senior Naval Staff officers; many of whom trusted the word of the RAF over their own naval aviators.

Royal Navy Fleet Air Arm expertise and advice had been ignored as usual and this came home to roost in a serious way during Operation Desert Storm. The GR1 aircraft was deployed to Kuwait to assist in the interdiction of Iraqi military airfields where the air defences were minimal compared with the Soviet Front. Approximately 24 of these Tornado GR aircraft were deployed to the combat theatre and very quickly eight were lost, mostly during low-level JP233 attacks on airfields.

An internal RAF investigation following Desert Storm found that only one of these eight losses was directly attributable to enemy fire. Six were attributed to unfamiliarity with the runway denial weapon and, separately, one to the flawed delivery at high level of a 'stick' of conventional high explosive bombs.

JP233 consisted of a very large and heavy canister that was carried under and flush with the aircraft fuselage. On weapon release by the aircrew at high speed and low level the whole canister was ejected downwards with small explosive cartridges. The many runway-cratering munitions inside were then dispersed along the runway before the canister hit the ground. Because of the very high cost of the weapon, the Tornado GR aircrew had not been allowed to do live firing exercises and this unfamiliarity produced aircraft handling problems that they mistook for the impact of enemy fire from the ground.

Weapon release was accompanied by a loud bang as the canister was ejected and at the same time the aircraft experienced major 'g' forces as the trim of the aircraft was radically changed – leading to a fierce upward rotation of the nose. Bearing in mind that this all took place at night over enemy territory one can understand what happened next. The aircrew became disorientated and believed they had been 'hit'. Thinking they had lost control of the aircraft and being at very low level, they ejected: the aircraft was lost and, at best, they were taken prisoner. One cannot blame the aircrew. They performed with great courage despite misguided Air Staff professional incompetence.

This was not the end of Tornado's weapon delivery problems. The Ministry having decided that the runway denial weapon delivery profile was suicidal, as suggested by the Directorate of Naval Air Warfare in the late 70's but ignored, the aircraft were then tasked with high level conventional iron bomb delivery – hoping to hit unseen targets in the featureless desert below with a 'stick' of about 6 Variable Time (VT) Fused bombs. These were all released by one press of the firing button but came off the aircraft at micro-second intervals so that weapon detonation over the target area would be spread out.

Sadly, it appears that these much-vaunted armchair experts in air warfare did not have their act together once again. When leaving the aircraft, the Variable Time fused bomb has a Safe Arm Device which prevents the bomb proximity-fuse from arming (going live) until it is well clear of the aircraft. When dropping a stick of bombs this interval needs to be increased substantially. If this is not done there is a danger of one bomb detecting the presence of the next bomb in line leading to the detonation of each bomb in turn with the last bomb exploding near the aircraft – known as the 'ladder effect'. That is precisely what caused the loss of one Tornado over Iraq.

Desert Storm was the first and only time that the Tornado GR has been tasked to conduct low-level direct attacks against targets that were defended by surface-to-air guns and missiles. It was a disaster and mainly due to the misleading advice given to Ministers during the procurement decision process.

How much did the GR 1/4 cost the taxpayer? Brief figures of declared and estimated costs are as follows.

Tornado GR 1/4 Costs.	
1979	
Initial Unit Cost 1979.	£37. 2 Million
Fleet of 147 aircraft.	£5. 5 Billion
Estimated In service Cost*.	£11 Billion
JP 233 Development Costs.	£10 Billion
Total	**£26. 5 Billion**

In today's Money (inflation linked Cost).	£144. 5 Billion
Without JP 233	£90 Billion
*Plus many aircraft/weapon system upgrades	

The 1990's heralded the approval of the upgrade of the GR1 to the GR4 Tornado in which the aircraft, designed initially for very low-level flight and attack, was converted to give it two new roles: a Close Air Support capability and a medium to high level Stand-Off capability (releasing weapons at some distance from the target). The multibillion pounds sterling JP 233 weapon system was unceremoniously discarded.

Over the next 13 years, more than 100 GR1s were extensively modified[15] at a cost of billions; the first GR4 flight taking place in April 1997. Much of this expenditure proved to be totally wasted – not resulting in any adequate operational return.

Despite the major cost and many publicity-garnishing, largely symbolic deployments of small numbers of aircraft, the Tornado Ground Attack and Reconnaissance aircraft has achieved very little in terms of the effective projection of British military power and political influence.

What they have achieved operationally is the destruction of many dilapidated pick-up trucks, mud huts and a few Jihadis. It represents an interesting bang for the buck equation–£1. 4 billion over Libya, about £4 billion over Syria/Iraq and heaven-knows how much in Afghanistan where they flew extended missions at high level but refused/were unable to react to urgent calls from

---

[15] The upgrades included Forward Looking Infra-Red (FLIR), wide angle Head Up Display (HUD), improved cockpit displays, Night Vision Goggles (NVG), new avionics including GPS and new weapons and sensors including the Storm Shadow cruise missile, the Brimstone air-to-ground missile, the Paveway III laser-guided bomb and Communications equipments.

ground forces for rapid Close Air Support: 24 hours-notice was demanded. The forsaken Harrier would respond in Afghanistan with 'wheels off the ground' just 15 minutes after the call for support was received.

The taxpayer may wish to be reminded/informed that when it was decided to send the Tornado GR 4 to Afghanistan, only 30 of the 134 aircraft in service were available for operational deployment and combat operations. The other 104 were sitting in hangars in the UK in various states of disrepair and maintenance.

Little of this tragic Tornado story has been made public within the UK. Nor do UK Government Ministers appear to have grasped that, despite all the misleading claims of the Air Staff, the RAF has been unable to defend the UK base from air attack for decades.

Over the past 20-odd years, Strategic Defence Reviews and Defence Policy Statements have recognised the changing map of possible world-wide threats to our security and economic prosperity.

In sum, the main thrust of this stated Strategic Policy underpins the operational need with

- learning from global operational experience;
- graduated response using easily deployable forces (carrier battle groups) rather than pre-positioning (land-based air);
- rapid and flexible response using military capability that has a qualitative edge.

It should therefore have followed that future UK Task Force operations would continue to be supported by a Carrier Battle Group, with an Amphibious Brigade if appropriate, that together:

- are capable of rapid response to an unexpected threat attack whether in the Strait of Hormuz, the South Atlantic or the South China Sea;
- can defend the Fleet and our merchant shipping from air attack in all-weather by day and by night;
- can project air and ground power ashore to deny an enemy the use of airspace/territory; and
- can deliver effective weapons against targets on the surface or on the ground.

How well did the modern RAF fit with this Policy? Would the Air Staff continue with their opposition to Carrier-based air power?

29

THE SECOND
'MAJOR UNTRUTH'.

I n 2001, the Navy fixed wing All Weather Fighter aircraft was
the Fighter Attack Sea Harrier FA2. According to our US Allies
it was the most capable Air Intercept Fighter aircraft in all of
Europe. It provided the Fleet and associated Task Forces with a
robust first line of air defence and air superiority. But the Air Staff
fought hard for the early withdrawal of Sea Harrier, then Harrier
and the Invincible class carriers from service. The Tornado Mafia
played a leading role in all this.

The term, Tornado Mafia, had been introduced covertly into
Ministry of Defence circles over the past few decades by the Royal
Air Force themselves, not by the Navy or by the Army. Specifically,
RAF personnel used the name to describe the numerical superiority and overwhelming influence of Tornado aircrew within their
single-service community – and in turn, within Whitehall. The
name is apt.

This Tornado team demonstrated to one and all that they were only
interested in the perpetuation of their own organisation, albeit at
a direct cost to global power projection through strike carrier and
other naval investment. They were a closed group: almost entirely
Tornado aficionados. They maintained an internal code of silence
and secrecy, forbidding their members from betraying the inadequacies of their aircraft to the government and to the public/

taxpayer. Such inadequacies and associated remedial costs were conveniently labelled 'Highly Classified' by the Air Staff to hide the truth from the public and from the Government.

In stark contrast to their aircraft's lack of utility as military combatants, they enjoyed an entirely partisan/biased influence with Ministers/Government that does not even start to satisfy the broader defence needs of our nation.

There is justification for deducing that at the turn of the century the Tornado Mafia devised a truly Machiavellian plan to discredit the Sea Harrier FA2: knowing full well that the Naval Staff did not have the resources or street-cred to challenge them. The Directorate of Naval Air Warfare had been dis-established in the early eighties by our Naval Staff masters – a seriously shortsighted decision by non-aviators.

Air Staff representative Air Marshal Sir Jock Stirrup and Minister of State for the Armed Forces, Lord Bach gave witness to the House of Commons Defence Select Committee in May 2002 concerning the planned withdrawal of the Sea Harrier FA2 from Service.

These two witnesses supported each other's misguided statements on actual aircraft capability of which clearly, neither had experience or knowledge. Either that or they intentionally misled the Committee. They denigrated the aircraft's capabilities without any substance to their claims/comments.

For example, although they both testified and agreed that Anti-Ship Sea-skimming Missiles represented the prime threat to our maritime assets, they seriously misled the Committee on this issue:

"Clearly Sea Harrier provided a useful defence against attacking aircraft, but in general terms it offers no protection against sea-skimming missiles

launched from ships, from submarines, from land or from aircraft standing off from distance.... The real issue here is that Sea Harrier does not help against sea-skimming missiles from wherever they are launched."

This was the second Major Untruth.

Sea Harrier FA2 was armed with AMRAAM and the Blue Vixen Radar. The AIM-120B AMRAAM (Advanced Medium Range Air-to-Air Missile) was specifically designed to intercept and destroy very small high-speed targets such as Sea-Skimming Missiles at long range – as was the Blue Vixen Radar. US/UK trials results showed emphatically that it did indeed have a very high probability of kill against these target types. It was arguably the most capable airborne anti-sea-skimming missile weapon system in the world.

As a result of this false high-level testimony to the Committee, the decision announced at the beginning of March 2002 by UK Armed Forces Minister Adam Ingram to phase out Sea Harrier FA2 by 2006 without replacement was confirmed. It made a mockery of all previous Strategic Defence Reviews, Defence Policy Statements and Joint Service Agreements.

The Naval Service is unique in its role of providing and defending Fleet/Joint Task Force operations for which it requires substantial sub-surface, surface and air weapons platforms at sea – rather than sitting in hangars on UK airfields. Such capability is essential, even when operating against supposedly third world Naval and Air Forces; or in pilotage waters where terrorist actions could threaten the Fleet and merchant shipping e. g. with hijacked aircraft, drones or swarm attacks.

In sharp contrast to the limitations and failings of UK land-based fighter aircraft programs and following its crucial air combat successes in the Falklands, ("Without the Sea Harrier, we would have lost the War" – Sir Henry Leach, First Sea Lord, 1982), the Sea Harrier served NATO interests with distinction over Iraq, Sierra Leone, Kosovo; sometimes being the only NATO fighter capable of operating in the adverse weather conditions that prevailed. For example, when weather conditions at shore bases in Italy were below limits during the Kosovo crisis, the Air Force units deployed there had no option but to cancel pre-planned operational missions – which were then undertaken by Sea Harriers from a Harrier Carrier.

The introduction to service of the FA2 variant in 1993 had signalled a major improvement in UK capability – which was studiously down-played/ignored by the Air Staff establishment. Its state-of-the-art Blue Vixen Radar coupled with the Beyond Visual Range AMRAAM gave it true All-Weather Fighter status and soon earned it an impressive reputation with our NATO allies during Atlantic Fleet Exercises and Fighter Weapons Meets. In Sierra Leone, the carrier-borne Sea Harrier proved to be the only UK fighter able to support our ground forces ashore with armed reconnaissance missions[16] and arguably provided a strong deterrent to rebel forces on the ground who might otherwise have engaged our own peace-keeping forces more vigorously. It has also made significant contributions to the policing of the No-Fly Zone over Iraq.

It was a multi-role, all-weather weapons system in its own right. It remained the only UK fighter aircraft capable of autonomous and effective all-weather Beyond Visual Range air intercept over land and sea. It responded rapidly to the operational need of

---

[16] The embarked RAF Harrier Squadron refused to fly these missions saying that they were unsure of being able to find their way back to the ship at the end of the sortie.

providing effective embarked air support of Fleet and Task Force units whenever and wherever it was called upon to do so in both exercise and combat and it has proved its value in support of UN ground and air operations. Its relatively low unit procurement cost gave unusual value for money.

Its flexibility of operational deployment would have allowed its effective use also in the air defence of the United Kingdom – unlike land-based air.

Without the embarked Sea Harrier, Fleet and UK Joint Task Force operations would now have to be conducted without proper air defence. And although the Minister had referred to the planned land-based Joint Future Combat Aircraft, Typhoon, being due in service by 2012, this new aircraft was to have no more Fleet Air Defence capability than Tornado.

With no carrier-borne fighter available for more than ten years, hard-earned Fleet Air Arm operational experience has been lost as well.

The Sea Harrier community of the Royal Navy Fixed Wing Fleet Air Arm consisted of a specially selected group of aviators and ground crew who were uniquely capable of meeting the rigorous demands of flying a single-seat, single-engine, multi-role all weather fighter whilst operating in all weathers by day and night from the deck of a ship at sea. The level of expertise within this community was arguably the highest in the UK and this statement is borne out by the track record of the Sea Harrier in peace and war.

Prior to the Sea Harrier entering service in 1979, there had been a gap of just two years since the decommissioning of the last of the UK Conventional Aircraft Carriers, HMS Ark Royal, in 1977. Even in this relatively short period of time, the experience level of the Fixed Wing Fleet Air Arm had been dangerously diluted.

This was noticeable at all levels of Sea Harrier operations and maintenance including pilots, engineers, ship's deck aircraft handlers, armourers, etc. Had the 1977-1979 gap been extended to six or more years, it is probable that the Top Gun expertise which was used to trial the new aircraft and create appropriate operational and safety procedures for it would have disappeared entirely. Further, the Falklands Campaign could not have been mounted.

The reality of this was not lost on the aircrew, engineers and maintenance ratings of the Sea Harrier Community. Having performed with distinction in peace and war throughout the previous twenty-odd years and having protected UK National and NATO Interests abroad with commendable success, this community wished to continue to serve the Nation and its Allies in the same dedicated way.

Flying missions in ground attack Harrier GR7s and 9s did not come close to maintaining the full level of Naval Air Warfare expertise. Although flying and ground crew billets have been generously made available by the USA Carrier community, the overall loss of sea-time and deck experience has rapidly eroded the hard-earned, multi-role, all weather operational expertise that has taken many decades to build. Neither promises nor limited financial inducements have persuaded enough invaluable personnel to stay while they wait 'in limbo' for a new Fixed Wing Fleet Air Arm to emerge.

The cost to the Nation of this loss of special expertise has been immense. Such war-fighting expertise is irreplaceable in the short or medium term. Further, it is highly likely that during any relearning process the cost to the nation could be felt:

- By a lower level of capability to deploy and react successfully to threat situations;

- By a disproportionately high accident and incident rate resulting in the loss of life and the loss of valuable new aircraft.

Britain is now less able to provide a robust defence for Task Force Operations Out-of-Area and this has inevitably led to a diminishment in the Nation's ability to support NATO or to wield global military power and political influence.

Following withdrawal of the Sea Harrier, the illogical decision to withdraw the Ground Attack Harrier and the fifth HMS Ark Royal from service rather than the obsolete Tornado was also clear evidence of Tornado Mafia influence.

It is understood that against National Security Council advice in the Strategic Defence Review of 2010 which had decided that the Tornado and not the Harrier should be withdrawn from service, our Prime Minister was prevailed upon to reverse this decision at the last minute during a secret meeting at Brize Norton with Tornado Mafia proponent, Sir Jock Stirrup. RAF Brize Norton provided vital support for all Tornado offshore operations and lay in the PM's constituency. Being relatively small and despite having an aircraft with a far better combat record and operational versatility, the voice of the Harrier community was drowned out by the volume of noise and misrepresentation emanating from the Tornado Mafia.

The later appointment of Air Commodore 'Rocky' Rochelle RAF to the position of Head of Carrier Enabled Power Projection was continuing evidence of the Tornado Mafia nepotism and the lack of operational wisdom within Whitehall–as was the appointment of Air Chief Marshal Sir Stuart Peach RAF to Chief of the Defence Staff. Rochelle was a Tornado GR navigator as was Peach, not a pilot: with no experience or expertise whatsoever of Carrier Strike operations and no hands-on expertise of carrier deck landings or naval air warfare. As such he was totally unsuited to and unqualified for leading Carrier Enabled Power Projection. This is a job that should have been, and should still be, filled by a Naval Sea Harrier/Harrier/F-35 qualified pilot with good deck experience.

Not surprisingly, the Tornado Mafia has now been transformed into the Typhoon Mafia. According to the Defence Procurement Agency and supported by Public Accounts Committee estimates of 2011, the land-based Typhoon program was initially expected to have cost the taxpayer at least £35 billion. The program cost now is understood to have reached £80 billion–i. e. more than eight times the cost of the Queen Elizabeth Carrier Project and more than three times the cost of the expected Trident replacement programme.

And what has the taxpayer got for this money? Certainly not global reach.

To date, about 160 Typhoon aircraft have been delivered at a unit life-time cost of £550 million (Hansard). Most of these aircraft require/ undergo expensive modification (some without a matching increase in the aircraft's utility) and only 30 or so are available for/capable of front-line 'multi-role' combat operations[17] at any one time. Tens of £ billions worth of aircraft are sitting unserviceable and non-operational in hangars. (As already experienced with its predecessor, the Tornado.)

It is now understood that the RAF intends to scrap 16 Eurofighter Typhoons as part of a project to save £ 800 million (USD1. 13 billion) on the running cost of the Service's combat aircraft fleet.

---

[17] Things are no better in Germany. A colleague there has pointed out that of the 60 or so Typhoon aircraft in service, only four have been available for front-line combat operations at any one time.

Some of these aircraft are barely 15 years old (the normal lifespan of such aircraft is 30 years plus).

It is extraordinary and bewildering to this taxpayer that some of these airframes have never flown since arriving at RAF Coningsby– one being ZJ940, which was delivered from the factory in 2007 and stripped for parts, having never ventured skyward since.

These plans to dismantle aircraft and harvest spare parts for use on the remainder of the Typhoon fleet were revealed on 29th January 2019 by RAF Air Command at High Wycombe, in Buckinghamshire, in response to a Freedom of Information (FOI) Act request.

The question must therefore be asked, "In contriving this mostly nugatory and extraordinary aircraft expenditure is the Typhoon Mafia completely in bed with the prime aircraft contractor, British Aerospace Systems (BAeS)–swallowing huge sums of taxpayers' money with little effective operational return?"

Despite major Typhoon Program costs, the RAF remains incapable of providing either:

- A viable air defence of the UK or
- Any form of effective, 24/7 air defence of the Fleet or Task Forces at sea at any range beyond 200 miles from mainland bases.

This replacement for the Tornado therefore represents yet another unjustifiably expensive collaborative project.

The Typhoon began life as an air staff requirement (ASR) for what was to be the European Fighter Aircraft (EFA). Although the ASR did initially require a supersonic Short Take Off & Vertical Landing (STOVL) aircraft, the Air Staff were persuaded by their international counterparts that a conventional take off & landing fighter would do. Was part of this compromise a result of the fact that only a STOVL variant could be operated from the deck of a carrier at sea? The Air Staff certainly had already demonstrated that they did not want to leave the door open for the Royal Navy Fleet Air Arm to maintain its independent existence.

The question needs to be asked, "what is the Euro-Fighter/ Typhoon role going to be now that the Cold War has ended and the air threat to the UK mainland base remains questionable?"- Like the Tornado, its sphere of influence as a land-based fighter is quite limited. It cannot be rapidly deployed around the world with the same facility as a Sea Harrier or the Future Joint Combat Aircraft (F-35B) because it cannot operate from aircraft carriers. What then, will be its job – or, indeed, the role of the RAF? It is difficult to see a role that justifies the Typhoon program costs.

You may well be inclined to think that air defence of the UK base is the proper role of the RAF and that the Typhoon fills this role adequately. I would suggest to you that the former is a reasonable assumption but that the latter is dangerously inaccurate.

The Typhoon with an unrefuelled combat radius of action of just 750 nautical miles is unable to defend the UK Base (its *raison d'être*) against the modern Russian air threat. Each Bear H or Blackjack bomber can launch up to 16 supersonic, convention- ally or nuclear armed ground attack cruise missiles[18] at a range of 1300 nm from their targets. UK does not have nearly enough Air Refuelling resources to extend the combat range of the Typhoon on a 24/7 on-task basis to deter/oppose this threat, so far as it is significant. Whether judged significant or not, it does call for a realistic deterrent capability.

---

[18] The Kh-101, 102 and Kh-555

The UK Base does not boast any effective hard kill air defences against this threat save for the ship-borne Sea Viper Missile—and there are insufficient T45 Guided Missile Destroyers to support both Fleet and UK Base Ballistic and Cruise Missile defence.

30

ONGOING PROPAGANDA
AND 'UNTRUTHS'.

We are experiencing more disingenuous Untruths as I write.

The Typhoon Mafia are now in charge of the propaganda war that attempts to expand the influence of the Royal Air Force. Inordinate celebrations in 2018 of the 100-year anniversary of the RAF took place all over the country and undoubtedly had a considerable impact on public opinion. But as Confucius might have said, "It is all a sham – a cover-up!" Shambles would have been a better word.

What do the public hear about time and time again?

- The Battle of Britain and the Dam Buster Raids,
- The Red Arrows,
- How successful have been the Tornado and the Typhoon Projects and,
- How the RAF won the Falklands War with just one bomb.

- and what should they be hearing?

Although we should indeed recall at least one of these two World War II events with pride, they should be remembered in the context of rather more telling and/or iconic achievements of our Armed Forces such as the Battle of the Atlantic, El Alamein, D-Day and more. The two much acclaimed achievements of the RAF are anachronistic in terms of modern warfare and of the perceived Strategic Threats to our National security and prosperity.

In the continuing propaganda deluge promoting the Battle of Britain there is no mention of the contribution of the Fleet Air Arm – 56 Royal Navy and Royal Marine pilots flew either with 804 or 808 Naval Air Squadron or with RAF Squadrons. Nor is it mentioned that some 500 or more of the pilots were from Commonwealth and allied nations, albeit flying in RAF colours. Critically there is no mention of the 1,000 ships and submarines of the Royal Navy and allied forces that denied the Germans any chance of successfully crossing the Channel with an invasion force. Hitler came to recognise the fallibility of Operation Sealion in the face of such naval power and postponed it in the late summer of 1940 – why doesn't Whitehall recognise this major part of the jigsaw puzzle?

The Battle of Britain was memorable but it did not save us from defeat by any means – it was an important battle at a bad time and contributed to overall victory but it did not win the war. Why else did the war continue for another five years?

Instead of World War II reminiscences, the public should now be hearing and the Government should be carefully considering how our current Armed Forces match up to the possibility of a new multi-dimensional military Cold War including the prime contenders, Russia and of course China. A detailed Threat Reduction Exercise should be conducted and the principal lessons from UK's contribution to the last Cold War should be key to governing a revised constitution of the three Services.

Two of these vital lessons are as follows.

- The effective air defence of the UK base by land-based air does not exist.
- It was Carrier air power that successfully deterred the Soviets. The earlier threat of the Soviet Bomber offensive against Northern Europe (including the UK) was effectively deterred by aircraft carriers of the U. S. Strike Fleet and the Royal Navy on patrol in the Northern approaches. According to senior Russian Generals, this show of Strike Carrier strength, insisted upon by President Reagan, is what convinced Gorbachev to end the Cold War and remove the Iron Curtain.

I well remember as a teenager how impressed I was when watching the Black Arrows practice their displays over RAF North Luffenham, Rutland. It is not at all surprising that the British public have been equally impressed with the performances of their successors, the Red Arrows. They are the public face of the RAF and represent the most important element of the Mafia Propaganda initiative – along with the Historic Memorial Flight operating out of Duxford. But despite their impressive air displays they do not in any sense represent the war-fighting capability that is necessary to defend our National Interests.

In contrast, in the 60's, two Royal Navy Fleet Air Arm aerobatic display teams were provided on a part time basis by front-line squadrons of carrier-borne aircraft: the Buccaneers of 'Fred's Five' and the Sea Vixens of 'Simon's Circus'. They were operational fighters that were ready to go to war – not a team of glorified second-line aircrew in training aircraft – and were great crowd pleasers at Farnborough and other air shows when not deployed at sea. They did represent Britain's true air power.

Nonetheless, the Air Staff has cleverly transformed the public face of air power with the Red Arrows and in doing so continues to hide the many serious land-based air deficiencies that have threatened our National and global security and continue to do so. Surely, these deficiencies must now be revealed to and properly recognised by our Government so that effective military air defence of the UK and its manifold offshore interests can be realised.

Sustained propaganda coupled with misleading information, even lies presented to Government Committees, Secretaries of State and Parliament have persuaded politicians and the public alike that the Tornado and Typhoon collaborative programs have been a success.

The truth of the matter concerning Tornado is revealed in Chapters 28 and 29 of this book. Hundreds of billions of pounds have been expended with no credible combat return on that investment in terms of deterrence or operations. Just a handful of clapped-out pickups and trucks, numerous mud huts and an uncertain number of Jihadis destroyed (or at least frightened). As given by the MoD and reported by the BBC News defence correspondent, Cyprus-based RAF aircraft have delivered 4,409 bombs and missiles over Syria and Iraq causing the deaths of 3,964 Jihadis. Main weapons delivered have been the Paveway Bomb (> £25,000 each), Hellfire Missiles from Drones (> £50,000 each) and Brimstone Missiles (approx. £175,000 each). By averaging out these costs one can reasonably suggest that just the weapons associated with the death of each terrorist cost the UK taxpayer about £80,000 – a total of over £315 million for weapons alone.

But this cost is relatively small when compared to the overall cost of delivering these weapons, including flight hours, fuel, logistics, pre-positioning and combat support (see Annex G). Defence analysts have estimated that the first three-years of the Iraq/Syria Expeditionary Air Wing 'Operation Shader' intervention (about 1600 attack missions) has already cost the taxpayer up to £4 Billion – more than the cost of the carrier HMS Queen Elizabeth – whilst contributing less than 5% of the Coalition air effort.

The Typhoon program is much publicised but is hardly more impressive and is certainly not cost-effective.

With some £60bn value of Typhoons residing in hangars at RAF stations, in various states of repair and modification, it seems to me that the RAF is alone responsible for the current £20 billion defence "black hole". This is not discussed in or released to the media because of the huge politically damaging waste of tax-payers' money and how it might affect defence sales. Why the RAF even ordered 160 of these aircraft is a mystery, especially as it has neither the pilots, the spares, the engineers or, indeed, the justified defence requirement for so many. The public should take note and it's time that the Defence Secretary and the Government took appropriate action.

In 1982, the onset of the misleading and quite dishonest Falklands propaganda campaign did not take long to materialise.

When the Navy played down the Falklands air victory, this opened the floodgates for the RAF propaganda machine that took imme-diate and sustained advantage of the general public's misconcep-tion that the Fleet Air Arm's Sea Harriers and their supporting cast were part of the Royal Air Force.

This is just another example of the propaganda and the 'Unholy war of Words' generated quite disgracefully by the RAF – propa-ganda that appears to be believed by the British public. After all, would a respected Military Service tell lies about such a matter of honour and integrity?

The tentacles of this deceit have stretched far and wide throughout the land and every effort has been made to ignore and discount the Fleet Air Arm air victory.

Post war, Commander Robin Kent MiD who had flown nearly 60 air defence war missions from HMS Invincible in Sea Harrier – protecting the San Carlos Beach Head, our Carrier Battle Group and our Ground Forces – and who had dropped more bombs on target than the Vulcan became Senior Naval Officer at RAF Linton-on-Ouse Flying Training Air Station. At the annual dinner celebrating the Falklands victory his personal distinguished and gallant service was totally ignored by the RAF community present and all attention was focused on the RAF Vulcan pilot who managed to hit the side of Port Stanley runway with just one of 21 bombs delivered. The two other Vulcan bombing missions carrying 42 bombs missed the runway entirely. At minimum, very bad manners, wouldn't you say?

If you read my first book you will appreciate that the Vulcan missions had zero effect on the way the Argentine conducted operations.

Whilst Robin was being insulted at Linton, I was privileged as the only Naval Officer to be invited to the Park Lane Banquet celebrating the 40th Anniversary of the World War II RAF Pathfinder squadrons. Air Vice-Marshal Bennet, the first Commanding Officer was the guest of honour and Air Chief Marshal Sir Michael Beetham was on the top table. I sat next to Group Captain Peter Townsend of Royal Family and World War II fame – a wonderful and gracious man–at a prestigious table hosted by a very close friend, Pat Barnard. I should mention at this point that Sir Michael had already been christened 'One-bomb Beetham' by the Fleet Air Arm – and I had played no small role in that. During the Dinner and quite unexpectedly I was honoured by being asked to stand up and be applauded by all the guests – but one attendee refused to applaud and just glared at me with utter venom in his eyes: Beetham. I really don't understand how I managed to offend such distinguished bastions of the military hierarchy. (The 'magic' continued in 2018:a close colleague was informed by an Air Marshal

working in Whitehall that "Sharkey still really stirs up the min-
ions there".)

Further to the unending fairy-tales about the RAF winning the
Air War in the Falklands, retired Chief of the Air Staff, Air Chief
Marshal Sir Peter Squire (RIP) wrote the Foreword entitled *"A
notable victory for Air Power"* to the Air Staff publication, *"RAF
in Op Corporate"*. This Foreword contains many misleading statements, the cumulative effect of which exaggerates the part played
by the RAF – whilst almost totally ignoring the convincing Air
Victory achieved by our carrier-borne Naval Aircraft and warships.
One of his most disingenuous comments concerns the operations
of the Nimrod Maritime Patrol Aircraft and is as follows:

> "The Nimrod's normal radius of action was some 1,900
> miles but, by the end of April, the hastily fitted air to
> air refuelling capability enabled them to provide direct
> support to the Task Force right down to the Falklands
> – and to monitor shipping in the inshore areas of the
> South Argentine ports."

This is a very seriously exaggerated statement of Nimrod participation. The Nimrod never ventured more than 600 miles
south of Ascension Island before or during the active confrontation, Ascension being 3500 miles north of the Islands. During
the two 600-mile missions that it did venture south of Ascension,
the Nimrod made only two reports to the Carrier Battle Group –
both were counter-productive – one misidentified a fishing fleet
as an Argentine Task Force and the other a container ship as the
Argentine aircraft carrier. Such misleading information resulted
from the fact that the Nimrod was not prepared to visually probe
its radar contacts for fear of being fired upon. To say that it provided direct support to the Task Force right down to the Falklands
is incorrect – it was never in evidence anywhere near the Falkland
Islands. And to state that the Nimrod monitored shipping in the

inshore areas of the South Argentina ports is beyond understanding and destroys the Publication's credibility. It would have taken a much bigger operation than the Black Buck Vulcan Missions to get a single Nimrod to the Islands and to the inshore areas of the South Argentina ports. That simply did not happen.

It was no surprise that the RAF made no mention of the Nimrod's prime role, anti-submarine warfare (ASW), when discussing the Falklands Operation. £ Billions had been spent on this capability with the Air Staff once more claiming effective global reach. Despite the existence of a valid Argentine submarine threat to our Task Force, no Nimrod ASW protection was provided.

The true facts about Nimrod ASW capability had been hidden from Ministers by perpetual spin. Post the Falklands, a senior Nimrod ASW pilot confided in me that the aircraft had only detected one submarine contact once every 5,000 flying hours. This disturbing truth has not prevented the continuation of contrived spin – as evidenced in a recent communication with a former Captain of Her Majesty's Submarine Sceptre.

"I was in the Directorate of Naval Warfare when the Air Staff insulted our intelligence by stating that if one Nimrod had a 30% chance of detecting a Russian Victor111 submarine (which was blatantly untrue) then 3 Nimrods would detect all submarines in a given area.

"The Army bought this and to my shame, some RN people also (they were of the old school of too many submariners reaching the higher ranks brigade) so it was quite a battle to restore sanity. In that, I had Fieldhouse on my side backed up by Woodward and some other lesser mortals.

"The only way I could get a Nimrod to detect me in Sceptre was to charge an active sono-buoy which did detect me as it swished down our flank."

It will be interesting to see if the multi-million-pound Nimrod successor, the P8 is any better. That is very much in doubt. (See Annex I, 'The Submarine Threat to Our Lifeblood – "Unseen" by MOD' for details and a summary of the status quo.)

In 1983, the Royal Navy Presentation Team was touring the country promoting the Naval Service and made not a single mention of the Sea Harrier Air War victory. The Fixed Wing Fleet Air Arm was not referred to in any way. Was the Fieldhouse directive going too far, was there collusion between the Air and Naval Staffs or was it a case of pervasive envy and jealousy by those who did not take part?

Whatever the reason, this omission was an own goal by the Naval Staff that contributed significantly to the success of the propaganda war waged under the Long-Term Plan.

31

A VERY PERSONAL VIEW
OF THE MoD.

I n 1976, when I entered the UK Ministry of Defence (MoD), I rather naively expected better things from our Whitehall system.

Very soon, I realised that the Ministry was a political battleground between individual Services and this internecine strife tended to cloud the main issue of defending UK interests effectively from those who might do us harm. The existence of internal political bickering made it difficult for front-line officers with pedigree to have appropriate access to and to provide accurate and logical advice to the Command and to the Chiefs of Staff. This in turn has prevented the latter from providing Ministers with appropriate advice on Defence Strategy and Procurement.

In the front line, symptoms of this enigma, competition for atten-tion from multiple voices, were evident during preparations for war in HMS Invincible, Falklands 1982. The ship's officers (as opposed to air group officers) had decided that it was unnecessary for the Commanding Officers of the Sea Harrier and Sea King squadrons to attend the Captain's daily War Briefing. Heads of Supply and Engineering Departments would be allowed to attend but not the leaders of the war-fighting squadrons. Direct unfiltered access to critical, current war-fighting expertise would not there-fore be available to the Command.

I was furious but after a short discussion with the very much more diplomatic Ralph Wykes-Sneyd, the Sea King Boss, I agreed that he should present our case to Commander 'Air' – and if that didn't work, then I would address the matter directly with JJ Black, our remarkable Captain. Ralph's initiative worked well. If it hadn't, the war would have taken a different course with some insane directives from the Admiral's Staff being blindly obeyed rather than studiously ignored. One such directive was, "Sea Harriers are not to transmit on their radars when on Combat Air Patrol". If we had not used our radar and therefore been detected by enemy aircraft, more than 450 enemy fighter-bomber sorties would not have aborted their missions against the San Carlos beachhead. That would have been a disaster.

Alongside the three Service Staffs in the Ministry lived an army of civil servants most of whom balked at having to make any decisions; preferring to leave such decisions and/or actions to committees – where deadlines were never set and so no-one could be held accountable for lack of progress or wasted funding. Leading this goliath of an army stood the Permanent Under-Secretaries (PUS) who headed each Civil Service Department and were the direct interface to the corresponding Secretary of State (SoS) – the Government Minister responsible for that department. And each Minister was in turn supported by his Civil Service Private Secretary. Few if any of these decision makers had any worthwhile broad military expertise or experience – but they had immense power.

For example, my early exposure to this 'power without accountability' occurred in the late 70's when we, the Naval Staff and the Air Staff together, prepared a Naval and Air Staff Requirement for the P3T Sea Eagle Air-to-Surface Missile for arming Buccaneers and Sea Harriers against the Soviet Fleet. The initial modest Requirement was for approximately 120 missiles. It was well-prepared and properly justified. When it got to the desk of the Minister for signature, the Rt. Hon. Fred Mulley, his civil service advisers quoted separate scientific studies and advised him that it would need only 5 missiles to sink the whole of the Soviet Northern Fleet (a complete joke). The Requirement was unceremoniously sent back to our Staff desks to be redone.

Let me briefly put this in context. We were at the height of the Cold War. If hostilities were to break out against the Soviets a massive fleet, hundreds of surface warships including powerful Amphibious Brigade vessels and troops, supported by squadrons of long-range bombers would have rounded the North Cape and descended on Northern Europe and Britain. I had specific knowledge of this threat from my service in the Intelligence Division of NATO AFNORTH Headquarters, Oslo, Norway in the early 70's (see Chapter 16). It would appear that our powerful civil service scientific advisers were blissfully unaware of the magnitude of this Soviet threat.

I recall two further occasions that exemplified a discernible lack of focus by the Minister on the defence matters in hand and gave rise to a certain level of astonishment/ merriment.

The first was when I was giving a formal presentation on Sea Harrier to the Defence Minister of France at RAF St. Morgan–where he was also given a guided tour and presentation on the Nimrod Maritime Patrol Aircraft. The French Minister was sartorially resplendent in a dark blue, pinstriped designer-suit with immaculate shoes, shirt, tie and manicure. Our Minister on the other hand did not abide by the same etiquette and his 'ensemble' was less than impressive–something that we the British public have become used to with many Labour politicians. On conclusion of my presentation, the French Minister very graciously accepted a Sea Harrier model from me, provided by British Aerospace. Then, to my complete astonishment Mr. Mulley asked me directly

337

in front of everyone, "And where is the Sea Harrier model for the British Defence Minister?"

How would you respond to that? Very quickly I replied, "You received your model more than a week ago at an earlier presentation, Minister". He did not appear to be well pleased.

The second occasion was very public. It occurred during the fly-past for the Queen's Jubilee Review of the Royal Air Force at RAF Finningley in 1977. The next morning our national newspapers recorded a front-page picture of the VIPs watching the show. Our Defence Minister (whose previous Cabinet posts had been Transport and then Education), sitting next to the Queen, was clearly fast asleep. By the time that the Minister entered the massive Main Building in Whitehall that morning, our Royal Marine contingent had already placed an armchair on each of the stairway landings (and there were many) with a neat sign saying, "Reserved for Fred". Once more, he was less than amused.

Putting the above anecdotes together, you will probably understand the dispiriting effect they were having on the Armed Forces in general. When a later Defence Permanent Undersecretary who, thanks to our democratic system of government, stands above the Chief of Defence Staff in the food chain, Mrs Ursula Brennan (whose background also had zero exposure to military matters) stated publicly that Civil Servants behind desks in Whitehall were just as important and should be paid at least as much as our front-line personnel in Afghanistan, this feeling of despair was exacerbated considerably. What price human life and sacrifice?

One must ask, should we be trusting the national security and military defence of Britain entirely to such individuals, some of whom clearly lack interest in and effective commitment to their appointed task? Or is there a better way of ensuring that they have all the right information upon which to make judgement? Chapter 32 below recommends such a way.

Without a change in procedures we are likely to remain back a century in time when our dedicated front-line forces and weapon systems were simply words on paper that could be manipulated at will and without justification or accountability – "cannon-fodder" was indeed the expression used by General Sir Nick Carter (CDS designate) in 2018.

After the Falklands Conflict I worked closely with General Sir Jeremy Moore, Royal Marines and he informed me that during War Cabinet meetings in 1982 Maggie Thatcher stated that she was prepared to lose 10,000 personnel to retake the Islands. There will always be casualties in war but this statement appeared to lack a proper balance between the ends and the means. There were only 1850 British citizens inhabiting the Islands.

The unholy war of words over recent decades represents a general theme of systemic sacrifice and disregard for the safety and security of our armed forces personnel, particularly by the Whitehall Establishment, and will probably be recorded as a shameful era in UK military history – complementing disgraces such as the Charge of the Light Brigade, World War I trench warfare and the indiscriminate bombing and annihilation of German cities in World War II.

In the process of deferring to the interests of the Loudest Voice and thereby denying our other armed force personnel adequate weapons and effective weapon systems during periods of prolonged peace, our leaders in Westminster have too often paid lip-service to countering the latent threats that are an ever-present danger to our economic prosperity and survival.

Is there an alternative
to the "Long Term Plan"?

Arguably, the 'achievements' of the covert Air Staff Long Term Plan have been limited to:

- the destruction of UK's ability to project effective global military and political power and influence;
- the creation of the much discussed "Black Hole" in Defence Budget Funding.

This situation must be rectified. It is as simple as that. But such rectification cannot take place without some effective changes in procedures within the Civil Service and the Ministry.

"You never change things by fighting the existing reality.

To change something, build a new model that makes the existing model obsolete."

Buckminster Fuller

You will have gathered from previous chapters that military strategy dictates that the UK needs to retain a rapidly deployable Air Defence and Combat Air Support capability for UK Task Force operations throughout the world. This capability can also be readily used for the defence of UK airspace and can only be reliably provided across the board by properly equipped Strike Carriers.

The UK has now reached a troubling watershed between

- Being able to project cost-effective global political and military power in defence of our Lifeblood and in support of National Policy,
- Relying on other nations and on some inappropriate UK-based weapon systems to protect those interests.

I would suggest that the current constitution of our Armed Forces and organisation and commercial practice within the Ministry of Defence is flawed. I would further suggest that each Armed Service should formally be required to justify its independent existence, constitution and associated weapon systems against the Government's declared Military Defence Priorities. Validation of all Armed Services' weapon procurement and maintenance plans is necessary. Such justification and validation was formally directed by Admiral Sandy Woodward when serving as Deputy Chief of Defence Staff in the late 80's. But the Central Staff Directive was only fulfilled by the Naval Staff who submitted a detailed formal Paper – the General Staff and the Air Staff failed to/refused to comply.

These measures are discussed at Annex G in a formal Submission to the House of Commons Defence Select Committee entitled "A Blueprint for Justification and Recovery".

Is it likely that the Ministry Air Staff and Whitehall will now bow to logic, to the laws of physics and aerodynamics and to the stated UK operational need and cease their attempts to deny the UK a fully capable Naval Service and Fixed Wing Fleet Air Arm?Or will they continue to attack the latter; thereby diverting attention away from Major Untruths and their own costly track record of impotence and incompetence? Human nature alone dictates that it will be the latter.

As with many aspects of the Long-Term Plan, the Typhoon Mafia will conduct its attacks covertly by carefully diverting our Government's attention away from dealing with the real threats to our Lifeblood.

A glaring example of how this may be achieved came to light in May 2018. The media publicised an extraordinary scheme generated by the Air Staff, British Aerospace Systems (BAeS) and a refreshed European Consortium to build a new 6th generation fighter, Tempest, to replace the Typhoon by 2050. Interestingly and with Brexit on the horizon, Aviation Week (October 2018) described this as a Dassault initiative between France and Germany.

Working within a Consortium or by Committee at whatever level has rarely been totally fruitful or cost-effective–one has to please everyone in order to arrive at a consensus and that often mitigates against addressing hard truths accurately. This Committee mentality has resulted in the overlapping of individual Armed Service Command and Control–a misguided concept that has led to the problem that UK Limited now faces i. e. three Services working together but against each other at the same time.

The launch of and reported initial major investment (£2 billion) in the Tempest Project after only 4 months of speculative design work appears to have short-circuited the system and surely requires some serious military justification before a penny more is spent. It would appear to represent panic stations by the Air Staff and BAeS because it ignores the proven process of initiating a project with a fully argued Staff Requirement followed by Competitive Tenders. It begs the question, "Who is in control of our National Military Defence – the Ministry or BAeS?"

Declared Strategic Policy continues to be centred upon Strike Carrier capability. Any aircraft Requirement should therefore reflect this under the title Naval/Air Staff Requirement. Without such joint input from the Royal Navy's Fleet Air Arm as well as the RAF it is more than likely that any final design of the Tempest will suffer from the same limitations as the Typhoon aircraft; that is to say non-carrier-capable, weight-critical, unsuitable for cost-effective modification to Carrier-capable status, unable to support First Echelon global deterrence and combat missions, and unable to defend the Homeland Base from threats around the globe.

It would be prudent to remember earlier major investment in and failure of other arguably questionable Projects such as the JP233 Runway Denial Weapon System, approximately £10 billion, 1979, and the Nimrod AWACS project, approximately £5 billion, 1985. Without more analysis and proper military justification, this Tempest project is likely to follow the same route of nugatory expenditure of scarce Defence Funds.

In the context of this declared land-based Tempest Project the fundamentals of declared Strategic Policy appear to have been largely ignored. The deployment of land-based combat aircraft to distant combat theatres requires the pre-positioning of massive logistic air support including air-to-air refuelling, the transport and rotation of supporting ground personnel, weapons, spare parts, fuel, food, ground defence and security systems, medical facilities, etc. Further, reliance on a land-based capability for the global defence of our national interests requires inordinate expenditure on fleets of multi-engine transport aircraft: expenditure that rivals the cost of the combat aircraft themselves[19]. All these costs far outweigh

---

[19] It is pertinent to note that Jane's Defence Weekly has reported the contracting out to L3 Commercial Training Solutions in Bournemouth, Dorset, of the training of 100 RAF multi-engine aircraft pilots.

those of a Carrier Battle Group and do not result in the necessary global versatility and capability demanded by successive Defence Reviews and Statements.

We should not forget that we have already wasted about £ 80 billion on the Typhoon project which is clearly unable to execute its prime role effectively, i. e. the defence of UK airspace against a possible major air-launched cruise missile onslaught.

The deficient and misleading claims about being able to convert Typhoon to carrier-capable status must also be applied to the inadvisable land-based Tempest Project.

Why 'inadvisable'?

The UK has already spent hundreds of billions of pounds on the dis-functional Tornado and Typhoon European collaborative programs; with the Propaganda machine convincing the public that it was money well spent – a blatant untruth. To ignore this and to follow the same disastrous procurement route must be described as criminally insane.

In parallel with the Tempest initiative, the Ministry is neglecting the need for an adequate number of fighter aircraft for the air groups of UK's two new carriers. Only 48 F-35B Lightning IIs have been ordered and the Loudest Voice is now trying to persuade the Treasury that the balance of F-35s (90 aircraft) should be land-based F-35As as these are cheaper. The Treasury appears to regard that as a very persuasive argument despite the fact that the F-35A is incapable of operating from a carrier – and therefore of no deterrence or policing value East of Suez, in the Asia-Pacific region or in the South Atlantic.

This is therefore yet another irresponsible way ahead.

A more sensible and cost-effective alternative to taking unproven/ disproven advice from the Loudest Voice would be for the Government to adopt the principles laid out in the Blue Print for Recovery provided at Annex G, i. e. impartially justifying all proposed military procurement in the light of utility, versatility and capability against the perceived threat.

For now, I commend the following comments from a notable Military Academic concerning this issue:

"Our Whitehall Mandarins and the British public might wish to consider that if an Organisation has to:

a. Depend so much on pervasive Public Relations,

b. Refer interminably to its distant past,

c. Actively fund and maintain a major presence in fields such as academia,

Then:

d. It must have a great fear that without misleading and dishonest PR the case for its independent existence in today's world would be extremely limited.

Public Relations initiatives always have an agenda. Frankly, one must ask what is the significance of the Battle of Britain and the Dambuster Raids? They are irrelevant to modern warfare. In stark contrast, submarines economically blockading Britain are a distinct reality/possibility. But the RAF don't want such a debate because legend and myth is their only weapon and without it, they are gone!"

The following remark from a very senior military colleague is also pertinent:

"One day all this concentration on hype instead of fighting power will come home to roost."

The Naval Service MUST start lobbying for its Air Arm, which it has not done to date. The issue behind misguided weapon system procurement is not so much The Loudest Voice as The Silent Voice.

When it comes to the need for action and armed combat our nation needs effective military leaders and war fighters with a jingoistic attitude and character–not political correctness, disgraceful propaganda and armchair Air Marshals, Generals and Admirals.

33

BEING IN HARM'S WAY
BECOMES A HABIT.

F ollowing my voluntary retirement from the Naval Service in
1985, my penchant for addressing challenges head-on and
overcoming setbacks continued and this is exemplified by the conclusion of my Turkish saga. It isn't always easy being a maverick.

I refer you back to Chapter 1.

Following my confrontation with Köksal in Marmaris after
leaving the Navy, my life continued to be somewhat testing – but
also gratifying.

Semiha's parents insisted on a divorce, much against my wishes.
But I realised that the mother/daughter relationship in Turkey is
a bond that would appear to be unbreakable: probably as a result
of the physical abuse suffered by most members of the fair sex in
the Islamic world.

Semiha told me amidst floods of tears that our time together was
over and she had to go and live with her family who desperately
needed money. The writing had been on the wall and now the
inevitable had been realised.

But the malicious intent and greed of her family had not yet run
its full course.

A few weeks later I was sitting with my good Turkish friend, Alpaslan Kalemçi, in his hotel when the police burst in to arrest me. Alpaslan questioned what was happening and was told that Semiha's family had accused me of stealing my own car! He accompanied me to the police station protesting my innocence but to no avail. As I was being fingerprinted like a common criminal, he called a lawyer who was well known for standing up for the rights of expatriates in Turkey. Fahri-bey lived in Marmaris and immediately arranged for my release from custody pending court action. He did explain to me that the mandatory sentence for stealing a car was a minimum of one year in jail. That was not something I relished. But when he had listened to chapter and verse about all the circumstances surrounding my arrest, he was reasonably optimistic about the eventual outcome. What appeared clear to everyone was that if I was sent to jail the family would find ways to appropriate all my possessions, the hotel development and my home.

But as I had already found, the police in Marmaris were well-balanced, generous in spirit and had no axe to grind against foreigners within their community. I was left in control of my own car pending the completion of court proceedings. No bail was required.

Fahri proved to be a wonderful defence attorney. Behind the scenes he lobbied all the most influential judges in the local area and paved the way for my eventual acquittal. He schooled me precisely how to behave in court; head-down, never looking at the judge in the eye and saying "Yes, your Honour" in Turkish whenever he nudged me on the shoulder.

After much time had elapsed and our divorce had been finalised, I was acquitted in court of any wrongdoing. Semiha and her family moved back to Istanbul and in our final meeting before she left, she made me promise faithfully not to contact her. I was terribly sad and still completely in love with her but I agreed. She had asked for very little from the divorce settlement and clearly remained very upset and very fond of me. When I did call her after three months, she asked me why I hadn't called before! I was taken aback but had already heard from another very good Turkish friend, Erdögan, a major local carpet dealer that a marriage had already been arranged for her with a rich member of the Istanbul élite. Further contact was therefore inappropriate.

I still miss her to this day.

The few months between Semiha leaving my home and then accompanying her family on their return to Istanbul were difficult. I had been devastated by the turn of events, had to cope with the loss of funding for and collapse of my hotel project, ongoing criminal court proceedings and, to make matters worse, occasionally saw her walking with her family along the promenade below my balcony. They never looked up–it was as though I didn't exist.

Marmaris had lost its sparkle and despite a continuing exercise routine my weight plunged down to less than nine stone, 57 kilos. True friends came to my rescue. Alpaslan became my main support and I spent many days by the pool at his hotel and most evenings with him at a local hostelry. Slowly but surely my self-respect returned and the pain started to disappear. But I was prone to some atypical behaviour.

This was evident during a visit by my two very supportive sons and their girlfriends on holiday from UK. One evening we all went around to the village of Içmilir at the western end of Marmaris Bay to visit one of my favourite watering holes–a bar owned by a retired Turkish naval officer. Two British holiday couples were also drinking there and, in very loud voices, were extolling the virtues of the labour MP, the Rt. Hon. Neil Kinnock. We could hardly hear ourselves think. Eventually I couldn't stand it anymore and said rather pointedly, "Excuse me, but we have heard quite enough about that red-headed Welsh git. Can't you keep your voices down?" They were not amused.

The two rather bulky men got up from their seats and approached.

"Hey, boyo! We are Welsh and proud of it. You have just insulted our wives."

"So, what? I didn't come here to listen to all that left-wing propaganda."

"You'd better apologise, or else!" It reminded me of the stand-off with the Welsh miner and his girlfriend in the Haverford West pub during flying training. They swaggered and tried to look as menacing as they could.

"No chance," I replied, "if you want to make something of it then let's step outside and I'll take you both on!" It wasn't a very clever thing to say but I was so stressed that I didn't really care, and my inebriation reinforced that.

As I got down from my bar stool, they backed off a little, briefly glanced at my two very tall and handy sons and one of them blurted out, "You just wait. We are both motorway police officers and if we ever catch you on our motorway, you'll be in real trouble!" Quite ludicrous! They turned and went back to their wives. Shortly afterwards, Kris said, "Come on Dad, I think it's time to go home." It was indeed.

Clearly, I was still on the edge. The next evening, we all stayed home in my apartment to watch that splendid film, "The Memphis Belle". I was thoroughly enjoying the movie when something extraordinary took place. Without any warning, my emotional dam burst. Tears filled my eyes, a lump in my throat prevented me from speaking and suddenly I was completely overwhelmed and sat sobbing uncontrollably in front of my lads. I didn't understand it, couldn't control it and felt thoroughly ashamed and at a loss. It is a moment I shall never forget. One of my lads came over to me, put his strong young arm around me and said, "It's all right Dad! We understand."

Shedding an involuntary tear is a phenomenon that seems to recur frequently whenever I am exposed especially to any air warfare documentary showing downed aircrew but also to news of people and animals in distress. Perhaps this is a symptom of an ongoing case of Post-Traumatic Stress Disorder (PTSD).

Be that as it may, this was all a precursor to the next unexpected romantic adventure in my life which began with mystery, excitement and hope but ended a few years later in disappointment.

After Semiha's departure, I began to return to my normal self; something I attribute mainly to the continued warm friendship of Alpaslan. We were sitting together one evening in a bar near to his hotel when a beautiful woman approached, grabbed me by the hand and said, "Come, I want you to meet a friend." Alpaslan smiled and nodded. He obviously knew who she was but I didn't have a clue. I went and sat at the bar between the two good-looking ladies.

The girl who had grabbed me said, "You don't remember me do you, Sharkey? I met you some time ago at one of Semiha's aerobic classes. My name is Abby, I am English and this is my friend Ziggy." I was thoroughly bemused and wondered what the hell was going on. "We were both reading our fortunes in our coffee cups the other day and mine told me that I was about to meet a handsome man who was well endowed and well-off. And you are that man." They both giggled.

Figure 42. The lovely Abby.

I couldn't help laughing and said, "You might be right about the former but not the latter!" We chatted aimlessly and in good humour for the rest of the evening. Alpaslan had a quiet word with me before he left.

"Take good care Sharkey. I'll explain more when I see you tomorrow."

By one o'clock in the morning, Ziggy had left and a very friendly Abby asked me very sweetly if I could give her a lift home. As she got out of the car she said, "I'll see you again at the pub, okay?"

The next morning Alpaslan explained his word of caution. Abby was married to Fikret Bayractoroğlu; a very prominent local figure and member of a very wealthy Istanbul family. "His brother is an extremely dangerous character, Saigün. If you are seen driving his wife around Marmaris you could be in a lot of trouble. It is illegal for anyone to be seen with another man's wife in his car. But worse than that, you would have to deal with Saigün."

When we got to know each other better, Abby related to me the level of violence that Saigün was capable of inflicting. He and a local mafia gang leader had been in a nightclub in Istanbul when the gang leader said something rude about his wife. Saigün exploded in fury. He smashed off the top of his crystal whiskey glass and ground the base deep into the man's face. It took 12 hours on the operating table to try to repair the damage. Saigün immediately knew that he had gone too far, jumped into his car with his wife and drove overnight to Fikret's house in Marmaris. For the next six weeks the house became like a fortress: guns everywhere and all occupants on full alert for the retribution that might come. The fact that no retribution materialised bears some testament to Saigün's fearsome reputation.

Although not yet aware of this incident, I took Alpaslan very seriously but at the same time was fascinated by Abby's interest in me. My self-esteem had still not fully recovered from the recent divorce. We met again in the bar as planned the following night. This time as I was dropping her home, she insisted that I go in and have a drink. "Don't worry, Fikret will be passed out on the couch with an empty bottle of whiskey at his side."

With considerable misgivings I briefly entered the home, saw him lying there, non-compos-mentis and my better judgment took over. I turned and left.

Two days later, she telephoned me saying that Fikret was away on business and asked me to come over to her house for a couple of drinks. She wanted to talk to me about something. Still intrigued by the situation, I agreed and soon found myself sitting next to her on the couch, enjoying a drink and some idle chat. Suddenly, she was looking at me with those seductive come and get me eyes and slowly undoing all the buttons on her blouse. To say I was tempted is a major understatement but instead of accepting the unspoken invitation I said, "Look, Abby, you are a very beautiful and desirable woman but I don't think you have told me what this is all about. Please tell me."

At last she explained what was on her mind, apart from gratuitous sex. Her story was convincing–but I was already open to being convinced.

Apparently, her marriage was a disaster area. Looking very much like Brooke Shields, she had been selected as one of the original four Virgin Atlantic girls but had thrown that opportunity away when she met Fikret and decided to come to Turkey. After marriage and initial happiness including the birth of a son, Erol, their relationship had become steadily worse because of Fikret's drinking–at least that was her story. The marriage had now become so bad that he and his family were planning to take away the child and throw her out. She was at her wit's end and didn't know what to do. That is why she had come to me.

"We have all noted that you as an Englishman have beaten the Turkish legal system and have survived false accusations against you in court. We also know you are a man of action and can look after yourself. Last but not least, I really like you." Flattery was getting her somewhere!

She went on to explain that Fikret's mother, an American citizen, had been thrown out by the family and she had tried to escape with her young child. They had caught her at the airport, beaten her escort savagely and had taken away the child.

"I need to get out of Turkey with Erol. Will you help me?"

Wow! Danger bells were ringing but I ignored them. Here was a new challenge for stepping into harm's way and another critical decision time in my life. I thought very quickly adding up the pros and cons of the situation. There was little to keep me in Turkey.

"Of course, I will. When do you want to leave?" I had been taken in hook, line and sinker.

"How soon can you arrange it?"

"Would tomorrow be soon enough?"

"Oh no! That is too quick. I have lots of things to sort out before leaving. Perhaps we should plan to go just before Christmas. Would that be okay?" It was then late September.

The ensuing three months became a rewarding distraction from my anguish over Semiha. Abby and I got to know each other well with many a covert meeting under a veil of secrecy–no mean feat in a small town like Marmaris. Slowly but surely, we were becoming very fond of each other, but our relationship remained largely platonic and was not fully consummated until the night before we flew out of Izmir.

My friendship with Erdögan, the carpet dealer, then proved to be very strong. I told him about the need to get Abby and Erol out of Turkey and he made a welcome suggestion. "My father is one of the most famous and feared bandits in the land. I shall speak to him for you and ask him to provide protection for you all at the airport." He was as good as his word. Armed protection was to be provided until the aircraft left Turkish soil; at the cost of just a few million Lire.

The simple plan was for Abby, Erol and her girlfriend to go to Izmir on an overnight shopping expedition. This was not unusual. I would go separately in my own car and we would stay the night together in a small hotel in the suburbs. My car would be looked after by my BMW garage while I was away. I would then have to return to Marmaris to complete the sale of my apartment.

Fikret proved to have been very suspicious of what might have been occurring during the previous three months and, as it turned out, his brother Saigün arranged a welcoming party at the airport, led by himself. Somehow details of our plan had been leaked.

The night before we left Marmaris, mother nature played a role that nearly put paid to all our plans. A massive rainstorm created flash flooding throughout the town thanks to the watershed created by the mountains surrounding us. In the early hours of the morning I was awoken by the phone ringing. When I tried to answer, the phone went dead. Concerned for her safety, I tried ringing Abby but was unable to get through. Grabbing a torch, I took the stairs down from the apartment and found that the promenade was completely flooded up to the top level of our entrance steps. Not fully realising the severity of the flooding and as it was starting to get light, I raced back upstairs to get my car keys then waded around to where the car was parked. The floodwater was halfway up the wheels of the car and the roadway leading to Alpaslan's hotel was a virtual torrent of water sweeping down to the promenade.

My phone was still dead and I wanted to get to the hotel, about half a mile away, hoping that the phones there would get through to Abby's home. Little did I realise that the road had several very shallow-gradient undulations and so I decided to drive slowly to the hotel rather than wade through all the floodwater. All was going well until halfway up the road. The water got deeper and deeper and eventually began rippling over the bonnet. Calamity struck. The engine died and as I opened the door the entire car interior was flooded. Not to be outdone, I decided to wade the rest of the way to the hotel in near waist-deep, very cold water which was moving rapidly, carrying with it all sorts of rubbish including tree branches and condoms.

Alpaslan welcomed my bedraggled, shivering figure with open arms and provided much-needed coffee. His phones were working and he called Abby's home to check that things were okay there. She was very relieved that I was okay and had indeed tried to call me. Optimistically, we agreed to stick to the plan if I could get the car going again when the flood subsided. We learned later that nearly 60 cars had been washed into the bay.

After a few hours, the road to the promenade was clear of water and I walked home to shower, change and get ready for the drive north. The big question remained: would the car start? Initially, the answer was no. The water had drained away but the seats were soaking. Several large bath towels were needed to make the driver's seat dry enough for the long journey. When I turned on the ignition and tried to start, there was absolutely no response. Our plan was in severe peril.

Good fortune came to my rescue. A huge truck pulled up alongside me and the driver offered to try using jump leads from his double-banked battery. As I turned the ignition switch there was a huge bang as the engine started and ticked over like a purring kitten. I kept the engine running as I collected my bags and set off on the long drive; only turning off the engine 300 kms later when I arrived at the BMW garage in Izmir. When I returned to collect the car, they explained that the large voltage from the truck's batteries had caused the starter motor to explode–thankfully after the engine had started.

It was such a pleasure and a relief when I found Abby waiting for me at the hotel. We were still not out of the woods but no news of Saigün or his men was good news. Naturally, we were booked into separate rooms on the same floor. After a very cosy evening in the small restaurant we retired to bed. Unable to sleep I laid a trail of my business cards from Abby's door to my own before drifting off. I was awoken by a beautiful naked goddess climbing into my bed and, for the first time, we made passionate love.

The following morning, breakfast went down very well indeed. And then the car arranged by our bandit friend arrived to take us to the airport. Crunch time had come!'

Halfway up the entrance road to the airport sat Saigün's large black Chevrolet limousine on the verge. But it was empty. Nervous tension rose as we entered the departure lounge. Amidst the melee of passengers, two very large and alert gentlemen stood out. They were ready for trouble. The nearest one to us looked over briefly and nodded. It was a sign that all was well. It transpired that Saigün and his gang of four had been intercepted by our protectors and taken at gunpoint to the airport manager's office where they were detained until our aircraft had taken off. Good for Erdögan and his father.

The first hurdle was over but there was more to come.

Abby's parents invited me to stay with the family in Crawley over Christmas where we got to know each other more in the biblical sense. But there were two levels of serious concern.

The first was that the Bayractoroğlu family had a long reach. Other fugitives from their malice had been followed to the UK and kneecapped. It was best to assume that they might well seek revenge in a similar manner and kidnap young Erol. We alerted the local police force to the situation who did as much as they could, keeping a watchful eye on the home and installing a panic button.

The second problem was equally tenuous and disturbing. I had to return to Turkey to arrange for the sale of my apartment and car as well as the shipment of all my worldly possessions to the UK–not a very edifying prospect. Fikret had called Abby's parents' home and demanded to speak to me. His message was clear: "If you come back to Turkey, I will kill you." My welcome mat no longer existed there, and I was up against the odds. Saigün had about six guns in his possession and was famous for being an expert knife thrower. I had no weapons and so I went shopping in London and bought a small high-powered crossbow and an arsenal of arrows for basic self-defence–it was better than nothing.

Another matter needing resolution was that for Abby to obtain a divorce from Fikret she had to remain domiciled in the UK for at least one year. We could then look elsewhere for a safe haven. In the meantime, there would be the constant threat of Erol being kidnapped and more revenge being sought. I discussed the matter with my superb solicitor, Charles Rutter of Wincanton. He gave me very good advice.

"Sharkey, no amount of police oversight or legal paperwork is going to provide adequate protection for Erol. He could be snatched at any time and moved out of the country on a light air-craft. You personally are the only defence against that. It looks as though you will have to go into hiding for the year."

He was quite right. We did so and as I was very well known throughout Southwest Britain as 'Sharkey Ward', I decided to change my name by deed poll to MacCartan-Ward, in recognition of my Irish ancestry.

In a matter of weeks, I had returned to Turkey and found the car in pristine condition but that was the least of my concerns. I was on full alert as I entered Marmaris and reached my apart-ment. I had no clue as to how far Fikret and his brother would go to exact revenge, but daylight hours appeared to be a sanctuary and any threat was likely to materialise after dark. So, by day I went around my business openly and spent the nights in nervous anticipation in the apartment–with the crossbow and arrows at the ready. A second visit was also necessary to sort out Abby's affairs and my own. She flew out separately and stayed in a hotel. It was risky business.

While she was in Marmaris, an ambush and assault were attempted on the pair of us but were foiled by the fortunate presence and intervention of Fahri-bey, my lawyer.

Finally, I was ready to leave Turkey for the last time. I chose to drive to Izmir in the small hours of the night to escape unwanted attention but Saigün had obviously been monitoring my movements. After starting the car, I realised something was wrong: it was not running smoothly and the engine was missing on at least one cylinder. As I approached the outskirts of Marmaris the big black Chevrolet limousine pulled out about 100 yards behind me. It was Saigün and his goons. Things were not looking so good. I slowly accelerated and as I reached about 70 mph the engine recovered its performance and ran very sweetly. Below 70 miles an hour it began to stutter again–it appeared that the bad boys had put some water in my petrol tank. There was only one solution: to keep the speed up all the way.

The mountainous road to Izmir passes through some wild and deserted scenery which meant that I was very much on my own; with thoughts of my military escape and evasion training running through my mind should the car stop. It was not an edifying prospect – I would be on a hiding to nothing.

Slowly but surely, the Chevy headlights behind grew smaller and smaller and finally disappeared after climbing the steep hillside at Akyaka on the road up to Muğla – about twenty miles from Marmaris. But I was taking no chances and continued to drive the little BMW at full speed until I reached Izmir–it was fortunate that I knew the road well.

The technicolour life of this Top Gun has continued in similar fashion. Eventually, I have ended up in the beautiful Island of Grenada in the Caribbean where once more 'attitude' has been able to contribute to my peace of mind. But that is another story.

I am thoroughly content with my lot; surrounded by many of the dogs that I have rescued and by some very true friends. My family in UK, especially my son Ashton, and in Canada are a constant comfort and delight to me.

I have only a few major regrets: the untimely and recent loss of my gallant eldest son, Kris; the accidental loss of my beloved brother, Michael; and the extraordinary and unjustifiable lack of support by Whitehall Mandarins, Politicians and Civil Servants for a robust Naval Service.

"Hands on" Conventional Carrier Deck Landing.

A Precise Approach Is Mandatory.

L anding on board a conventional aircraft carrier in a fighter aircraft presents significant challenges that are not experienced when operating from an airfield ashore. Deck landing into arrestor wires by day is a high workload, high skill task requiring 100% concentration and extremely precise control of speed, aircraft attitude and glide path – both vertically and laterally. Any diversion from the prescribed approach parameters can and does result in various undesirable effects.

Too high an approach speed can cause the hooked wire to break leaving the aircraft with not enough residual speed to take off again but too much speed to stop on the deck: resulting in the loss of the aircraft.

Aircraft attitude (the angle of attack that the aircraft wings are presented to the air stream) must be accurately controlled. Too high a nose attitude at the resultant low speed will cause the loss of lift from the wing surfaces and the aircraft will rapidly sink towards the stern of the ship. Too low a nose attitude will result in an increase in air speed, giving the aircraft to much inertia for the arrestor wire to cope with – and the latter will break.

Maintenance of the prescribed glide path as given by the stabilised landing sight is necessary to ensure that the hook does indeed catch a wire. If you are too low on the glide path, the hook can bounce over all the wires (or you may crash into the stern of the ship). If you are too high on the glide slope, your hook will miss the wires.

In other words, the correct air speed, attitude/angle of attack and glide slope must be maintained in a stable fashion all the way down the approach path to the deck.

Undercarriage Strength.

A stable approach means that the inertia of the aircraft, both horizontal and vertical, remains constant to the touchdown point where there is no reduction in rate of descent of the aircraft (as with landing on an airfield) and the forces that the aircraft under-carriage have to contain are markedly higher than for airfield landings. Some have observed in the past that a carrier deck landing is almost akin to a "crash on deck" – the forces involved are so large. The undercarriage strength also has to take account of the movement of the ship, particularly a pitching deck and "ship heave".

The Pitching Deck. With the deck pitching around the ship's centre of gravity in heavy seas a severe upward momentum of the deck can be experienced at the touchdown point. This upward momentum needs to be taken into account in undercarriage strength as it effectively creates an increased downward force of the aeroplane on touchdown.

Ship Heave. This is caused by the ship being moved bodily up and down by heavy seas and has a similar impact on the undercarriage strength as the effects of ship pitch.

The Geometry of the Glide Path.

The prescribed glide path for deck landing (as indicated to the pilot by the deck landing sight) is, by virtue of simple geometry, steeper than that experienced ashore. On land, the prescribed glide path is 3°. But the land is stationary. With the ship moving at up to 30 knots away from the aircraft on the approach, the deck landing sight is set at 4° which gives the aircraft a net approach path through the air of just 3°. Aircraft handling for maintaining the glide slope is therefore the same for landings ashore and landings on the deck. It is of course important to recognise that if the ship's deck is pitching 2°, this leaves only 1° of clearance between the aircraft flight path and the stern of the ship. Any reduction in the prescribed glide path and this clearance, through for example the adoption of a flared landing technique, would therefore be totally unacceptable from a practical and a flight safety point of view.

The touchdown area where the tail hook of the aircraft catches the arrestor wire is extremely small and any lapse in concentration can cause pilots to miss the wires completely or, catastrophically, to impact the stern of the ship. As if this was not enough, the flow of the wind over the deck often creates turbulence (a 'burble' or a 'hole') just behind the ship causing a loss of wing lift. This has to be anticipated by applying a small amount of power. Even in calm, benign sea conditions this can represent a major challenge to any carrier deck pilot.

Ground Cushion on Landing: Aircraft Strength Implications.

When an aircraft lands on an airfield ashore it encounters a 'ground cushion' when its height above the runway is at about 10 feet. This condition is caused by the interaction between the flat surface of the ground and the airflow across the aircraft's wings. This automatically causes a reduction in the rate of descent of the aircraft, a side-effect of which is that the aircraft stays airborne longer and touches down further along the runway. If the pilot also reduces rate of descent by "flaring" the aircraft, the ground cushion effect will be exaggerated and the aircraft will touch down smoothly further down the runway without placing heavy forces on the undercarriage system. Catching a wire on a carrier deck using this technique would be extremely difficult if not impossible.

When landing on a carrier, with the deck approximately 60 feet above the sea surface, there is no ground cushion. If there was, it would make landing on board more difficult and more dangerous because the essence of a good approach to the deck is to continue the prescribed glide slope all the way to the deck without any reduction (or increase) in the steady rate of descent. This allows the point of impact of the deck hook on the deck to be more precisely achieved – allowing the aircraft to "catch a wire". Any flaring prior to touch down (even the smallest amount) will cause the aircraft to miss the wires. A side-effect of this type of approach is that a heavy force is applied to the landing gear on touchdown and, hence, the landing gear needs to be much more robust (and heavy) than its land-based counterpart.

The arresting hook system appears simple but represents a major challenge for aircraft design. The dynamic interaction between the aircraft and the arresting system at around 135 knots is massive and reliably bringing the aircraft to a controlled halt in around 350 feet is a difficult and dangerous challenge.

'Close In' Approach Problems.

The "burble" behind the ship, as referred to above, can cause an increase in the rate of descent of the aircraft as it approaches the stern of the ship. An obvious danger, this has to be anticipated by the pilot applying a small amount of power in order to maintain the prescribed flight path to the required impact point of the deck hook amidst the wires. If too much power is applied, the aircraft's rate of descent will be reduced and the aircraft will flare, missing the wires.

When you are learning to deck land, one of the golden rules is always to concentrate on the cues given by the deck landing sight and NEVER to attempt to "fly the deck" (which is precisely what a flared landing would require). That is because the landing sight is fully stabilised and is positioned so that if you do follow its cues, your hook will catch a wire because you are maintaining the prescribed steady glide path all the way to the deck. The deck can move considerably in heavy seas and that movement must be totally ignored by the pilot if he is to land on board safely.

In rough seas with the ship pitching, rolling and heaving, the challenge becomes much greater. Conducting night deck landings in poor weather represents the most difficult and challenging flying task that any military pilot will face in any environment. In such conditions it is quite impossible for a pilot to "fly the deck" safely or to employ a flared landing technique.

The Landing Sight.

In very brief terms, the landing sight sits to the left of the carrier runway approximately half-way down the deck. It is fully stabilized in order to remove the effects of ship roll and pitch. What the pilot sees on the approach is a long horizontal bar of green datum lights in the centre of which is a bright white light known as the 'meat ball'. When the pilot is precisely on the glide path, he sees all the lights in line. If he starts to go high above the glide path, he sees the meat ball rising above the green datums. If he starts to go low, he sees the meat ball descending below the datums.

The datums are pre-positioned in height above the deck for each aircraft type–each type having a particular height of the pilot's eye above the deck hook when in the approach configuration. If the pilot flies a perfect glide path touchdown with the meat ball in line with the datums, the aircraft deck hook will catch the target arrestor wire.

Annex B

Letter by John Lehman, Former Secretary of the US Navy.

Written with a focus on tail hookers/chasers [carrier aviators] but it applies to all three of the naval forces – aviators, surface warriors, and submariners.

" The swaggering-flyer mystique forged over the past century has been stymied in recent years by political correctness.

We celebrate the 100th anniversary of U. S. naval aviation this year, but the culture that has become legend was born in controversy, with battleship admirals and Marine generals seeing little use for airplanes. Even after naval aviators proved their worth in World War I, naval aviation faced constant conflict within the Navy and Marine Corps, from the War Department, and from sceptics in congress. Throughout the interwar period, its culture was forged largely un-noted by the public.

It first burst into the American consciousness 69 years ago when a few carrier aviators changed the course of history at the World War II Battle of Midway. For the next three years, the world was fascinated by these glamorous young men who, along with the Leathernecks, dominated the newsreels of the war in the Pacific. Most were sophisticated and articulate graduates of the Naval

Academy and the Ivy League, and as such, they were much favoured for Pathé News interviews and War Bond tours. Their casualty rates from accidents and combat were far higher than other branches of the naval service, and aviators were paid nearly a third more than non-flying shipmates. In typical humour, a pilot told one reporter: "We don't make more money, we just make it faster."

Landing a touchy World War II fighter on terra firma was difficult enough, but to land one on a pitching greasy deck required quite a different level of skill and sangfroid. It took a rare combination of hand-eye coordination, innate mechanical sense, instinctive judgment, accurate risk assessment, and most of all, calmness under extreme pressure. People with such a rare combination of talents will always be few. The current generation of 9-G jets landing at over 120 knots hasn't made it any easier.

By war's end, more than 100 carriers were in commission. But when Louis Johnson replaced the first Secretary of Defense, Jim Forrestal—himself one of the original naval aviators in World War I—he tried to eliminate both the Marine Corps and naval aviation. [As is happening now in the UK.]

Korea.

By 1950 Johnson had ordered the decommissioning of all but six aircraft carriers. Most historians count this as one of the important factors in bringing about the invasion of South Korea, supported by both China and the Soviet Union. After that initial onslaught, no land airbases were available for the Air Force to fight back, and all [US] air support during those disastrous months came from the USS Valley Forge (CV-45), the only [US] carrier left in the western Pacific. She was soon joined by the other two carriers remaining in the Pacific. [UK had three carriers on station throughout.]

Eventually, enough land bases were recovered to allow the Air Force to engage in force, and more carriers were recommissioned, manned by World War II vets hastily recalled to active duty.

By the time of the armistice, the Cold War was well underway and for the next 43 years naval aviation was at the leading edge of the conflict around the globe. As before, aviators suffered very high casualties throughout. Training and operational accidents took a terrible toll. Jet fighters on straight decks operating without the sophisticated electronics or reliable ejection seats that evolved in later decades had to operate come hell or high water as one crisis followed another in the Taiwan Strait, Cuba, and many lesser-known fronts.

Between1953 and 1957, hundreds of naval aviators were killed in an average of 1,500 crashes per year, while others died when naval intelligence gatherers like the EC-121 were shot down by North Koreans, Soviets, and Chinese. In those years carrier aviators had only a one-in-four chance, 25%, of surviving 20 years of service.

Vietnam and the Cold War

The Vietnam War was an unprecedented feat of endurance, courage, and frustration in ten years of constant combat. Naval aviators flew against the most sophisticated Soviet defensive systems and highly trained and effective Vietnamese pilots. But unlike any previous conflict, they had to operate under crippling civilian political restrictions, well known, telegraphed, to the enemy. Antiaircraft missiles and guns were placed in villages and other locations known to be immune from attack. The kinds of targets that had real strategic value were protected by U. S. civilians while hundreds of aviators' lives and thousands of aircraft were lost attacking easily rebuilt bridges and "suspected truck parks," as the U. S. government itself indulged its academic game theories.

Stephen Coonts' *Flight of the Intruder* brilliantly expressed the excruciating frustration from this kind of combat. Scores of naval aviators were killed or taken prisoner. More than 100 squadron commanders and executive officers were lost. The heroism and horror of the POW experience for men such as John McCain and Jim Stockdale were beyond anything experienced since the war with Japan.

Naturally, when these men hit liberty ports, and when they returned to their bases between deployments, their partying was as intense as their combat. The legendary stories of Cubi Point, Olongapo City, and the wartime 'Tailhook conventions' in Las Vegas grew with each passing year.

Ending the Cold War.

Perhaps the greatest and least known contribution of naval aviation was its role in bringing the Cold War to a close. President Ronald Reagan believed that the United States could win the Cold War without combat.

Along with building the B-1 and B-2 bombers and the Peacekeeper missile, and expanding the Army to 18 divisions, President Reagan built the 600-ship Navy and, more important, approved the Navy recommendation to begin at once pursuing a forward strategy of aggressive exercising around the vulnerable coasts of Russia. This demonstrated to the Soviets that we could defeat the combined Warsaw Pact navies and use the seas to strike and destroy their vital strategic assets with carrier-based air power.

Nine months after the President's inauguration, three U. S. and two Royal Navy carriers executed offensive exercises in the Norwegian Sea and Baltic. In this and subsequent massive exercises there and in the northwest Pacific carried out every year, carrier aircraft proved that they could operate effectively in ice and fog, penetrate the best defences, and strike all of the bases and nodes of the Soviet strategic nuclear fleet.

Subsequent testimony from members of the Soviet General Staff attested that this was a major factor in the deliberations and the loss of confidence in the Soviet government that led to its collapse.

During those years naval aviation adapted to many new policies, the removal of the last vestiges of institutional racial discrimination, and the first winging of women as naval aviators and their integration into ships and squadrons.

'Break the Culture'

1991 marked the dissolution of the Warsaw Pact and the end of the Cold War. But as naval aviation shared in this triumph, the year also marked the start of tragedy.

The Tailhook Convention that took place in September that year began a scandal with a negative impact on naval aviation that continues to this day. The over-the-top parties of combat aviators were overlooked during the Vietnam War but had become accidents waiting to happen in the post war era.

Whatever the facts of what took place there, it set off investigations within the Navy, the Department of Defense, the Senate, and the House that were beyond anything since the investigations and hearings regarding the Pearl Harbour attack. Part of what motivated this grotesquely disproportionate witch hunt was pure partisan politics and the deep frustration of Navy critics (and some envious begrudgers within the Navy) of the glamorous treatment accorded to the Navy and its aviators in Hollywood and the media, epitomised by the movie Top Gun.

Patricia Schroeder (D-CO), chair of the House Armed Services Committee investigation, openly and repeatedly declared that her mission was to "break the culture," of naval aviation. One can make the case that she succeeded.

What has changed in naval aviation since Tailhook? First, we should review the social/cultural, and then professional changes. Many but not all were direct results of Tailhook.

'De-Glamorisation' of Alcohol. Perhaps in desperation, the first reaction of Pentagon leadership to the congressional witch hunt was to launch a massive global jihad against alcohol, tellingly described as "de-glamorisation."

While alcohol was certainly a factor in the Tailhook scandal, it was absolutely not a problem for naval aviation as a whole. There was no evidence that there were any more aviators with an alcohol problem than there were in the civilian population, and probably a good deal fewer.

As a group, naval aviators have always been fastidious about not mixing alcohol and flying. But social drinking was always a part of off-duty traditional activities like hail-and-farewell parties and especially the traditional Friday happy hour. Each Friday on every Navy and Marine air station, most aviators not on duty turned up at the officers' club at 1700 to relax and socialise, tell bad jokes, and play silly games like "dead bug."

But there was also an invaluable professional function because happy hours provided a kind of sanctuary where junior officers could roll the dice with commanders, captains, and admirals, ask questions that could never be asked while on duty, listen avidly to the war stories of those more senior, and absorb the lore and mores of the warrior tribe.

When bounds of decorum were breached, or someone became over-refreshed, as occasionally happened, they were usually taken care of by their peers. Only in the worst cases would a young junior officer find himself in front of the skipper on Monday morning. Names like Mustin Beach, Trader Jon's, Miramar, and Oceana were a fixed part of the culture for anyone commissioned before 1991.

A similar camaraderie took place in the chiefs' clubs, the acey-deucy clubs, and the sailors' clubs. Now all of that is gone.

Most officers' and non-commissioned officers' clubs were closed and happy hours banned. A few clubs remain, but most have been turned into family centres for all ranks and are, of course, empty.

No officers dare to be seen with a drink in their hand. The JOs do their socialising as far away from the base as possible, and all because the inquisitors blamed the abuses of Tailhook '91 on alcohol abuse. It is fair to say that naval aviation was slow to adapt to the changes in society against alcohol abuse and that corrections were overdue, especially against tolerance of driving while under the influence.

But once standards of common sense were ignored in favour of "political correctness," there were no limits to the spread of its domination.

Not only have alcohol infractions *anonymously reported* on the hot-line become career-enders, but *suspicions* of sexual harassment, homophobia, telling of risqué jokes, and speech likely to offend now-favoured groups all find their way into fitness reports. And if actual hot-line investigations are then launched, that is usually the end of a career, regardless of the outcome. There is now absolutely zero-tolerance for any missteps whatsoever in these areas.

Turning Warriors into Bureaucrats

On the professional side, it is not only the zero-tolerance of infractions of political correctness but the smothering effects of the explosive growth of bureaucracy in the Pentagon.

When the Department of Defense was created in 1947, the headquarters staff was limited to 50 billets. Today, 750,000 full-time equivalents are on the headquarters staff. This has gradually expanded the time and cost of producing weapon systems, from the 3 years from-concept-to-deployment of Polaris, to the projected 24 years of the F-35. As an example, when the SR71 project was given the go-ahead, the plane was designed, new materials and fuel invented, and the first flight of the bird was accomplished in 22 months.

But even more damaging, these congressionally created new bureaucracies are demanding more and more meaningless paperwork from the operating forces. According to the most recent rigorous survey, each Navy squadron must prepare and submit some 980 different written reports annually, most of which are never read by anyone but still require tedious gatherings of every kind of statistic for every aspect of squadron operations. As a result, the average aviator now spends a very small fraction of his or her time on duty actually flying. This is the reason pilots of the Navy and Air Force are resigning and joining the airlines. They want to fly! It is the reason that the Air Force is short 2000 pilots as of today. I don't have the number for the Navy, but they are short also.

Job satisfaction has steadily declined. In addition to paperwork, the bureaucracy now requires officers to attend mandatory courses in sensitivity to women's issues, sensitivity to and integration of openly homosexual personnel, and how to reintegrate into civilian society when leaving active duty.

This of course is perceived as an outrageously massive waste of time by aviators and is offensive to them in the inherent assumption that they are no longer officers and gentlemen but somehow coarse brutes who will abuse women and gays, and not know how to dress or hold a fork in civilian society unless taught by GS-12s.

One of the greatest career burdens added to naval aviators since the Cold War has been the Goldwater-Nichols requirement to have served at least four years of duty on a joint staff to be considered for flag, and for junior officers to have at least two years of such joint duty even to screen for command.

As a result, the joint staffs in Washington and in all the combatant commands have had to be vastly increased to make room. In addition, nearly 250 new Joint Task Force staffs have been created to accommodate these requirements. Thus, when thinking about staying in or getting out, young Navy and Marine aviators look forward to far less flight time when not deployed, far more paperwork, and many years of mind-numbing staff duty.

Zero-Tolerance Is Intolerable

Far more damaging than bureaucratic bloat is the intolerable policy of "zero-tolerance" applied by the Navy and the Marine Corps. One strike, one mistake, one DUI, and you are out.

The Navy has produced great leaders throughout its history. In every era the majority of naval officers are competent but not outstanding. But there has always been a critical mass of fine leaders. They tended to search for and recognise the qualities making up the right stuff, as young JOs looked up the chain and emulated the top leaders, while the seniors, in turn, looked down and identified and mentored youngsters with promise.

By nature, these kinds of war-winning leaders make mistakes when they are young and need guidance—and often protection from the system.

Today, alas, there is much evidence that this critical mass of such leaders is being, or has been, lost.

Chester Nimitz put his whole squadron of destroyers on the rocks by making mistakes. But while being put in purgatory for a while, he was protected by those seniors who recognised a potentially great leader. In today's Navy, Nimitz would instantly be gone. Any seniors trying to protect him would themselves be accused of a career-ending cover-up.

Because the best aviators are calculated risk-takers, they have always been particularly vulnerable to the system. But now in the age of political correctness and zero-tolerance, they are rapidly becoming an endangered species.

Today, a young officer with the right stuff is faced on commissioning with making a ten-year commitment if he or she wants to fly, which weeds out some with the best potential. Then after winging and an operational squadron tour, they know well the frustrations outlined here. They have seen many of their role models bounced out of the Navy for the bad luck of being breath-alysed after two 12oz beers or allowing risqué forecastle follies.

'Dancing on the Edge of a Cliff'

They have not seen senior officers put their own careers on the line to prevent injustice. They see before them at least 14 years of sea duty interspersed with six years of bureaucratic staff duty in order to be considered for flag rank. And now they see all that family separation and sacrifice as equal to dancing on the edge of a cliff. One tiny mistake or an anonymous and unjust accusation or mere suspicion of *possible* homophobia, racism or sexism and they are over. They can no longer count on a sea-daddy coming to their defence.

Today, the right kind of officers with the right stuff still decide to stay for a career, but many more, a majority, are putting in their letters (resigning) in numbers that make a critical mass of future stellar leaders impossible. In today's economic environment, retention numbers look somewhat okay, but those statistics are misleading.

Much hand-wringing is being done among naval aviators (active-duty, reserve, and retired) about the remarkable fact that there has only been one aviator chosen as Chief of Naval Operations during the past 30 years. For most of the last century, there were always enough outstanding leaders among aviators, submariners, and surface warriors to ensure a rough rotation among the communities when choosing a CNO.

The causes of this sudden change are not hard to see. Vietnam aviator losses severely thinned the ranks of leaders and mentors; Tailhook led to the forced or voluntary retirement of more than 450 carrier aviators, including many of the very finest, like Bob Stumpf, former skipper of the Blue Angels.

There are, of course, the armchair strategists and think-tankers who herald the arrival of unmanned aerial vehicles as totally eliminating the need for naval aviators and their entire culture, since future naval flying will be done from unified bases in Nevada, with operators requiring a culture rather closer to computer geeks.

This is highly unlikely.

As the aviator culture fades from the Navy, what is being lost?Great naval leaders have and will come from each of the communities and have absorbed virtues from all of them. But each of the three communities has its unique cultural attributes. Submariners are imbued with the precision of engineering mastery and the chess players' adherence to the disciplines of the long game; surface sailors retain the legacy of John Paul Jones, David G. Farragut and Arleigh "31 Knot" Burke and have been the principal repository of strategic thinking and planning. Aviators have been the principal source of offensive thinking, best described by Napoleon as "L'audace, l'audace, toujours l'audace!" (Audacity, audacity, always audacity!)

Those attributes of naval aviators—willingness to take intelligent calculated risk, self-confidence, even a certain swagger—that are absolutely invaluable in wartime are the very ones that make them particularly vulnerable in today's zero-tolerance Navy. The political correctness police, the thought police, like Inspector Javert in Les Misérables, are out to get them and they are relentless.

The history of naval aviation is one of constant change and challenge. While the current era of massive and choking bureaucracy and of killing political correctness, with its new requirements of integrating women, transgenders, and openly gay individuals, is indeed challenging, it can probably be dealt with without compromising naval excellence. But what does truly challenge the future of the naval services is the mindless pursuit of zero-tolerance. A Navy led by men and women who have never made a serious mistake will be a Navy that will fail."

Dr. Lehman was the 65th Secretary of the Navy and a member of the 9/11 Commission.

His testament above can for the most part be read across to the history of the UK Armed Services and of Fleet Air Arm and Royal Marine fighter pilots. (Our Marine pilots were already flying with distinction in World War I combat – well before there was any Royal Air Force – and have been doing so ever since.)

A recent supportive viewpoint was presented by Ace Jewell, CDR, USN (ret) now about 88 years old and a fighter pilot in 3 wars. (Few of his ilk remain.)

> "Drones will not be late to briefings, start fights at happy hour, destroy clubs, attempt to seduce others' dates, purchase huge watches, insult other services, sing O'Leary's Balls, dance on tables, yell "Show us yer tits!", or do all of the other things that we know win wars."

In a similar vein, Churchill wrote:

> 'We are now fighting for our lives and cannot afford to confine Army appointments to persons who have excited no hostile comment in their career.'

Winston Churchill
Note to CIGS 19 October 1940

ROYAL NAVY FIXED WING CARRIER OPERATIONS SINCE 1948.

This Annex provides a brief outline of 19 events, crises, conflicts and deterrence in which fixed-wing aircraft carriers
were deployed in support of UK Government policy since 1948.
They show that the availability of sea-based tactical aviation adds
immensely to the nation's overall deterrent capability. On several occasions no other form of intervention was initially possible.
More significant is the inability of potential aggressors to deter
the deployment of aircraft carriers into areas supposedly dominated by land-based aircraft. The myth of vulnerability is belied
by experience.

Palestine 1948

Naval aircraft from HMS *Ocean* covered the final evacuation
of British forces from Palestine in May 1948. RAF aircraft had
already been evacuated and only carrier-borne naval aircraft were
capable of providing the protection required.

Korea 1950-53

HMS *Triumph* joined the USS *Valley Forge* to strike at North
Korean targets shortly after N Korea attacked the South in June

1950. The British aircraft carriers *Triumph, Theseus, Glory* and *Ocean* provided all the UK's tactical strike and fighter operations throughout the 3 years of the war. RAF involvement was limited to transport flights into safe airfields and some flying-boat MPA patrols in the open ocean off Japan. RN carrier aircraft flew thousands of effective sorties.

Suez 1956

This was a combined assault on Egypt by British and French carrier-borne and land-based aircraft. In the British operations, the RN deployed 3 fixed-wing carriers, *Eagle, Albion* and *Bulwark* plus 2 helicopter carriers, *Ocean* and *Theseus*. Because of their ability to gain better position, the strike carriers reacted more quickly to calls for offensive air support than RAF aircraft in distant Cyprus and Malta. Despite only having one-third of the total British strike fighters embarked, RN strike fighters flew two-thirds of the strike sorties and their aircraft spent longer over the target area. RAF aircraft had long transits from their bases, carried less weapons and could spend little time on task, most of that at high level to conserve fuel.

Levant 1958

US/UK assistance sought to protect Lebanon and (land-locked) Jordan against Iraqi aggression. *Eagle* provided support for airborne and amphibious forces deployed into theatre. RAF transport aircraft flying British troops into Jordan were protected by carrier-borne fighters since RAF fighter bases were too far away for their aircraft to be effective.

Korea 1960

UN forces including an RN carrier deployed to the Yellow Sea on exercises aimed at deterring the North from launching a renewed attack on the South. Deterrence succeeded. There was no RAF involvement since no land-bases were close enough.

Kuwait 1961

British forces deployed to Kuwait to defend it against threatened Iraqi aggression. HMS *Bulwark* arrived with 42 RM Commando within 24 hours (since good intelligence had put her in the right place) and used its helicopters to deploy and support them. British troops were flown into Kuwait by RAF transport with only what they stood up in – they had to requisition vehicles and wait for RN amphibious shipping to bring in more. Strike carrier HMS *Victorious* took several days to arrive with her battle group from the South China Sea but brought the 'complete package of air power' that subsequently dominated the area. A single RAF Hunter squadron had deployed to Kuwait from Bahrain but lacked fuel, ammunition, spares and most of all GCI radar coverage other than that provided by *Bulwark*. RAF transport was being used to fly in troops and so none was available to support the Hunters which left once *Victorious* arrived. The need for the RN to support land-based aircraft led to the second commando-carrier, HMS *Albion*, being fitted with better surveillance radar (Type 965).

Confrontation with Indonesia 1963-66

Britain and the Commonwealth supported the Malaysian Government against Indonesian aggression and deployed forces from all 3 Services. The Far East Fleet provided a considerable deterrent against Indonesian escalation and the presence of its strike carriers posed a threat that Indonesia could not counter. Carrier and air group transits of high-visibility international waters such as the Sunda Strait added to their deterrence value. Land-based air could not provide such a visible deterrent.

A decisive role in support of the Royal Marines and Army was played by the Navy's Commando Helicopters flying several thousands of hours operating from *Albion* and *Bulwark* in succession and mostly from Forward Air Bases ashore in unusually demanding conditions over a period of 4-5 years.

The Air Force had a presence of Whirlwind and Belvedere helicopters and Twin Pioneers. But the RAF's refusal to delegate operational control of helicopter tasking to the Ground Commander and the strict observance of RAF aircrew duty time or monthly aircraft flying hours limits were great obstacles to their effectiveness. In contrast Naval helicopter squadrons had great rapport with the Army and Royal Marines and applied practical exceptions to such limitations.

The Commando Ship gave invaluable back up for the aircraft deployed ashore and incidentally was the main form of lift for RAF helicopters from Singapore to Borneo.

East African Mutinies 1964

Following a mutiny by Tanganyikan Army units in January 1964, Britain was asked to provide assistance. HMS *Centaur* was at Aden and embarked 45 RN Commando, 16/5 Lancers with their vehicles and 2 RAF Helicopters in addition to her normal air group. The subsequent assault was 'a Model of how flexible carriers are and how quickly they can act'. (Another example of RAF being taken into action by an RN carrier.) *Centaur* was capable of launching her normal air group although at times it would have been a 'squeeze'.

Defence of Zambia 1965

Following UDI by Rhodesia, the Zambian Government requested air defence arrangements from the UK. HMS *Eagle* was positioned from 23 November to 7 December 1965 pending the arrival of RAF fighters.

Beira Patrol 1965-66

Followed on from Zambia assistance above. Britain undertook to enforce UN sanctions preventing tankers from entering Beira with oil for Rhodesia. Only carriers could search the vast areas of sea involved in the months it took the RAF to build up an MPA base and deploy aircraft to it. *Eagle* and *Ark Royal* were both involved for considerable periods at sea.

Aden 1967

British forces were evacuated from Aden in November 1967 covered by HMS Victorious with an RN task force off shore. RAF aircraft were among the forces evacuated and therefore relied on RN carrier-borne aircraft for their defence while they did so.

Suez 1967

HMS Victorious, on her way home from the Far East, passed through the Suez Canal and then flew Sea Vixens on airborne standby/alert ready to assist Israeli forces while 801 Sqn Buccaneer Mk 2 acted as tankers. That they were eventually not called on for combat was a great disappointment for the aircrew involved.

Belize 1972.

A show of strength by Buccaneers from *Ark Royal* prevented a threatened invasion of British Honduras (Belize) by Guatemala. Land-based air was too far away and could do nothing.

South Atlantic 1982

Carrier/ship-borne Naval All-Weather Fighters (Sea Harrier) and helicopters were fundamental to the success of the campaign which would not have been possible without them. Significantly the RAF Ground Attack Harrier needed carriers/*Atlantic Conveyor* to get them into action. [The RAF myth that its land-based fighter aircraft could protect the Fleet at sea throughout the oceans of the world was completely destroyed.]

Kuwait 1991

USN carriers played a big part in the coercive all-arms forces that drove Iraqi forces out of Kuwait; HMS *Ark Royal* operated in the Eastern Mediterranean in a containment role that was not, in the event, used.

Bosnia/Former Yugoslavia 1992-96

RN and USN carriers operated in support of UN and NATO operations in the former Yugoslavia. Carriers were able to position clear of weather which sometimes limited RAF and coalition operations from land bases. The UK Government ordered one carrier to be available constantly in case it proved necessary to withdraw British forces under fire–since land-based aircraft could not guarantee to do so and did not have the valuable mix of fighters and helicopters close to the scene of action.

Afghanistan 2001

During the US-led invasion of Afghanistan, October 2001, Bagram Airfield was secured by a team from the British Special Boat Service and B and C Companies from 40 Commando, Royal Marines – delivered by UK Carrier.

Sierra Leone 2002

HMS *Illustrious* provided air support in the form of Sea Harrier armed reconnaissance missions and a national command centre for British forces that rescued UN forces in Sierra Leone providing a secure base that could not be located or attacked by the terrorists ashore.

Iraq 2003

HMS *Ark Royal* operated in her alternative helicopter role with Sea Kings and RAF Chinooks embarked to land RM commandoes on the Al Faw Peninsula. Later, Sea Harrier FA2 fighter aircraft assisted the U. S. Navy in enforcing the no-fly zone over Iraq.

Libya 2011

But for the withdrawal of HMS *Ark Royal* and the Royal Navy Harrier GR9 squadrons (SDSR 2010), Britain could have supplied in theatre, rapid response, fighter combat offensive air support for the Libyan Operation–as supplied effectively by the French and Italian aircraft carriers and the USS *Kearsage*. Instead, British rotary wing air power was deployed to great operational effect in HMS *Ocean* in the form of the Apache helicopters of the Army Air Corps (flown by both AAC and RN pilots) and the Sea King AEW helicopters of the Royal Navy. These resources provided the 24/7 offensive air support that was not available from land-based air situated 600 nautical miles from the theatre of action.

David Hobbs
Crail
February 2011

Operations in which the RAF has relied on RN Aircraft Carriers to get into and sustain operations.

Although the RAF would have politicians believe that it is a mobile force, there are many examples of where it could not have deployed aircraft, aircrew and maintainers into conflict zones without aircraft carriers. Once deployed, the RAF then relied on sea-borne bulk supplies of fuel and ammunition which, in turn, needed the RN to maintain control of the sea supply routes with its aircraft carriers playing a prominent role. Examples include:

Russia 1919

British forces deployed into Russia against Bolsheviks in 1919 needed air support most of which was transported into theatre in RN aircraft/seaplane carriers and then deployed ashore.

Palestine 1929

Aircraft from HMS *Courageous* landed to support British troops in action in Palestine.

Norway 1940

RAF aircraft based in the UK had insufficient range to be effective in operations over Norway after the German invasion. Most support came from carrier-borne aircraft but the only effective RAF involvement came from Gladiator and Hurricane fighters landed from the aircraft carriers *Glorious* and *Furious*. The carriers also gave navigational and technical support.

Malta 1940-42

RAF fighters had insufficient range to fly to Malta from Gibraltar after Italy entered the war and the only way to get Hurricanes and Spitfires to Malta was to fly them off the decks of RN and USN aircraft carriers. There would have been no fighters in Malta without them. HMS *Ark Royal* 3 was lost returning from flying Spitfires to Malta.

North Africa 1941-42

Most of the fighters in the Desert Air Force relied on sea control to get them there and numbers were carried in aircraft carriers such as HMS *Furious*.

Sumatra 1942

RAF fighters did not have the range to reinforce Allied forces in South East Asia as the Japanese advanced in early 1942. HMS *Indomitable* ferried and flew off Hurricanes to Sumatra which could not, otherwise, have got there.

Pacific 1945

RN escort carriers ferried RAF Mosquito bombers and their secret 'Highball' bouncing bombs to Australia in 1945. They were intended to operate from the decks of fleet carriers to attack Japanese warships in the home islands but the USN refused to allow them to do so. The RN put considerable effort into training their crews.

Korea 1950-53

Although the RAF did not operate combat aircraft in the Korean War, it did supply Meteor fighters to 77 Squadron of the RAAF which did operate. They were ferried to Iwakuni in Japan in British aircraft carriers including HMS *Unicorn*. Without her, the RAAF could not have supported the Squadron in action.

Confrontation 1963-66

During the Indonesian Confrontation against Malaysia, the RAF relied on RN commando-carriers to ferry helicopters to Borneo. They lacked the range to fly there.

East African Mutiny 1964

2 RAF Belvedere helicopters were embarked in HMS *Centaur*; they had no other means of reaching the scene of action.

South Atlantic 1982

RAF Harriers and Chinook helicopters had no means of reaching the conflict other than Atlantic Conveyor and the decks of Hermes and Invincible. They relied on the RN radar/air defence environment and RN supplies of fuel and weapons to be effective, neither of which would have been there without the carriers.

Iraq 2003

RAF Chinooks embarked in HMS Ark Royal 5 took part in the amphibious assault by Royal Marines on the Al Faw peninsula. Again, they lacked the range to operate from a land-base and needed the aircraft carrier to take them to the fight.

David Hobbs, Crail, February 2011.

Annex E

WORDS OF WISDOM FROM DR. ANTHONY WELLS.

"... the United States is addressing interests in the strategic context, not in a piecemeal or ad hoc way. In 2014 the European Union issued a Maritime Security Strategy, and the United Kingdom issued a National Strategy for Maritime Security. Both of these showed positive trends, a revitalization of the maritime domain in grand strategy. Furthermore, the American Chief of Naval Operations and the British First Sea Lord have jointly issued a vision for deeper cooperation in the next fifteen years, how best to work together to pursue mutual strategic interests. Their declaration is a good starting point for our analysis and discussion.

At the heart of this analysis is the core concept of "strategy" itself. There can be many definitions, perhaps in the eye of the beholder. Nonetheless, it is essential that we have a framework; otherwise our future strategy may be built on shifting sands. There are two separate concepts: the ways and means to implement strategic goals, and the core strategic goals themselves. The latter is about what it is that we are trying to achieve and why, while the former is about how to do it—and it is easy to slip into the how without fully analysing the why. We can address "naval power" and its characteristics, and the individual benefits for example of various naval capabilities, forward persistent presence, manoeuvre, flexibility to use the sea commons, overwhelming combined force, logistics, and so forth. This is not strategy but well understood and defined aspects of multiple naval means: surface, subsurface, air, space, amphibious, nuclear deterrence, and special forces. Strategy is fundamentally about what the United States and the United Kingdom want to do, and why, in order to protect and enhance their well defined perceptions and written statements of their national interests. Once those interests are defined and prioritized, it behoves both nations to consider "how to create the environment and means with which to both control and achieve favourable outcomes," however these may be defined. Influencing and controlling the behaviour of others, whether state players or other actors, good or bad, in the best interests of the United States and the United Kingdom are the natural corollaries to what both countries define as their top priorities.

Admiral Sir George Zambellas, the First Sea Lord, and Admiral Jonathan Greenert, former Chief of Naval Operations, have done a sterling job in their joint paper, Combined Seapower: A Shared Vision for Royal Navy—United States Navy Cooperation. It is the way ahead for both navies, together and in unison, for at least the next fifteen years. What may need more emphasis is the question of what indeed the core national strategic interests are. Both admirals have brilliantly articulated the "how," with a fine shopping list of operational and technical issues, force mixes, exercises, joint training, forward-deployed joint and combined operations, intelligence, and personnel exchanges. They have clearly defined the absolute necessity for protecting, and controlling when necessary, the sea lines of communication and seaborne trade. But both countries' political, public, and media elites need to hear why the two combined navies are the best means to advance the national interests while restricting and, if necessary, denying any potential adversaries the same ability. The right words are vital in this debate: that sea power in its myriad US-UK combined format will offer both countries' leaderships the optimal means, together with diplomatic and economic means, to achieve favourable outcomes.

The substance of strategic expeditionary naval diplomacy and warfare, its core, characteristic value, is its ability to signal, influence, deter, and, at worst case, provide the full range of measured force to meet all known and projected military-political-economic contingencies. This is the key lesson of naval history, and grand strategy.

Manoeuvring a fleet, of whatever composition, scenario, or local tactical situation, is predicated on the measured application of both implied and actual force. A full US-UK battle force of surface, subsurface, air, space, and special forces, grouped with a large amphibious force (which can include a Marine Expeditionary Force, with its organic air group), enables penetration and occupation of the most challenging threat region with extraordinary lethal force. The combined strength of a US-UK naval task force would make it, therefore, not just formidable but an instrument of strategic power. The history of the last fifteen years is a sad reflection on the fallacy of committing land forces to situations that were strategically untenable. Historically the United States and the United Kingdom have committed large armies, essentially "people's armies" led by career professionals, only in the face of the most threatening odds. Large standing armies, eating up national treasure, offer no strategic value unless the intent is to overrun, like Adolf Hitler, neighbours with brutal force. The "On and From the Sea" strategy offers a much more diverse and affordable set of strategic options, with forward presence and manoeuvrability crucial as instruments of not just national power but diplomatic signalling. The essence of maritime strategy resides therefore in these innate characteristics, put simply by one famous example. When asked if Napoleon could invade England, Admiral John Jervis responded, "I do not say they [the French] cannot come, I only say they cannot come by sea." This summarizes a critical strategic point, and within it lies the strategy that led to Napoleon's demise and to the end of French conquests during the Napoleonic era. As in countless scenarios in the past, the navies of the United States and the United Kingdom can launch forces onto land in measured and strategically placed ways when necessary, while controlling the seas and air above. Once the strategic advantages of combined US-UK naval forces are fully articulated, it becomes axiomatic that the maritime domain becomes the single best arena for protecting and enhancing the vital national interests of the United States and the United Kingdom.

The "Statement of Intent Regarding Enhanced Cooperation on Carrier Operations and Maritime Power Projection" (signed by the British secretary for defence and the American secretary of defense in January 2012) is a means to an end, but it is not a strategy. The strategic concepts described above call for a resolute statement of joint national resolve to use the sea and naval forces as "the primary means" to secure the vital national interests of the United States and the United Kingdom. The latter, with a lower gross national product and hence less available investment for defense, may have to transfer resources from the army budget to the Royal Navy. The great traditions and core capabilities of the British Army can be preserved, with perhaps a much larger reserve army and a reduced permanent, career force level. Resources will have to be found for the Royal Navy, and this is the most likely, perhaps only, practical outcome. It may be that the US Army too will have to be significantly reduced, in order to fund not just the O/no-class SSBN replacement but also the forward presence and logistics sustainment that the new strategy dictates.

The "shared vision" for the US Navy and the Royal Navy, articulated by their two fine leaders, is a fitting end to our study. We end on a most positive note—that the cooperation and historical links of both navies will not only endure but be enhanced with new energy and vision, reflecting the hallmark of both navies: that people are the single most important factor and that there is no substitute for good leadership. Both the United States Navy and the Royal Navy are in highly capable hands.

Fear God and Dread Nought."

Books Celebrating Fleet Air Arm Achievements.

'Royal Naval Air Service: 1912-1918', by Brad King.

'Sailor in the Air', by Vice Admiral Sir Richard Bell Davies VC CB DSO AFC.

'Air War in the Falklands 1982' – Osprey.

'Sea Harrier over the Falklands', by Commander Sharkey Ward DSC AFC.

'The Fleet Air Arm Handbook', by David Wragge.

'Wings on my Sleeve' by Captain Eric 'Winkle' Brown CBE DSC AFC RN. Published by Weidenfeld and Nicolson.

'The Disastrous Fall and Triumphant Rise of the Fleet Air Arm' by Henry Adlam Lt Cdr Ret'd. Published by Pen and Sword.

And David Hobbs' books:

'Taranto and Naval Air Warfare in the Mediterranean 1940 – 1945', due for publication in 2020/21.

'A Century of Carrier Aviation–1909 to 2009'.

'British Aircraft Carriers–1908 to 2013'.

'The Royal Navy's Air Service in the Great War–1914 to 1918'.

'The Dawn of Carrier Strike–1919 to 1940'.

'The British Pacific Fleet–1944 to 1948'.

'Aircraft Carrier Victorious–1941 to 1968'.

'The British Carrier Strike Fleet after 1945–1945 to 2015'.

"A Blueprint for Justification and Recovery"

House of Commons Defence Select Committee Inquiry, ''Modernising Defence Programme''.

"A Blueprint for Justification and Recovery."

MEMORANDUM

To: **The House of Commons Defence Committee**
From: **Commander N D MacCartan-Ward RN DSC AFC**.
Reference: NDMA/HCDC/MDP dated 01 April 2018.

NEW INQUIRY:
MODERNISING DEFENCE PROGRAMME (MDP)

Date: 01 April 2018.

This Submission is supported by:
   Rear-Admiral ESJ Larken RN DSO
   Captain Colin Hamilton RN
   Commander Graham J Edmonds RN

G H Bennett (Associate Professor, Plymouth University)

SUBJECT: A Blueprint for Justification and Recovery.

Introduction

1. The UK has now reached a troubling watershed between
   a. Being able to project cost-effective global political and military power in defence of our Lifeblood and in support of National Policy,
   b. Relying on other nations and on some inappropriate UK-based weapon systems to protect those interests.

2. This Submission suggests that:
   a. The current constitution of our Armed Forces and the 'organisation, efficiency management and business and commercial practices in the Ministry of Defence (MoD)' is flawed and fails to support 1. a. , above.
   b. Each Armed Service should formally justify its independent existence, constitution and associated weapon systems against HMG's Military Defence Priorities.
   c. Budgetary assignments between each Armed Service should be flexible, on a firm Joint Service basis.

Assumptions

3. The UK's principal vulnerability to military attack/aggression is globally based and, in large measure, lies on or under the high seas against our Trade Routes, Energy Supply Routes, Undersea Communications Cables and our Overseas Territories, including our Exclusive Economic Zones (EEZs) – our 'Lifeblood'.

4. "Deployed boots on the ground" are essential to success in any land-based campaign. "Deployed Navy warships

on and under the sea" are essential for deterring those that might harm our Prime National Interest, our Lifeblood. Such physical presence requires the global capability of supporting air power which cannot be reliably or effectively provided 24/7 by land-based air power especially beyond the NATO geographic area.

5. It is unlikely that Russia (or another major power) would have an interest in provoking a major war in Europe or conduct pre-emptive strikes on the UK. Any intent for ballistic missile attack on the UK Base by a Rogue Nation is most unlikely actually to occur. Ultimate shield in both cases is ensured by the nuclear deterrent.

6. There is no foreseeable risk of a military invasion of Britain's shores. Should a risk develop in the future, the Naval Service will be required to provide the first line of defence and deterrence – as in World War II.

7. So-called 'Grey Warfare', undertaken by for instance cyber resources or public disinformation, will continue to be a vulnerability.

8. It is a Government obligation to fund properly the capabilities referred to at 1. a. , above.

What should the MDP mean for the size and shape of the Armed Forces? Which capabilities should the MDP be seeking to retain and augment? Which should it be seeking to restructure or dispose of?

9. With our current limited capability to project effective military power and deterrence beyond the NATO area, MDP should herald a radical and comprehensive Justification Process leading to a new funding balance between the

Armed Forces that reflects our Nation's Prime Military Defence Interest. In pursuit of this, National Threat Reduction Exercises should be adopted. A basic premise of these exercises must be to understand our limitations as a small maritime island nation with middle-rank developed economy.

10. As part of the NATO Alliance the UK should therefore contribute to the deterrent effect of the Alliance with practical and effective capabilities that are within our means and that also serve our particular global national interests as an island nation.

11. UK's military contribution to NATO should be examined critically and revised/reshaped:
    a. Leaving the Land-Based Air and Ground Defence of the continental European land-mass mainly to its constituent Nations;
    b. Concentrating UK's military contribution on a robust maritime capability centred on a properly funded and equipped Naval Service, including a Royal Marine led, rapid-reaction Amphibious Brigade Group.

Land-Based Forces–Ground

12. General Sir Nick Carter's comment in the press that the UK does not have the military wherewithal to challenge the Russian threat is a truism but fails to put into context our Island Nation status. Heavy tanks and artillery are not needed for the direct defence of the UK Base – see assumption at paragraph 6 above. The retention and quantity of such weapon systems for this purpose needs to be validated. However, UK needs to be able to deploy at decent notice one properly provisioned Division to support NATO within the NATO geographic area, but not beyond.

It should not be stationed permanently abroad (i. e. no re-creation of BAOR).

13. Further, there is a case for our European NATO partners maintaining an effective establishment of appropriate heavy weapon systems and robust Army infrastructures (including personnel) to deter incremental aggression over their borders.

Conclusion.

14. The question to be addressed by our Government must be:

'Can or should Britain continue to invest in and 'protect the UK Base' with heavy armour and maintain a large Army when the defence of our principal global national interest, which demands a core maritime capability, is not receiving adequate funding?'

Land-Based Forces – Air

15. The constitution of UK's military air assets is seriously out of balance in the context of paragraph 1. a. , above. Global Land Force and Naval operations need to have 24/7 Combat Air Support for effective deterrence, offence and defence and this has not been available beyond the immediate NATO area without extreme cost during and as a direct result of the 'gapping' of our Carrier Strike capability.

16. A comprehensive Threat Reduction Exercise would validate this observation, leading to a major and essential reallocation of resources particularly with regard to:
a.   The size of our land-based Combat Aircraft Fleet, and,

b. The non-cost-effectiveness of independent Expeditionary Air Wing Operations.

Combat Aircraft Defence of the UK Base

17. The Typhoon with an unrefuelled combat radius of action of just 750 nm is unable to defend the UK Base (its raison d'être) against the modern Russian air threat. Each Bear H or Blackjack bomber can launch up to 16 supersonic, conventionally or nuclear armed ground attack cruise missiles[20] at a range of 1300 nm from their targets. UK does not have nearly enough Air Refuelling resources to extend the combat range of the Typhoon on a 24/7 on-task basis to deter/oppose this threat, so far as it is significant. Whether judged significant or not, it does call for a realistic deterrent capability.

18. The UK Base does not boast any effective hard kill air defences save for the ship-borne Sea Viper Missile–and there are insufficient T45 Guided Missile Destroyers to support both Fleet and UK Base Ballistic and Cruise Missile defence.

19. Sufficient capability to deter Russia from hazarding or being seen to hazard the UK Base is essential. This is public and political reality. But our Red line is that there should be no re-creation of RAF Germany (e. g. RAF Balkans). Continental Allies must provide such resources/ capability.

20. The main, currently-available defence against the realisation of an unlikely Russian air offensive against the UK Base would be deployment of the US Navy Strike Carrier

---

[20] The Kh-101, 102 and Kh-555.

Striking Fleet, supported when operational by UK Aircraft Carriers and Guided Missile Warships.

21. The operational effectiveness/cost-effectiveness of the 160-strong Typhoon Fleet is questionable. It should be radically reduced in size. This would represent a logical and handsome saving in Defence funds without hazarding national security.

Expeditionary Air Wing (EAW) Operations

22. EAW Operations have been re-introduced following the gapping in UK Carrier Strike Capability which has been vital to the success of most Expeditionary Task Force Operations since World War II.

23. This represents a costly departure from historical precedent in terms of funding as well as true global reach. This cost is not commensurate with the relatively modest achievements by land-based air in or immediately adjacent to the NATO area against undefended targets without any air threat: as in the Libya conflict and now the Iraq/Syria conflict against Daesh/ISIS.

24. 903 EAW deployment to Cyprus for operations in Iraq/Syria has resulted in many pickups, trucks and small buildings being destroyed and Jihadis killed but at considerable cost in terms of Defence (and Defence Contingency?) Funds. [As given by the MoD and reported by the BBC News defence correspondent, Cyprus-based RAF aircraft have delivered 4,409 bombs and missiles over Syria and Iraq causing the deaths of 3,964 Jihadis. Main weapons delivered have been the Paveway Bomb (> £25,000 each), Hellfire Missiles from Drones (> £50,000 each) and Brimstone Missiles (approx. £175,000 each). By

averaging out these costs one can reasonably suggest that just the weapons associated with the death of each terrorist cost the UK taxpayer about £80,000 – a total of over £315 million for weapons alone.]

25. Various defence analysts have estimated the true Air cost of the Libyan venture as approximately £1. 5 billion. The three-year Iraq/Syria air intervention (about 1600 attack missions) has already cost the taxpayer up to £4 billion – more than the cost of the carrier HMS Queen Elizabeth – whilst contributing less than 5% of the Coalition air effort.

26. Comments in the press by a Typhoon Squadron Commander as well as statistics from a well-known defence commentator, Howard Wheeldon, after his visit to Akrotiri, Cyprus indicate that each 8-hour 903 EAW attack mission cost approximately £2,200,000.

Single Attack Mission Cost					
		Per Flight hour	Mission Length	Weapons delivered Cost	Total
2 Tornados	2	£35,000	8		£560,000
2 Typhoons	2	£70,000	8		£1,120,000
1 Voyager	1	£20,000	8		£160,000
1 Sentinel	1	£20,000	8		£160,000
Paveway IV	1			£25,000	£25,000
Brimstone	1			£175,000	£175,000
				Total	**£2,200,000**

27. If two targets were attacked on each Attack Mission delivering 1 Paveway & 1 Brimstone, the total cost of 800 missions would be £1. 76 billion.

28. If 400 additional Attack Missions were flown without weapon release, this would cost £800,000,000: giving a total for 1200 missions of £2. 56 billion.

29. This leaves many further missions to be costed, including a large number of Reaper sorties.

30. Further costs have been accrued with the major logistic support train to and from Britain involving Voyager, C-130J Hercules, C-17 and A400M Atlas aircraft.

31. Personnel support costs, e. g. at RAF Brize Norton and Akrotiri (8,900*) over a three-year period at approximately £35,000 p. a. amount to a further £ 934,500,000 – totalling £3. 5 billion. (*Almost 2,500 personnel greater than that of the invaluable and now threatened Corps of the Royal Marines.)

Conclusion

32. EAWs cannot be considered a cost-effective way of conducting Military Operations against low-value undefended targets. A return to Maritime-Based Expeditionary Task Force Operations with true global reach is considered essential.

Maritime Forces
Decline of the Naval Service

33. Our Naval Service has been reduced, and drastically so, over the past two decades following successive Defence Reviews. The root causes of this steady decline in global Maritime capability include:
   a. Lack of political, Civil Service and academic recognition of this paper's Assumptions (3-8 above);

b. Lack of control of Single Service rivalry and in-fighting within MoD – it is notable that the single service with the greater senior-officer availability are those that seem most influential in Academia. Trenchard's first view of the proposal to form an independent RAF is pertinent. [21]

c. The excessive influence within Cabinet, MoD, NSC and Parliamentary Academic Adviser teams of some academic cadres steered by unbalanced 'expert' briefing;

d. A lack of 'reliable and robust justification' when addressing the Operational Requirements for and Procurement of major weapon systems;

e. Deficient MoD contracting with and contract control of UK Defence Contractors, for instance without effective penalty clauses within Contracts to protect the end Customer;

f. The anachronistic and counter-productive arbitrary three-way split in Military Defence Funding.

34. These 'root causes' led to the proposal concerning the withdrawal of HMSs Albion and Bulwark from Service and further cuts to Royal Marine personnel. There was a lack of military justification behind this proposal and it was opportune that the Defence Committee conducted a formal Inquiry into the matter. The published Report HC 622[22] on the future of the Royal Marines and our Amphibious Warships challenged the proposal strongly and is a fine example of a sensible, if necessarily sectoral,

---

[21] "a service beyond control of the Army and Navy would be very liable to lose its sense of proportion and be drawn towards the spectacular".

[22] HC 622 Published on 4 February 2018, 'Sunset for the Royal Marines? The Royal Marines and UK amphibious capability' is in itself a Threat Reduction Exercise and provides a significant example of the utility and value of such an Exercise.

Threat Reduction Exercise – entailing the detailed 'Justification or Not' of such proposals.

Increasing Global Challenges

35. Global military threats to our national Lifeblood continue to proliferate.

36. These include:
   a. Modern Diesel Submarines which are very difficult to detect and are being procured by Major Powers, Rogue Nations and some Third World countries. The availability of submarines with Air Independent Propulsion (AIP) systems[23] represents a 'game-changer' for ASW and ASuW resources, allowing these conventional boats to remain silently submerged for up to 2 or 3 weeks – as opposed to 2 or 3 days – and pose a significant threat to our Lifeblood. MPA aircraft, when available, have little if any capability against this threat.
   b. Mobile Land-Based and Sea-based Anti-Ship Missile Systems.
   c. The emergence of Asymmetric Warfare including the possibility of Swarm Attacks in the Strait of Hormuz and other trade-route chokepoints.

Paras b. and c. above indicate a very strong need for a powerful Defence Suppression capability (as with the F-18 Growler aircraft).

37. These threats cannot be countered effectively by Land-Based Air or Ground Forces.

---

[23] http://www.public.navy.mil/subfor/underseawarfaremagazine/Issues/Archives/issue_13/propulsion. htm

38. Nor can the threat to our Undersea Communication Cables be so countered. In its Report to the Committee dated Dec 1, 2017, the Policy Exchange Think Tank considered that 'Undersea Cables were Indispensable, insecure' and that 'Britain, as an island nation, was particularly vulnerable.'[24]

Conclusion

39. A major increase in Naval Service equipment and capability is essential–and could, without harm to our National Security and Military Defence, be compensated for by a calibrated reduction in those elements of the Army and Royal Air Force that are not relevant to the prime threats to our Lifeblood.

Should the MoD be seeking further increases in defence spending?

40. If the Government introduces a program of Armed Forces Justification through the medium of Threat Reduction, it is likely that 'the Black Hole' in Defence Funding can be reduced, if not eliminated. This will in turn allow a return to responsible funding that may need marginal increases.

41. There needs to be equally robust and critical justification of the charges being made by the Defence Industry for new weapon systems and for the maintenance of current weapon systems/platforms. Immediate examples include:
   a.   The upkeep of the obsolete Tornado GR4 – more than £7 billion since Harrier withdrawal (NAO figures);

---

[24] https://policyexchange.org.uk/publication/undersea-cables-indispensable-insecure/

b. The continuing cost of the Typhoon Program (no longer effective in its primary role against the Russian threat) – now estimated to be more than £80 billion;
c. The size of the F-35 Program;
d. The equally extraordinary planned cost of each Type 26 Guided Missile Frigate:

Direct Comparison–UK v Foreign Warship Costs	
UK Type 45 Daring–Guided Missile Destroyer	£633,000,000
UK Type 26–Guided Missile Frigate (plus undeclared weapon system costs)	£1,233,000,000
US FFG(X)–new Guided Missile Frigate	£354,000,000
French new Frigates	£585,000,000

Conclusions.

42. Validation of all Armed Services' weapon procurement and maintenance plans is necessary.

43. Current MoD Contractual Procedures appear to have failed to protect the interest of the Armed Forces as end-customers.

How can the MoD reform itself to improve its business, commercial and procurement practices? How can it set realistic efficiency targets?

44. A principal root cause of misguided Defence Procurement and excessive Equipment Costs lies within the MoD itself. While single-service interests and mutual barriers continue to rule without impartial oversight and associated Justification of Priorities, the current defence spending malaise is certain to continue. MoD cannot efficiently and fairly 'reform itself' – but it must be reformed.

What lessons can be learned from past defence reviews to inform and improve the outcome of the MDP? Who should the MoD be consulting externally?

45. Lack of a mandatory Threat Reduction process has led to misguided decisions which have in turn led to the irresponsible demise in UK's ability to project military power and deterrence on a global basis. The arbitrary three-way split of Defence Funding between the Services continues to be illogical, counter-productive and anachronistic.

46. A principal factor for ensuring UK's continuing political and military influence in the world, thereby ensuring the sustainment of our island nation Lifeblood, must be a marked diminution in the overwhelming influence of Land-Based Air Academia in Whitehall whose advices have led to the regrettable gap in Carrier Strike and the associated near emasculation of effective Naval Service world-reach.

47. It should be noted and understood that:
    a. More than 80% of all effective Air Power Projections/Interventions since World War II have been conducted by the aircraft of British and United States Carrier Battle Groups;
    b. Other Nations recognise this and reflect it by utilising the expert advices of Naval Warfare trained Academics (75%) and not Land-Based Air Academics (less than 25%);
    c. Retired Officers who are proven experts in their own fields (e. g. Naval Air Warfare a. o. t. Land-Based Air Warfare) and are not gagged by successive Governments are far more able to provide accurate Threat Reduction advice – as demonstrated by the recent Amphibious Warfare/Royal Marine Inquiry.

What are the implications of examining Defence separately from the wider consideration of national security capabilities?

48. Such separation would allow the realistic recognition of the Military measures necessary for the global defence of our Lifeblood – without which our economic and commercial prosperity cannot be guaranteed.

Black Buck Fuel Costs– Falklands 1982

Range from Ascension, 3500 nm
63 Bombs (one on target)
4 Shrikes (one target destroyed)

tual mbing issions	No.	*No. Tankers per mission	*Give Away gallons/ Tanker	Total Give away fuel gallons	**Cost/ gallon	Sub total	Operation Cost Running Total
3	13	10000	390000	£4		£1,560,000	£1,560,000

ccording to RAF participants up to 15 refuelling tankers were launched for each mission to account for any serviceability. These fuel figures are therefore conservative.

Today's prices.

tual rike issions ee note 1 low)	No.	No. Tankers per mission	Give Away gallons/ Tanker	Total Give away fuel gallons	Cost/ gallon	Sub total	Operation Cost Running Total
4	13	10000	520000	£4		£2,080,000	£3,640,000

orted rborne issions ee note below)	No.	No. Tankers per mission	Used/Ditched gallons/ Tanker	Total used fuel gallons	Cost/ gallon	Sub total	Operation Cost Running Total
12	13	75000	1170000	£4		£4,680,000	£8,320,000

Transit to & from UK	No.	No. Aircraft	Fuel gallons/ aircraft	Fuel gallons	Cost/ gallon	Sub total	Total Cost
	2	17	75000	255000	£4	£1,020,000	£9,340,000

Fuel Cost per Bomb/ Shrike on Target				No. on Target	Operation Cost	Cost per Bomb/ Shrike on Target
				2	£9,340,000	£4,670,000

Fuel Cost per Bomb/ Shrike delivered				No. delivered	Operation Cost	Cost per Bomb/ Shrike delivered
				68	£9,340,000	£137,353

By contrast:

Fuel Cost of Harrier Bombing Mission from Carrier	A/C	Bombs/ aircraft		Fuel gallons/ aircraft	Cost/ gallon	Sub total	Cost/ Bomb delivered
	1	5		500	£4	£2,000	£400

Note 1.

Post-war inspections revealed that only one target was destroyed by the Shrike missiles fired. That was a radar-laid anti-aircraft gun positioned on the southern edge of Port Stanley town.

Note 2.

Following the war, an RAF team was formed to analyse all land-based air operations associated with Operation Corporate. One of the members of that team provided the following information.

"There were a total of 12 Black Buck missions that launched from Ascension Island that had to be aborted in flight. This resulted in a massive amount of fuel being jettisoned by the Victor tankers prior to being able to land back on the airfield.

On one of these aborted missions the Vulcan pilot reported cabin pressurisation failure when the aircraft reached altitude. It was not until after all the aircraft had landed that the cause for the pressurisation failure was established: one of the small cockpit windows had been left open!"

The Submarine Threat to Our Lifeblood – "Unseen" by MOD?

MEMORANDUM

To: **The House of Commons Defence Select Committee**
Copy to: **Secretary of State**
           First Sea Lord
           Admiral the Rt. Hon Lord West of Spithead GCB DSC PC

From: Commander N D MacCartan-Ward DSC AFC
Reference: JOAF/NDMW dated 10 January 2018.

**Subject: The Submarine Threat to Our Lifeblood –
         "Unseen" by MOD?**

Date: 10 January 2018.

Executive Summary.

i.   This paper is focused mainly on assessing the track record
     of the Anti-Submarine Warfare (ASW) capabilities of UK's
     Maritime Patrol Aircraft (MPA). Prior to the ongoing P8

Poseidon procurement, UK's recent experience has centred on the Nimrod aircraft which is no longer in service.

ii. The paper also addresses the Surface Search (ASuW) role of MPA and assesses this capability particularly in relation to our Navy's global open ocean needs and responsibilities.

iii. An increasing number of modern diesel submarines (which are very difficult to detect and pose a significant threat to our trade, energy supplies and undersea communications) are now being procured by Major Powers, Rogue Nations and some Third World countries.

iv. The availability of such submarines with Air Independent Propulsion (AIP) systems represents a 'game-changer' for ASW and ASuW resources, allowing these conventional boats to remain submerged for up to 2 or 3 weeks – as opposed to 2 or 3 days.

v. Expert comments provided are drawn from retired senior Naval Submariners and Surface Warfare practitioners who have in depth experience of joint ASW/ ASuW operations with the Nimrod and other MPA aircraft.

vi. Considerable doubt is expressed concerning MPA ASW effectiveness in the autonomous detection, location and subsequent prosecution of submarines.

vii. It is agreed that, when available, MPA have been very useful in the ASuW role by discouraging conventional submarines from 'snorkelling' at periscope depth to recharge their batteries–a result which can be achieved by any friendly radar-fitted aircraft or drone. However, the introduction of Air Independent Propulsion (AIP) boats diminishes this capability markedly.

viii.   The cost-effectiveness of procuring sophisticated and expensive MPA aircraft such as the P8 Poseidon as opposed to other more affordably priced aircraft that are available to conduct the ASW and ASuW support role effectively is challenged.

Preamble.

1. While our *classe politique* and the National Security Advisor concentrates on domestic affairs rather than the Military Defence of our national interests, an alarming threat to our global maritime interests is proliferating unseen under the waves. An increasing number of modern diesel submarines are now being procured by Major Powers, Rogue Nations and some Third World countries. The cumulative market for global expenditure on military submarines will reach over US$300 Billion over the next decade[25] – new battery technologies, Air Independent Propulsion (AIP)[26] systems and longer-range missiles make them increasingly potent and difficult to detect.

2. As so many nations have decided to invest in submarines one can assume that they have concluded that the best ASW/ASuW platform with the least chance of being detected is, as one RAN Warfare Officer termed them, 'a black tube of death' (another submarine).

3. Chief of the Defence Staff, Air Chief Marshal Sir Stuart Peach (December 15, 2017, 12:01am, The Times):

---

[25] The Global Submarines and MRO Market 2017-2027 -https://www. reportlinker. com/p05236673

[26] http://www. public. navy. mil/subfor/underseawarfaremagazine/Issues/ Archives/issue_13/propulsion. htm

"Britain's trade and internet are at risk of catastrophic damage from any Russian attack on underwater communications cables, the head of the armed forces has warned. … Therefore, we must continue to develop our maritime forces, with our allies, to match Russian fleet Modernisation."

4. In its Report to the Committee dated Dec 1, 2017 https://policyexchange. org. uk/publication/undersea-cables-indispensable-insecure/, the Policy Exchange Think Tank considered that "Undersea Cables were Indispensable, insecure" and that "Britain, as an island nation, was particularly vulnerable [to the submarine threat]."

5. In recent evidence to the Committee, former First Sea Lord Admiral Sir George Zambellas described UK anti-submarine defence as "inadequate" and criticised poor SSN availability.

6. It would appear that the crux of this matter lies in Sir Stuart's statement that *"we must continue to develop our maritime forces"* to counter this threat – not just to our undersea cables but also to our trade and energy supplies. Logically, such development must be cost-effective and operationally effective.

Aim.

7. To assess the utility, cost-effectiveness and global operational effectiveness of past and 'present' UK MPA aircraft in the ASW and ASuW roles in the open ocean and littoral environments.

Introduction.

8. This paper has drawn heavily on the in-depth experience of Senior Submariners and Naval Warfare experts (not all of whom are named). It takes stock of the situation concerning effective investment in reliable ASW and ASuW assets.

9. The professional skills and commitment of RAF air and ground crews are not in question. They must be credited with the fastidious execution of all instructions emanating from their Operational Commanders.

10. However, the paper does raise serious questions concerning:
    a. MOD's persuasive and optimistic view of the ASW effectiveness of MPA undertaking area (e. g. open ocean) anti-submarine search.
    b. The 'alternative' history that has been presented to politicians and the public including the execution of the air war in the Falklands War, particularly the part played by MPA.

Background – Case Studies and observations by senior operators.

11. The MoD has always been fully cognisant of a submarine threat. Since before World War II and up until the 1980's, the UK has countered it predominantly by Anti-Submarine Frigates, Destroyers, Helicopters, Hunter Killer Submarines (both SSN & SSK), Sigint and access to US fixed underwater arrays (SOSUS).

12. In the 1960's and 70's, MoD persuaded Ministers that Maritime Patrol Aircraft were also "essential" to counter this threat.

13. The terminology "essential" was probably an exaggeration and has proven to be less than accurate. Many £ billions of

taxpayers' money have been invested first in the Shackleton and Nimrod fleets (and now, expectedly, in the Poseidon fleet)–with arguably poor operational ASW results that appear to have been unseen by our Secretaries of State and our Government.

An observation by a Nimrod MPA pilot 1982.

14. At a post Falklands gathering in Rosyth in 1982, a senior Nimrod pilot reported anonymously (he asked his name not to be revealed) that "the mean time between submarine detections by the Nimrod and its Sonobuoys was just one submarine detection every 5000 flying hours[27]". Based on strictly applied RAF crew duty times and harmony rules this equates to 625 eight-hour missions at a conservative cost of more than £100 million (at £20,000 per hour) for one detection. This regrettable record does not appear to have been communicated to or acknowledged by MoD and it does raise hard questions as to the efficacy of the MPA Nimrod anti-submarine capability.

15. This lack of candour led to more dependence on the Nimrod force (instead of Hunter Killers, ASW Helicopters or Surface Warships) than was probably justified or wise.

Russian Submarine in the Med.

16. According to the Wall Street Journal[28], it appears that the US fleet in the Eastern Mediterranean was unable to detect and track the Russian diesel boat that launched cruise missiles into Syria in September 2017 against Jihadi troops (the

---

[27] The effect on Nimrod aircrew morale and their ability to concentrate on their electronic and sonar weapon systems to achieve the task in hand must have been counter-productive, to say the least.

[28] https://www. wsj. com/articles/a-russian-ghost-submarine-its-u-s-pursuers-and-a-deadly-new-cold-war-1508509841

Veliky Novgorod a Varshavyanka [NATO Kilo] class SSK of the Black Sea Fleet). The US P8 Poseidon Maritime Patrol Aircraft operating from Italy was reportedly unable to detect or track the submarine.

17. However, as is clearly explained at paragraph 19, below, the Mediterranean Sea provides a benign environment for the clandestine operation of submarines and the key to detecting a diesel boat in the Med is to be able to catch it when it is 'snorkelling' at Periscope Depth to recharge its batteries. This requires a lot of luck and a major multiple-asset/Combined Arms ASW operation that may or may not be successful/ effective. This is especially difficult with the introduction and proliferation of submarines fitted with Air Independent Propulsion (AIP) systems that allow a submarine to stay totally submerged for weeks rather than days.

18. This case study, if correct, indicates little improvements in combined ASW capability in the Mediterranean during two decades to the present. The contribution of MPAs in direct ASW mode would appear to be very low.

The Mediterranean – NATO's Southern Flank.

19. Undetected threats within this Sea, whether submarine or other, represent a serious challenge to NATO's Southern Flank.

20. The Navy Ops ASW desk officer in J3/J7 Division at CinCSouth NATO HQ in Naples in the early 90s recorded the following experience.

> "Anti-Submarine Warfare [ASW] was one of the trick-
> iest elements of Med maritime warfare and to address
> the issue I was tasked by the CinC, Adm J T Howe USN
> (later Director NSA), to write a paper on the Problems

and Issues of ASW in the Med. This was brought about by the embarrassing fact that once Russian submarines entered the Med from the Atlantic they could not be relocated until they exited. The paper was well received but the inevitable conclusion was that when a submarine is east of the Alboran Basin (where the Sound Surveillance System [SOSUS] arrays are laid) locating any type of submarine was / is very difficult. The main sea lane is, of course, from the Straits of Gibraltar to the Suez Canal and it is very, very noisy and busy. The Med is very polluted, has complex sea mounts, narrow straits (e. g. Sicily to Malta to Tripoli), sub-tectonic plates, volcanos, can be saltier than the oceans and has lots of wrecks.

In my time at the desk and during the numerous Southern Region Exercises (Southern Region is 80% sea-water) there was never ever an unalerted detection of either a SSN or SSK–save but once when a Spanish Navy AV8B Harrier was on a low-level exercise mission (via various refuelling stops) to attack a US CVN. In the Western Basin south of the Balearics the Harrier overflew a surfacing SSK and, breaking radio silence, was able to report the unalerted detection via his FC net.

I'm not surprised the P8 failed. So did the P3s, Nimrods and Atlantiques!"

MPA ASW Experience of Senior Submariners/Senior Seaman Officers.

21. Admiral Sir Sandy Woodward GBE KCB (Captain SSKs TIRELESS and GRAMPUS and SSN WARSPITE 1970-72; Captain Submarine Sea Training 1974-75; Flag Officer First

Flotilla 1981-83 (including Commander Carrier Battle Group, Falklands Campaign 1982 and later, Flag Officer Submarines) provided the following viewpoint:

"I was fortunate enough to fly on board a Nimrod during an antisubmarine exercise. A target submarine had been provided under the waves in a restricted area. No matter how it tried with its various sensors, the Nimrod was unable to detect the submarine. Eventually, it asked the submarine to launch a green smoke grenade to provide the submarine's location. I was not impressed."

He also gave the opinion:

"In my extensive experience, the Nimrod had never made an unalerted detection of a submarine." (Alerted detections give the MPA some chance.)

22. Rear Admiral Jeremy Larken DSO (Captain SSK OSIRIS 1970-71; Commander Submarine Sea Training 1975; Captain SSN VALIANT 1977; Captain Third Submarine Squadron 1978-81 (6xSSN; 2xSSK and close liaison with USN on submarines search tactics)) provided this viewpoint:

"I'm not current with MPA ASW capabilities. The US has always been better at it than us, but historically we have set the bar low[29]. I believe it is true that no Nimrod (or Shackleton) ever localised a submarine with sonobuoys to within the Mk. 46 torpedo

---

[29] It is of considerable import to note that after the end of the Cold War the U. S. Navy lowered its interest in MPA/ASW resources believing that 'the Russian Navy's submarine fleet was in rusty decline and not considered a threat' – not the case today. www. jhuapl. edu/techdigest/TD/td2403/Brooks. pdf .

weapon-detection envelope. Additionally, the Nimrod surface recce capability in 1982 was counter-productive – blithely identifying a container ship [south of Ascension] as the Vincento de Mayo carrier using the then new, 'clever profiling search radar'."

23. A further senior Submariner provided the following more detailed comments:

a. I spent most of my years in the RN at sea in submarines including commanding PORPOISE, REVENGE, REPULSE and SCEPTRE and spent some significant time operating with or avoiding MPA.

b. In the SSK OTTER, where I was the XO, and then in PORPOISE we were the target submarine for Mk 44s, Mk 46s, Stingray (as well as Tigerfish) and spent many hours vectoring in 'lost' MPA to find us. The naive presumption in aiding them was that it saved time and enhanced in-contact operator training time. The reality was that their area search capability was probably terrible–but did anyone quantify that capability?

c. To enhance RN/RAF Submarine/MPA cooperation and whilst I was CO of PORPOISE, I offered SOO Air (MPA) and his boss a trip at sea for a couple of days to witness life in an SSK and to see at first hand an exercise against 2 Frigates supported by 2 Nimrods. Our orders: the SSK, was to snort until attacked by either Nimrod or frigate and attempt to attack the frigates. We fronted up at the appropriate hour in the correct position (known to all forces) and I obeyed the Operation Order, "gulping" on one diesel. Both Nimrods operated all their detection kit and roughly knowing where we were still could not detect us. Both RAF officers watched with amazement from the periscopes the underside of Nimrods flying over the top still unable to detect us.

d. However, a Nimrod did help us once in gaining contact on a Soviet surface ship up in the Arctic Circle, for which I was grateful. On the many occasions operating as the loyal opposition, as either a Whisky or Foxtrot SSK, against UK and NATO ships in a variety of exercises and JMCs, MPA never detected us.

e. In my time in SSBNs much of it was spent evading Blue Forces (mainly MPA that covered wide areas) that were searching for Soviet submarines–which we were also trying to evade! I know that Nimrod never detected any of the SSBNs that I served in. My time in SCEPTRE was equally dismissive of Nimrod MPA on the few occasions we operated together.

f. Despite the foregoing, MPA have been extremely useful for ASuW work which I believe has had national benefits in the arena of Fishery Protection, Reconnaissance, Shadowing and other purposes–whether that has made them cost effective [for ASW], I very much doubt it.

g. My advice to the Secretary of State and the Defence Select Committee would be for a trial to be conducted with the P8s against a Modern submarine threat monitored by a powerful team of non-Air Force ASW experts on board and which was subsequently analysed by an independent authority; only then could a proper Cost/Benefit analysis be made."

24. A senior Naval Warfare Officer, Captain Colin Hamilton, (Served in ASW Leander frigates and Flag Officer Flotilla1 Flagship from 1969-1985; also in Maritime Tactical School) provided the following viewpoint:

"The only thought that strikes me is the assumption [without any proof or justification] that MPA were intended/capable of independent search for submarines over large areas. I don't believe the RN ever accepted that position. When we gave them expanses of ocean to search ahead of an Exercise Battle Group (JMOTS/JMC), it was always the case that they needed cueing to a target submarine after detection by SOSUS or some task group asset and could only act as a relocation asset. It was very seldom if ever that they relocated the submarine. It is however true that their area radar search encouraged diesel submarines to stay down."

25. This view is supported by very recent comments retrieved from a senior analyst at the Joint, RN/RAF, Analysis Centre at Teddington (JAAC) where all serious sonar records are analysed. He is quoted as saying that:

"Nimrods were not a lot of good at area search. They were good at keeping conventional submarines 'on their toes' with their radars and 'maybe OK'[30] at prosecuting submarines detected by SOSUS, etc. But "Area" search and above all "Detection" in the vast oceans was NOT their strong point."

26. The experience of these distinguished Maritime professionals adds considerable weight to the disclosure at paragraph 14, above, by the senior Nimrod pilot.

MPA ASuW in support of Fleet operations.

---

[30] It is believed that after the precise location of an exercise submarine had been given to Nimrod MPA aircraft through the launching of a green smoke grenade, the MPA would launch sonobuoys and carry out prescribed search routines around the given location. Even though they rarely if ever detected the submarine in this search, they would file a carefully worded exercise report to JACC confirming "the successful conduct of the prescribed ASW search pattern".

27. The global operational availability on task of land-based Surface Search (ASuW) aircraft merits clinical analysis. During the author's time flying from the old HMS Ark Royal and then HMS Invincible in home waters and abroad, there was rarely a Shackleton or Nimrod MPA active or available in support of fleet operations–even when operating with the American fleet in the GRIUK gap practicing 'launching a nuclear strike on the Soviets'.

28. The RAF maintained strict Command and Control of their MPA. Aircraft could be allocated to a maritime exercise, operation or mission but the Naval Task Group (TG) staff would still have to request MPA support from the RAF Tasking Authority. The request could be refused–it often was, as in Desert Storm when the Iraqis were mining the Northern Gulf and MPA area search was required. The Tasking Authority had only to say that it has a 'higher priority task'; one not involving direct or indirect support of the TG. Such Tasking Authority refusals immediately dilute or remove the number of MPA aircraft available to the TG Commander[31].

29. Scarce defence funds have been/are being invested in a Fleet Support MPA capability that has not been globally demonstrated. This has arguably prevented investment in more operationally effective and available ASW/ASuW assets (Hunter Killer Subs, Helicopters, Surface Warships and Drones).

---

[31] This is a matter of considerable concern with respect to effective future global operations – both for MPA and for Carrier-borne aircraft. Allocation of resources must give priority to Combined Arms in defence of the Fleet and other global interests. Tasking Control of Task Group assets, including MPA, must be enjoyed by the on-site TG Commander and not maintained by land based Authorities who are distant from a combat theatre – whether littoral or open ocean.

30. One must not forget that when there is a perceived submarine or surface threat to our trade routes, our energy supplies, our undersea communications and our fleet at sea, there needs to be a 24/7 ability to search for, interrogate and prosecute such a threat. ASuW remains an integral part of this need. However, the global availability of land-based MPA for such sustained operations must be considered in serious doubt and this raises equally serious questions concerning the cost/benefit equation of such an asset.

31. As suggested at paragraph 23. f, above, national benefits from MPA ASuW local deployment in the arena of Fishery Protection, Reconnaissance, Shadowing and other purposes have been realised but it is reasonable to propose that these littoral tasks around the Homeland base could be executed effectively by much cheaper ASW/ASuW aircraft and Drones. The CN-235 MPA / HC-144 Ocean Sentry, Saab 2000 MPA and Airbus Military C295 MPA would appear to be very capable alternatives; with the latter's unit cost of approximately £50 million comparing very favourably with that of Poseidon at £330 million. We could afford up to 60 MPA aircraft rather than 9 Poseidons – 18 would be a reasonable Fleet size allowing the permanent deployment of 2-aircraft ASW/ASuW flights to Akrotiri and to the Falklands (where trouble is brewing yet again).

32. The questions that are now of great import and operational significance and that should be urgently addressed are:
    a. "With only 9 Poseidons in the MPA fleet of which only 6 may be available at any one time, will combat/deterrent operations offshore take full priority over the routine policing of National Waters?"
    b. "And if so, will the Task Group Commander be given full Command and Control of supporting MPA [and embarked F-35B Squadrons/supporting Sigint/EW assets]?"

How has this situation been allowed to develop?

33. There appear to be two answers to this question:
    a. MOD has not been in receipt of accurate, substantiated MPA ASW data and has therefore been unable to advise Ministers and the public as to the actual operational effectiveness of MPA aircraft in the ASW and ASuW roles.
    b. Internal MOD politics between the Services (as well as inaccurate data) appear to have prevented the detailed operational justification of Nimrod MPA and now the P8 Poseidon aircraft.

Misrepresentation appears to have taken place.
History of the Falklands War.

34. An example of such misrepresentation may be found in the Foreword to the undated PDF document entitled, "RAF in Op Corporate" which was provided by the retired Chief of the Air Staff, Sir Peter Squire. His Foreword entitled, "A notable victory for Air Power", made/inferred many historically inaccurate and unsubstantiated statements. In particular, these included the following:

> "The Nimrod's normal radius of action was some 1,900 miles but, by the end of April, the hastily fitted air to air refuelling capability **enabled them to provide direct support to the Task Force right down to the Falklands – and to monitor shipping in the inshore areas of the South Argentine ports**."

35. This claim is embarrassingly inaccurate (and does not record Nimrod's failure to provide any direct ASW/ASuW support to the Carrier Battle Group). During two 600-mile ASuW missions in which the Nimrod ventured south of Ascension, it made only two reports to the Carrier Battle Group – both were

counter-productive – one misidentified a fishing fleet as an Argentine Task Force and the other a container ship as the Argentine aircraft carrier. This misleading contact report on the container ship occurred when the Carrier Battle Group was 2,000 miles further South. The Nimrod was never in evidence anywhere near the Falkland Islands. And to state that the Nimrod 'monitored shipping in the inshore areas of the South Argentina ports' is beyond understanding.

36. This view is supported by one of our Senior Submariners:

"I was running the Submarine Operations Cell CTF 311 for Flag Officer Submarines and CINCFLEET in 1982 and covered the entire Falklands Campaign. We worked hand in glove with HQ18 GP RAF on all operational matters. I can confirm that the only significant [land-based] RAF contributions to OPERATION CORPORATE were the single Vulcan attacks on Port Stanley Airfield supported by at least 10 Victor Tankers in refuelling relays. These operations delivered just one bomb on the airstrip. I am not aware of a single significant operational contribution by Nimrod at any stage."

A recent Presentation on MPA effectiveness by MOD/RAF to Members of Parliament.

37. Despite all experience to the contrary, a group of MPs (in the last Government) was informed by MOD/MPA spokesmen that "two MPA could clear the North Atlantic of submarines in a week". This claim is unjustified and unsubstantiated by analysis.

38. Question:Was the P8 Poseidon Procurement decision based on this fallacious claim?

Express article by Martin Docherty-Hughes, SNP MP for West Dunbartonshire – 11 Jan 18[32].

39. This Express article demonstrates the total/misplaced belief that some of our MPs have in MPA ASW capability – presumably without any detailed knowledge of actual operational capabilities or shortfalls. The following sentence puts the statement by the MOD/MPA spokesmen at paragraph 37 above into some perspective:

> *"After Russian submarines entered Scottish territory on multiple occasions the UK had to ask NATO allies to send <u>17 spy planes</u> to hunt the submarines between January and November."*

Were these 'hunts' successful? Perhaps the DSC should send Mr. Docherty-Hughes (and others) a copy of this Memorandum with Annexes?

Issues arising and questions demanding attention.

40. The effective options for detecting and locating a submarine have proved to be Towed Arrays (surface ship) or Submarines and on occasion ASW Helicopters operating where practicable with SOSUS, leading to location within attacking parameters by SSNs. Within the Mediterranean, SSNs do best but any initial area detection is very difficult. (Please see testimony above at paragraphs 21 to 26.)

41. The ASW contribution by MPA has appeared to be little at best, beyond limiting SSKs re-charging batteries at periscope depth– using surface search radar, and hence limiting SSK mobility

---

[32] https://www. express. co. uk/news/uk/903095/uk-military-france-germany-scotland-russia-submarine-defence-cuts-Martin-Docherty-Hughes

and hence capability – a task made almost impossible with the introduction of Air Independent Propulsion (AIP) boats.

42. That MPA resources have received major funding over many decades would appear to raise questions of objective operational capability analysis moving upwards within the central MOD staff Operational Requirements community.

43. It is now understood that the new US Mk 54 torpedo is being procured for UK's Poseidon aircraft even though serious doubt continues to be expressed over the capability that it will provide[33]:

> "In April 2003, Raytheon was awarded a sole source contract for the production of the Mk 54. Full rate production began in October 2004. In March 2010 the Fifth Fleet requested improvements in the Mk 54's performance against diesel-electric submarines via an Urgent Operational Need Statement (UONS). This led to a software Block Upgrade (BUG) program which began testing in August 2011 and which continues, having been criticised by the DOT&E for using unrealistic proxies for threat submarines. "[3]

> "The FY14 DOT&E report assessed the Mk 54 (BUG) torpedo as not operationally effective in its intended role. "During operationally challenging and realistic scenarios, the Mk 54 (BUG) demonstrated below threshold performance and exhibited many of the same failure mechanisms observed during the FY 2004 initial operational testing". Shortfalls were also identified with the employing platforms' tactics and tactical

---

[33] https://en. wikipedia. org/wiki/Mark_54_MAKO_Lightweight_Torpedo

documentation, and interoperability problems with some platform fire control systems."

44. Scarce defence funds have therefore been/are being invested in a Fleet Support MPA capability that has not been objectively analysed or globally demonstrated. Arguably, this has prevented investment in more operationally effective and available ASW/ASuW assets (Hunter Killer Subs, Helicopters, Surface Warships and Drones). For example, the Spearfish heavyweight torpedo currently fitted to RN submarines as an anti-ship and anti-submarine weapon, has proven to be exceptionally effective and reliable–and it is British.

45. This lack of objective analysis and candid communication over many years may have [has] led to more resources being assigned to MPA forces at the expense of SSKs, ASW Helicopters or Surface Warships than may have been justified or wise.

46. Should we not be putting our limited defence funds into Hunter Killer Submarines, Surface Warships (including Carriers) with their ASW helicopters and Drones that can do the job on a global basis?

Internal MOD politics.

47. The Naval Staff has enjoyed the leadership of several submariner First Sea Lords; all of whom were arguably 'obliged to presume' that the Nimrod MPA could detect threat submarines and did not have available any concrete evidence beyond personal experience to prove otherwise.

48. It is worthy of consideration that it was the integrity of our First Sea Lords that put them at a disadvantage in the 'game' of internal MOD politics. In 1983, Sir John Fieldhouse told the

author of this paper that he didn't want to challenge the RAF because he was "about to become the Chief of the Defence Staff and did not wish to appear partisan".

49. Such integrity reportedly led Sir John to ask the returning victorious Carrier Battle Group Commander, Sir 'Sandy' Woodward in 1982, "to keep a low public profile concerning the Falklands victory". As a result, and within less than a year after the Falklands conflict, the Royal Navy Presentation Team that was touring the country did not make a single reference to the Fixed Wing Fleet Air Arm and the success of the Sea Harrier in the air war. This left the door wide open for the RAF to mislead the nation with a PR blitz.

50. The same non-partisan integrity may also be the reason why the failed £3 billion upgrade to the clearly dysfunctional and obsolete Nimrod fleet was apparently not robustly challenged at the turn-of-the-century by the Naval Staff and the subsequent Chief of the Defence Staff, the now Admiral of the Fleet Lord Boyce.

Discussion.

51. The nub of the matter here is that our global vulnerability to the emergent conventional submarine threat has been/is being enhanced by misguided procurement based on inaccurate/unproven data.

52. The land-based P8 Poseidon may indeed be somewhat more capable at ASW and ASuW than the Nimrod MPA but to what degree (especially in the light of new battery technologies, Air Independent Propulsion (AIP) systems and longer-range missiles) – and at what cost? And if the RAF retains the mantle of MPA Tasking Authority rather than delegating the same to

deployed Maritime Forces/Task Groups, will operational Fleet units continue to be denied reliable MPA support?

53. There is certainly much utility for MPA ASuW in littoral/home waters but this could be much more cost-effectively achieved by alternative aircraft and/or indeed Satellite Surveillance. With regard to open ocean/global MPA utility and availability, that utility and availability remains very much in doubt.

54. Meanwhile, in the light of this blossoming submarine threat, we do not have enough globally-capable "submarine killers": that is to say, Hunter Killer Submarines, ASW Warships with Merlin Helicopters and Drones.

55. Will the proposed new class of Type 31e Frigate have a robust ASW/ASuW capability? It will be too late to ask this question after the frigates have been built. The initial order is £1. 25 billion for five general purpose frigates at £250 million per Type 31e. Does this price include fitting of the necessary weapon systems such as a Hull Mounted Sonar, weapons storage for an embarked ASW Helicopter and Air Defence Missiles? Or will the fitting of these be retrospective at considerable extra cost?

56. Para 55 above also raises the question: why do our Fleet ASW Helicopters not have a substantial anti-surface ship weapon for launch at targets well over the horizon? Without such, our new destroyers and frigates will be extremely vulnerable to surface attack even by third world or rogue nations.

Conclusion.

57. Our Nation has been/is being misinformed concerning the cost-effectiveness, operational effectiveness and global reach of Maritime Patrol Aircraft as ASW and, to a lesser extent, as ASuW platforms.

58. The continued major/excessive investment of defence funds in the MPA weapon system does not appear to have taken note of game-changing technologies such as Air Independent Propulsion (AIP) systems and has therefore weakened our global ASW capability–by reducing justifiable investment in more cost-effective and operationally available ASW/ASuW platforms. These could include drones and UAVs with sonobuoys.

Recommendations.

59. In the light of all the above, the open ocean ASW capability of current MPA aircraft should be demonstrated in a tightly governed trial. This ASW trial should be conducted outside the continental shelf with a P8 against a Modern submarine 'threat' (both nuclear and conventional with AIP) and should be monitored by a powerful team of non-Air Force ASW experts on board. The subsequent analysis by an approved independent authority would then allow the first reliable Cost/Benefit assessment to be made of the utility of this weapon system.

60. Command and Control of MPA [and Sigint, EW and Fighter] aircraft supporting Fleet operations offshore should be fully vested in the deployed/on-site Task Group Command.

61. The Defence Select Committee and our new Secretary of State for Defence may wish to address these matters with some urgency and make appropriate changes to the planned UK Armed Forces Order of Battle.

Annex J

The Need for Justification of the Armed Services and their Weapon Systems: Fixed Wing Combat Aircraft.

MEMORANDUM

To: **The House of Commons Defence Select Committee**
Copy to: **Secretary of State for Defence**
First Sea Lord

From: **Cdr N D MacCartan-Ward DSC AFC**

Reference: **Towards the 2020 Strategic Defence and Security Review.**

Date: **19 January 2020.**

This Submission is supported by:

Dr. Anthony R Wells
Rear Admiral Sir Robert Woodard KCVO DL
Rear Admiral Bob Love OBE CB FREng

Rear Admiral Bruce Williams CBE
Commodore Michael Clapp CB
Captain John Hall CBE
Captain Graham Meredith
Captain Colin Hamilton
Captain Peter Hore
Lieutenant-Colonel Ewen Southby-Tailyour OBE RM
Commander David A Hobbs MBE
Commander Ed Featherstone
Commander Graham Edmonds
    Commander Mike Evans
Commander Paul Fisher
Lieutenant-Commander Lester May
Major David Jeremy
Richard Shuttleworth RN

Evaluating Expenditure on British Military Fixed Wing Combat Aircraft since the Carrier Decision of 1966/7 and the Operational Return on Investment – the Creation of the "Black Hole".

Figure 42. The Carrier-capable Naval Fighter Wing Harrier Combat Air Support Aircraft.

Executive Summary.

1. This Memorandum seeks to evaluate and justify (or otherwise)
    British military investment in
    a. Land-based non-carrier-capable fixed wing combat air-
        craft, and,
    b. Carrier-capable fixed wing combat aircraft since the 1966/7
        Carrier decision. In doing so it underpins the vital strategic
        and tactical reality that the effective global projection of
        British air power in defence of the National Interest is most
        economically achieved by carrier-borne air groups.

2. It summarises original costs, inflation-linked costs and then
    addresses the operational return/combat success realised for
    each aircraft group.

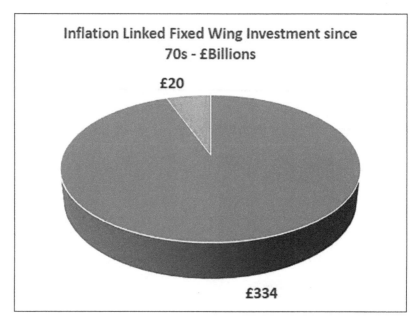

Figure 43. Fixed Wing Investment Imbalance.

3. It reveals a disturbing imbalance of investment between land-
    based and carrier-capable fixed wing aircraft. That investment

disparity does not reflect established UK Strategic Policy which is now centred upon Strike Carrier utility and deterrence value.

4. It suggests that the lack of combat success and of deployed combat utility by land-based fighter aircraft, as iterated at Annex B, provides little justification for this imbalance and that associated costs have been a prime causative factor in the generation of the "Black Hole" in Defence spending. Effective deployment of these land-based assets to combat theatres overseas requires time-consuming pre-positioning and the utilisation of major air-bridge logistic/combat support, the aircraft program costings of which are included in Tables 1 and 2 at Annex A.

5. It concludes that:
   a. The major investment in non-carrier-capable land-based fixed wing aircraft has not been justified by combat theatre achievement or by global utility.
   b. Such investment has prevented adequate, threat-related expenditure on more flexible and rapidly deployable weapons platforms in support of Strategic Maritime Policy including surface warships, submarines, carrier-capable aircraft and Strike Carrier platforms.

6. It recommends that Ministers
   a. should review and justify (or otherwise) urgently the continuing major investment in land-based non-carrier-capable aircraft and
   b. should revive and maintain a robust fleet and carrier-borne capability that has served us so effectively in terms of cost, deterrence and combat since the start of World War II.

7. It further recommends that the Government/Defence Select Committee should now analyse and justify (or otherwise)

expenditure on army weapon systems over the same period – especially heavy armour and artillery – and relate this to the perceived threat and stated Strategic Maritime Policy. Such analysis is beyond the scope of this Memorandum.

Introduction

8. The taxpayer and the government are probably not fully aware of the magnitude of investment that has been made in land-based British military fixed wing combat aircraft and their deployment-support platforms since 1966/7. This Memorandum provides a concise but not necessarily comprehensive review of that investment and measures its effectiveness in terms of successful combat/deterrence operations worldwide.

9. During this period, some major costs have been kept hidden from the public by the Ministry of Defence, especially for Tornado, Nimrod and, now, Typhoon in-service modifications and support. With regard to the latter and after 2003, the Ministry of Defence refused to release updated cost-estimates on the grounds of 'commercial sensitivity'. This eventually led to criticism of the program by the Public Accounts Committee 2011 Report into the "Management of the Typhoon Project". The timeline of the Typhoon Program up to 2015 is provided at Annex C and reveals the mismanagement and general confusion associated with this collaborative program.

10. Unfortunately, full lifetime cost-in-service figures for the Typhoon aircraft have been hidden from the public domain and are difficult to establish. The Chair of the public Accounts Committee, the Rt. Hon. Mrs. Margaret Hodge, deemed it likely that program costs were likely to rise to at least £55 Billion. Limited exposure to ongoing major Typhoon modification programs supports that suggestion.

11. Figures given for the initial unit cost of individual aircraft types are drawn mainly from MoD/Government records and Defence Procurement Agency figures. Estimates given for the hidden cost of in-service modifications to each aircraft type are considered conservative.

12. Table 1 at Annex A summarises the original costs of each listed program. Table 2 provides inflation-linked costs for the same programs up to 2019.

13. A list of combat operations associated with each type of aircraft is provided at Annex B.

The Origins of the Investment Imbalance in Combat Aircraft.

14. In the late 60's, Ministers were persuaded fraudulently that global 24/7 air defence of the Fleet and of allied merchant shipping at sea could be conducted effectively by land-based air and that aircraft carriers were therefore not required. Subsequent events have shown that they, the Government, had received misleading advice – and without proper justification or demonstration.

15. Since then, the RAF has filled the MoD with many more senior staff officers than the other two Services and has sponsored a large group of Academics specialising in land-based air warfare. This was much to their single service benefit. It enabled them to have overwhelming and unjustified influence in the corridors of power on all air matters.

16. Unfortunately, the Royal Navy had a higher ratio of its personnel deployed in the front line and hence were unable to follow suit (see graph below). Further, their Lordships focussed predominantly on the acquisition of fleet escorts, submarines

and Anti-Submarine Warfare and this led to a neglect of carri-
er-borne air power and of Naval Air Warfare proven expertise.
This neglect was best exemplified by the closure of the Naval
Staff's Directorate of Naval Air Warfare in the early 80's. As
RAF influence increased exponentially, Royal Navy Fleet Air
Arm influence decreased markedly.

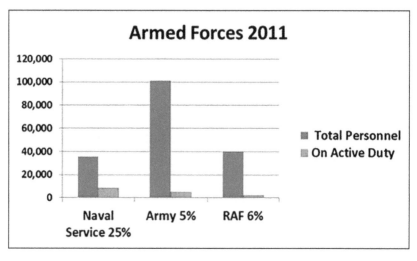

Figure 44a. Active Duty Ratios.

17. The advices of the land-based air aficionados within MoD
and of associated Academics within Cabinet Offices and
elsewhere in Whitehall have been accepted without question
by Ministers, few of whom understood that global military
power and deterrence depended on a robust deployed presence under the sea, on the sea surface and in the air above
the Fleet. The end result of this, as demonstrated by recent
history, has been the steep decline of investment in the carrier-borne Fixed Wing Fleet Air Arm, in the Naval Service and
in Britain's Strategic Military and Political Power Projection
and Deterrence Capability.

Scope.

18. This Memorandum does not address the in-service cost of our two new carriers and of the joint F-35B program. Nor does it address the comparative cost of land-based fixed wing airfields, establishments, logistic support and personnel structures that are needed to enable Expeditionary Air Wing (EAW) deployment to combat theatres relatively close offshore such as the Middle East. SDSR 2020 may wish to address the cost and effectiveness of such EAW operations, particularly bearing in mind their comparative lack of more distant First Echelon global deployability, utility and flexibility. It is of note that the combined personnel numbers of just two of the supporting airfields, Brize Norton and Akrotiri, Cyprus during the EAW operations over Syria and Iraq exceeded 8,000 – more than the total strength of the Corps of Royal Marines whose global utility represents a vital part of declared Maritime Strategy. In cost-effective contrast, ships' crews for each of our two new carriers number 679–with further accommodation for 900 Air Group and Royal Marine personnel.

Investment in Fixed Wing Aircraft other than the carrier-capable Harrier and Sea Harrier.

The Tornado Multi-Role Combat Aircraft (MRCA).
Tornado F1/F3 – Air Defence Vehicle (ADV).

19. Costs.

a) Initial unit cost, 1979:	£42 million.
b) Estimated in life cost (147 aircraft):	£9 billion.
c) Estimate of in-service modifications:	£15 billion.
This represents a total but conservative initial program cost of:	£24 billion.

20. The modifications to the Tornado ADV variant tried in vain to provide it with its specified operational capability and were on-going since day one. In the mid-80s, a retired Chief of the Air Staff, Sir Keith Williamson, then working for Marconi admitted on television that the aircraft *"might as well have cement inside the radar dome because it didn't work at all"* – hence it became known as the 'Blue circle' radar. Problems with the new radar and lack of an effective air-to-air weapon system continued through the 90s; as did extensive and expensive modification programs. Despite this, MoD/Air repeatedly informed Parliament that the aircraft was fully operational.

21. A desk officer in MOD/DNLP in the late 80s considers that this Memorandum's given Tornado costs might have been underestimated. "The shenanigans of the Tornado Program were held up to be an example of how not to do it. They removed money from the front end of the program (development phase) to make it look better and then over the ensuing years spent many times more than the initial sum saved to modify the aircraft and its systems to get back to the original design specs – which they never achieved."

Combat Operations.

22. The Tornado F1/F3 ADV has not been able to contribute in any significant way to British/Allied combat/deterrence operations offshore. Its lack of a working weapon system left the United Kingdom completely vulnerable to Soviet air attack up until the end of the Cold War and beyond. When deployed to the Arabian Gulf during the Iraq war, it flew nugatory combat air patrol missions over the sea well away from the theatre of active operations.

Tornado GR1/4 – Ground Attack and Reconnaissance.

23. Costs.

a) Initial unit cost, 1979:	£37 million.
b) Estimated initial in life cost (138 aircraft):	£8 billion.
c) Estimate of in-service modifications:	£15 billion.
This represents a total but conservative program cost* of:	£23 billion.

*Choosing to extend the life of and operate the Tornado GR4 in Afghanistan cost the taxpayer a further £7. 5 billion (National Audit Office estimate) whereas keeping Harrier in service for operations in Afghanistan over the same period would have cost the taxpayer approximately £1. 1 billion. This unnecessary additional cost could have paid for our two new carriers with some change left over.

24. Designed for the low-level nuclear interdiction of Soviet runways and other targets, the development of the GR1/4 (and of the F1/3) suffered from the collaborative demands of our European partners who insisted on a shorter and smaller aircraft than originally designed. As a result, it had limited range and manoeuvrability especially when carrying a war load.

25. The Tornado GR1 was provided with a special to type Runway Denial Weapon System known as the JP 233. The Tornado GR4 was provided with the Storm Shadow cruise missile for the interdiction of hardened targets. (see below for further information)

Combat Operations.

26. Although the Tornado GR1/4 has been deployed in small numbers for combat operations over Iraq, Bosnia (based in Italy), Libya, Afghanistan and Syria, its track record has been less

than remarkable – predominately achieving the destruction of pick-up trucks, mud huts and small groups of Jihadi fighters.

27. In Iraq, Desert Storm, eight aircraft were lost in quick succession but a formal inquiry found that only one of these was due to enemy action. The remainder of the losses reportedly resulted from unfamiliarity with the JP 233 delivery profile as well as from 'finger trouble' and a basic lack of air warfare munitions expertise. That is not to say that the GR aircrew did not display remarkable courage during the low-level attacks that they carried out by night.

28. Over Kosovo, it was engaged in ground support operations but, when prevented from taking off from its Italian base through bad weather, these operations were successfully conducted by the Sea Harrier FA2 operating from our carrier.

29. The Tornado GR support operations over Libya were conducted from UK, Italy and Cyprus with major tanker and logistic support at an estimated deployment cost of at least £1. 4 billion. Their response to urgent Combat Air Support requests was limited (almost non-existent) as were the results of ordnance delivery, whether iron bombs or the Storm Shadow cruise missile. Storm Shadow deliveries suffered from misfires, guidance failure and warhead failure and was totally ineffective. SDSR 2010 had just removed our carriers and Harriers from service – and these had been the only UK fixed wing assets capable of providing reliable and timely urgent Support missions.

30. Similar limited Tornado operations were conducted over Syria at an estimated cost of £4 billion.

31. In Afghanistan, Tornado GR4 has been significantly less successful than the Royal Navy Fighter Wing and RAF Harrier

squadrons that preceded it. This shortfall is a direct result, in part, of its poor aerodynamic performance at altitude and in hot weather as well as certain serious airworthiness problems resulting from airframe age.

32. There is also the question of the RAF ethos being brought into play. In Parliament during the Prime Minister's debate on SDSR 2010, one well known Labour speaker said that his son had just got back from Afghanistan (40 Commando RM) and had told him that *"when the RAF was asked at one stage to supply cover/close air support, the troops were told that 'no RAF aircraft were programmed to fly that day'."*

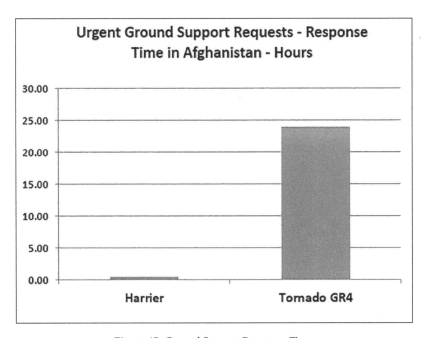

Figure 45. Ground Support Response Times.

JP 233 Runway Denial Weapon System for Tornado GR1.

33. Cost.

  a) Development cost, 1979:   £10 billion.
  b) Production and in-service cost: Not Known.

Combat Operations.

34. Its disastrous first operational deployment on the Tornado GR1 in Desert Storm led to its immediate withdrawal from service.

Storm Shadow cruise missile for Tornado GR4 and Typhoon.

35. The initial procurement decision (circa 2002) for this missile for the RAF and for the Royal Navy Tomahawk was made by the MoD/Air department (EC Deep Strike) who were responsible for ordering all Strike Weapons including cruise missiles. Initial orders were as follows and did not reflect weapon type combat utility or Strategic Policy. What was the operational justification for 900 Storm Shadow missiles?

Tomahawk (TacTom)–Block 4 – for Submarines	
Missile Range	**1500 nm+**
Cost per Unit	**US$550,000**
Number ordered for RN use	**65**
Total Cost	**US$36 million**

Storm Shadow – for the GR4	
Missile Range	**400 nm**
Cost per Unit	**US$750,000**
Number ordered for RAF use	**900**
Total Cost	**US$675 million***

36. These Storm Shadow costs* did not include the price of the warhead and other production/support measures. The latter raised the cost per missile to £900,000 giving a total initial procurement cost of £810 million. Costs of development and of modifying Typhoon for deployment of this missile have not been released.

Combat Operations.

37. The Storm Shadow missile was removed from the French Navy air armament inventory because of its unreliability and poor performance; including misfires, failure to guide to the target and warhead malfunctions. This intelligence fits well with reports that at least five of the eight missiles fired by Tornado in support of "Odyssey Dawn", Libya, were either misfires or failed to guide to or hit their intended targets. No proof of targets successfully interdicted by Storm Shadow has been declared.

Nimrod AWACS.

38. This ill-considered attempt to duplicate the United States AWACS capability in the mid-80s is understood to have cost the taxpayer not less than:£5 billion.

Nimrod MRA/MPA.

39. Cost.

a) Initial unit cost:	Not Known.
b) Estimated in life cost	£15 billion.
c) In-service modifications, 1997:	£3 billion.
This represents a total but conservative program cost of:	£18 billion.

Combat Operations.

40. This land-based aircraft was significant by its absence from the effective direct support of Operation Corporate in the Falklands, 1982, and from all other conflicts engaged in since that time.

Typhoon–Eurofighter.

41. Cost.

a) Initial unit cost, Defence Procurement Agency (1998)*:	£92.2 million.
b) Initial estimated in life cost, (160 aircraft):	£22 billion.
c) Estimate of in-service modifications:	£25 billion.
This represents a total but conservative program cost of:	£47 billion.

* This did not include related development costs (approx. £4 billion).

42. Annex C provides a detailed timeline concerning the development of the aircraft (which is still ongoing) and some of the declared costings up to 2015.

43. Those commentators who highlight the cost of our two new carriers repeatedly (at £6. 2 billion) often blame their procurement for the "Black Hole in Defence Spending". The exponential rising cost of the Typhoon program (and the cost of the Tornado programs before it) would appear to be a much more logical and demonstrable cause of the "Black Hole". Paragraphs 44 to 48, below, provide justification for this statement.

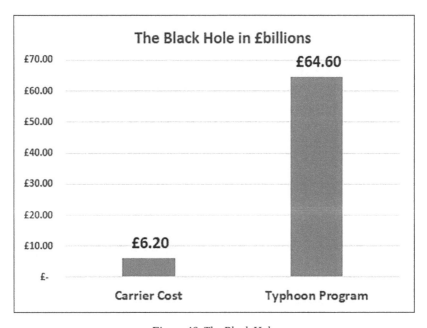

Figure 46. The Black Hole.

44. The initial order of Typhoon aircraft was for 232 airframes. In 2006, this order was reduced to 160 aircraft; almost simultaneously with an order by Saudi Arabia for 72 aircraft. But the Saudi's were only charged £72 million per airframe–£20 million less than cost that the RAF was initially contracted to pay: representing a subsidy to Saudi Arabia of £1. 44 billon – at tax-payers' expense. (This almost equals the contracted initial cost of one of our two new carriers.)

45. Typhoon was procured in collaboration with European partners to provide air defence of the United Kingdom against the Soviet air threat during the Cold War. That threat is now non-existent and the current Russian air threat against the United Kingdom base is considered unlikely to materialise. However, if it does, the Typhoon with an unrefuelled combat radius of action of just 750 nm will be unable to defend the UK Base (its *raison d'être*) against the modern Russian air threat. Each Russian long-range bomber can launch up to 16 supersonic, conventionally or nuclear armed ground attack cruise missiles[34] at a range of 1300 nm from their targets. UK does not have nearly enough Air Refuelling resources to extend the combat range of the Typhoon on a 24/7 on-task basis and at sufficient strength to deter/oppose this threat. Only carrier air power coupled with Type 45 Daring Destroyer missiles have this capability.

46. Typhoon is a land-based fighter aircraft initially designed for single role capability and is entirely unsuitable for conversion to carrier deck operations. Hence its utility in the context of our national maritime defensive strategy and task force operational capability offshore is minimal.

47. Despite this, Ministers have been persuaded that major modifications should be carried out to give the aircraft a working air-to-ground capability. All Typhoon aircraft have required/undergo expensive modifications (many without a matching increase in the aircraft's global utility) and only 30 or so are available for/capable of front-line 'multi-role' combat operations[35] at any one time. As a result, £ Billions worth of aircraft

---

[34] The Kh-101, 102 and Kh-555.

[35] Things are no better in Germany. A colleague there has pointed out that of the 60 or so Typhoon aircraft in service, only four have been available for front-line combat operations at any one time.

are sitting unserviceable and non-operational in hangars. (A similar situation to that experienced by the Tornado Program.)

48. In the context of fiscal constraint and operational logic, this ongoing Typhoon modification program must be considered an unnecessary waste of National Defence Budget funding. This is particularly so in the light of the Royal Air Force desire to procure Joint Strike Fighter aircraft to replace the limited capability of the Tornado GR4. The new aircraft will be mul-tirole and will provide all the air to ground capability required – provided that it is carrier-capable, i. e. the F-35B Lightning II.

Combat Operations.

49. It appears unlikely that the Typhoon aircraft will ever be deployed on First Echelon expeditionary task force combat operations outside the NATO area. Libya and Syria deploy-ments were Second Echelon – requiring pre-positioning and major air-bridge logistic support.

Return on investment for non-carrier-capable fixed wing combat aircraft.

50. Overall Costs.
   a) The total original investment in non-carrier-capable fixed wing combat aircraft is estimated at something more than **£155 billion** (see Annex A, Table 1).
   b) When adjusted for inflation to the year 2019, this total investment figure reaches nearly **£344 billion** (see Annex A, Table 2).
   c) The averaged inflation-linked expenditure from 1979 to 2019 for the non-carrier -capable fast jet fleet as a whole stands at **£8. 8 billion** per annum.

This investment has resulted in very limited participation and success by these aircraft in combat/deterrence operations offshore. The twenty-six enemy aircraft shot down by Britain's air forces since 1948 have been at the hands of carrier-borne Naval aircraft. Surface warships have shot down a similar number.

Investment in the carrier-capable Sea Harrier and the Harrier.

Sea Harrier FRS Mark1.

51. Costs.

a) Initial unit cost, 1979:	£12 million.
b) Estimated in life cost (34 aircraft):	£1.1 billion.
c) Estimate of in-service modifications:	N/A
This represents a total but conservative program cost of:	£1.1 billion.

52. This aircraft was procured to provide the fleet at sea with the ability to intercept Soviet shadowing aircraft. It was introduced to service in 1979 and during the next three years was developed by the Royal Navy Fleet Air Arm into an exceptional fighter combat aircraft and a reasonably adequate all-weather interceptor.

Combat Operations.

53. This versatile carrier-borne fighter aircraft distinguished itself in the Falklands war by shooting down 25 Argentinian fighters, ground attack aircraft and logistic support aircraft and deterring attacks (turning the enemy aircraft away) from over 450 Argentinian strike aircraft missions by Mirage V and Skyhawk ground attack aircraft.

54. It represented the difference between success and failure in the air war to retake the Falkland Islands.

Sea Harrier FA2.

55. Costs.

a) Initial unit cost, 1988:	£24 million.
b) Estimated in life cost (56 aircraft):	£2.2 billion.
c) Estimate of in-service modifications:	N/A
This represents a total but conservative program cost of:	£2.2 billion.

56. This carrier-borne aircraft was developed from the Sea Harrier FRS Mk1 and was fitted with a state-of-the-art, beyond visual range weapons system consisting of the Blue Vixen Radar and the AMRAAM missile. It was admired by all our NATO military partners as the most capable area interceptor within the European fighter inventory.

Combat Operations.

57. The FA2 distinguished itself with its versatility and reliability:
   a. Policing the no-fly zone over Iraq alongside our American allies;
   b. Policing the no-fly zone over Kosovo and conducting air to ground missions when land-based aircraft were prevented from flying;
   c. Flying armed reconnaissance missions over Sierra Leone in support of UN ground forces.

58. Its early withdrawal from service was a most regrettable example of MoD misjudgement. It removed the fleet's long-range air defence capability, was operationally illogical and paid no regard whatsoever to its excellent track record and its

recognised capability for the effective defence and support of global task force operations.

Harrier GR3 through GR9.

59. Costs.

a) Averaged Initial unit cost, 1988:	£20 million.
b) Estimated in life cost (100 aircraft):	£3.6 billion.
c) Estimate of in-service modifications:	£5 million.
This represents a total but conservative program cost of:	£4.1 billion.

60. This outstanding ground attack and low-level reconnaissance aircraft served the nation well for almost 40 years. Following the withdrawal of the Sea Harrier from service, it became the only carrier-capable fast jet military aircraft in service with the Royal Air Force and the Royal Navy.

Combat Operations.

61. The Harrier GR3 distinguished itself flying ground attack missions from our carriers in combat in the Falklands war. Its demonstration of firepower was instrumental in the surrender of Goose Green to the 2nd Battalion the Parachute Regiment.

62. The Harrier GR7/9 recent service in Afghanistan with Royal Navy Fighter Wing and Royal Air Force squadrons was highly successful and much applauded by our allies in theatre. First-hand reports from returning squadrons indicate that it represented a most in-demand close air support aircraft within the combat zone.

The Sea Harrier and Harrier–Return on Investment.

63. Overall Costs.
   a) The total original investment in the Sea Harrier and the Harrier is estimated at just over **£6 billion** (see Annex A, Table 1).
   b) When adjusted for inflation to the year 2019, this investment figure reaches £20. **4 billion** (see Annex A, Table 2).
   c) The averaged inflation linked expenditure from 1979 to 2019 for the Harrier fleet as a whole stands at £523 **million** per annum.

64. During their years in service, the Sea Harriers and Harriers have accumulated significantly more combat success than the combined efforts of all their more expensive non-carrier-capable, British, fast jet, fixed wing counterparts.

Summary.

65. In summary,
   a) Government investment in fast jet military aircraft during the last 50 years has for the most part been inadequately justified and, in many cases, ill-considered and non-cost-effective.
   b) The carrier-capable Sea Harrier and Harrier GR programs have cost the taxpayer an inflation linked sum of £523 **million per annum** since 1979 and have demonstrated a remarkable return on investment in terms of successful combat operations offshore. This success in combat far outweighs the cumulative achievements of all other military fast jet aircraft in the UK inventory.
   c) Very much greater investment in non-carrier-capable military fixed wing aircraft has cost the nation an inflation-linked sum of **£8. 8 billion per annum** over the same

period and has contributed significantly to the "Black Hole in Defence Spending". The return on this investment in terms of successful combat operations offshore has, by comparison, been negligible and is likely to remain so.

d) Our carrier-capable aircraft have therefore demonstrated conclusively an order greater cost-effectiveness and operational value for money as well as demonstrating significant effectiveness and reliability in combat capability and flexibility.

66. Admiral Sir Michael Layard, KCB, CBE: letter to the Daily Telegraph, 25 October 2010:

"I am disturbed by Con Coughlin's "sea blindness". (A fighter falls prey to politics–23 October).

He laudably criticises the Government's crass and dangerous decision to disband the unique Harrier Force in favour of the less capable, more costly, more manpower intensive Tornado. However, he misses a vital point on flexibility.

The Harrier is not only a most effective land-based aircraft it also operates from the Royal Navy's aircraft carriers (as in the Falklands campaign) and projects force from the sea around the world, thus bringing an immense dimension to its usefulness.

Dismissing the Harrier early in favour of the near obsolete Tornado will not only take the better aeroplane out of play but will also leave a huge gap in Britain's maritime capability."

https://www. telegraph. co. uk/ comment/letters/8086127/

Echoes-of-previous-Conservative-defence-cuts-put-the-Falkland-Islands-at-risk. html

Conclusions.

67. It is concluded that
   a. The major investment in non-carrier-capable land-based fixed wing aircraft has not been justified by combat theatre achievement or by global utility.
   b. Such investment has prevented adequate, threat-related expenditure on more flexible and rapidly deployable weapons platforms in support of declared Strategic Maritime Policy including surface warships, submarines, carrier-capable aircraft and associated Strike Carrier platforms.

Recommendations.

68. It is recommended that Ministers
   a. should review and justify (or otherwise) urgently the continuing major investment in land-based non-carrier-capable aircraft and
   b. should revive and maintain a robust fleet and carrier-borne capability that has served us so effectively in terms of cost, deterrence and combat since the start of World War II.

69. Further to the above, it is recommended that the Government/ Defence Select Committee should now analyse and justify (or otherwise) expenditure on army weapon systems over the same period – especially heavy armour and artillery – and relate this to the perceived threat and stated Strategic Maritime Policy. This analysis is beyond the scope of this Memorandum. (However and regarding operational utility, it is of note that our heavy tanks failed to be of use during Desert Storm in Iraq, being initially unable to advance more than 2. 5 miles per

day and were left behind when "Stormin' Norman" required 25 miles per day. US and French tanks were able to achieve this target.)

(Appendix) Annex A. Table of investment in British military Fixed Wing combat aircraft since 1967.

Table 1. Original Costs.

Non-Carrier Capable Investment Costs–£ Millions

	No. Aircraft	Initial unit cost	Fleet Initial In life cost	Develop. cost	Est. Modn's	Total Program Cost
Tornado ADV 1979	147	£42	£9,261		£15,000	£24,261
Tornado GR 1979	138	£37	£7,659		£15,000	£22,659
JP 233 1979				£10,000		£10,000
Nimrod MPA 1979	23		£15,000		£3,000	£18,000
Nimrod AWACS 1985				£5,000		£5,000
E-3D Sentry 1990	7					
Typhoon 1998	160	£92	£22,128		£25,000	£47,128
Hercules C-130J2000	25	£92	£3,461			£3,461
C17A Globemaster 2001	8	£151	£1,812			£2,512
Raytheon Sentinel 2008	5	£170	£1,275		£486	£1,761
Voyager 2011	14		£13,000			£13,000
RC-135W Rivet J. 2013	3					£450
A400M Atlas 2014	16	£179	£4,284			£4,284
P8 MPA	9	£333	£4,500			£4,500
					Total	£157,01

Carrier Capable Investment Costs–£ Millions

Sea Harrier Mk1 '79	34	£12	£612			£612
Sea Harrier FA2 '85	56	£24	£2,016			£2,016
Harrier GR5/7/9 '83	100	£20	£3,000		£500	£3,500
					Total	£6,128

See next page for Table of the costs adjusted for inflation.
http://www.thisismoney.co.uk/historic-inflation-calculator

Table 2. Inflation-linked Costs.

Non-Carrier Capable Investment Costs–£ Millions–Inflation-Linked to 2019

	No. Aircraft	Initial unit cost	Fleet Initial In life cost	Develop. cost	Est. Modn's	Total Program Cost
Tornado ADV 1979	147	£222	£48,951		£1,500	£50,451
Tornado GR 1979	138	£195	£40,365		£1,500	£41,865
AP 233 1979				£53,000		£53,000
Nimrod MPA 1979	23		£79,000		£4,800	£83,800
Nimrod AWACS 1985				£14,800		£14,800
E-3D Sentry 1990	7					
Typhoon 1998	160	£165	£39,600		£25,000	£64,600
Hercules C-130J2000	25	£147	£5,513			£5,513
C17A Globemaster 2001	8	£240	£2,880			£2,880
Raytheon Sentinel 2008	5	£217	£1,628		£486	£2,114
Voyager 2011	14		£15,300			£15,300
RC-135W Rivet J. 2013	3					£488
A400 M 2014	16	£189	£4,524			£4,524
P8 MPA	9	£333	£4,500			£4,500

					Land Based Aircraft	£343,834
Carrier Capable Investment Costs–£Millions						
Sea Harrier Mk1 '79	34	£63	£3,213			£3,213
Sea Harrier FA2 '85	56	£71	£5,964			£5,964
Harrier GR5/7/9 '83	100	£65	£9,750		£1,478	£11,228
					Carrier Capable Aircraft	**£20,405**

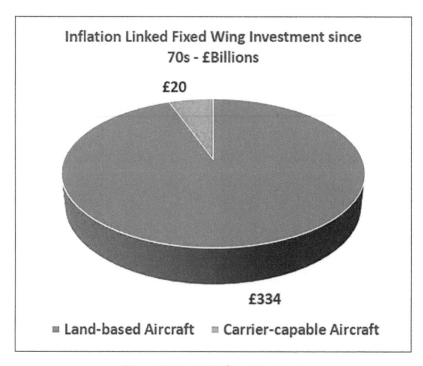

Figure 47. Fast Jet Military Investment.

(Appendix) Annex B. A list of successful combat operations associated with each Group of aircraft.

Land-Based Air other than Harrier/Sea Harrier.

Aircraft Type	Combat Achievement
Tornado F1/F3.	**None.**
Tornado GR1/4.	**Iraq – Desert Storm.** Eight aircraft lost with little return.
	Kosovo. Close Air Support of own forces when the weather permitted land-based flying.
	Libya. Extremely expensive and ineffective.
	Afghanistan. Close Air Support of own forces but much less effective than the Harrier GR7/9. Extremely expensive and ineffective.
	Syria. Provided less than 5% of coalition effort. Generally expensive and ineffective.
Nimrod MRA/MPA.	**1982.** Surveillance of the seas adjacent to Ascension Island.
	Zero presence or participation in the active combat theatre during the battle for the Falklands.

Typhoon. **None.** (Fighter Escort for Tornados in Libya and Syria was against a non-existent air threat.)

Carrier-capable Sea Harrier and Harrier.

<u>Aircraft Type</u> <u>Combat Achievement</u>

Sea Harrier FRS Mk1. **Falklands, 1982.**
1500 war missions/sorties flown. 98% mission availability to the Command.

25 air-to-air kills in combat.

Deterred/turned away over 450 Argentinian aircraft bombing missions.

Dozens of interdiction, close air support and reconnaissance missions flown.

Disablement and sinking of the Narwhal intelligence gathering trawler.

Detecting and deterring the approach of the Argentine Carrier Battle Group during the latter's pincer movement with the Belgrano.

Sea Harrier FA2. **Iraq.** Policing the no-fly zone over Iraq alongside our American allies.

Bosnia/Kosovo. Policing the no-fly zone and conducting air to ground

466

missions when land-based aircraft were prevented from flying.

Sierra Leone. Flying armed reconnaissance missions in support of UN ground forces.

Harrier GR3 through GR9.

Falklands,1982.
Up to 126 ground attack missions flown from aircraft carriers.

Enabled Parachute Regiment victory at Goose Green.

Bosnia/Kosova. Several hundred missions flown from Italy.

Afghanistan. Hundreds of highly successful Close Air Support missions flown and much applauded by our allies and ground forces in Theatre.

(Appendix) Annex C. Typhoon Timeline up to 2015.

1972.
RAF issues Air Staff Target 396 (AST-396), a requirement for a STOVL aircraft to replace the Harrier and Jaguar fleets.

AST-403, specification revised for an air superiority fighter. STOVL requirement dropped and AST-409 lead to the development of Harrier GR5.

Mid-1970s–France, Germany and UK initiate the European Combat Aircraft (ECA) program.

1979.
Following differing requirements (particularly French requirement for carrier compatibility) BAe and MBB propose the European Combat Fighter (ECF)

1981.
Development of different national prototypes and continued differences over specification lead to cancellation of ECF program.

Panavia partners (Germany, Italy and UK) launch Agile Combat Aircraft (ACA) program. Following failure of Germany and Italy to fund development the UK MoD pays £80m prototype, the Experimental Aircraft Program (EAP).

1983.
May–contract for production of EAP prototype signed.

The UK, France, Germany, Italy and Spain launch Future European Fighter Aircraft (F/EFA) program. Aircraft to have short takeoff and landing (STOL) and beyond visual range (BVR) capabilities.

1984.
France reiterates requirement for carrier capable version. The UK, Germany and Italy opt out and establish new EFA program.

1985.
France officially withdraws, commences ACX project.

27 October–EAP demonstrator rolled out at BAe Warton.

1986.
June–Eurofighter GmbH established.

8 August–EAP makes its first flight. Configuration closely matches final Eurofighter design.

Rolls-Royce, MTU Aero Engines, FiatAvio (now Avio) and ITP form EuroJet Turbo GmbH for development of EJ200.

Cost of the program has reached £180 million, but West German and Italian governments wavered on the agreement and the three main industrial partners had to provide another £100 million to keep it afloat.

1988.
23 November–contracts signed for production of demonstrator engines and airframes.

1990.
EuroRADAR formed for development of <u>ECR-90</u> (CAPTOR) radar.

1991.
1 May–last flight of EAP demonstrator.

1992.
EuroDASS formed for development of defensive aids sub system (DASS.) Initially only UK and Italy participate. When Eurofighter enters service only RAF aircraft will exploit all capabilities of DASS.

July–Germany announces intention to withdraw from the DASS element.

Negotiations begin to reduce costs. As a single engine aircraft is ruled out Germany decides to fit cheaper systems, e. g. F/A-18's APG-65 in place of ECR-90, and delay its service entry by two years. Germany eventually participates in all systems.

December–renamed Eurofighter 2000.

1994.
27 March–maiden flight of first development aircraft, DA1 from DASA at Manching with RB199 engines.

6 April–maiden flight of second development aircraft, DA2 from BAe Warton. DA2 also flew with RB199s.

1995.
4 June–maiden flight of Italian DA3, the first with EJ200 engines.

1996.
31 August–Spanish DA6 becomes the first two-seater to fly.

1997.
The estimated cost is £17 billion

27 January–first flight of DA7 from Turin.

24 February–maiden flight of German DA5, first aircraft to be fitted with ECR-90.

14 March–maiden flight of UK's DA4, the second two-seater and last of the seven development aircraft.

1998.
PUS for the Armed Forces told the House of Commons that the European Fighter Aircraft would "be a major project, costing the UK about £7 billion". It was soon apparent that a more realistic estimate was £13 billion, made up of £3. 3 billion development costs plus £30 million per aircraft

January–first aerial refuelling trials, involving DA2 and an RAF VC10 tanker. The first production contract was signed on 30

January 1998 between Eurofighter GmbH, Eurojet and NETMA. The procurement totals were as follows: the UK 232, Germany 180, Italy 121, and Spain 87. Production was again allotted according to procurement: British Aerospace (37. 42%), DASA (29. 03%), Aeritalia (19. 52%), and CASA (14. 03%).

30 January–NETMA and Eurofighter <u>GmbH</u> sign production and support contracts for 620 aircraft.

September–"Typhoon" name adopted, announced as strictly for export contracts. There is some controversy as the last aircraft to bear the name was the Hawker Typhoon, a World War II aircraft, and contracts were signed for production of 148 Tranche 1 aircraft and procurement of long lead-time items for Tranche 2 aircraft.

1999.
Eurofighter International established as single contracting-management company to handle all export sales.

2000.
8 March–first export sale, 60 ordered and 30 options by Greece (but delayed, maybe cancelled).

16 May–UK commits to MBDA Meteor BVRAAM, leading to significant benefits for export prospects, with an in-service date (ISD) of December 2011. In December 2002, France, Germany, Spain and Sweden joined the British in a $1. 9bn contract for Meteor on Typhoon. The protracted contract negotiations pushed the ISD to August 2012, and it was further put back by Eurofighter's failure to make trials aircraft available to the Meteor partners. Meteor is in production and first deliveries to the RAF were scheduled for Q4 2012 but full clearance on Typhoon is not planned until mid-2016.

7 July–DA2 emerges from ten month stand down with latest avionics. Finished in black to reduce cosmetic effect of 490 pressure transducers applied to airframe.

2002.

5 April–Instrumented Production Aircraft (IPA2) makes maiden flight from Turin.

11 April–IPA 3 makes maiden flight from EADS Military Aircraft, Manching, Germany.

15 April–IPA 1 makes maiden flight from BAE Warton.

2 July–Austria announces acquisition of 24 Typhoons, later reduced to 18.

23 July–"Typhoon" name officially adopted as in-service name by four partner nations.

21 November–DA6, flying out of Getafe, crashes. Twin engine failure is blamed. . [3]

2003.

Estimated cost risen to £20 billion and the in-service date of 2003, defined as the date of delivery of the first aircraft to the RAF, was 54 months (four and a half years) late.

After 2003 the Ministry of Defence refused to release updated cost-estimates on the grounds of 'commercial sensitivity'.

13 February–first series production aircraft, GT001 flies from Manching. This is the first of Germany's 180 aircraft.

14 February–in the space of just over an hour Italy's IT001 and Britain's BT001 make their maiden flights.

17 February–Spain's ST001 flies from EADS Military Aircraft, Getafe, Spain.

30 June–"type acceptance" signed, marking formal delivery of aircraft to the partner nations.

October–integration of Meteor begins.

2004.
27 June–two RAF Typhoon T1s depart UK for Singapore for marketing and training.

15 December–UK confirms purchase of second batch of 89 aircraft, the last nation to commit to "Tranche 2" production of 236 aircraft.

2005.
April–Singapore drops the Typhoon from its shortlist to supply the country's next generation fighter.

16 December–the *Aeronautica Militare Italiana* (Italian Air Force) declares the Typhoon's initial operational capability and sets it on quick reaction alert from Grosseto Air Base.

21 December–Saudi Arabia agrees to a purchase of an unspecified number of Typhoons with the UK Ministry of Defence.

2006.
January–first AMI operational squadron formed.

February–first operational mission undertaken by the Italian Air Force as Eurofighter Typhoon defends the airspace over Turin during the 2006 Winter Olympics.

31 March–first RAF operational squadron formed.

August 18–announcement of Saudi Arabia signing a contract to buy 72 planes from the UK.

October 03–100th production aircraft delivered.

2007
May–Eurofighter Development Aircraft 5 made the first flight with the CAPTOR-E radar demonstrator.

12 July–the first Eurofighter for Austria is delivered to the Austrian Air Force.

Germany estimated the system cost (each aircraft and training, plus spare parts) at 120 million euros and said it was in perpetual increase.

June 17 Germany ordered 31 aircraft of Tranche 3A for 2,800 million euros, leading to a system cost of 90 million euros per aircraft.

2008.
January 16–the first Tranche 2 Eurofighter Typhoon makes its first flight.

March, the final aircraft out of Tranche 1 was delivered to the German Air Force, with all successive deliveries being at the Tranche 2 standard.

June, RAF Air Chief Marshal Sir Glenn Torpy suggested that the RAF fleet might only be 123 jets, instead of 232.

October 21, the first two of 91 Tranche 2 aircraft, ordered four years before, were delivered to RAF Coningsby and the Eurofighter nations were considering splitting the 236-fighter Tranche 3 into two parts

October 22–first flight of Typhoon in Royal Saudi Air Force livery.

2009.
Eurojet attempts to find funding to test a thrust vectoring nozzle (TVN) on a flight demonstrator.

May 14, Gordon Brown confirmed that the UK would move ahead with the third batch purchase.

June 12–first Saudi Typhoons delivered.

July, the contract for the first part, Tranche 3A, signed for 112 aircraft split across the four partner nations, including 40 aircraft for the UK, 31 for Germany, 21 for Italy and 20 for Spain. These 40 aircraft were said to have fully covered the UK's obligations in the project by Air Commodore Chris Bushell, because of cost overruns in the project.

November 25–200th Typhoon delivered.

The German BW-Plan 2009 indicated that Germany intended to equip/retrofit their Eurofighters with the AESA Captor-E from 2012, but the contract award was delayed until at least mid-2014.

Tranches explained:

Production is divided into three tranches. Tranches are a production / funding distinction, and do not necessarily imply an incremental increase in capability with each tranche. Tranche 3 is based on late Tranche 2 aircraft with improvements added. Tranche 3 has been split into A and B. Tranches are further divided up into production standard / capability blocks and funding / procurement batches, though these do not coincide, and are not the same thing; egthe Eurofighter designated FGR4 by the RAF is a Tranche 1, block 5.

Batch 1 covered block 1, but batch 2 covered blocks 2, 2B and 5.

2010.
August 24–a Spanish Eurofighter crashes in Spain, killing a Saudi pilot

December 22–250th Typhoon delivered.

December–The Spanish MoD put the cost of their Typhoon project up to December that year 11. 718 billion euros, up from an original 9. 255 billion euros and implying a system cost for their 73 aircraft of 160 million euros each.

2011.
The National Audit Office estimated the UK's "total programme" cost was £37 billion.

The UK's Committee of Public Accounts reported that the mismanagement of the project had helped increase the cost of each aircraft by 75%. It is also suggested that the program cost was "likely to rise to at least **£55 billon".** The Defence Secretary Liam Fox responded that "I am determined that in the future such projects are properly run from the outset, and I have announced reforms to reduce equipment delays and cost overruns".

April 14–Liam Fox admitted that Britain's Eurofighter Typhoon jets were grounded in 2010 due to shortage of spare parts. The RAF was "cannibalising" aircraft for spare parts in a bid to keep the maximum number of Typhoons operational on any given day. The MoD warned the problems were likely to continue until 2015.

22 June–the partner nations agreed to fund development of the Captor-E radar, with entry into service planned for 2015.

2012.

July–Philip Hammond suggested that a follow-on buy of F-35A aircraft would be determined by the Strategic Defence and Security Review in 2015, with the aim of replacing UK's Typhoons around 2030. The UK is to decide what mix of manned and unmanned aircraft to replace its Eurofighters with sometime between 2015 and 2020

December 21–Oman orders 12 Eurofighter Typhoons.

2013.

The RAF seeks to develop conformal fuel tanks (CFT) for their Typhoons to free up underwing space for weapons, and all Tranche 3 aircraft are fitted to accept these tanks

June–Chris Bushell of Selex ES warned that the failure of European nations to invest in an AESA radar was putting export orders at risk.

In November BAE stated that work on an AESA radar continued, to protect exports.

December 4–400th Typhoon delivered.

2014.

Funding for upgrades comes from export customers. However, the four original partner nations have been reluctant to invest further in the program. None of the partner nations have confirmed an order for Tranche 3Bs, which would have been "optimized for future higher-tempo air-to-air and strike operations", and Germany has cut its own orders short to avoid the model.

The second element of the Phase 1 Enhancements package known as 'P1Eb was announced, allowing "Typhoon to realise both its air-to-air and air-to-ground capability to full effect".

Tranche 3 aircraft ESM/ECM enhancements have been focused on improving radiating jamming power with antenna modifications, while EuroDASS is reported to offer a range of new capabilities, including the addition of a digital receiver, extending band coverage to low frequencies (VHF/UHF) and introducing an interferometric receiver with extremely precise geolocation functionalities. On the jamming side, EuroDASS is looking to low-band (VHF/UHF) jamming, more capable antennae, new ECM techniques, while protection against missile is to be enhanced through a new passive MWS in addition to the active devices already on board the aircraft.

February–first flight of a Eurofighter equipped with a "mass model" of the Captor-E radar

At Farnborough MoD awarded BAE Systems a £72 million contract to conduct national-specific testing on a prototype AESA system.

July – twelve RAF Tranche 2 Typhoons had been upgraded with Phase 1 Enhancement (P1E) capability to enable them to use the Paveway IV guided bomb; the Tranche 1 version had used the GBU-12 Paveway II in combat over Libya.

The RAF aims to upgrade their Typhoons to carry the Storm Shadow cruise missile and Brimstone air-to-ground missile by 2018 to ensure they have manned aircraft configured with strike capabilities by the time the Tornado GR4 is retired in 2019.

The MoD is funding research for a common launcher system for the Typhoon that could drop the Selective Precision Effects at Range (Spear) III networked precision-guided weapon planned for the F-35.

RAF Tranche 1 Typhoons are too structurally and technically different from later models and will be will be placed in storage or sold and, in 2015 or 2016, the older models will be switched out for Tranche 2 and 3 versions, a process which will remove the Tranche 1 aircraft from service around 2020 to be stripped for parts to support newer versions to lower costs.

November 19–the contract to upgrade to the Captor-E was signed at the offices of EuroRadar lead Selex ES in Edinburgh, in a deal worth £1bn.

Availability of the radar, for Tranche 2 and 3A aircraft, was anticipated by 2016-17, however there are to date no orders for the radar system and it is not expected to be in service until 2021.

December 12–First full trial installation of Brimstone missile.

2015.
Airbus flight tested a package of aerodynamic upgrades for the Eurofighter that included fuselage strakes and leading-edge root extensions which increases wing lift by 25% resulting in an increased turn rate, tighter turning radius, and improved nose-pointing ability at low speed with angle of attack values around 45% greater than on the standard aircraft and roll rates up to 100% higher.

Eurofighter's Laurie Hilditch said these improvements should increase subsonic turn rate by 15% and give the Eurofighter the sort of "knife-fight in a phone box" turning capability enjoyed by rivals such as Boeing's F/A-18E/F or the Lockheed Martin F-16, without sacrificing the transonic and supersonic high-energy agility inherent to its delta wing-canard configuration Oct – SDSR decides to retain some of the Tranche 1 aircraft to increase the number of front-line squadrons from five to seven and to boost the out-of-service date from 2030 to 2040 as well as implementing the Captor-E AESA radar in later tranches.

Due to the limited ground attack capabilities of RAF Typhoons in the campaign against ISIS, the RAF has delayed the retirement of one squadron of Tornados and is attempting to bring forward the deployment of Brimstone missiles on Typhoon to 2017.

Accidents

By June 2014, there had been two fatal crashes in about 240,000 flight hours, flown by 406 aircraft, delivered to six different air forces.

- On 21 November 2002, the Spanish twin-seat Typhoon prototype DA-6 crashed due to a double engine flameout caused by surges of the two engines at 45,000 ft. The two crew members escaped unhurt and the aircraft crashed in a military test range near Toledo, some 70 miles (110 km) from its base at Getafe

- On 23 April 2008 a Royal Air Force Typhoon FGR4, tail number ZJ943, made a wheels–up landing at the US Navy's NAS China Lake, in the United States. The aircraft was severely damaged and was returned to the UK on 27 October 2008. It was stored in a hardened aircraft shelter at 11 Squadron for some time, before being stripped of most usable parts and moved to storage at RAF Shawbury on 29 July 2015. [304][305] The pilot from 17 Squadron did not sustain any significant injury. It is thought the pilot may have forgotten to deploy the undercarriage or that for some reason he was not alerted to the fact that the undercarriage was not deployed.

- On 24 August 2010, a Spanish twin-seat Typhoon crashed at Spain's Morón Air Base moments after take-off for a routine training flight. It was being piloted by a Lieutenant Colonel of the Royal Saudi Arabian Air Force, who was killed, and a Spanish Air Force Major, who ejected safely. Following this incident, the German Air Force grounded its 55 planes on 16 September 2010, amidst concerns that after ejecting successfully the pilot had fallen to his death. In response to the crash's investigation, the RAF temporarily grounded all Typhoon training flights on 17 September 2010. Quick Reaction Alert duties were unaffected. On 21 September, the RAF announced that the harness system had been sufficiently modified to enable routine flying from RAF Coningsby. The Austrian Air Force also said that all its aircraft had been cleared for flight. On 24 August 2010, the ejection seat manufacturer Martin Baker commented: ". . . under certain conditions, the quick release fitting could be unlocked using the palm of the hands, rather than the thumb and fingers and that this posed a risk of inadvertent release", and added that a modification had been rapidly developed and approved "to eliminate this risk" and was being fitted to all Typhoon seats.

- On 9 June 2014, the Spanish Air Ministry announced that a Typhoon had crashed at Spain's Morón Air Base on landing after a routine training flight. The sole pilot, Captain Fernando Lluna Carrascosa of the Spanish Air Force, who had over 600 Eurofighter flying hours, died in the crash. The aircraft was one of the 46 aircraft of the Air Force's 111 and 113 squadrons. The cause of the accident was unclear.

- On 23 June 2014, a Typhoon of the German Air Force suffered a mid-air collision with a Learjet 35A, which crashed near Olsberg, Germany. The severely damaged Eurofighter made a safe landing at Nörvenich Air Base.

CPSIA information can be obtained
at www.ICGtesting.com
Printed in the USA
LVHW052132120820
663009LV00021B/2442